AFRICAN
GAME TRAILS

◆

Mr. Roosevelt and one of his big lions

From a photograph by Kermit Roosevelt

AFRICAN GAME TRAILS

Theodore Roosevelt

AN ACCOUNT OF THE

AFRICAN WANDERINGS

OF AN

AMERICAN HUNTER-NATURALIST

Peter Capstick, Series Editor

St. Martin's Press
New York

To the Reader:

The editors and publishers of the Peter Capstick Adventure Library faced significant responsibilities in the faithful reprinting of Africa's great hunting books of long ago. Essentially, they saw the need for each text to reflect to the letter the original work, nothing having been added or expunged, if it was to give the reader an authentic view of another age and another world.

In deciding that historical veracity and honesty were the first considerations, they realized that it meant retaining many distasteful racial and ethnic terms to be found in these old classics. The firm of St. Martin's Press, Inc., therefore wishes to make it very clear that it disassociates itself and its employees from the abhorrent racial-ethnic attitudes of the past which may be found in these books.

History is the often unpleasant record of the way things actually were, not the way they should have been. Despite the fact that we have no sympathy with the prejudices of decades past, we feel it better—and indeed, our collective responsibility—not to change the unfortunate facts that were.

—Peter Hathaway Capstick

Library of Congress Cataloging-in-Publication Data

Roosevelt, Theodore.
    African game trails.
    Reprint. Originally published: New York: Scribner, 1910.
    "From Peter Capstick's library."
    1. Hunting—Africa, East. 2. Africa, East—
Description and travel. I. Title.
√SK252.R64   1988   799.29676   88-11533
    ISBN 0-312-02151-8

First Edition

10 9 8 7 6 5 4 3 2 1

Teddy Roosevelt is one of my oldest friends. I cannot count the campfires we have shared in the deepest New Jersey woods, our hackles bristling in the death of twilight, like gamecocks, at the whiff of lion or the sweet odor of buffalo. Fifty times I have stood at Kermit's side in his leopard charges, and as often with Teddy when he shot his elephants.

That Teddy had been dead twenty-one years before I was born had not a whit to do with the reality of the matter. He was my first real hunting pal at a time when I needed one. I grew up mostly alone, a slavish waif of dream and adventure, building huts in the deep, rich evergreens of the family estate, hiding there with my books. Teddy's was always on top of the stack.

It is strange for me to write of the man who, possibly more than any other in those early years, influenced my African hunting career. If I slit my eyes through the leaping tongues of flame, I can almost hear his high, nearly falsetto voice, the only remnant of a once frail body. Despite poor eyesight, Roosevelt overcame his childhood health problems and went on to more than live up to the formidable stature of his father, scion of a wealthy mercantile family that included the Knickerbockers and that had been in America since 1649.

There is another special feature of this particular reprint. The first edition, which appeared in 1910 and from which this edition has been reproduced, was a gift from Roosevelt to my great-uncle, The Hon. John Henry Capstick, Republican Congressman for the Fifth Congressional District of New Jersey from 1914 to the year of his death in office in 1918. John Capstick and the late President were friends and fellow sportsmen who particularly enjoyed wingshooting together.

I so well remember the neatly folded letter from the ex-President to my great-uncle in which the former expresses the wish that they might enjoy more quail shooting before long. It accompanied the gift of *African Game Trails*. The letter is long gone, together with my Red Ryder BB gun, my skates, and my wartime Messerschmitt 109 model, into that hidden whirlpool somewhere in the darker regions that gulps and belches with satisfaction after ingesting such fare from one's childhood and youth.

As I got to know my boyhood hero better, I was fascinated to learn that Roosevelt's first wife, Alice Hathaway Lee, bore the same family name as I do, mine having been passed down from my mother's line. The links intrigued me greatly as I grew older. The Roosevelts and the Capsticks were strangely destined to cross spoor and I consider myself honored to be able to help make available this fresh edition of a grand tale.

Born in 1858 in New York City to a family of great wealth and social prominence, Theodore Roosevelt could so easily have succumbed to a life of pampered ease. Instead, he overcame considerable health problems in his youth and went on to be the twenty-sixth President of the United States, bringing to that high office a record of significant reform and a reputation for such a universal thirst for knowledge and accomplishment that many historians consider him to be the most scholarly, versatile, and talented leader since the days of Thomas Jefferson.

Prolific writer and historian, Roosevelt was also a fearless politician and explorer, a mountaineer, hunter/conservationist, naturalist, cattle rancher, soldier, and a Harvard Phi Beta Kappa graduate with a profound understanding of classical literature. He quickly showed his leadership qualities—the kind of qualities that would encourage him to be one of the first Americans, including his great friend Carl Akeley, to undertake such an exhaustive and adventurous safari into British East Africa. *African Game Trails* is the story of that pioneer safari and collecting expedition, starting as it did with Roosevelt's arrival in Mombasa in April 1909 and concluding with his departure for home via Khartoum in March 1910.

A few insights into Roosevelt's life before this historic undertaking are in order. While still President, he enacted thoroughgoing legislation that was destined to save 125 million acres of America's wilderness areas and their delicate ecosystems from commercial development and ruin, eclipsing similar efforts of the previous three U.S. presidents. Generations of Americans have Roosevelt to thank for their being able to escape the horrors and stress of urban life into numerous wildlife refuges, national parks, forestry reserves, and hunting areas. His farsighted action in reorganizing the National Forest Service and his fearless handling of critics mark him as a hunter/conservationist decades before such issues were widely understood and increasingly accepted.

Roosevelt's heroic role as leader of the 1st U.S. Volunteer Cavalry, the famed "Rough Riders," in the charge up Kettle Hill in Cuba in 1898 during the Battle of Santiago at the time of the Spanish-American War made him a household name throughout the States. He once said: "No triumph of peace is quite so great as the supreme triumph of war." These words sound a little strange when one recalls that Roosevelt was awarded the Nobel Peace Prize in 1906 for his mediating role in the Russo-Japanese

War. Bellicose and forthright, Roosevelt was nonetheless an artful politician who knew when to exercise caution. His dealings with the Japanese are proof of this skill, one he carried over into everyday life.

The recipient of many honors, including membership of the prestigious Explorers Club, Roosevelt enjoyed the kind of profile that made it inevitable that his safari plans should attract great attention from the media and from ordinary citizens, whole congregations of whom regularly prayed for his safety in special services while he was hunting and collecting in Africa.

The Smithsonian Institution commissioned Roosevelt and his party to collect specimens in Africa for the National Museum in Washington, D.C., such specimens ranging from the "Kenia Dormouse" to elephant, lion, and white rhinoceros. Birds, reptiles, and plants completed the massive array of specimens. The logistics of the taxidermy alone were astonishing, especially when one considers the lack of sophisticated transport in most areas and the huge distances over which so many tons of valuable material had to be safely transported. Edward Heller, the eminent mammologist and ecologist, supervised this aspect of the expedition. He was a gleaming star in the world of naturalism who held Roosevelt's accomplishments in this area in such high regard that he once stated: "I constantly felt while with him that I was in the presence of the foremost naturalist of our time, as indeed I was." Roosevelt was a keen observer and such a talented field naturalist that Heller collaborated with him in the production of *Life Histories of African Game Animals*, which appeared in 1914.

It was none other than the legendary Frederick Courteney Selous who played a major role in arranging the Roosevelt safari. He had dedicated his book *African Nature Notes and Reminiscenses* to Roosevelt in 1908, while Roosevelt was still in office. The book was the final result of earlier encouragement by the then President, who first invited Selous to the White House in 1905. Selous was greatly impressed by the breadth of Roosevelt's interest in and knowledge of wildlife. Roosevelt had read previous works by Selous and we can safely assume that this urged him to one day hunt in Africa and try to experience something of the thrills and challenges peculiar to African big game.

Free at last of the responsibilities of the Presidency, Roosevelt, his son Kermit, several prominent naturalists, and a horde of newsmen set sail for Mombasa, via Naples, Aden, and Suez. Selous joined the party in Italy and whetted their collective appetites with his unique stories of African hunting. The ship docked in torrential rain in Mombasa, from where the Roosevelt party traveled on the British Acting Governor's special train to Nairobi.

This event marked the beginning of the great safari era. R. J. Cunninghame, regarded as the first professional hunter, and Leslie Tarlton of the Nairobi firm of Newland and Tarlton were the field managers of the entire expedition. They are handsomely credited by Roosevelt for their expertise, Cunninghame being a particularly fine companion for the ex-President because of his Cambridge education and extensive travels on behalf of the British Museum. It is curious that Roosevelt consistently misspells Cunninghame's name throughout.

The Roosevelt safari, which covered vast areas of today's Kenya and Uganda as well as part of the then Lado and down the Nile to Khartoum, initiated the industry of safari, one of the greatest foreign-exchange earners in African history. Roosevelt's book was by far the most important book by an American at the time on what had previously been an overwhelmingly British domain in Kenya and other non-German areas. It opened the continent to those who had the means to replace the "Grand Tour" of Europe as a rite of American or British passage. Now, it was all safari. . . .

It is quite impossible to comment on the Roosevelt safari and expedition at any length without treading on the text itself. This would be like revealing the end of a Hitchcock movie by a low whisper during the preliminary credits, such are the delights and adventures that await you.

A few words, however, seem appropriate concerning some of the people who featured in the Roosevelt experience in British East Africa. One of the snippets of information I found concerned the nickname the Swahili-speaking safari staff gave their important visitor. He was named *Bwana Tumbo* in reference to his sizeable stomach. Far from being an insult, this honorific indicated that Roosevelt was seen as a powerful and important personality to whom many people showed deference. Roosevelt also took a keen and constant interest in the various tribesmen he met during his African travels, taking the trouble to get to know their names and something about their lifestyles in the case of gunbearers and other safari staff members.

Contrary to what one sometimes reads, Selous did not accompany Roosevelt as a professional hunter; the two men merely met socially on a number of occasions during that year. The ex-President was the guest of Sir Alfred and Lady Pease at their ranch on the Athi Plains, where he took his first lions. Pease dedicated his splendid *The Book of the Lion* to his distinguished safari guest, who also wrote a brief preface to the forthcoming book while still in East Africa. Pease's book features in this series.

The Hill cousins, Clifford and Harold, also hosted Roosevelt on a hunt, the three men getting along extremely well together. Bill Judd, another famous hunter who had hunted with Cunninghame in Portuguese East Africa before the turn of the century, also took Roosevelt out. The story goes that he lost the honor of heading the Roosevelt safari because of the toss of a coin. He was eventually gored to death by an elephant.

Philip Percival, doyen of the professional hunting community and the founding president of the eventual East African Professional Hunters' Association, entertained Roosevelt as did a host of other dignitaries. The tremendous hospitality showered on the party and the wild beauty of the African bush vividly impressed Roosevelt, who said: " . . . every one—behaved as if each was my host and felt it incumbent on him to give me a good time."

One wonders what would have happened had Roosevelt's generous hosts and hunting companions made just one fatal error of judgment in the field and their world-famous guest been injured or even killed. Here, Denys Finch Hatton's unnerving experience with the then Prince of Wales on safari comes to mind: "HRH" wanted a picture of a charging rhino. This was set up, Finch Hatton covering any eventuality of the provoked charge. He was obliged to drop the beast before it got too close to the heir to the British throne.

According to J. A. Hunter, the Prince exploded with rage at his hunter's action. Finch Hatton coolly told his client that had he not shot the rhino and had it killed the visiting Royal instead, he, Finch Hatton, would have had to "go behind a tree and blow my brains out." Fortunately, nothing of the like happened during the Roosevelt trip, although Roosevelt did kill two lions on the Kapiti Plains "without any professional hunters being present." This was a huge risk and one can only imagine the international furor had Roosevelt died on safari as the result of a hunting miscalculation. He was a hardened outdoorsman and my guess is that he must have been difficult at times to manage.

It must not be forgotten that the Roosevelt safari was

far, far more than a chest-thumping expedition. Roosevelt had arranged for a full porter's load of classical literature, his famous Pigskin Library, to accompany him. He even had other classics added to it en route. The esthete in him mingled with the tough hunter/naturalist—he often read "beside the carcass of a beast I had killed, or else waiting for camp to be pitched."

I consider the Foreword to this book, written by Roosevelt upon his arrival in Khartoum in March 1910, to be among the most astonishingly evocative and charming pages ever written about the spirit of safari. I have quoted from it, crediting Roosevelt, in previous books of mine, and finer words have never passed through my typewriter. Roosevelt's words may well be the signpost pointing toward the end of an era where ignorant but well-meaning preservationists would dictate in error to the true veterans of the bushveld, to the detriment of the wild animals and wilder habitat that composed Roosevelt's Pleistocene. In fact, we shall never see it again.

Teddy Roosevelt knew what was coming, the glistening, chip-edged scythe of civilization that would mercilessly slice away forever the grace and "hidden spirit of the wilderness" that made him not only a great observer and chronicler of a time past but a prophet of its demise. He knew, probably with dampened eye, that which would come as surely as the locusts, drought, plague, famine, and poachers.

In *African Game Trails* he has caught the essence of the early East Africa and has passed it down to us " . . . changed only by the slow change of the ages through time everlasting." Perhaps it went a bit faster than he fancied but he has left us the acrid waft of campfire, the nasal sludge of swamp and the sharp smell of danger. Teddy and Kermit Roosevelt were there, the right personalities in the right place and at the right time. Here they have left their record.

The one thing nobody could guard against on that momentous expedition was malaria. Roosevelt was to suffer recurring bouts of the disease in years to come and this doubtless contributed to his early death on 6 January 1919 at home on Long Island, New York. He was buried "without splendor or parade" at Sagamore Hill, his Long Island home and hunting lodge.

African Game Trails has been a standard item in every library of hunting Africana since it first appeared in print. It represents the success, from the American viewpoint, of someone who sowed a dream in the American psyche to go to Africa and experience the hunt and to bring back qualities that would enhance the hard-core manliness, love of the outdoors, and the strength of person and nation that became America.

I can only hope this great American would have been as proud of us as we are of him, who have taken the time to know him better through this book. Join him and the good things that were.

Peter Hathaway Capstick

TO
KERMIT ROOSEVELT
MY SIDE-PARTNER
IN OUR
"GREAT ADVENTURE"

FOREWORD

"I speak of Africa and golden joys"; the joy of wandering through lonely lands; the joy of hunting the mighty and terrible lords of the wilderness, the cunning, the wary, and the grim.

In these greatest of the world's great hunting-grounds there are mountain peaks whose snows are dazzling under the equatorial sun; swamps where the slime oozes and bubbles and festers in the steaming heat; lakes like seas; skies that burn above deserts where the iron desolation is shrouded from view by the wavering mockery of the mirage; vast grassy plains where palms and thorn-trees fringe the dwindling streams; mighty rivers rushing out of the heart of the continent through the sadness of endless marshes; forests of gorgeous beauty, where death broods in the dark and silent depths.

There are regions as healthy as the northland; and other regions, radiant with bright-hued flowers, birds and butterflies, odorous with sweet and heavy scents, but, treacherous in their beauty, and sinister to human life. On the land and in the water there are dread brutes that feed on the flesh of man; and among the lower things, that crawl, and fly, and sting, and bite, he finds swarming foes far more evil and deadly than any beast or reptile; foes that kill his crops and his cattle, foes before which he himself perishes in his hundreds of thousands.

The dark-skinned races that live in the land vary widely. Some are warlike, cattle-owning nomads; some till the soil and live in thatched huts shaped like beehives; some are fisherfolk; some are ape-like naked savages, who dwell in the woods and prey on creatures not much wilder or lower than themselves.

The land teems with beasts of the chase, infinite in number and incredible in variety. It holds the fiercest beasts of ravin, and the fleetest and most timid of those beings that live in undying fear of talon and fang. It holds the largest and the smallest of hoofed animals. It holds the mightiest creatures that tread the earth or swim in its rivers; it also holds distant kinsfolk of these same creatures, no bigger than woodchucks, which dwell in crannies of the rocks, and in the tree tops. There are antelope smaller than hares, and antelope larger than oxen. There are creatures which are the embodiments of grace; and others whose huge ungainliness is like that of a shape in a nightmare. The plains are alive with droves of strange and beautiful animals whose like is not known elsewhere; and with others even stranger that show both in form and temper something of the fantastic and the grotesque. It is a never-ending pleasure to gaze at the great herds of buck as they move to and fro in their myriads; as they stand for their noontide rest in the quivering heat haze; as the long files come down to drink at the watering-places; as they feed and fight and rest and make love.

The hunter who wanders through these lands sees sights which ever afterward remain fixed in his mind. He sees the monstrous river-horse snorting and plunging beside the boat; the giraffe looking over the tree tops at the nearing horseman; the ostrich fleeing at a speed that none may rival; the snarling leopard and coiled python, with their lethal beauty; the zebras, barking in the moonlight, as the laden caravan passes on its night march through a thirsty land. In after years there shall come to him memories of the lion's charge; of the gray bulk of the elephant, close at hand in the sombre woodland; of the buffalo, his sullen eyes lowering from under his helmet of horn; of the rhinoceros, truculent and stupid, standing in the bright sunlight on the empty plain.

These things can be told. But there are no words that can tell the hidden spirit of the wilderness, that can reveal its mystery, its melancholy, and its charm. There is delight in the hardy life of the open, in long rides rifle in hand, in the thrill of the fight with dangerous game. Apart from this, yet mingled with it, is the strong attraction of the silent places, of the large tropic moons, and the splendor of the new stars; where the wanderer sees the awful glory of sunrise and sunset in the wide waste spaces of the earth, unworn of man, and changed only by the slow change of the ages through time everlasting.

THEODORE ROOSEVELT.

KHARTOUM, *March* 15, 1910.

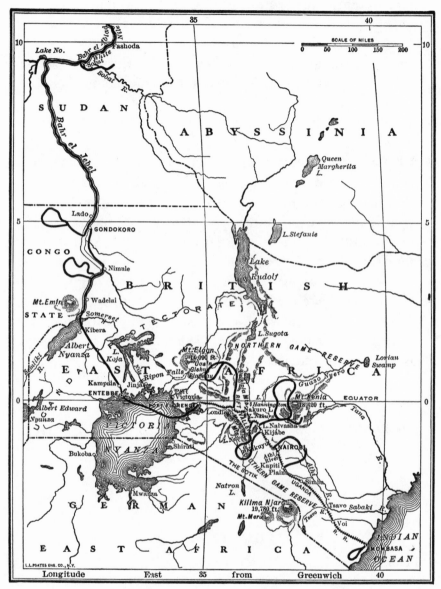

Map showing Mr. Roosevelt's route and hunting trips in Africa

CONTENTS

CONTENTS

CHAPTER IX

CHAPTER X

CHAPTER XI

CHAPTER XII

CHAPTER XIII

CHAPTER XIV

CHAPTER XV

ILLUSTRATIONS

He loved the great game as if he were their father.

—Anglo-Saxon Chronicle.

Tell me the course, the voyage, the ports and the new stars.

—Bliss Carman.

AFRICAN GAME TRAILS

CHAPTER I

A RAILROAD THROUGH THE PLEISTOCENE

The great world movement which began with the voyages of Columbus and Vasco da Gama, and which has gone on with ever-increasing rapidity and complexity until our own time, has developed along a myriad lines of interest. In no way has it been more interesting than in the way in which it has brought into sudden, violent, and intimate contact phases of the world's life history which would normally be separated by untold centuries of slow development. Again and again, in the continents new to peoples of European stock, we have seen the spectacle of a high civilization all at once thrust into and superimposed upon a wilderness of savage men and savage beasts. Nowhere, and at no time, has the contrast been more strange and more striking than in British East Africa during the last dozen years.

The country lies directly under the equator; and the hinterland, due west, contains the huge Nyanza lakes, vast inland seas which gather the head-waters of the White Nile. This hinterland, with its lakes and its marshes, its snow-capped mountains, its high, dry plateaus, and its forests of deadly luxuriance, was utterly unknown to white men half a century ago. The map of Ptolemy in the second century of our era gave a more accurate view of the lakes, mountains, and head-waters of the Nile than the maps published at the beginning of the second half of the nineteenth century, just before Speke, Grant, and Baker made their great trips of exploration and adventure. Behind these explorers came others; and then adventurous missionaries, traders, and elephant hunters; and many men, whom risk

1

did not daunt, who feared neither danger nor hardship, traversed the country hither and thither, now for one reason, now for another, now as naturalists, now as geographers, and again as government officials or as mere wanderers who loved the wild and strange life which had survived over from an elder age.

Most of the tribes were of pure savages; but here and there were intrusive races of higher type; and in Uganda, beyond the Victoria Nyanza, and on the head-waters of the Nile proper, lived a people which had advanced to the upper stages of barbarism, which might almost be said to have developed a very primitive kind of semi-civilization. Over this people—for its good fortune—Great Britain established a protectorate; and ultimately, in order to get easy access to this new outpost of civilization in the heart of the Dark Continent, the British Government built a railroad from the old Arab coast town of Mombasa westward to Victoria Nyanza.

This railroad, the embodiment of the eager, masterful, materialistic civilization of to-day, was pushed through a region in which nature, both as regards wild man and wild beast, did not and does not differ materially from what it was in Europe in the late Pleistocene. The comparison is not fanciful. The teeming multitudes of wild creatures, the stupendous size of some of them, the terrible nature of others, and the low culture of many of the savage tribes, especially of the hunting tribes, substantially reproduces the conditions of life in Europe as it was led by our ancestors ages before the dawn of anything that could be called civilization. The great beasts that now live in East Africa were in that by-gone age represented by close kinsfolk in Europe; and in many places, up to the present moment, African man, absolutely naked, and armed as our early paleolithic ancestors were armed, lives among, and on, and in constant dread of, these beasts, just as was true of the men to whom the cave lion was a nightmare of terror, and the mammoth and the woolly rhinoceros possible but most formidable prey.

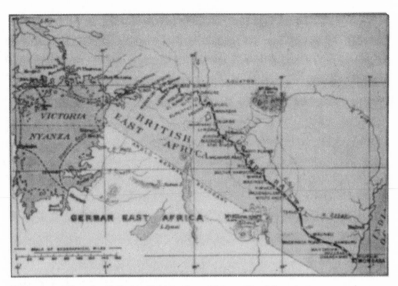

Map of the Uganda Railway, British East Africa. Total length from Mombasa on the Indian Ocean to Port Florence on Lake Victoria Nyanza, 581 miles

This region, this great fragment out of the long-buried past of our race, is now accessible by railroad to all who care to go thither; and no field more inviting offers itself to hunter or naturalist, while even to the ordinary traveller it teems with interest. On March 23, 1909, I sailed thither from New York, in charge of a scientific expedition sent out by the Smithsonian, to collect birds, mammals, reptiles, and plants, but especially specimens of big game, for the National Museum at Washington. In addition to myself and my son Kermit (who had entered Harvard a few months previously), the party consisted of three naturalists: Surgeon-Lieut. Col. Edgar A. Mearns, U.S.A., retired; Mr. Edmund Heller, of California, and Mr. J. Alden Loring, of Owego, N. Y. My arrangements for the trip had been chiefly made through two valued English friends, Mr. Frederick Courteney Selous, the greatest of the world's big-game hunters, and Mr. Edward North Buxton, also a mighty hunter. On landing we were to be met by Messrs. R. J. Cuninghame and Leslie Tarlton, both famous hunters; the latter an Australian, who served through the South African war; the former by birth a Scotchman, and a Cambridge man, but long a resident of Africa, and at one time a professional elephant hunter—in addition to having been a whaler in the Arctic Ocean, a hunter-naturalist in Lapland, a transport rider in South Africa, and a collector for the British Museum in various odd corners of the earth.

We sailed on the *Hamburg* from New York—what headway the Germans have made among those who go down to the sea in ships!—and at Naples trans-shipped to the *Admiral*, of another German line, the East African. On both ships we were as comfortable as possible, and the voyage was wholly devoid of incidents. Now and then, as at the Azores, at Suez, and at Aden, the three naturalists landed, and collected some dozens or scores of birds—which next day were skinned and prepared in my room, as the largest and best fitted for the purpose. After reaching Suez the ordinary tourist type of passenger ceased to be predominant; in his place there were Italian officers going out to a desolate coast town on the edge of Somaliland; missionaries, German, English, and American; Portuguese civil officials; traders of different nationalities; and planters and military and civil officers bound to German and British East Africa. The Englishmen included planters, magistrates, forest officials, army officers on leave from India, and other army officers going out to take command of black native levies in out-of-the-way regions where the English flag stands for all that makes life worth living. They were a fine set, these young Englishmen, whether dashing army officers or capable civilians; they reminded me of our own men who have reflected such honor on the American name, whether in civil and military positions in the Philippines and Porto Rico, working on the Canal Zone in Panama, taking care of the custom-houses in San Domingo, or serving in the army of occupation in Cuba. Moreover, I felt as if I knew most of them already, for they might have walked out of the pages of Kipling. But I was not as well prepared for the corresponding and equally interesting types among the Germans, the planters, the civil officials, the officers who had commanded, or were about to command, white or native troops; men of evident power and energy, seeing whom made it easy to understand why German East Africa has

We would gather on deck around Selous to listen to tales
of strange adventures

From a photograph by Kermit Roosevelt

thriven apace. They are first-class men, these English and Germans; both are doing in East Africa a work of worth to the whole world; there is ample room for both, and no possible cause for any but a thoroughly friendly rivalry; and it is earnestly to be wished, in the interest both of them and of outsiders, too, that their relations will grow, as they ought to grow, steadily better—and not only in East Africa but everywhere else.

On the ship, at Naples, we found Selous, also bound for East Africa on a hunting trip; but he, a veteran whose first hunting in Africa was nearly forty years ago, cared only for exceptional trophies of a very few animals, while we, on the other hand, desired specimens of both sexes of all the species of big game that Kermit and I could shoot, as well as complete series of all the smaller mammals. We believed that our best work of a purely scientific character would be done with the mammals, both large and small.

No other hunter alive has had the experience of Selous; and, so far as I now recall, no hunter of anything like his

A baobab-tree, Mombasa
From a photograph by Kermit Roosevelt

experience has ever also possessed his gift of penetrating observation joined to his power of vivid and accurate narration. He has killed scores of lion and rhinoceros and hundreds of elephant and buffalo; and these four animals are the most dangerous of the world's big game, when hunted as they are hunted in Africa. To hear him tell of what he has seen and done is no less interesting to a naturalist than to a hunter. There were on the ship many men who loved wild nature, and who were keen hunters of big game; and almost every day, as we steamed over the hot, smooth waters of the Red Sea and the Indian Ocean, we would gather on deck around Selous to listen to tales of those strange adventures that only come to the man who has lived long the lonely life of the wilderness.

Kermit Roosevelt and R. J. Cuninghame preparing to
take pictures

On April 21 we steamed into the beautiful and picturesque harbor of Mombasa. Many centuries before the Christian era, dhows from Arabia, carrying seafarers of Semitic races whose very names have perished, rounded the Lion's Head at Guardafui and crept slowly southward along the barren African coast. Such dhows exist to-day almost unchanged, and bold indeed were the men who first steered them across the unknown oceans. They were men of iron heart and supple conscience, who fronted inconceiv-

able danger and hardship; they established trading stations
for gold and ivory and slaves; they turned these trading
stations into little cities and sultanates, half Arab, half negro.
Mombasa was among them.   In her time of brief splendor
Portugal seized the
city; the Arabs won
it back; and now Eng-
land holds it. It lies just
south of the equator,
and when we saw it the
brilliant green of the
tropic foliage showed
the town at its best.

F. C. Selous
From a photograph by W. N. McMillan

We were welcomed
to Government House
in most cordial fash-
ion by the acting Gov-
ernor, Lieutenant-
Governor Jackson, who
is not only a trained
public official of long
experience but a first-
class field naturalist
and a renowned big-
game hunter; indeed I
could not too warmly
express my apprecia-
tion of the hearty and
generous courtesy with
which we were received
and treated alike by the official and the unofficial world
throughout East Africa.   We landed in the kind of torrential downpour that only comes in the tropics; it reminded
me of Panama at certain moments in the rainy season.
That night we were given a dinner by the Mombasa Club;
and it was interesting to meet the merchants and planters
of the town and the neighborhood as well as the officials.

The former included not only Englishmen but also Germans and Italians; which is quite as it should be, for at least part of the high inland region of British East Africa can be made one kind of "white man's country"; and to achieve this white men should work heartily together, doing scrupulous justice to the natives, but remembering that progress and development in this particular kind of new land depend exclusively upon the masterful leadership of the whites, and that therefore it is both a calamity and a crime to permit the whites to be riven in sunder by hatreds and jealousies. The coast regions of British East Africa are not suited for extensive white settlement; but the hinterland is, and there everything should be done to encourage such settlement. Non-white aliens should not be encouraged to settle where they come into rivalry with the whites (exception being made as regards certain particular individuals and certain particular occupations).

R. J. Cuninghame, known to the Swahilis as "Bwana Medivu," the master with the beard

From a photograph by Edmund Heller

There are, of course, large regions on the coast and in

the interior where ordinary white settlers cannot live, in which it would be wise to settle immigrants from India, and there are many positions in other regions which it is to the advantage of everybody that the Indians should hold, because there is as yet no sign that sufficient numbers of white men are willing to hold them, while the native blacks, although many of them do fairly well in unskilled labor, are not yet competent to do the higher tasks which now fall to the share of the Goanese, and Moslem and non-Moslem Indians. The small merchants who deal with the natives, for instance, and most of the minor railroad officials, belong to these latter classes. I was amused, by the way, at one bit of native nomenclature in connection with the Goanese. Many of the Goanese are now as dark as most of the other Indians; but they are descended in the male line from the early Portuguese adventurers and conquerors, who were the first white men ever seen by the natives of this coast. Accordingly to this day some of the natives speak even of the dark-skinned descendants of the subjects of King Henry the Navigator as "the whites," designating the Europeans specifically as English, Germans, or the like; just as in out-of-the-way nooks in the far Northwest one of our own red men will occasionally be found who still speaks of Americans and Englishmen as "Boston men" and "King George's men."

One of the government farms was being run by an educated colored man from Jamaica; and we were shown much courtesy by a colored man from our own country who was practising as a doctor. No one could fail to be impressed with the immense advance these men represented as compared with the native negro; and indeed to an American, who must necessarily think much of the race problem at home, it is pleasant to be made to realize in vivid fashion the progress the American negro has made, by comparing him with the negro who dwells in Africa untouched, or but lightly touched, by white influence.

In such a community as one finds in Mombasa or Nairobi one continually runs across quiet, modest men whose lives have been fuller of wild adventure than the life of a viking leader of the ninth century. One of the public officials whom I met at the Governor's table was Major Hinde. He had at one time served under the government of the Congo Free State; and, at a crisis in the fortunes of the

Mr. Roosevelt saying good-by in the Mombasa station
From a photograph by Kermit Roosevelt

State, when the Arab slave-traders bade fair to get the upper hand, he was one of the eight or ten white men, representing half as many distinct nationalities, who overthrew the savage soldiery of the slave-traders and shattered beyond recovery the Arab power. They organized the wild pagan tribes just as their Arab foes had done; they fought in a land where deadly sickness struck down victor and vanquished with ruthless impartiality; they found their commissariat as best they could wherever they happened to be; often they depended upon one day's victory to furnish the ammunition with which to wage the morrow's battle; and ever they had to be on guard no less against the thousands of cannibals in their own ranks than against the thousands of cannibals in the hostile ranks, for, on whichever side they fought, after every battle the warriors of the man-eating tribes watched their chance to butcher the wounded indiscriminately and to feast on the bodies of the slain.

The most thrilling book of true lion stories ever written is Colonel Patterson's "The Man-eaters of Tsavo." Colonel Patterson was one of the engineers engaged, some ten or twelve years back, in building the Uganda Railway; he was in charge of the work, at a place called Tsavo, when it was brought to a complete halt by the ravages of a couple of man-eating lions which, after many adventures, he finally killed. At the dinner at the Mombasa Club I met one of the actors in a blood-curdling tragedy which Colonel Patterson relates. He was a German, and, in company with an Italian friend, he went down in the special car of one of the English railroad officials to try to kill a man-eating lion which had carried away several people from a station on the line. They put the car on a siding; as it was hot the door was left open, and the Englishman sat by the open window to watch for the lion, while the Italian finally lay down on the floor and the German got into an upper bunk. Evidently the Englishman must have fallen asleep, and the lion, seeing him through the window, entered the carriage by the door to get at him. The Italian waked to find the lion standing on him with its hind feet, while its fore paws were on the seat as it killed the unfortunate Englishman, and the German, my informant, hearing the disturbance, leaped out of his bunk actually onto the back of the lion. The man-eater, however, was occupied only with his prey; holding the body in his mouth he forced his way out through the window-sash, and made his meal undisturbed but a couple of hundred yards from the railway carriage.

The day after we landed we boarded the train to take what seems to me, as I think it would to most men fond of natural history, the most interesting railway journey in the world. It was Governor Jackson's special train, and in addition to his own party and ours there was only Selous; and we travelled with the utmost comfort through a naturalist's wonderland. All civilized governments are now realizing that it is their duty here and there to preserve, unharmed,

Train on the Uganda Railway
From a photograph by Kermit Roosevelt

tracts of wild nature, with thereon the wild things the destruction of which means the destruction of half the charm of wild nature. The English Government has made a large game reserve of much of the region on the way to Nairobi, stretching far to the south, and one mile to the north, of the track. The reserve swarms with game; it would be of little value except as a reserve; and the attraction it now offers to travellers renders it an asset of real consequence to the whole colony. The wise people of Maine, in our own country, have discovered that intelligent game preservation, carried out in good faith, and in a spirit of common-sense as far removed from mushy sentimentality as from brutality, results in adding one more to the State's natural resources of value; and in consequence there are more moose and deer in Maine to-day than there were forty years ago; there is a better chance for every man in Maine, rich or poor, provided that he is not a game butcher, to enjoy his share of good hunting; and the number of sportsmen and tourists attracted to the State adds very appreciably to the means of livelihood of the citizen. Game reserves should not be established where they are detrimental to the interests of large bodies of settlers, nor yet should they be nominally established in regions so remote that the only men really interfered with are those who respect the law, while a premium is thereby put on the activity of the unscrupulous persons who are eager to break it. Similarly, game laws should be drawn primarily in the interest of the whole people, keeping steadily in mind certain facts that ought to be self-evident to every one above the intellectual level of those well-meaning persons who apparently think that all shooting is wrong and that man could continue to exist if all wild animals were allowed to increase unchecked. There must be recognition of the fact that almost any wild animal of the defenceless type, if its multiplication were unchecked while its natural enemies, the dangerous carnivores, were killed, would by its simple increase crowd man off the planet; and of the further fact that, far short of such increase, a time speedily comes when the existence of too much game is incompatible with the interests, or indeed the existence, of the cultivator. As in most other matters, it is only the happy mean which is healthy and rational. There should be certain sanctuaries and nurseries where game can live and breed absolutely unmolested; and elsewhere the laws should so far as possible provide for the continued existence of the game in sufficient numbers to allow a reasonable amount of hunting on fair terms to any hardy and vigorous man fond of the sport, and yet not in sufficient numbers to jeopard the interests of the actual settler, the tiller of the soil, the man whose well-being should be the prime object to be kept in mind by every statesman. Game butchery is as objectionable as any

Mr. Roosevelt, Governor Jackson, Mr. Selous, and Dr. Mearns, riding
in front of the engine on the way to Kapiti
From a photograph by Kermit Roosevelt

other form of wanton cruelty or barbarity; but to protest against all hunting of game is a sign of softness of head, not of soundness of heart.

In the creation of the great game reserve through which
the Uganda Railway runs the British Government has
conferred a boon upon mankind, and no less in the enact-
ment and enforcement of the game laws in the African
provinces generally. Of course experience will show where,
from time to time, there must be changes. In Uganda
proper buffaloes and hippos throve so under protection as
to become sources of grave danger not only to the crops but
to the lives of the natives, and they had to be taken off the
protected list and classed as vermin, to be shot in any number at any time; and only the great demand for ivory
prevented the necessity of following the same course with
regard to the elephant; while recently in British East
Africa the increase of the zebras, and the harm they did to
the crops of the settlers, rendered it necessary to remove a
large measure of the protection formerly accorded them,
and in some cases actually to encourage their slaughter;
and increase in settlement may necessitate further changes.
But, speaking generally, much wisdom and foresight, highly
creditable to both government and people, have been
shown in dealing with and preserving East African game
while at the same time safeguarding the interests of the
settlers.

On our train the locomotive was fitted with a comfortable seat across the cow-catcher, and on this, except at meal-
time, I spent most of the hours of daylight, usually in company with Selous, and often with Governor Jackson, to
whom the territory and the game were alike familiar. The
first afternoon we did not see many wild animals, but birds
abounded, and the scenery was both beautiful and interesting. A black-and-white hornbill, feeding on the track, rose
so late that we nearly caught it with our hands; guinea-fowl
and francolin, and occasionally bustard, rose near by; brilliant rollers, sun-birds, bee-eaters, and weaver-birds flew
beside us, or sat unmoved among the trees as the train
passed. In the dusk we nearly ran over a hyena; a year
or two previously the train actually did run over a lioness

Mr. Roosevelt and some members of his caravan

From a photograph by Kermit Roosevelt

one night, and the conductor brought in her head in triumph.
In fact, there have been continual mishaps such as could
only happen to a railroad in the Pleistocene! The very
night we went up there was an interruption in the telegraph
service due to giraffes having knocked down some of the
wires and a pole in crossing the track; and elephants have
more than once performed the same feat. Two or three
times, at night, giraffes have been run into and killed; once
a rhinoceros was killed, the engine being damaged in the
encounter; and on other occasions the rhino has only just
left the track in time, once the beast being struck and a
good deal hurt, the engine again being somewhat crippled.
But the lions now offer, and have always offered, the chief
source of unpleasant excitement. Throughout East Africa
the lions continually take to man-eating at the expense of
the native tribes, and white hunters are continually being
killed or crippled by them. At the lonely stations on the
railroad the two or three subordinate officials often live
in terror of some fearsome brute that has taken to haunting
the vicinity; and every few months, at some one of these
stations, a man is killed, or badly hurt by, or narrowly
escapes from, a prowling lion.

The stations at which the train stopped were neat and
attractive; and besides the Indian officials there were
usually natives from the neighborhood. Some of these
might be dressed in the fez and shirt and trousers which
indicate a coming under the white man's influence, or
which, rather curiously, may also indicate Mohammedan-
ism. But most of the natives are still wild pagans, and
many of them are unchanged in the slightest particular
from what their forefathers were during the countless ages
when they alone were the heirs of the land—a land which
they were utterly powerless in any way to improve. Some
of the savages we saw wore red blankets, and in deference
to white prejudice draped them so as to hide their nakedness. But others appeared—men and women—with literally not one stitch of clothing, although they might have

rather elaborate hair-dresses, and masses of metal ornaments on their arms and legs. In the region where one tribe dwelt all the people had their front teeth filed to sharp points; it was strange to see a group of these savages, stark naked, with oddly shaved heads and filed teeth, armed with primitive bows and arrows, stand gravely gazing at the train as it rolled into some station; and none the less strange, by the way, because the locomotive was a Baldwin, brought to Africa across the great ocean from our own country. One group of women, nearly nude, had their upper arms so tightly bound with masses of bronze or copper wire that their muscles were completely malformed. So tightly was the wire wrapped round the upper third of the upper arm, that it was reduced to about one-half of its normal size; and the muscles could only play, and that in deformed fashion, below this unyielding metal bandage. Why the arms did not mortify it was hard to say; and their freedom of use was so hampered as to make it difficult to understand how men or women whose whole lives are passed in one or another form of manual labor could inflict upon themselves such crippling and pointless punishment.

Next morning we were in the game country, and as we sat on the seat over the cow-catcher it was literally like passing through a vast zoological garden. Indeed no such railway journey can be taken on any other line in any other land. At one time we passed a herd of a dozen or so of great giraffes, cows and calves, cantering along through the open woods a couple of hundred yards to the right of the train. Again, still closer, four waterbuck cows, their big ears thrown forward, stared at us without moving until we had passed. Hartebeests were everywhere; one herd was on the track, and when the engine whistled they bucked and sprang with ungainly agility and galloped clear of the danger. A long-tailed straw-colored monkey ran from one tree to another. Huge black ostriches appeared from time to time. Once a troop of impalla, close by the track, took fright; and as the beautiful creatures fled we saw now

one and now another bound clear over the high bushes. A
herd of zebra clattered across a cutting of the line not a
hundred yards ahead of the train; the whistle hurried their
progress, but only for a moment, and as we passed they
were already turning round to gaze. The wild creatures
were in their sanctuary, and they knew it. Some of the
settlers have at times grumbled at this game reserve being
kept of such size; but surely it is one of the most valuable
possessions the country could have. The lack of water in
parts, the prevalence in other parts of diseases harmful to
both civilized man and domestic cattle, render this great
tract of country the home of all homes for the creatures of
the waste. The protection given these wild creatures is
genuine, not nominal; they are preserved, not for the
pleasure of the few, but for the good of all who choose to
see this strange and attractive spectacle; and from this nursery and breeding-ground the overflow keeps up the stock
of game in the adjacent land, to the benefit of the settler
to whom the game gives fresh meat, and to the benefit of
the whole country because of the attraction it furnishes to
all who desire to visit a veritable happy hunting ground.

Soon after lunch we drew up at the little station of
Kapiti Plains, where our safari was awaiting us; "safari"
being the term employed throughout East Africa to denote
both the caravan with which one makes an expedition and
the expedition itself. Our aim being to cure and send home
specimens of all the common big game—in addition to as
large a series as possible of the small mammals and birds
—it was necessary to carry an elaborate apparatus of
naturalists' supplies; we had brought with us, for instance,
four tons of fine salt, as to cure the skins of the big beasts
is a herculean labor under the best conditions; we had
hundreds of traps for the small creatures; many boxes
of shot-gun cartridges in addition to the ordinary rifle
cartridges which alone would be necessary on a hunting
trip; and, in short, all the many impedimenta needed if
scientific work is to be properly done under modern con-

ditions. Few laymen have any idea of the expense and pains which must be undergone in order to provide groups of mounted big animals from far-off lands, such as we see

A large American flag was floating over my own tent
From a photograph by Kermit Roosevelt

in museums like the National Museum in Washington and the American Museum of Natural History in New York. The modern naturalist must realize that in some of its branches his profession, while more than ever a science, has also become an art. So our preparations were neces-

sarily on a very large scale; and as we drew up at the station
the array of porters and of tents looked as if some small
military expedition was about to start. As a compliment,
which I much appreciated, a large American flag was floating over my own tent; and in the front line, flanking this
tent on either hand, were other big tents for the members
of the party, with a dining tent and skinning tent; while behind were the tents of the two hundred porters, the gun-

The askaris and porters drawn
In front of the tent stood the men in two lines; the first containing the
From a photograph

bearers, the tent boys, the askaris or native soldiers, and
the horse boys or saises. In front of the tents stood the
men in two lines; the first containing the fifteen askaris,
the second the porters with their headmen. The askaris
were uniformed, each in a red fez, a blue blouse, and white
knickerbockers, and each carrying his rifle and belt. The
porters were chosen from several different tribes or races to
minimize the danger of combination in the event of mutiny.
Here and there in East Africa one can utilize ox wagons,
or pack trains of donkeys; but for a considerable expedition
it is still best to use a safari of native porters, of the type
by which the commerce and exploration of the country have

always been carried on. The backbone of such a safari is generally composed of Swahili, the coast men, negroes who have acquired the Moslem religion, together with a partially Arabicized tongue and a strain of Arab blood from the Arab warriors and traders who have been dominant in the coast towns for so many centuries. It was these Swahili trading caravans, under Arab leadership, which, in their quest for ivory and slaves, trod out the routes which the

up in line to greet us
fifteen askaris, the second the porters with their headmen
by Edmund Heller

early white explorers followed. Without their work as a preliminary the work of the white explorers could not have been done; and it was the Swahili porters themselves who rendered this work itself possible. To this day every hunter, trader, missionary, or explorer must use either a Swahili safari or one modelled on the Swahili basis. The part played by the white-topped ox wagon in the history of South Africa, and by the camel caravan in North Africa, has been played in middle Africa by the files of strong, patient, childlike savages, who have borne the burdens of so many masters and employers hither and thither, through and across, the dark heart of the continent.

Equatorial Africa is in most places none too healthy a place for the white man, and he must care for himself as he would scorn to do in the lands of pine and birch and frosty weather. Camping in the Rockies or the North Woods can with advantage be combined with "roughing it"; and the early pioneers of the West, the explorers, prospectors, and hunters, who always roughed it, were as hardy as bears, and lived to a hale old age, if Indians and accidents per-

Our first camp, Kapiti Plains station, on a bare, dry
From a photograph

mitted. But in tropic Africa a lamentable proportion of the early explorers paid in health or life for the hardships they endured; and throughout most of the country no man can long rough it, in the Western and Northern sense, with impunity.

At Kapiti Plains our tents, our accommodations gener-ally, seemed almost too comfortable for men who knew camp life only on the Great Plains, in the Rockies, and in the North Woods. My tent had a fly which was to protect it from the great heat; there was a little rear extension in which I bathed—a hot bath, never a cold bath, is almost a tropic necessity; there was a ground canvas, of vital moment in a land of ticks, jiggers, and scorpions; and a cot to sleep on, so as to be raised from the ground. Quite a contrast to life on the round-up! Then I had two tent boys to see after my belongings, and to wait at table as well as in the tent. Ali, a Mohammedan mulatto (Arab and negro), was the chief of the two, and spoke some English, while under him was "Bill," a speechless black boy; Ali being particularly faithful and efficient. Two other Moham-

plain covered with brown and withered grass
by Edmund Heller

medan negroes, clad like the askaris, reported to me as my gun-bearers, Muhamed and Bakari; seemingly excellent men, loyal and enduring, no trackers, but with keen eyes for game, and the former speaking a little English. My two horse boys, or saises, were both pagans. One, Hamisi, must have had in his veins Galla or other non-negro blood; derived from the Hamitic, or bastard Semitic, or at least non-negro, tribes which, pushing slowly and fitfully south-ward and south-westward among the negro peoples, have created an intricate tangle of ethnic and linguistic types from the middle Nile to far south of the equator. Hamisi always wore a long feather in one of his sandals, the only

ornament he affected.   The other sais was a silent, gentle-
mannered black heathen; his name was Simba, a lion,
and as I shall later show he was not unworthy of it.   The
two horses for which these men cared were stout, quiet
little beasts; one, a sorrel, I named Tranquillity, and the
other, a brown, had so much the coblike build of a zebra
that we christened him Zebra-shape.   One of Kermit's
two horses, by the way, was more romantically named after
Huandaw, the sharp-eared steed of the Mabinogion.   Cuninghame, lean, sinewy, bearded, exactly the type of hunter
and safari manager that one would wish for such an expedition as ours, had ridden up with us on the train, and at
the station we met Tarlton, and also two settlers of the
neighborhood, Sir Alfred Pease and Mr. Clifford Hill.
Hill was an Africander.   He and his cousin, Harold Hill,
after serving through the South African war, had come to
the new country of British East Africa to settle, and they
represented the ideal type of settler for taking the lead in the
spread of empire.   They were descended from the English
colonists who came to South Africa in 1820; they had never
been in England, and neither had Tarlton.   It was exceedingly interesting to meet these Australians and Africanders,
who typified in their lives and deeds the greatness of the
English Empire, and yet had never seen England.

As for Sir Alfred, Kermit and I were to be his guests
for the next fortnight, and we owe primarily to him, to his
mastery of hunting craft, and his unvarying and generous
hospitality and kindness, the pleasure and success of our
introduction to African hunting.   His life had been one
of such varied interest as has only been possible in our own
generation.   He had served many years in Parliament;
he had for some years been a magistrate in a peculiarly responsible post in the Transvaal; he had journeyed and
hunted and explored in the northern Sahara, in the Soudan,
in Somaliland, in Abyssinia; and now he was ranching
in East Africa.   A singularly good rider and one of the best
game shots I have ever seen, it would have been impossible

to have found a kinder host or a hunter better fitted to teach us how to begin our work with African big game.

At Kapiti station there was little beyond the station buildings, a "compound" or square enclosure in which there were many natives, and an Indian store. The last was presided over by a turbaned Mussulman, the agent of other Indian traders who did business in Machakos-boma,

Porters and their tents
From a photograph by J. Alden Loring

a native village a dozen miles distant; the means of communication being two-wheeled carts, each drawn by four humped oxen, driven by a wellnigh naked savage.

For forty-eight hours we were busy arranging our outfit; and the naturalists took much longer. The provisions were those usually included in an African hunting or exploring trip, save that, in memory of my days in the West, I included in each provision box a few cans of Boston baked beans, California peaches, and tomatoes. We had plenty of warm bedding, for the nights are cold at high altitudes, even under the equator. While hunting I wore heavy shoes, with hobnails or rubber soles; khaki trousers, the knees faced with leather, and the legs buttoning tight from the knee to below the ankle, to avoid the need of leggings; a khaki-colored army shirt; and a sun helmet, which I wore in deference to local advice, instead of my beloved and far more convenient slouch hat. My rifles were an army Springfield, 30-calibre, stocked and sighted to suit myself; a Winchester 405; and a double-barrelled 500–450 Holland, a beautiful weapon presented to me by some English friends.*

Kermit's battery was of the same type, except that instead of a Springfield he had another Winchester shooting the army ammunition, and his double-barrel was a Rigby. In addition I had a Fox No. 12 shot-gun; no better gun was ever made.

There was one other bit of impedimenta, less usual for African travel, but perhaps almost as essential for real enjoyment even on a hunting trip, if it is to be of any length.

* Mr. E. N. Buxton took the lead in the matter when he heard that I intended making a trip after big game in Africa. I received the rifle at the White House, while I was President. Inside the case was the following list of donors:

LIST OF ZOOLOGISTS AND SPORTSMEN WHO ARE DONORS OF A DOUBLE ELEPHANT RIFLE TO THE HON. THEODORE ROOSEVELT, PRESIDENT U. S. A.

IN RECOGNITION OF HIS SERVICES ON BEHALF OF THE PRESERVATION OF SPECIES BY MEANS OF NATIONAL PARKS AND FOREST RESERVES, AND BY OTHER MEANS

E. N. BUXTON, ESQ.
RT. HON. LORD AVEBURY, D.C.L. ("The Pleasures of Life," etc.)
MAJOR-GEN. SIR F. REGINALD WINGATE, K.C.B. (Governor-General of the Soudan.)
SIR EDMUND G. LODER, BART.
HON. N. C. ROTHSCHILD.
THE EARL OF LONSDALE. (Master of Hounds.)
SIR R. G. HARVEY, BART.
THE RT. HON. LORD CURZON OF KEDLESTON, G.C.S.I., G.C.I.E.
ST. GEORGE LITTLEDALE, ESQ.
DR. P. CHALMERS MITCHELL, F.R.S., F.Z.S. (Secretary of the Zoological Soc.)
C. E. GREEN, ESQ. (Master of Essex Hounds.)

This was the "Pigskin Library," so called because most of the books were bound in pigskin. They were carried in a light aluminum and oil-cloth case, which, with its contents, weighed a little less than sixty pounds, making a load for one porter. Including a few volumes carried in the various bags, so that I might be sure always to have one with me, and Gregorovius, read on the voyage outward, the list was as printed in Appendix F.

It represents in part Kermit's taste, in part mine; and, I need hardly say, it also represents in no way all the books we most care for, but merely those which, for one reason or another, we thought we should like to take on this particular trip.

I used my Whitman tree army saddle and my army field-glasses; but, in addition, for studying the habits of the game, I carried a telescope given me on the boat by a fellow-traveller and big-game hunter, an Irish hussar captain from India—and incidentally I am out in my guess if this same Irish hussar captain be not worth watching should his country ever again be engaged in war. I had

---

F. C. SELOUS, ESQ. ("A Hunter's Wanderings," etc.)
COUNT BLÜCHER.
LIEUT.-COL. C. DELMÉ RADCLIFFE, C.M.G., M.V.O.
MAURICE EGERTON, ESQ.
LORD DESBOROUGH, C.V.O.
CAPTAIN M. McNEILL.
CLAUDE H. TRITTON, ESQ.
J. TURNER-TURNER, ESQ.
HON. L. W. ROTHSCHILD, M.P.
RT. HON. SIR E. GREY, BART., M.P. (Foreign Secretary and author of "Dry Fly Fishing.")
SIR M. DE C. FINDLAY, C.M.G. (British Minister at Dresden.)
C. PHILLIPPS-WOLLEY, ESQ., F.R.G.S. ("Sport in the Caucasus.")
RT. HON. SIR G. O. TREVELYAN, BART., D.C.L. ("The American Revolution.")
WARBURTON PIKE, ESQ.
SIR WM. E. GARSTIN, G.C.M.G.
HIS GRACE THE DUKE OF BEDFORD, K.G. ("A Great Estate.")
HER GRACE THE DUCHESS OF BEDFORD.
LORD BRASSEY, G.C.B., M.V.O. (Owner of *The Sunbeam*.)
HON. T. A. BRASSEY. (Editor of the *Naval Annual*.)
RHYS WILLIAMS, ESQ.
MAJOR-GEN. A. A. A. KINLOCH, C.B. ("Large Game in Thibet.")

a very ingenious beam or scale for weighing game, designed and presented to me by my friend, Mr. Thompson Seton. I had a slicker for wet weather, an army overcoat, and a mackinaw jacket for cold, if I had to stay out overnight in the mountains. In my pockets I carried, of course, a knife, a compass, and a water-proof match-box. Finally, just before leaving home, I had been sent, for good luck, a gold-mounted rabbit's foot, by Mr. John L. Sullivan, at one time ring champion of the world.

Our camp was on a bare, dry plain, covered with brown and withered grass. At most hours of the day we could see round about, perhaps a mile or so distant, or less, the game feeding. South of the track the reserve stretched for a long distance; north it went for but a mile, just enough to prevent thoughtless or cruel people from shooting as they went by in the train. There was very little water; what we drank, by the way, was carefully boiled. The drawback

---

Sir Wm. Lee-Warner, K.C.S.I. ("The Protected Princes of India.")
The Rt. Rev. the Lord Bishop of London.
Major-Gen. Dalrymple White.
Colonel Claude Cane.
Rt. Hon. Sydney Buxton, M.P. (Postmaster General, "Fishing and Shooting.")
Major C. E. Radclyffe, D.S.O.
Sir A. E. Pease, Bart. ("Cleveland Hounds.")
Sir H. H. Johnston, K.C.B., G.C.M.G. ("The Uganda Protectorate.")
Abel Chapman, Esq. ("Wild Spain.")
J. G. Millais, Esq., F.Z.S. ("A Breath from the Veldt.")
E. Lort-Phillips, Esq. (Author of ornithological works.)
R. Kearton, Esq., F.Z.S. ("Wild Nature's Ways.")
J. H. Gurney, Esq., F.Z.S. (Works on ornithology.)
F. J. Jackson, C.B., C.M.G., Lieut.-Governor East African Protectorate. ("Big Game," Badminton Library.)
Col. Sir F. Lugard, K.C.M.G., C.B., D.S.O.
Lady Lugard. ("A Tropical Dependency.")
Sir Clement L. Hill, K.C.B., M.P. (Late Head of the African Department; Foreign O.)
Sir H. Seton-Karr, M.P., C.M.G. ("My Sporting Holidays.")
Captain Boyd Alexander. ("From the Niger to the Nile.")
Sir J. Kirk, K.C.B., G.C.M.G. (Dr. Livingstone's companion, 1858–64.)
Moreton Frewen, Esq.
The Earl of Warwick.
P. L. Sclater, Esq., D.Sc., Ph.D. (Late Sec. Zool. Soc.)
Col. J. H. Patterson, D.S.O. ("The Man-Eaters of Tsavo.")

to the camp, and to all this plains region, lay in the ticks, which swarmed, and were a scourge to man and beast. Every evening the saises picked them by hundreds off each horse; and some of our party were at times so bitten by the noisome little creatures that they could hardly sleep at night, and in one or two cases the man was actually laid up for a couple of days; and two of our horses ultimately got tick fever, but recovered.

In mid-afternoon of our third day in this camp we at last had matters in such shape that Kermit and I could

My first "tommy" (Thomson's gazelle)
From a photograph by Edmund Heller

begin our hunting; and forth we rode, he with Hill, I with Sir Alfred, each accompanied by his gun-bearers and sais, and by a few porters to carry in the game. For two or three miles our little horses shuffled steadily northward across the desolate flats of short grass until the ground began to rise here and there into low hills, or koppies, with rock-strewn tops. It should have been the rainy season, the season of "the big rains"; but the rains were late, as the parched desolation of the landscape bore witness; nevertheless there were two or three showers that afternoon. We soon began to see game, but the flatness of the country and the absence of all cover made stalking a matter of diffi-

culty; the only bushes were a few sparsely scattered mimosas; stunted things, two or three feet high, scantily leaved,
but abounding in bulbous swellings on the twigs, and in
long, sharp spikes of thorns. There were herds of hartebeest and wildebeest, and smaller parties of beautiful gazelles. The last were of two kinds, named severally after
their discoverers, the explorers Grant and Thomson; many
of the creatures of this region commemorate the men—
Schilling, Jackson, Neuman, Kirke, Chanler, Abbot—
who first saw and hunted them and brought them to the
notice of the scientific world. The Thomson's gazelles, or
Tommies as they are always locally called, are pretty, alert
little things, half the size of our prongbuck; their big
brothers, the Grant's, are among the most beautiful of
all antelopes, being rather larger than a whitetail deer,
with singularly graceful carriage, while the old bucks carry
long lyre-shaped horns.

Distances are deceptive on the bare plains under the
African sunlight. I saw a fine Grant, and stalked him in
a rain squall; but the bullets from the little Springfield
fell short as he raced away to safety; I had underestimated
the range. Then I shot, for the table, a good buck of the
smaller gazelle, at two hundred and twenty-five yards; the
bullet went a little high, breaking his back above the
shoulders.

But what I really wanted were two good specimens, bull
and cow, of the wildebeest. These powerful, ungainly
beasts, a variety of the brindled gnu or blue wildebeest of
South Africa, are interesting creatures of queer, eccentric
habits. With their shaggy manes, heavy forequarters, and
generally bovine look, they remind one somewhat of our
bison, at a distance, but of course they are much less bulky,
a big old bull in prime condition rarely reaching a weight of
seven hundred pounds. They are beasts of the open plains,
ever alert and wary; the cows, with their calves, and one or
more herd bulls, keep in parties of several score; the old
bulls, singly, or two or three together, keep by themselves,

A herd of zebra and hartebeest

One of the interesting features of African wild life is the close association and companionship
so often seen between two totally different species of game

From photographs by Kermit Roosevelt

or with herds of zebra, hartebeest, or gazelle; for one of the interesting features of African wild life is the close association and companionship so often seen between totally different species of game.　Wildebeest are as savage as they are suspicious; when wounded they do not hesitate to charge a man who comes close, although of course neither they nor

Head of the wildebeest bull shot by Mr. Roosevelt

From a photograph by Edmund Heller

any other antelopes can be called dangerous when in a wild state, any more than moose or other deer can be called dangerous; when tame, however, wildebeest are very dangerous indeed, more so than an ordinary domestic bull.　The wild, queer-looking creatures prance and rolick and cut strange capers when a herd first makes up its mind to flee from a stranger's approach; and even a solitary bull will sometimes plunge and buck as it starts to gallop off; while a couple

Mr. Roosevelt in Africa in his hunting costume

From a photograph by Edmund Heller

of bulls, when the herd is frightened, may relieve their feelings by a moment's furious battle, occasionally dropping to their knees before closing. At this time, the end of April, there were little calves with the herds of cows; but in many places in equatorial Africa the various species of antelopes seem to have no settled rutting time or breeding time; at least we saw calves of all ages.

Our hunt after wildebeest this afternoon was successful; but though by velt law each animal was mine, because I hit it first, yet in reality the credit was communistic, so to speak, and my share was properly less than that of others. I first tried to get up to a solitary old bull, and after a good deal of manœuvring, and by taking advantage of a second rain squall, I got a standing shot at him at four hundred yards, and hit him, but too far back. Although keeping a good distance away, he tacked and veered so, as he ran, that by much running myself I got various other shots at him, at very long range, but missed them all, and he finally galloped over a distant ridge, his long tail switching, seemingly not much the worse. We followed on horseback; for I hate to let any wounded thing escape to suffer. But meanwhile he had run into view of Kermit; and Kermit— who is of an age and build which better fit him for successful breakneck galloping over unknown country dotted with holes and bits of rotten ground—took up the chase with enthusiasm. Yet it was sunset, after a run of six or eight miles, when he finally ran into and killed the tough old bull, which had turned to bay, snorting and tossing its horns.

Meanwhile I managed to get within three hundred and fifty yards of a herd, and picked out a large cow which was unaccompanied by a calf. Again my bullet went too far back; and I could not hit the animal at that distance as it ran. But after going half a mile it lay down, and would have been secured without difficulty if a wretched dog had not run forward and put it up; my horse was a long way back, but Pease, who had been looking on at a distance, was mounted, and sped after it. By the time I had reached my horse Pease was out of sight; but riding hard for some miles I overtook him, just before the sun went down, standing by the cow which he had ridden down and slain. It was long after nightfall before we reached camp, ready for a hot bath and a good supper. As always thereafter with anything we shot, we used the meat for food and preserved the skins for the National Museum. Both the cow and the bull were fat and in fine condition; but they were covered with ticks, especially wherever the skin was bare. Around the eyes the loathsome creatures swarmed so as to make complete rims, like spectacles; and in the armpits and the groin they were massed so that they looked like barnacles on an old boat. It is astonishing that the game should mind them so little; the wildebeest evidently dreaded far more the biting flies which hung around them; and the maggots of the bot-flies in their nostrils must have been a sore torment. Nature is merciless indeed.

The next day we rode some sixteen miles to the beautiful hills of Kitanga, and for over a fortnight were either Pease's guests at his farm—ranch, as we should call it in the West —or were on safari under his guidance.

CHAPTER II

ON AN EAST AFRICAN RANCH

THE house at which we were staying stood on the beautiful Kitanga hills. They were so named after an Englishman, to whom the natives had given the name of Kitanga; some years ago, as we were told, he had been killed by a lion near where the ranch house now stood; and we were shown his grave in the little Machakos graveyard. The house was one story high, clean and comfortable, with a veranda running round three sides; and on the veranda were lion skins and the skull of a rhinoceros. From the house we looked over hills and wide lonely plains; the green valley below, with its flat-topped acacias, was very lovely; and in the evening we could see, scores of miles away, the snowy summit of mighty Kilimanjaro turn crimson in the setting sun. The twilights were not long; and when night fell, stars new to northern eyes flashed glorious in the sky. Above the horizon hung the Southern Cross, and directly opposite in the heavens was our old familiar friend the Wain, the Great Bear, upside down and pointing to a North Star so low behind a hill that we could not see it. It is a dry country, and we saw it in the second year of a drought; yet I believe it to be a country of high promise for settlers of white race. In many ways it reminds one rather curiously of the great plains of the West, where they slope upward to the foot-hills of the Rockies. It is a white man's country. Although under the equator, the altitude is so high that the nights are cool, and the region as a whole is very healthy. I saw many children, of the Boer immigrants, of English settlers, even of American missionaries, and they looked sound and well. Of course, there was no real identity in any feature; but again and again the landscape struck me by its general likeness to the

cattle country I knew so well.   As my horse shuffled forward,
under the bright, hot sunlight, across the endless flats or
gently rolling slopes of brown and withered grass, I might
have been on the plains anywhere, from Texas to Montana;
the hills were like our Western buttes; the half-dry water-

Sir Alfred, Lady, and Miss Pease, on ranch steps with rhino and lion
skulls and lion skins
From a photograph by Kermit Roosevelt

courses were fringed with trees, just as if they had been
the Sandy, or the Dry, or the Beaver, or the Cottonwood,
or any of the multitude of creeks that repeat these and
similar names, again and again, from the Panhandle to the
Saskatchewan.   Moreover a Westerner, far better than an
Easterner, could see the possibilities of the country.   There
should be storage reservoirs in the hills and along the rivers

—in my judgment built by the government, and paid for by the water-users in the shape of water-rents—and irrigation ditches; with the water stored and used there would be an excellent opening for small farmers, for the settlers, the actual home-makers, who, above all others, should be encouraged to come into a white man's country like this of the highlands of East Africa. Even as it is, many settlers do well; it is hard to realize that right under the equator the conditions are such that wheat, potatoes, strawberries, apples, all flourish. No new country is a place for weaklings; but the right kind of man, the settler who makes a success in similar parts of our own West, can do well in East Africa; while a man with money can undoubtedly do very well indeed; and incidentally both men will be leading their lives under conditions peculiarly attractive to a certain kind of spirit. It means hard work, of course; but success generally does imply hard work.

The plains were generally covered only with the thick grass on which the great herds of game fed; here and there small thorn-trees grew upon them, but usually so small and scattered as to give no shelter or cover. By the occasional watercourses the trees grew more thickly, and also on the hills and in the valleys between. Most of the trees were mimosas, or of similar kind, usually thorny; but there were giant cactus-like euphorbias, shaped like candelabra, and named accordingly; and on the higher hills fig-trees, wild olives, and many others whose names I do not know, but some of which were stately and beautiful. Many of the mimosas were in bloom, and covered with sweet-smelling yellow blossoms. There were many flowers. On the dry plains there were bushes of the color and size of our own sage-brush, covered with flowers like morning-glories. There were also wild sweet-peas, on which the ostriches fed; as they did on another plant with a lilac flower of a faint heliotrope fragrance. Among the hills there were masses of singularly fragrant flowers like pink jessamines, growing on bushes sometimes fifteen feet high or over.   There were white flowers that smelt like narcissus, blue flowers, red lilies, orange tiger-lilies, and many others of many kinds and colors, while here and there in the pools of the rare rivers grew the sweet-scented purple lotus-lily.

There was an infinite variety of birds, small and large, dull-colored and of the most brilliant plumage.   For the most part they either had no names at all or names that meant nothing to us.   There were glossy starlings of many kinds; and scores of species of weaver finches, some brilliantly colored, others remarkable because of the elaborate nests they built by communities among the trees.   There were many kinds of shrikes, some of them big, parti-colored birds, almost like magpies, and with a kestrel-like habit of hovering in the air over one spot;   others very small and prettily colored.   There was a little red-billed finch with its outer tail feathers several times the length of its head and body.   There was a little emerald cuckoo, and a tiny thing, a barbet, that looked exactly like a kingfisher four inches long.   Eared owls flew up from the reeds and grass.   There were big, restless, wonderfully colored plantain-eaters in the woods; and hornbills, with strange swollen beaks.   A true lark, colored like our meadow-lark (to which it is in no way related) sang from bushes; but the clapper-lark made its curious clapping sounds (apparently with its wings like a ruffed grouse) while it zigzagged in the air.   Little pipits sang overhead like our Missouri skylarks.   There were night-jars; and doves of various kinds, one of which uttered a series of notes slightly resembling the call of our whippoorwill or chuckwills widow.   The beautiful little sun-birds were the most gorgeous of all.   Then there were bustards, great and small, and snake-eating secretary birds, on the plains; and francolins, and African spurfowl with brilliant naked throats, and sand grouse that flew in packs uttering guttural notes.   The wealth of bird life was bewildering.   There was not much bird music, judged by the standards of a temperate climate; but the bulbuls, and one or two warblers, sang very sweetly.   The naturalists

caught shrews and mice in their traps; mole rats with vel-
vety fur, which burrowed like our pocket gophers; rats
that lived in holes like those of our kangaroo rat; and one
mouse that was striped like our striped gopher. There were
conies among the rocks on the hills; they looked like squat,
heavy woodchucks, but their teeth were somewhat like
those of a wee rhinoceros, and they had little hoof-like nails
instead of claws. There were civets and wild-cats and
things like a small mongoose. But the most interesting
mammal we saw was a brilliantly colored yellow and blue,
or yellow and slate, bat, which we put up one day while
beating through a ravine. It had been hanging from a
mimosa twig, and it flew well in the strong sunlight, looking like some huge, parti-colored butterfly.

It was a settled country, this in which we did our
first hunting, and for this reason all the more interesting.
The growth and development of East and Middle Africa
are phenomena of such absorbing interest, that I was delighted at the chance to see the parts where settlement
has already begun before plunging into the absolute wilderness. There was much to remind one of conditions in
Montana and Wyoming thirty years ago; the ranches
planted down among the hills and on the plains still teeming with game, the spirit of daring adventure everywhere
visible, the hope and the heart-breaking disappointment, the
successes and the failures. But the problem offered by the
natives bore no resemblance to that once offered by the
presence of our tribes of horse Indians, few in numbers
and incredibly formidable in war. The natives of East
Africa are numerous; many of them are agricultural or pastoral peoples after their own fashion; and even the bravest
of them, the warlike Masai, are in no way formidable as
our Indians were formidable when they went on the war-
path. The ranch country I first visited was in what was
once the domain of the Wakamba, and in the greater part
of it the tribes still dwell. They are in most ways primitive
savages, with an imperfect and feeble social, and therefore

Mr. Roosevelt and Medlicott at the spot where we nooned on the first (unsuccessful) day
of lion hunting in the Lucania Donga

From a photograph by Kermit Roosevelt

military, organization; they live in small communities under
their local chiefs; they file their teeth, and though they wear
blankets in the neighborhood of the whites, these blankets
are often cast aside; even when the blanket is worn, it is often
in such fashion as merely to accentuate the otherwise absolute nakedness of both sexes. Yet these savages are cattle-
keepers and cattle-raisers, and the women do a good deal of
simple agricultural work; unfortunately, they are waste-
fully destructive of the forests. The chief of each little village is recognized as the official headman by the British
official, is given support, and is required to help the authorities keep peace and stamp out cattle disease—the two most
important functions of government so far as the Wakamba
themselves are concerned. All the tribes have their herds
of black, brown, and white goats, of mottled sheep, and
especially of small humped cattle. The cattle form their
pride and joy. During the day each herd is accompanied
by the herdsmen, and at night it is driven within its boma,
or circular fence of thorn-bushes. Except for the milk,
which they keep in their foul, smoky calabashes, the natives
really make no use of their cattle; they do not know how
to work them, and they never eat them even in time of
starvation. When there is prolonged drought and conse-
quent failure of crops, the foolish creatures die by the hundreds when they might readily be saved if they were willing
to eat the herds which they persist in treating as ornaments
rather than as made for use.

Many of the natives work for the settlers, as cattle-
keepers, as ostrich-keepers, or, after a fashion, as laborers.
The settlers evidently much prefer to rely upon the natives
for unskilled labor rather than see coolies from Hindostan
brought into the country. At Sir Alfred Pease's ranch, as
at most of the other farms of the neighborhood, we found
little Wakamba settlements. Untold ages separated employers and employed; yet those that I saw seemed to get
on well together. The Wakamba are as yet not sufficiently
advanced to warrant their sharing in the smallest degree in

the common government; the "just consent of the governed" in their case, if taken literally, would mean idleness, famine, and endless internecine warfare. They cannot govern themselves from within; therefore they must be governed from without; and their need is met in highest fashion by firm and just control, of the kind that on the whole they are

Tree with Wakamba beehives, Kitanga
From a photograph by Edmund Heller

now getting. At Kitanga the natives on the place sometimes worked about the house; and they took care of the stock. The elders looked after the mild little humped cattle—bulls, steers, and cows; and the children, often the merest toddlers, took naturally to guarding the parties of pretty little calves, during the daytime, when they were separated from their mothers. It was an ostrich-farm, too; and in the morning and evening we would meet the great birds, as they went to their grazing-grounds or returned to the ostrich boma, mincing along with their usual air of foolish stateliness, convoyed by two or three boys, each

with a red blanket, a throwing stick, copper wire round his
legs and arms, and perhaps a feather stuck in his hair.

There were a number of ranches in the neighborhood—
using "neighborhood" in the large Western sense, for they
were many miles apart. The Hills, Clifford and Harold,
were Africanders; they knew the country, and were work-

Percival and his oxen starting off for the giraffes
From a photograph by Kermit Roosevelt

ing hard and doing well; and in the midst of their work
they spared the time to do their full part in insuring a successful hunt to me, an entire stranger. All the settlers I
met treated me with the same large and thoughtful courtesy
—and what fine fellows they were! And their wives even
finer. At Bondoni was Percival, a tall sinewy man, a fine
rider and shot; like so many other men whom I met, he
wore merely a helmet, a flannel shirt, short breeches or
trunks, and puttees and boots, leaving the knee entirely
bare. I shall not soon forget seeing him one day, as he
walked beside his twelve-ox team, cracking his long whip,
while in the big wagon sat pretty Mrs. Percival with a puppy,
and a little cheetah cub, which we had found and presented

to her and which she was taming. They all—Sir Alfred, the Hills, every one—behaved as if each was my host and felt it peculiarly incumbent on him to give me a good time; and among these hosts one who did very much for me was Captain Arthur Slatter. I was his guest at Kilimakiu, where he was running an ostrich-farm; he had lost his right hand, yet he was an exceedingly good game shot both with his light and his heavy rifles.

At Kitanga, Sir Alfred's place, two Boers were working, Messrs. Prinsloo and Klopper. We forgathered, of course, as I too was of Dutch ancestry; they were strong, upstanding men, good mechanics, good masons, and Prinsloo spoke English well. I afterward stopped at the farm of Klopper's father, and at the farm of another Boer named Loijs;

Sir Alfred with cheetah cub, Botha

From a photograph by Kermit Roosevelt

and I met other Boers while out hunting—Erasmus, Botha, Joubert, Meyer. They were descendants of the Voortrekkers with the same names who led the hard-fighting farmers northward from the Cape seventy years ago; and were kinsfolk of the men who since then have made these names honorably known throughout the world. There must of course be many Boers who have gone backward under the stress of a hard and semi-savage life; just as in our communities of the frontier, the backwoods, and the lonely mountains, there are shiftless "poor whites" and "mean whites," mingled with the sturdy men and women who have laid deep the foundations of our national greatness. But

personally I happened not to come across these shiftless
"mean white" Boers. Those that I met, both men and
women, were of as good a type as any one could wish for
in his own countrymen or could admire in another nation-
ality. They fulfilled the three prime requisites for any
race: they worked hard, they could fight hard at need, and
they had plenty of children. These are the three essential
qualities in any and every nation; they are by no means
all-sufficient in themselves, and there is need that many
others should be added to them; but the lack of any one of
them is fatal, and cannot be made good by the presence
of any other set of attributes.

It was pleasant to see the good terms on which Boer and
Briton met. Many of the English settlers whose guest I
was, or with whom I hunted—the Hills, Captain Slatter,
Heatley, Judd—had fought through the South African war;
and so had all the Boers I met. The latter had been for
the most part members of various particularly hard-fighting
commandos; when the war closed they felt very bitterly,
and wished to avoid living under the British flag. Some
moved West and some East; those I met were among the
many hundreds, indeed thousands, who travelled northward
—a few overland, most of them by water—to German East
Africa. But in the part in which they happened to settle
they were decimated by fever, and their stock perished of
cattle sickness; and most of them had again moved northward, and once more found themselves under the British
flag. They were being treated precisely on an equality with
the British settlers; and every well-wisher to his kind, and
above all every well-wisher to Africa, must hope that the
men who in South Africa fought so valiantly against one
another, each for the right as he saw it, will speedily grow
into a companionship of mutual respect, regard, and consideration such as that which, for our inestimable good fortune, now knits closely together in our own land the men
who wore the blue and the men who wore the gray and
their descendants. There could be no better and manlier

people than those, both English and Dutch, who are at this moment engaged in the great and difficult task of adding East Africa to the domain of civilization; their work is bound to be hard enough anyhow; and it would be a lamentable calamity to render it more difficult by keeping alive a bitterness which has lost all point and justification, or by failing to recognize the fundamental virtues, the fundamental characteristics, in which the men of the two stocks are in reality so much alike.

Messrs. Klopper and Loijs, whose farms I visited, were doing well; the latter, with three of his sons, took me out with pride to show me the dam which they had built across a dry watercourse, so as to make a storage reservoir when the rains came. The houses were of stone, and clean and comfortable; the floors were covered with the skins of buck and zebra; the chairs were home-made, as was most of the other furniture; the "rust bunks," or couches, strongly and gracefully shaped, and filled with plaited raw hide, were so attractive that I ordered one to take home. There were neatly kept little flower-gardens, suffering much from the drought; there were ovens and out-buildings; cattle-sheds for the humped oxen and the herds of pretty cows and calves; the biltong was drying in smoke-houses; there were patches of ground in cultivation, for corn and veg-

Klopper and Prinsloo, the two Boers working on Sir Alfred's Ranch

From a photograph by Kermit Roosevelt

etables; and the wild velt came up to the door-sills, and the wild game grazed quietly on all sides within sight of the houses. It was a very good kind of pioneer life; and there could be no better pioneer settlers than Boers such as I saw.

The older men wore full beards, and were spare and sinewy. The young men were generally smooth-faced or mustached, strongly built, and rather shy. The elder women were stout, cordial, motherly housewives; the younger were often really pretty. At their houses I was received with hearty hospitality, and given coffee or fresh milk, while we conversed through the medium of the sons or daughters who knew a little English. They all knew that I was of Dutch origin, and were much interested when I repeated to them the only Dutch I knew, a nursery song which, as I told them, had been handed down to me by my own forefathers, and which in return I had repeated, so many, many times, to my children when they were little. It runs as follows, by the way; but I have no idea how the words are spelled, as I have no written copy; it is supposed to be sung by the father, who holds the little boy or little girl on his knee, and tosses him or her up in the air when he comes to the last line:

> Trippa, troppa, tronjes,
> De varken's in de boonjes,
> De koejes in de klaver,
> De paardeen in de haver,
> De eenjes in de water-plass!
> So groot myn kleine (here insert the
>   little boy's or little girl's name) wass!

My pronunciation caused trouble at first; but I think they understood me the more readily because doubtless their own usual tongue was in some sort a dialect; and some of them already knew the song, while they were all pleased and amused at my remembering and repeating it; and we were speedily on a most friendly footing.

The essential identity of interest between the Boer and British settlers was shown by their attitude toward the district commissioner, Mr. Humphery, who was just

Heads of first two big lions shot by Mr. Roosevelt
From a photograph by Kermit Roosevelt

leaving for his biennial holiday, and who dined with us in our tent on his way out. From both Boer farmer and English settler—and from the American missionaries also—

I heard praise of Humphery, as a strong man, not in the
least afraid of either settler or native, but bound to do
justice to both, and, what was quite as important, *sympa-
thizing with the settlers and knowing and understanding
their needs*. A new country in which white pioneer settlers
are struggling with the iron difficulties and hardships of
frontier life is above all others that in which the officials
should be men having both knowledge and sympathy with
the other men over whom they are placed and for whom
they should work.

My host and hostess, Sir Alfred and Lady Pease, were
on the best terms with all their neighbors, and their friendly
interest was returned; now it was the wife of a Boer farmer
who sent over a basket of flowers, now came a box of
apples from an English settler on the hills; now Prinsloo
the Boer stopped to dinner; now the McMillans—American friends, of whose farm and my stay thereon I shall
speak later—rode over from their house on the Mua Hills,
with their guest, Selous, to take lunch. This, by the way,
was after I had shot my first lions, and I was much pleased
to be able to show Selous the trophies.

My gentle-voiced hostess and her daughter had seen
many strange lands and strange happenings; as was natural with a husband and father of such adventure-loving
nature. They took a keen interest, untinged by the slightest
nervousness, in every kind of wild creature from lions and
leopards down. The game was in sight from the veranda
of the house almost every hour of the day. Early one morning, in the mist, three hartebeests came right up to the
wire fence, two-score yards from the house itself; and the
black-and-white striped zebra, and ruddy hartebeest, grazed
or rested through the long afternoons in plain view, on the
hill-sides opposite.

It is hard for one who has not himself seen it to realize
the immense quantities of game to be found on the Kapiti
Plains and Athi Plains and the hills that bound them.
The common game of the plains, the animals of which I

saw most while at Kitanga and in the neighborhood, were the zebra, wildebeest, hartebeest, Grant's gazelle, and "tommies" or Thomson's gazelle; the zebra, and the hartebeest, usually known by the Swahili name of kongoni, being by far the most plentiful. Then there were impalla, mountain reedbuck, duiker, steinbuck, and dimin-

Some of the naturalists' porters and skinners
From a photograph by J. Alden Loring

utive dikdik. As we travelled and hunted we were hardly ever out of sight of game; and on Pease's farm itself there were many thousand head; and so there were on Slatter's. If wealthy men who desire sport of the most varied and interesting kind would purchase farms like these they could get, for much less money, many times the interest and enjoyment a deer-forest or grouse-moor can afford.

The wildebeest or gnu were the shyest and least plentiful, but in some ways the most interesting, because of the queer streak of ferocious eccentricity evident in all their actions. They were of all the animals those that were most exclusively dwellers in the open, where there was neither hill nor bush. Their size and their dark bluish hides, sometimes showing white in the sunlight, but more often black, rendered them more easily seen than any of their companions. But hardly any plains animal of any size makes any effort to escape its enemies by eluding their observation. Very much of what is commonly said about "protective coloration" has no basis whatever in fact. Black and white are normally the most conspicuous colors in nature (and yet are borne by numerous creatures who have succeeded well in the struggle for life); but almost any tint, or combination of tints, among the grays, browns and duns, harmonizes fairly well with at least some surroundings, in most landscapes; and in but a few instances among the larger mammals, and in almost none among those frequenting the open plains, is there the slightest reason for supposing that the creature gains any benefit whatever from what is loosely called its "protective coloration." Giraffes, leopards, and zebras, for instance, have actually been held up as instances of creatures that are "protectingly" colored and are benefited thereby. The giraffe is one of the most conspicuous objects in nature, and never makes the slightest effort to hide; near by its mottled hide is very noticeable, but as a matter of fact, under any ordinary circumstances any possible foe trusting to eyesight would discover the giraffe so far away that its coloring would seem uniform, that is, would because of the distance be indistinguishable from a general tint which really might have a slight protective value. In other words, while it is possible that the giraffe's beautifully waved coloring may under certain circumstances, and in an infinitesimally small number of cases, put it at a slight disadvantage in the struggle for life, in the enormous majority of cases — a majority so great as to make the remaining cases negligible — it has no effect whatever, one way or the other; and it is safe to say that under no conditions is its coloring of the slightest value to it as affording it "protection" from foes trusting to their eyesight. So it is with the leopard;

it is undoubtedly much less conspicuous than if it were black—and yet the black leopards, the melanistic individuals, thrive as well as their spotted brothers; while on the whole it is probably slightly more conspicuous than if it were nearly unicolor, like the American cougar. As compared with the cougar's tawny hide the leopard's coloration represents a very slight disadvantage, and not an advantage, to the beast; but its life is led under conditions which make either the advantage or the disadvantage so slight as to be negligible; its peculiar coloration is probably in actual fact of hardly the slightest service to it from the "protective" stand-point, whether as regards escaping from its enemies or approaching its prey. It has extraordinary facility in hiding, it is a master of the art of stealthy approach; but it is normally nocturnal and by night the color of its hide is of no consequence whatever; while by day, as I have already said, its varied coloration renders it slightly more easy to detect than is the case with the cougar.

All of this applies with peculiar force to the zebra, which it has also been somewhat the fashion of recent years to hold up as an example of "protective coloration." As a matter of fact the zebra's coloration is not protective at all; on the contrary it is exceedingly conspicuous, and under the actual conditions of the zebra's life probably never hides it from its foes; the instances to the contrary being due to conditions so exceptional that they may be disregarded. If any man seriously regards the zebra's coloration as "protective," let him try the experiment of wearing a hunting suit of the zebra pattern; he will speedily be undeceived. The zebra is peculiarly a beast of the open plains, and makes no effort ever to hide from the observation of its foes. It is occasionally found in open forest; and may there now and then escape observation simply as any animal of any color—a dun hartebeest or a nearly black bushbuck—may escape observation. At a distance of over a few hundred yards the zebra's coloration ceases to be conspicuous simply because the distance has caused it to lose all its distinctive character—that is, all the quality which could possibly make it protective. Near by it is always very conspicuous, and if the conditions are such that any animal can be seen at all, a zebra will catch the eye much more quickly than a Grant's gazelle, for instance. These gazelles, by the way, although much less conspicuously colored than the zebra, bear when young, and the females even when adult, the dark side stripe which characterizes all sexes and ages of the smaller gazelle, the tommy; it is a very conspicuous marking, quite inexplicable on any theory of protective coloration. The truth is that no game of the plains is helped in any way by its coloration in evading its foes and none seeks to escape the vision of its foes. The larger game animals of the plains are always walking and standing in conspicuous places, and never seek to hide or take advantage of cover; while, on the contrary, the little grass and bush antelopes, like the duiker and steinbuck, trust very much to their power of hiding, and endeavor to escape the sight of their foes by lying absolutely still, in the hope of not being made out against their background. On the plains one sees the wildebeest farthest off and with most ease; the zebra and hartebeest next; the gazelles last.

The wildebeest are very wary. While the hunter is still a long way off the animal will stop grazing and stand with head raised, the heavy shoulders and short neck making it unmistakable. Then, when it makes up its mind to allow no closer approach, it brandishes its long tail, springs and plunges, runs once or twice in semicircles, and is off, the head held much lower than the shoulders, the tail still lashing; and now and then a bull may toss up the dust with its horns. The herds of cows and calves usually contain one or two or more bulls; and in addition, dotted here and there over the plain, are single bulls or small parties of bulls, usually past their prime or not yet full grown. These bulls are often found in the company of hartebeests or zebras; and stray zebras and hartebeests are often found with the wildebeest herds. The stomachs of those I opened contained nothing but grass; they are grazers, not browsers. The hartebeest are much faster, and if really frightened speedily leave their clumsy-looking friends behind; but the wildebeest, as I have seen them, are by far the most wary. The wildebeest and zebra seemed to me to lie down less freely than the hartebeest; but I frequently came on herds of both lying down during the heat of the day. Sometimes part of the herd will stand drowsily erect and the rest lie down. Near Kitanga there were three wildebeest which were usually found with a big herd of hartebeest, and which regularly every afternoon lay down for some hours, just as their friends did. The animal has a very bovine look; and though called an antelope it is quite as close kin to the oxen as it is to many of the other beasts also called antelope. The fact is that antelope is not an exact term at all, but merely means any hollow-horned ruminant which the observer happens to think is not a sheep, goat, or ox. When, with Linnæus, the first serious effort at the systematization of living nature began, men naturally groped in the effort to see correctly and to express what they saw. When they came to describe the hollow-horned ruminants, they, of course, already had names at hand for anything that looked like one of the domestic creatures with which they were familiar; and as "antelope" was also already a name of general, though vague, currency for some wild creatures, they called everything an antelope that did not seem to come in one of the more familiar domestic categories. Study has shown that sheep and goats grade into one another among the wild species; and the so-called antelopes include forms differing from one another quite as sharply as any of them differ from their kinsfolk that are represented in the farm-yard.

Zebra share with hartebeest the distinction of being the most abundant game animal on the plains, throughout the whole Athi region. The two creatures are fond of associating together, usually in mixed herds; but sometimes there will merely be one or two individuals of one species in a big herd of the other. They are sometimes, though less frequently than the hartebeest, found in open bush country; but they live in the open plains by choice.

I could not find out that they had fixed times for resting, feeding, and going to water. They and the hartebeests formed the favorite prey of the numerous lions of the neighborhood; and I believe that the nights, even the moonlight nights, were passed by both animals under a nervous strain of apprehension, ever dreading the attack of their arch enemy, and stampeding from it. Their stampedes cause the utmost exasperation to the settlers for when in terror of the real or imaginary attack of a lion, their mad, heedless rush takes them through a wire fence as if it were made of twine and pasteboard. But a few months before my arrival a mixed herd of zebra and hartebeest, stampeded either by lions or wild dogs, rushed through the streets of Nairobi, several being killed by the inhabitants, and one of the victims falling just outside the Episcopal church. The zebras are nearly powerless when seized by lions; but they are bold creatures against less formidable foes, trusting in their hoofs and their strong jaws; they will, when in a herd, drive off hyena or wild dogs, and will turn on hounds, if the hunter is not near. If the lion is abroad in the daytime, they, as well as the other game, seem to realize that he cannot run them down; and though they follow his movements with great alertness, and keep at a respectful distance, they show no panic. Ordinarily, as I saw them, they did not seem very shy of men; but in this respect all the game displayed the widest differences, from time to time, without any real cause, that I could discern, for the difference. At one hour, or on one day, the zebra and hartebeest would flee from our approach when half a mile off; and again they would permit us to come within a couple of hundred yards before moving slowly away. On two or three occasions at lunch herds of zebra remained for half an hour watching us with much curiosity not over a hun-

dred yards off.   Once, when we had been vainly beating for
lions at the foot of the Elukania ridge, at least a thousand
zebras stood, in herds, on every side of. us, throughout
lunch; they were from two to four hundred yards distant,
and I was especially struck by the fact that those which
were to leeward and had our wind were no more alarmed
than the others.   I have seen them water at dawn and sunset, and also in the middle of the day; and I have seen
them grazing at every hour of the day, although I believe
most freely in the morning and evening.   At noon and until
the late afternoon those I saw were quite apt to be resting,
either standing or lying down.   They are noisy.   Hartebeests merely snort or sneeze now and then; but the shrill,
querulous barking of the "bonte quaha," as the Boers call
the zebra, is one of the common sounds of the African plains,
both by day and night.   It is usually represented in books by
the syllables "qua-ha-ha"; but of course our letters and syllables were not made to represent, and can only in arbitrary
and conventional fashion represent, the calls of birds and
mammals; the bark of the bonte quagga or common zebra
could just as well be represented by the syllables "ba-wa-
wa," and as a matter of fact it can readily be mistaken for
the bark of a shrill-voiced dog.   After one of a herd has
been killed by a lion or a hunter its companions are particularly apt to keep uttering their cry.   Zebras are very
beautiful creatures, and it was an unending pleasure to
watch them.   I never molested them save to procure specimens for the museums, or food for the porters, who like
their rather rank flesh.   They were covered with ticks
like the other game; on the groin, and many of the tender-
est spots, the odious creatures were in solid clusters; yet the
zebras were all in high condition, with masses of oily yellow
fat.   One stallion weighed six hundred and fifty pounds.

The hartebeest—Coke's hartebeest, known locally by
the Swahili name of kongoni—were at least as plentiful,
and almost as tame as the zebras.   As with the other game
of equatorial Africa, we found the young of all ages; there

seems to be no especial breeding time, and no one period
among the males corresponding to the rutting season among
northern animals.   The hartebeests were usually insepara-
ble companions of the zebra; but though they were by preference beasts of the bare plain, they were rather more
often found in open bush than were their striped friends.
There are in the country numerous ant-hills, which one sees
in every stage of development, from a patch of bare earth
with a few funnel-like towers, to a hillock a dozen feet high
and as many yards in circumference.   On these big ant-
hills one or two kongoni will often post themselves as look-
outs, and are then almost impossible to approach.   The
bulls sometimes fight hard among themselves, and although
their horns are not very formidable weapons, yet I knew of
one case in which a bull was killed in such a duel, his chest
being ripped open by his adversary's horns; and now and
then a bull will kneel and grind its face and horns into the
dust or mud.   Often a whole herd will gather around and
on an ant-hill, or even a small patch of level ground, and
make it a regular stamping ground, treading it into dust
with their sharp hoofs.   They have another habit which
I have not seen touched on in the books.   Ordinarily their
droppings are scattered anywhere on the plain; but again
and again I found where hartebeests—and more rarely
Grant's gazelles—had in large numbers deposited their
droppings for some time in one spot.   Hartebeest are
homely creatures, with long faces, high withers, and showing when first in motion a rather ungainly gait, but they
are among the swiftest and most enduring of antelope, and
when at speed their action is easy and regular.   When
pursued by a dog they will often play before him—just as
a tommy will—taking great leaps, with all four legs inclined backward, evidently in a spirit of fun and derision.
In the stomachs of those I killed, as in those of the zebras,
I found only grass and a few ground plants; even in the
open bush or thinly wooded country they seemed to graze
and not browse.   One fat and heavy bull weighed 340

pounds; a very old bull, with horns much worn down 299; and a cow in high condition 315.

The Grant's gazelle is the most beautiful of all these plains creatures; it is about the size of a big white-tail deer; one heavy buck which I shot, although with poor horns, weighed 171 pounds. The finest among the old bucks have beautiful lyre-shaped horns, over two feet long, and their

Vulture raven or white-necked raven
From a photograph by J. Alden Loring

proud, graceful carriage and lightness of movement render them a delight to the eye. As I have already said, the young and the females have the dark side stripe which marks all the tommies; but the old bucks lack this, and their color fades into the brown or sandy of the dry plains far more completely than is the case with zebra or kongoni. Like the other game of the plains they are sometimes found in small parties, or else in fair-sized herds, by themselves, and sometimes with other beasts; I have seen a single fine buck in a herd of several hundred zebra and kongoni. The Thomson's gazelles, hardly a third the weight of their

larger kinsfolk, are found scattered everywhere; they are
not as highly gregarious as the zebra and kongoni, and are
not found in such big herds; but their little bands—now a
buck and several does, now a couple of does with their
fawns, now three or four bucks together, now a score of
individuals—-are scattered everywhere on the flats. Like
the Grants, their flesh is delicious, and they seem to have
much the same habits. But they have one very marked
characteristic: their tails keep up an incessant nervous
twitching, never being still for more than a few seconds at
a time, while the larger gazelle in this part of its range
rarely moves its tail at all. They are grazers and they
feed, rest, and go to water at irregular times, or at least
at different times in different localities; and although they
are most apt to rest during the heat of the day, I have
seen them get up soon after noon, having lain down for a
couple of hours, feed for an hour or so, and then lie down
again. In the same way the habits of the game as to mi-
gration vary with the different districts, in Africa as in
America. There are places where all the game, perhaps
notably the wildebeests, gather in herds of thousands, at
certain times, and travel for scores of miles, so that a district which is teeming with game at one time may be almost
barren of large wild life at another. But my information
was that around the Kapiti Plains there was no such complete and extensive shift. If the rains are abundant and
the grass rank, most of the game will be found far out in
the middle of the plains; if, as was the case at the time
of my visit, there has been a long drought—the game will
be found ten or fifteen miles away, near or among the foot-
hills.

Unless there was something special on, like a lion or
rhinoceros hunt, I usually rode off followed only by my
sais and gun-bearers. I cannot describe the beauty and
the unceasing interest of these rides, through the teeming
herds of game. It was like retracing the steps of time for
sixty or seventy years, and being back in the days of Corn-

wallis Harris and Gordon Cumming, in the palmy times of the giant fauna of South Africa. On Pease's own farm one day I passed through scores of herds of the beautiful and wonderful wild creatures I have spoken of above; all told there were several thousands of them. With the exception of the wildebeest, most of them were not shy, and I could have taken scores of shots at a distance of a couple of hundred yards or thereabout. Of course, I did not shoot at anything unless we were out of meat or needed the skin for the collection; and when we took the skin we almost always took the meat too, for the porters, although they had their rations of rice, depended for much of their wellbeing on our success with the rifle.

These rides through the wild, lonely country, with only my silent black followers, had a peculiar charm. When the sky was overcast it was cool and pleasant, for it is a high country; as soon as the sun appeared the vertical tropic rays made the air quiver above the scorched land. As we passed down a hill-side we brushed through aromatic shrubs and the hot pleasant fragrance enveloped us. When we came to a nearly dry watercourse, there would be beds of rushes, beautiful lilies and lush green plants with staring flowers; and great deep-green fig-trees, or flat-topped mimosas. In many of these trees there were sure to be native beehives; these were sections of hollow logs hung from the branches; they formed striking and characteristic features of the landscape. Wherever there was any moisture there were flowers, brilliant of hue and many of them sweet of smell; and birds of numerous kinds abounded. When we left the hills and the wooded watercourses we might ride hour after hour across the barren desolation of the flats, while herds of zebra and hartebeest stared at us through the heat haze. Then the zebra, with shrill, barking neighs, would file off across the horizon, or the high-withered hartebeests, snorting and bucking, would rush off in a confused mass, as unreasoning panic succeeded foolish confidence. If I shot anything, vultures of several kinds, and the tall, hideous

marabou storks, gathered before the skinners were through
with their work; they usually stayed at a wary distance,
but the handsome ravens, glossy-hued with white napes,
big-billed, long-winged, and short-tailed, came round more
familiarly.

I rarely had to take the trouble to stalk anything; the
shooting was necessarily at rather long range, but by manœuvring a little, and never walking straight toward a beast,
I was usually able to get whatever the naturalists wished.
Sometimes I shot fairly well, and sometimes badly. On
one day, for instance, the entry in my diary ran: "Missed
steinbuck, pig, impalla and Grant; awful." On another
day it ran in part as follows: "Out with Heller. Hartebeest, 250 yards, facing me; shot through face, broke neck.
Zebra, very large, quartering, 160 yards, between neck
and shoulder. Buck Grant, 220 yards, walking, behind
shoulder. Steinbuck, 180 yards, standing, behind shoulder."
Generally each head of game bagged cost me a goodly
number of bullets; but only twice did I wound animals
which I failed to get; in the other cases the extra cartridges
represented either misses at animals which got clean away
untouched, or else a running fusillade at wounded animals
which I eventually got. I am a very strong believer in
making sure, and, therefore, in shooting at a wounded animal as long as there is the least chance of its getting off.
The expenditure of a few cartridges is of no consequence
whatever compared to the escape of a single head of game
which should have been bagged. Shooting at long range
necessitates much running. Some of my successful shots at
Grant's gazelle and kongoni were made at 300, 350, and
400 yards; but at such distances my proportion of misses
was very large indeed—and there were altogether too many
even at shorter ranges.

The so-called grass antelopes, the steinbuck and duiker,
were the ones at which I shot worst; they were quite plentiful, and they got up close, seeking to escape observation
by hiding until the last moment; but they were small, and

when they did go they rushed half hidden through the grass and in and out among the bushes at such a speed, and with such jumps and twists and turns, that I found it wellnigh impossible to hit them with the rifle. The few I got were generally shot when they happened to stand still.

On the steep, rocky, bush-clad hills there were little klipspringers and the mountain reedbuck or Chanler's reedbuck, a very pretty little creature. Usually we found the reedbuck does and their fawns in small parties, and the bucks by themselves; but we saw too few to enable us to tell whether this represented their normal habits. They fed on the grass, the hill plants, and the tips of certain of the shrubs, and were true mountaineers in their love of the rocks and rough ground, to which they fled in frantic haste when alarmed. They were shy and elusive little things, but not wary in the sense that some of the larger antelopes are wary. I shot two does with three bullets, all of which hit. Then I tried hard for a buck; at last, late one evening, I got up to one feeding on a steep hill-side, and actually took ten shots to kill him, hitting him no less than seven times.

Occasionally we drove a ravine or a range of hills by means of beaters. On such occasions all kinds of things were put up. Most of the beaters, especially if they were wild savages impressed for the purpose from some neighboring tribe, carried throwing-sticks, with which they were very expert; as indeed were some of the colonials, like the Hills. Hares, looking and behaving much like small jackrabbits, were plentiful both on the plains and in the ravines, and dozens of these were knocked over; while on several occasions I saw francolins and spurfowl cut down on the wing by a throwing-stick hurled from some unusually dexterous hand.

The beats, with the noise and laughter of the good-humored, excitable savages, and the alert interest as to what would turn up next, were great fun; but the days I enjoyed most were those spent alone with my horse and gun-bearers.

We might be off by dawn, and see the tropic sun flame splendid over the brink of the world; strange creatures rustled through the bush or fled dimly through the long grass, before the light grew bright; and the air was fresh and sweet as it blew in our faces. When the still heat of noon drew near I would stop under a tree, with my water canteen and my lunch. The men lay in the shade, and the hobbled pony grazed close by, while I either dozed or else watched through my telescope the herds of game lying down or standing drowsily in the distance. As the shadows lengthened I would again mount, and finally ride homeward as the red sunset paled to amber and opal, and all the vast, mysterious African landscape grew to wonderful beauty in the dying twilight.

CHAPTER III

LION HUNTING ON THE KAPITI PLAINS

THE dangerous game of Africa are the lion, buffalo, elephant, rhinoceros, and leopard. The hunter who follows any of these animals always does so at a certain risk to life or limb; a risk which it is his business to minimize by coolness, caution, good judgment, and straight shooting. The leopard is in point of pluck and ferocity more than the equal of the other four; but his small size always renders it likely that he will merely maul, and not kill, a man. My friend, Carl Akeley, of Chicago, actually killed barehanded a leopard which sprang on him. He had already wounded the beast twice, crippling it in one front and one hind paw; whereupon it charged, followed him as he tried to dodge the charge, and struck him full just as he turned. It bit him in one arm, biting again and again as it worked up the arm from the wrist to the elbow; but Akeley threw it, holding its throat with the other hand, and flinging its body to one side. It luckily fell on its side with its two wounded legs uppermost, so that it could not tear him. He fell forward with it and crushed in its chest with his knees until he distinctly felt one of its ribs crack; this, said Akeley, was the first moment when he felt he might conquer. Redoubling his efforts, with knees and hand, he actually choked and crushed the life out of it, although his arm was badly bitten. A leopard will charge at least as readily as one of the big beasts, and is rather more apt to get his charge home, but the risk is less to life than to limb.

There are other animals often or occasionally dangerous to human life which are, nevertheless, not dangerous to the hunter. Crocodiles are far greater pests, and far more often man-eaters, than lions or leopards; but their shooting is not accompanied by the smallest element of risk. Poisonous snakes are fruitful sources of accident, but they are actuated only by fear, and the anger born of fear. The hippopotamus sometimes destroys boats and kills those in them; but again there is no risk in hunting him. Finally, the hyena, too cowardly ever to be a source of danger to the hunter, is sometimes a dreadful curse to the weak and helpless. The hyena is a beast of unusual strength, and of enormous power in his jaws and teeth, and thrice over would he be dreaded were fang and sinew driven by a heart of the leopard's cruel courage. But though the creature's foul and evil ferocity has no such backing as that yielded by the angry daring of the spotted cat, it is yet fraught with a terror all its own; for on occasion the hyena takes to man-eating after its own fashion. Carrion-feeder though it is, in certain places it will enter native huts and carry away children or even sleeping adults; and where famine or disease has worked havoc among a people, the hideous spotted beasts become bolder and prey on the survivors. For some years past Uganda has been scourged by the sleeping sickness, which has ravaged it as in the Middle Ages the Black Death ravaged Europe. Hundreds of thousands of natives have died. Every effort has been made by the government officials to cope with the disease; and among other things sleeping-sickness camps have been established, where those stricken by the dread malady can be isolated and cease to be possible sources of infection to their fellows. Recovery among those stricken is so rare as to be almost unknown, but the disease is often slow, and months may elapse during which the diseased man is still able to live his life much as usual. In the big camps of doomed men and women thus established there were, therefore, many persons carrying on their avocations much as in an ordinary native village. But the hyenas speedily found that in many of the huts the inmates were a helpless prey. In 1908 and throughout the early part of 1909 they grew constantly bolder, haunt-

Kermit Roosevelt, Sir Alfred Pease, and Mr. Roosevelt at the carcass of first big lion

ing these sleeping-sickness camps, and each night entering them, bursting into the huts and carrying off and eating the dying people. To guard against them each little group of huts was inclosed by a thick hedge; but after a while the hyenas learned to break through the hedges, and continued their ravages; so that every night armed sentries had to patrol the camps, and every night they could be heard firing at the marauders.

The men thus preyed on were sick to death, and for the most part helpless. But occasionally men in full vigor are attacked. One of Pease's native hunters was seized by a hyena as he slept beside the camp-fire, and part of his face torn off. Selous informed me that a friend of his, Major R. T. Coryndon, then administrator of Northwestern Rhodesia, was attacked by a hyena but two or three years ago. At the time Major Coryndon was lying, wrapped in a blanket, beside his wagon. A hyena, stealthily approaching through the night, seized him by the hand, and dragged him out of bed; but as he struggled and called out, the beast left him and ran off into the darkness. In spite of his torn hand the major was determined to get his assailant, which he felt sure would soon return. Accordingly, he went back to his bed, drew his cocked rifle beside him, pointing toward his feet, and feigned sleep. When all was still once more, a dim form loomed up through the uncertain light, toward the foot of the bed; it was the ravenous beast returning for his prey; and the major shot and killed it where it stood.

A few months ago a hyena entered the outskirts of Nairobi, crept into a hut, and seized and killed a native man. At Nairobi the wild creatures are always at the threshold of the town, and often cross it. At Governor Jackson's table, at Government House, I met Mr. and Mrs. Sandiford. Mr. Sandiford is managing the railroad. A few months previously, while he was sitting, with his family, in his own house in Nairobi, he happened to ask his daughter to look for something in one of the bedrooms.

She returned in a minute, quietly remarking, "Father, there's a leopard under the bed." So there was; and it was then remembered that the house-cat had been showing a marked and alert distrust of the room in question—very probably the leopard had gotten into the house while trying to catch her or one of the dogs. A neighbor with a rifle was summoned, and shot the leopard.

Hyenas not infrequently kill mules and donkeys, tearing open their bellies, and eating them while they are still alive. Yet when themselves assailed they usually behave with abject cowardice. The Hills had a large Airedale terrier, an energetic dog of much courage. Not long before our visit this dog put up a hyena from a bushy ravine, in broad daylight, ran after it, overtook it, and flew at it. The hyena made no effective fight, although the dog—not a third its weight—bit it severely, and delayed its flight so that it was killed. During the first few weeks of our trip I not infrequently heard hyenas after nightfall, but saw none. Kermit, however, put one out of a ravine or dry creek-bed—a donga, as it is locally called—and though the brute had a long start he galloped after it and succeeded in running it down. The chase was a long one, for twice the hyena got in such rocky country that he almost distanced his pursuer; but at last, after covering nearly ten miles, Kermit ran into it in the open, shooting it from the saddle as it shambled along at a canter growling with rage and terror. I would not have recognized the cry of the hyenas from what I had read, and it was long before I heard them laugh. Pease said that he had only once heard them really laugh. On that occasion he was watching for lions outside a Somali zareba. Suddenly a leopard leaped clear over the zareba, close beside him, and in a few seconds came flying back again, over the high thorn fence, with a sheep in its mouth; but no sooner had it landed than the hyenas rushed at it and took away the sheep; and then their cackling and shrieking sounded exactly like the most unpleasant kind of laughter. The normal death of very old lions, as

they grow starved and feeble—unless they are previously
killed in an encounter with dangerous game like buffalo—
is to be killed and eaten by hyenas; but of course a lion
in full vigor pays no heed to hyenas, unless it is to kill one
if it gets in the way.

During the last few decades, in Africa, hundreds of
white hunters, and thousands of native hunters, have been
killed or wounded by lions, buffaloes, elephants, and rhinos.
All are dangerous game; each species has to its grewsome
credit a long list of mighty hunters slain or disabled. Among
those competent to express judgment there is the widest
difference of opinion as to the comparative danger in hunting the several kinds of animals. Probably no other hunter
who has ever lived has combined Selous's experience with
his skill as a hunter and his power of accurate observation
and narration. He has killed between three and four
hundred lions, elephants, buffaloes, and rhinos, and he
ranks the lion as much the most dangerous, and the rhino
as much the least, while he puts the buffalo and elephant
in between, and practically on a par. Governor Jackson
has killed between eighty and ninety of the four animals;
and he puts the buffalo unquestionably first in point of formidable capacity as a foe, the elephant equally unquestionably second, the lion third, and the rhino last. Stigand
puts them in the following order: lion, elephant, rhino,
leopard, and buffalo. Drummond, who wrote a capital
book on South African game, who was for years a professional hunter like Selous, and who had fine opportunities
for observation, but who was a much less accurate observer
than Selous, put the rhino as unquestionably the most dangerous, with the lion as second, and the buffalo and elephant
nearly on a level. Samuel Baker, a mighty hunter and good
observer, but with less experience of African game than any
one of the above, put the elephant first, the rhino second,
the buffalo seemingly third, and the lion last. The experts
of greatest experience thus absolutely disagree among themselves; and there is the same wide divergence of view

among good hunters and trained observers whose opportunities have been less. Mr. Abel Chapman, for instance,
regards both the elephant and the rhino as more danger-

Clifford Hill's Kikuyu ostrich boys as they beat the tall grass tor lion on the
third day of lion hunting at Killima (Hill) Ugami, when we got two large
and one small one. The boys had their bows and arrows for protection
From a photograph by Kermit Roosevelt

ous than the lion; and many of the hunters I met in East
Africa seemed inclined to rank the buffalo as more dangerous than any other animal. A man who has shot but a

dozen or a score of these various animals, all put together, is not entitled to express any but the most tentative opinion as to their relative prowess and ferocity; yet on the whole it seems to me that the weight of opinion among those best fitted to judge is that the lion is the most formidable opponent of the hunter, under ordinary conditions. This is my own view. But we must ever keep in mind the fact that the surrounding conditions, the geographical locality, and the wide individual variation of temper within the ranks of each species, must all be taken into account. Under certain circumstances a lion may be easily killed, whereas a rhino would be a dangerous foe. Under other conditions the rhino could be attacked with impunity, and the lion only with the utmost hazard; and one bull buffalo might flee and one bull elephant charge, and yet the next couple met with might show an exact reversal of behavior.

At any rate, during the last three or four years, in German and British East Africa and Uganda, over fifty white men have been killed or mauled by lions buffaloes, elephants, and rhinos; and the lions have much the largest list of victims to their credit. In Nairobi church-yard I was shown the graves of seven men who had been killed by lions, and of one who had been killed by a rhino. The first man to meet us on the African shore was Mr. Campbell, Governor Jackson's A.D.C., and only a year previously he had been badly mauled by a lion. We met one gentleman who had been crippled for life by a lioness. He had marked her into some patches of brush, and coming up, tried to put her out of one thick clump. Failing, he thought she might have gone into another thicket, and walked toward it; instantly that his back was turned, the lioness, who had really been in the first clump of brush, raced out after him, threw him down, and bit him again and again before she was driven off. One night we camped at the very spot where, a score of years before, a strange tragedy had happened. It was in the early days of the opening of the country, and an expedition was going toward Uganda; one of

R. J. Cuninghame   Sir Alfred Pease   Mr. Roosevelt

Mr. Roosevelt weighing a lioness (shot by him) which the porters brought in entire amid great rejoicings and chantings

From a photograph by Kermit Roosevelt

the officials in charge was sleeping in a tent with the flap
open. There was an askari on duty; yet a lion crept up,
entered the tent, and seized and dragged forth the man.
He struggled and made outcry; there was a rush of people,
and the lion dropped his prey and bounded off. The
man's wounds were dressed, and he was put back to bed in
his own tent; but an hour or two after the camp again grew
still, the lion returned, bent on the victim of whom he had
been robbed; he re-entered the tent, seized the unfortunate wounded man with his great fangs, and this time
made off with him into the surrounding darkness, killed
and ate him. Not far from the scene of this tragedy,
another had occurred. An English officer named Stewart,
while endeavoring to kill his first lion, was himself set on and
slain. At yet another place we were shown where two
settlers, Messrs. Lucas and Goldfinch, had been one killed
and one crippled by a lion they had been hunting. They
had been following the chase on horseback, and being men
of bold nature, and having killed several lions, had become
too daring. They hunted the lion into a small piece of
brush and rode too near it. It came out at a run and was
on them before their horses could get under way. Goldfinch was knocked over and badly bitten and clawed; Lucas went to his assistance, and was in his turn knocked
over, and the lion then lay on him and bit him to death.
Goldfinch, in spite of his own severe wounds, crawled
over and shot the great beast as it lay on his friend.

Most of the settlers with whom I was hunting had met
with various adventures in connection with lions. Sir
Alfred had shot many in different parts of Africa; some
had charged fiercely, but he always stopped them. Captain Slatter had killed a big male with a mane a few months
previously. He was hunting it in company with Mr. Humphery, the district commissioner of whom I have already
spoken and it gave them some exciting moments for when
hit it charged savagely. Humphery had a shot-gun loaded
with buckshot, Slatter his rifle. When wounded, the lion

charged straight home, hit Slatter, knocking him flat and rolling him over and over in the sand, and then went after the native gun-bearer, who was running away—the worst possible course to follow with a charging lion. The mechanism of Slatter's rifle was choked by the sand, and as he rose to his feet he saw the lion overtake the fleeing man, rise on his hind legs like a rearing horse—not springing— and strike down the fugitive. Humphery fired into him with buckshot, which merely went through the skin; and some minutes elapsed before Slatter was able to get his rifle in shape to kill the lion, which, fortunately, had begun to feel the effect of his wounds, and was too sick to resume hostilities of its own accord. The gun-bearer was badly but not fatally injured. Before this, Slatter, while on a lion hunt, had been set afoot by one of the animals he was after, which had killed his horse. It was at night and the horse was tethered within six yards of his sleeping master. The latter was aroused by the horse galloping off, and he heard it staggering on for some sixty yards before it fell. He and his friend followed it with lanterns and drove off the lion, but the horse was dead. The tracks and the marks on the horse showed what had happened. The lion had sprung clean on the horse's back, his fore claws dug into the horse's shoulders, his hind claws cutting into its haunches, while the great fangs bit at the neck. The horse struggled off at a heavy run, carrying its fearsome burden. After going some sixty yards the lion's teeth went through the spinal cord, and the ride was over. Neither animal had made a sound, and the lion's feet did not touch the earth until the horse fell.

While a magistrate in the Transvaal, Pease had under him as game officer a white hunter, a fine fellow, who underwent an extraordinary experience. He had been off some distance with his Kaffir boys, to hunt a lion. On his way home the hunter was hunted. It was after nightfall. He had reached a region where lions had not been seen for a long time, and where an attack by them was unknown.

He was riding along a trail in the darkness, his big boar-
hound trotting ahead, his native "boys" some distance
behind.   He heard a rustle in the bushes alongside the
path, but paid no heed, thinking it was a reedbuck.   Immediately afterward two lions came out in the path behind
and raced after him.   One sprang on him, tore him out
of the saddle, and trotted off holding him in its mouth, while
the other continued after the frightened horse.   The lion
had him by the right shoulder, and yet with his left hand
he wrenched his knife out of his belt and twice stabbed it.
The second stab went to the heart and the beast let go of
him, stood a moment, and fell dead.   Meanwhile, the dog
had followed the other lion, which now, having abandoned
the chase of the horse, and with the dog still at his heels,
came trotting back to look for the man.   Crippled though
he was, the hunter managed to climb a small tree;   and
though the lion might have gotten him out of it, the dog
interfered.   Whenever the lion came toward the tree the
dog worried him, and kept him off until, at the shouts and
torches of the approaching Kaffir boys, he sullenly retired,
and the hunter was rescued.

Percival had a narrow escape from a lion, which nearly
got him, though probably under a misunderstanding.   He
was riding through a wet spot of ground, where the grass
was four feet high, when his horse suddenly burst into a
run and the next moment a lion had galloped almost alongside of him.   Probably the lion thought it was a zebra, for
when Percival, leaning over, yelled in his face, the lion
stopped short.   But he at once came on again, and nearly
caught the horse.   However, they were now out of the tall
grass, and the lion gradually drew up when they reached
the open country.

The two Hills, Clifford and Harold, were running an
ostrich-farm.   The lions sometimes killed their ostriches
and stock;   and the Hills in return had killed several lions.
The Hills were fine fellows;   Africanders, as their forefathers for three generations had been, and frontiersmen of

the best kind. From the first moment they and I became fast friends, for we instinctively understood one another, and found that we felt alike on all the big questions, and looked at life, and especially the life of effort led by the pioneer settler, from the same stand-point. They reminded me, at every moment, of those Western ranchmen and home-makers with whom I have always felt a special sense of companionship and with whose ideals and aspirations I have always felt a special sympathy. A couple of months before my visit, Harold Hill had met with a rather unpleasant adventure. He was walking home across the lonely plains, in the broad daylight, never dreaming that lions might be abroad, and was un-armed. When still some

One of the native beaters and gun-bearers
From a photograph by Edmund Heller

miles from his house, while plodding along, he glanced up and saw three lions in the trail only fifty yards off, staring fixedly at him. It happened to be a place where the grass was rather tall, and lions are always bold where there is the slightest cover; whereas, unless angered, they are cautious on bare ground. He halted, and then walked slowly to one side; and then slowly forward toward his house. The lions followed him with their eyes, and when he had passed they rose and slouched after him. They were not pleasant followers, but to hurry would have been fatal; and he walked slowly on along the road, while for a mile he kept catching

glimpses of the tawny bodies of the beasts as they trod
stealthily forward through the sunburned grass, alongside
or a little behind him. Then the grass grew short, and the
lions halted and continued to gaze after him until he disappeared over a rise.

Everywhere throughout the country we were crossing
were signs that the lion was lord and that his reign was
cruel. There were many lions, for the game on which they
feed was extraordinarily abundant. They occasionally took
the ostriches or stock of the settlers, or ravaged the herds
and flocks of the natives, but not often; for their favorite food was yielded by the swarming herds of kongoni
and zebras, on which they could prey at will. Later we
found that in this region they rarely molested the buffalo,
even where they lived in the same reedbeds; and this though
elsewhere they habitually prey on the buffalo. But where
zebras and hartebeests could be obtained without effort,
it was evidently not worth their while to challenge such
formidable quarry. Every "kill" I saw was a kongoni or
a zebra; probably I came across fifty of each. One zebra
kill, which was not more than eighteen hours old (after
the lapse of that time the vultures and marabouts, not to
speak of the hyenas and jackals, leave only the bare bones),
showed just what had occurred. The bones were all in
place, and the skin still on the lower legs and head. The
animal was lying on its belly, the legs spread out, the neck
vertebra crushed; evidently the lion had sprung clean on
it, bearing it down by his weight while he bit through the
back of the neck, and the zebra's legs had spread out as the
body yielded under the lion. One fresh kongoni kill showed
no marks on the haunches, but a broken neck and claw
marks on the face and withers; in this case the lion's hind
legs had remained on the ground, while with his fore paws
he grasped the kongoni's head and shoulders, holding it
until the teeth splintered the neck bone.

One or two of our efforts to get lions failed, of course;
the ravines we beat did not contain them, or we failed to

make them leave some particularly difficult hill or swamp—
for lions lie close.   But Sir Alfred knew just the right place
to go to, and was bound to get us lions—and he did.

One day we started from the ranch house in good season for an all-day lion hunt.   Besides Kermit and myself,
there was a fellow-guest, Medlicott, and not only our host,

The start for the first day's lion hunting
From a photograph by Kermit Roosevelt

but our hostess and her daughter; and we were joined by
Percival at lunch, which we took under a great fig-tree at
the foot of a high, rocky hill.   Percival had with him a little
mongrel bull-dog, and a Masai "boy," a fine, bold-looking
savage, with a handsome head-dress and the usual formidable
spear; master, man, and dog evidently all looked upon any
form of encounter with lions simply in the light of a spree.

After lunch we began to beat down a long donga, or dry
watercourse—a creek, as we should call it in the Western

plains country. The watercourse, with low, steep banks, wound in curves, and here and there were patches of brush, which might contain anything in the shape of lion, cheetah, hyena, or wild dog. Soon we came upon lion spoor in the sandy bed; first the footprints of a big male, then those of a lioness. We walked cautiously along each side of the donga, the horses following close behind so that if the

View of rock where we lunched on the day we got the first four lions
From a photograph by Lady Pease

lion were missed we could gallop after him and round him up on the plain. The dogs—for besides the little bull, we had a large brindled mongrel named Ben, whose courage belied his looks—began to show signs of scenting the lion; and we beat out each patch of brush, the natives shouting and throwing in stones, while we stood with the rifles where we could best command any probable exit. After a couple of false alarms the dogs drew toward one patch, their hair bristling, and showing such eager excitement that it was evident something big was inside; and in a moment one of the boys called, "simba" (lion), and pointed with his finger. It was just across the little ravine, there about four yards wide and as many feet deep; and I shifted my posi-

Noon at Ugami.   Sir Alfred Pease bending over behind Mr. Roosevelt
From a photograph by Kermit Roosevelt

tion, peering eagerly into the bushes for some moments before I caught a glimpse of tawny hide; as it moved, there was a call to me to "shoot," for at that distance, if the lion charged, there would be scant time to stop it; and I fired into what I saw. There was a commotion in the bushes, and Kermit fired; and immediately afterward there broke out on the other side, not the hoped-for big lion, but two cubs the size of mastiffs. Each was badly wounded and we finished them off; even if unwounded, they were too big to take alive.

This was a great disappointment, and as it was well on in the afternoon, and we had beaten the country most apt to harbor our game, it seemed unlikely that we would have another chance. Percival was on foot and a long way from his house, so he started for it; and the rest of us also began to jog homeward. But Sir Alfred, although he said nothing, intended to have another try. After going a mile or two he started off to the left at a brisk canter; and we, the other riders, followed, leaving behind our gun-bearers, saises, and porters. A couple of miles away was another donga, another shallow watercourse with occasional big brush patches along the winding bed; and toward this we cantered. Almost as soon as we reached it our leader found the spoor of two big lions; and with every sense acock, we dismounted and approached the first patch of tall bushes. We shouted and threw in stones, but nothing came out; and another small patch showed the same result. Then we mounted our horses again, and rode toward another patch a quarter of a mile off. I was mounted on Tranquillity, the stout and quiet sorrel.

This patch of tall, thick brush stood on the hither bank—that is, on our side of the watercourse. We rode up to it and shouted loudly. The response was immediate, in the shape of loud gruntings, and crashings through the thick brush. We were off our horses in an instant, I throwing the reins over the head of mine; and without delay the good old fellow began placidly grazing, quite unmoved by the ominous sounds immediately in front.

I sprang to one side; and for a second or two we waited, uncertain whether we should see the lions charging out ten yards distant or running away. Fortunately, they adopted the latter course. Right in front of me, thirty yards off, there appeared, from behind the bushes which had first screened him from my eyes, the tawny, galloping form of a big maneless lion. Crack! the Winchester spoke; and as the soft-nosed bullet ploughed forward through his flank the lion swerved so that I missed him with the second shot; but my third bullet went through the spine and forward into his chest. Down he came, sixty yards off, his hind quarters dragging, his head up, his ears back, his jaws open and lips drawn up in a prodigious snarl, as he endeavored to turn to face us. His back was broken; but of this we could not at the moment be sure, and if it had merely been grazed, he might have recovered, and then, even though dying, his charge might have done mischief. So Kermit, Sir Alfred, and I fired, almost together, into his chest. His head sank, and he died.

This lion had come out on the left of the bushes; the other, to the right of them, had not been hit, and we saw him galloping off across the plain, six or eight hundred yards away. A couple more shots missed, and we mounted our horses to try to ride him down. The plain sloped gently upward for three-quarters of a mile to a low crest or divide, and long before we got near him he disappeared over this. Sir Alfred and Kermit were tearing along in front and to the right, with Miss Pease close behind; while Tranquillity carried me, as fast as he could, on the left, with Medlicott near me. On topping the divide Sir Alfred and Kermit missed the lion, which had swung to the left, and they raced ahead too far to the right. Medlicott and I, however, saw the lion, loping along close behind some kongoni; and this enabled me to get up to him as quickly as the lighter men on the faster horses. The going was now slightly downhill, and the sorrel took me along very well, while Medlicott, whose horse was slow, bore to the right and joined the other two men. We gained rapidly, and, finding out this, the lion suddenly halted and came to bay in a slight hollow, where the grass was rather long. The plain seemed flat, and we could see the lion well from horseback; but, especially when he lay down, it was most difficult to make him out on foot, and impossible to do so when kneeling.

We were about a hundred and fifty yards from the lion, Sir Alfred, Kermit, Medlicott, and Miss Pease off to one side, and slightly above him on the slope, while I was on the level, about equidistant from him and them. Kermit and I tried shooting from the horses; but at such a distance this was not effective. Then Kermit got off, but his horse would not let him shoot; and when I got off I could not make out the animal through the grass with sufficient distinctness to enable me to take aim. Old Ben the dog had arrived, and, barking loudly, was strolling about near the lion, which paid him not the slightest attention. At this moment my black sais, Simba, came running up to me and took hold of the bridle; he had seen the chase from the line of march and had cut across to join me. There was no other sais or gun-bearer anywhere near, and his action was plucky, for he was the only man afoot, with the lion at bay. Lady Pease had also ridden up and was an interested spectator only some fifty yards behind me.

Now, an elderly man with a varied past which includes rheumatism does not vault lightly into the saddle; as his sons, for instance, can; and I had already made up my mind that in the event of the lion's charging it would be wise for me to trust to straight powder rather than to try to scramble into the saddle and get under way in time. The arrival of my two companions settled matters. I was not sure of the speed of Lady Pease's horse; and Simba was on foot and it was of course out of the question for me to leave him. So I said, "Good, Simba, now we'll see this thing through," and gentle-mannered Simba smiled a shy appreciation of my tone, though he could not understand the words. I was still unable to see the lion when I knelt, but he was now standing up, looking first at one group of horses and then at the other, his tail lashing to and fro, his head held low, and his lips dropped over his mouth in peculiar fashion, while his harsh and savage growling rolled thunderously over the plain.   Seeing Simba and me

"Ben" worrying the second big lion before it died, and when we were afraid it could yet charge

From a photograph by Kermit Roosevelt

on foot, he turned toward us, his tail lashing quicker and quicker.   Resting my elbow on Simba's bent shoulder, I took steady aim and pressed the trigger; the bullet went in between the neck and shoulder, and the lion fell over on his side, one foreleg in the air.   He recovered in a moment and stood up, evidently very sick, and once more faced me, growling hoarsely.   I think he was on the eve

of charging. I fired again at once, and this bullet broke
h s back just behind the shoulders; and with the next I
killed him outright, after we had gathered round him.

These were two good-sized maneless lions; and very
proud of them I was. I think Sir Alfred was at least as
proud, especially because we had performed the feat alone,
without any professional hunters being present. "We
were all amateurs, only gentleman riders up," said Sir
Alfred. It was late before we got the lions skinned. Then
we set off toward the ranch, two porters carrying each lion
skin, strapped to a pole; and two others carrying the cub
skins. Night fell long before we were near the ranch; but
the brilliant tropic moon lighted the trail. The stalwart
savages who carried the bloody lion skins swung along at
a faster walk as the sun went down and the moon rose
higher; and they began to chant in unison, one uttering a
single word or sentence, and the others joining in a deep-
toned, musical chorus. The men on a safari, and indeed
African natives generally, are always excited over the death
of a lion, and the hunting tribes then chant their rough
hunting songs, or victory songs, until the monotonous,
rhythmical repetitions make them grow almost frenzied.
The ride home through the moonlight, the vast barren landscape shining like silver on either hand, was one to be remembered; and above all, the sight of our trophies and of
their wild bearers.

Three days later we had another successful lion hunt.
Our camp was pitched at a waterhole in a little stream
called Potha, by a hill of the same name. Pease, Medlicott,
and both the Hills were with us, and Heller came too; for
he liked, when possible, to be with the hunters so that he
could at once care for any beast that was shot. As the
safari was stationary, we took fifty or sixty porters as beaters. It was thirteen hours before we got into camp that
evening. The Hills had with them as beaters and water-
carriers half a dozen of the Wakamba who were working
on their farm. It was interesting to watch these naked

savages, with their filed teeth their heads shaved in curious patterns and carrying for arms little bows and arrows. Before lunch we beat a long, low hill. Harold Hill was

Kermit Roosevelt and cheetah shot by him
From a photograph by Edmund Heller

with me; Medlicott and Kermit were together. We placed ourselves, one couple on each side of a narrow neck, two-thirds of the way along the crest of the hill; and soon after we were in position we heard the distant shouts of the beaters as they came toward us, covering the crest and the tops of the slopes on both sides. It was rather disconcerting to find how much better Hill's eyes were than mine. He saw everything first, and it usually took some time before he could make me see it. In this first drive nothing came my way except some mountain reedbuck does, at which I did not shoot. But a fine male cheetah came to Kermit, and he bowled it over in good style as it ran.

Then the beaters halted, and waited before resuming their march until the guns had gone clear round and established themselves at the base of the farther end of the hill. This time Kermit, who was a couple of hundred yards from me, killed a reedbuck and a steinbuck. Suddenly Hill said, "Lion," and endeavored to point it out to me, as it crept cautiously among the rocks on the steep hill-side, a hundred and fifty yards away. At first I could not see it; finally I thought I did and fired, but, as it proved, at a place just above him. However, it made him start up, and I immediately put the next bullet behind his shoulders; it was a fatal shot; but, growling, he struggled down the hill, and I fired again and killed him. It was not much of a trophy, however, turning out to be a half-grown male.

We lunched under a tree, and then arranged for another beat. There was a long, wide valley, or rather a slight depression in the ground—for it was only three or four feet below the general level—in which the grass grew tall, as the soil was quite wet. It was the scene of Percival's adventure with the lion that chased him. Hill and I stationed ourselves on one side of this valley or depression, toward the upper end; Pease took Kermit to the opposite side; and we waited, our horses some distance behind us. The beaters were put in at the lower end, formed a line across the valley, and beat slowly toward us, making a great noise.

They were still some distance away when Hill saw three lions, which had slunk stealthily off ahead of them through the grass. I have called the grass tall, but this was only by comparison with the short grass of the dry plains. In the depression or valley it was some three feet high. In such grass a lion, which is marvellously adept at hiding,

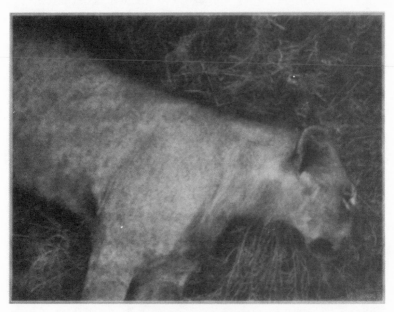

The third male lion shot by Mr. Roosevelt
From a photograph by Edmund Heller

can easily conceal itself, not merely when lying down, but when advancing at a crouching gait. If it stands erect, however, it can be seen.

There were two lions near us, one directly in our front, a hundred and ten yards off. Some seconds passed before Hill could make me realize that the dim yellow smear in the yellow-brown grass was a lion; and then I found such difficulty in getting a bead on him that I overshot. However, the bullet must have passed very close—indeed, I think it just grazed him—for he jumped up and faced us,

growling savagely. Then, his head lowered, he threw his
tail straight into the air and began to charge. The first
few steps he took at a trot, and before he could start into a
gallop I put the soft-nosed Winchester bullet in between the
neck and shoulder. Down he went with a roar; the wound
was fatal, but I was taking no chances, and I put two more
bullets in him. Then we walked toward where Hill had
already seen another lion—the lioness, as it proved. Again
he had some difficulty in making me see her; but he succeeded and I walked toward her through the long grass,
repressing the zeal of my two gun-bearers, who were stanch,
but who showed a tendency to walk a little ahead of me
on each side, instead of a little behind. I walked toward
her because I could not kneel to shoot in grass so tall; and
when shooting off-hand I like to be fairly close, so as to be
sure that my bullets go in the right place. At sixty yards I
could make her out clearly, snarling at me as she faced me;
and I shot her full in the chest. She at once performed a
series of extraordinary antics, tumbling about on her head,
just as if she were throwing somersaults, first to one side
and then to the other. I fired again, but managed to shoot
between the somersaults, so to speak, and missed her.
The shot seemed to bring her to herself, and away she tore;
but instead of charging us she charged the line of beaters.
She was dying fast, however, and in her weakness failed
to catch any one; and she sank down into the long grass.
Hill and I advanced to look her up, our rifles at full cock,
and the gun-bearers close behind. It is ticklish work to
follow a wounded lion in tall grass, and we walked carefully,
every sense on the alert. We passed Heller, who had been
with the beaters. He spoke to us with an amused smile.
His only weapon was a pair of field-glasses, but he always
took things as they came, with entire coolness, and to be
close to a wounded lioness when she charged merely interested him. A beater came running up and pointed toward
where he had seen her, and we walked toward the place.
At thirty yards distance Hill pointed, and, eagerly peering,

I made out the form of the lioness showing indistinctly through the grass. She was half crouching, half sitting, her head bent down; but she still had strength to do mischief. She saw us, but before she could turn I sent a bullet through her shoulders; down she went, and was dead when we walked up. A cub had been seen, and another full-grown lion, but they had slunk off and we got neither.

This was a full-grown, but young, lioness of average size; her cubs must have been several months old. We took her entire to camp to weigh; she weighed two hundred and eighty-three pounds. The first lion, which we had difficulty in finding, as there were no identifying marks in the plain of tall grass, was a good-sized male, weighing about four hundred pounds, but not yet full-grown; although he was probably the father of the cubs.

We were a long way from camp, and, after beating in vain for the other lion, we started back; it was after nightfall before we saw the camp-fires. It was two hours later before the porters appeared, bearing on poles the skin of the dead lion, and the lioness entire. The moon was nearly full, and it was interesting to see them come swinging down the trail in the bright silver light, chanting in deep tones, over and over again, a line or phrase that sounded like:

"Zou-zou-boulé ma ja guntai; zou-zou-boulé ma ja guntai."

Occasionally they would interrupt it by the repetition in unison, at short intervals, of a guttural ejaculation, sounding like "huzlem." They marched into camp, then up and down the lines, before the rows of small fires; then, accompanied by all the rest of the porters, they paraded up to the big fire where I was standing. Here they stopped and ended the ceremony by a minute or two's vigorous dancing amid singing and wild shouting. The firelight gleamed and flickered across the grim dead beasts, and the shining eyes and black features of the excited savages, while all around the moon flooded the landscape with her white light.

CHAPTER IV

ON SAFARI. RHINO AND GIRAFFE

WHEN we killed the last lions we were already on safari, and the camp was pitched by a waterhole on the Potha, a half-dried stream, little more than a string of pools and reedbeds, winding down through the sun-scorched plain. Next morning we started for another waterhole at the rocky hill of Bondoni, about eight miles distant.

Safari life is very pleasant, and also very picturesque. The porters are strong, patient, good-humored savages, with something childlike about them that makes one really fond of them. Of course, like all savages and most children, they have their limitations, and in dealing with them firmness is even more necessary than kindness; but the man is a poor creature who does not treat them with kindness also, and I am rather sorry for him if he does not grow to feel for them, and to make them in return feel for him, a real and friendly liking. They are subject to gusts of passion, and they are now and then guilty of grave misdeeds and shortcomings; sometimes for no conceivable reason, at least from the white man's stand-point. But they are generally cheerful, and when cheerful are always amusing; and they work hard, if the white man is able to combine tact and consideration with that insistence on the performance of duty the lack of which they despise as weakness. Any little change or excitement is a source of pleasure to them. When the march is over they sing; and after two or three days in camp they will not only sing, but dance when another march is to begin. Of course at times they suffer greatly from thirst and hunger and fatigue, and at times they will suddenly grow sullen or rebel without what seems to us any adequate cause; and they have an inconsequent

94

type of mind which now and then leads them to commit follies all the more exasperating because they are against their own interest no less than against the interest of their employer. But they do well on the whole, and safari life is attractive to them. They are fed well; the government requires that they be fitted with suitable clothes and given small tents, so that they are better clad and sheltered than they would be otherwise; and their wages represent money which they could get in no other way. The safari repre-

The caravan on safari at Potha
In single file came the long line of burden-bearers
From a photograph by Kermit Roosevelt

sents a great advantage to the porter; who in his turn alone makes the safari possible.

When we were to march, camp was broken as early in the day as possible. Each man had his allotted task, and the tents, bedding, provisions, and all else were expeditiously made into suitable packages. Each porter is supposed to carry from fifty-five to sixty pounds, which may all be in one bundle or in two or three. The American flag, which flew over my tent, was a matter of much pride to the porters, and was always carried at the head or near the head of the line of march; and after it in single file came the long line of burden-bearers. As they started, some of them would blow on horns or whistles and others beat little tomtoms; and at intervals this would be renewed again and again throughout the march; or the men might suddenly begin to chant, or merely to keep repeating in unison some one word or one phrase which, when we asked to have it translated, might or might not prove to be entirely meaningless. The headmen carried no burdens, and the tent boys hardly anything, while the saises walked with the spare horses. In addition to the canonical and required costume of blouse or jersey and drawers, each porter wore a blanket, and usually something else to which his soul inclined. It might be an exceedingly shabby coat; it might be, of all things in the world, an umbrella, an article for

The American flag was always at the head or near the head of the line of march
The caravan on safari at Potha
From a photograph by Kermit Roosevelt

which they had a special attachment. Often I would see a porter, who thought nothing whatever of walking for hours at mid-day under the equatorial sun with his head bare, trudging along with solemn pride either under an open umbrella, or carrying the umbrella (tied much like Mrs. Gamp's) in one hand, as a wand of dignity. Then their head-gear varied according to the fancy of the individual. Normally it was a red fez, a kind of cap only used in hot climates, and exquisitely designed to be useless therein because it gives absolutely no protection from the sun. But one would wear a skin cap; another would suddenly put one or more long feathers in his fez; and another, discarding the fez, would revert to some purely savage head-dress which he would wear with equal gravity whether it were, in our eyes really decorative or merely comic. One such head-dress, for instance, consisted of the skin of the

Stopping for luncheon at Bondoni rocks

From a photograph by Edmund Heller

top of a zebra's head, with the two ears. Another was made of the skins of squirrels, with the tails both sticking up and hanging down. Another consisted of a bunch of feathers woven into the hair, which itself was pulled out into strings that were stiffened with clay. Another was really too intricate for description because it included the man's natural hair, some strips of skin, and an empty tin can.

If it were a long journey and we broke it by a noonday halt, or if it were a short journey and we reached camp ahead of the safari, it was interesting to see the long file of men approach. Here and there, leading the porters, scattered through the line, or walking alongside, were the askaris, the rifle-bearing soldiers. They were not marksmen, to put it mildly, and I should not have regarded them as particularly efficient allies in a serious fight; but they were excellent for police duty in camp, and were also of use in preventing collisions with the natives. After the leading askaris might come one of the headmen; one of whom, by the way, looked exactly like a Semitic negro, and always travelled with a large dirty-white umbrella in one hand; while another, a tall, powerful fellow, was a mission boy who spoke good English; I mention his being a mission boy because it is so frequently asserted that mission boys never turn out well. Then would come the man with the flag, followed by another blowing on an antelope horn, or perhaps beating an empty can as a drum; and then the long line of men, some carrying their loads on their heads, others on their shoulders, others, in a very few cases, on their backs. As they approached the halting place their spirits rose, the whistles and horns were blown, and the improvised drums beaten, and perhaps the whole line would burst into a chant.

On reaching the camping ground each man at once set about his allotted task, and the tents were quickly pitched and the camp put in order, while water and firewood were fetched. The tents were pitched in long lines, in the first of which stood my tent, flanked by those of the other white men and by the dining tent. In the next line were the cook tent, the provision tent, the store tent, the skinning tent, and the like; and then came the lines of small white tents for the porters. Between each row of tents was a broad street. In front of our own tents in the first line an askari was always pacing to and fro; and when night fell we would kindle a camp-fire and sit around it under the stars. Before each of the porters' tents was a little fire, and beside it stood the pots and pans in which the porters did their cooking. Here and there were larger fires, around which the gun-bearers or a group of askaris or of saises might gather. After nightfall the multitude of fires lit up the darkness and showed the tents in shadowy outline; and around them squatted the porters, their faces flickering from dusk to ruddy light, as they chatted together or suddenly started some snatch of wild African melody in which all their neighbors might join. After a while the talk and laughter and singing would gradually die away, and as we white men sat around our fire, the silence would be unbroken except by the queer cry of a hyena, or much more rarely by a sound that always demanded attention—the yawning grunt of a questing lion.

If we wished to make an early start we would breakfast by dawn and then we often returned to camp for lunch. Otherwise we would usually be absent all day, carrying our lunch with us. We might get in before sunset or we might be out till long after nightfall; and then the gleam of the lit fires was a welcome sight as we stumbled toward them through the darkness. Once in, each went to his tent to take a hot bath; and then, clean and refreshed, we sat down to a comfortable dinner, with game of some sort as the principal dish.

On the first march after leaving our lion camp at Potha I shot a wart-hog. It was a good-sized sow, which, in company with several of her half-grown offspring, was grazing near our line of march; there were some thorn-trees which gave a little cover, and I killed her at a hundred and eighty yards, using the Springfield, the lightest and handiest of all my rifles. Her flesh was good to eat, and the skin, as with all our specimens, was saved for the National Museum. I did not again have to shoot a sow, although I killed half-grown pigs for the table, and boars for specimens. This sow and her porkers were not rooting, but were grazing

Making camp at Bondoni

From a photograph by Kermit Roosevelt

as if they had been antelope; her stomach contained nothing but chopped green grass. Wart-hogs are common throughout the country over which we hunted. They are hideous beasts, with strange protuberances on their cheeks; and when alarmed they trot or gallop away, holding the tail perfectly erect with the tassel bent forward. Usually they are seen in family parties, but a big boar will often be alone. They often root up the ground, but the stomachs of those we shot were commonly filled with nothing but grass.

If the weather is cloudy or wet they may be out all day long, but in hot, dry weather we generally found them abroad only in the morning and evening. A pig is always a comical animal; even more so than is the case with a bear, which also impresses one with a sense of grotesque humor—and this notwithstanding the fact that both boar and bear may be very formidable creatures. A wart-hog standing alertly at gaze, head and tail up, legs straddled out, and ears cocked forward, is rather a figure of fun; and not the less so when with characteristic suddenness he bounces round with a grunt and scuttles madly off to safety. Wart-hogs are beasts of the bare plain or open forest, and though they will often lie up in patches of brush they do not care for thick timber.

After shooting the wart-hog we marched on to our camp at Bondoni. The gun-bearers were Mohammedans, and the dead pig was of no service to them; and at their request I walked out while camp was being pitched and shot them a buck; this I had to do now and then, but I always shot males, so as not to damage the species.

Next day we marched to the foot of Kilimakiu Mountain, near Captain Slatter's ostrich-farm. Our route lay across bare plains thickly covered with withered short grass. All around us as we marched were the game herds, zebras and hartebeests, gazelles of the two kinds, and now and then wildebeests. Hither and thither over the plain, crossing and recrossing, ran the dusty game trails, each with its myriad hoof-marks; the round hoof-prints of the zebra, the heart-shaped marks that showed where the hartebeest herd had trod, and the delicate etching that betrayed where the smaller antelope had passed. Occasionally we crossed the trails of the natives, worn deep in the hard soil by the countless thousands of bare or sandalled feet that had trodden them. Africa is a country of trails. Across the high veldt, in every direction, run the tangled trails of the multitudes of game that have lived thereon from time immemorial. The great beasts of the marsh and the forest

made therein broad and muddy trails which often offer
the only pathway by which a man can enter the sombre
depths.   In wet ground and dry alike are also found the
trails of savage man.   They lead from village to village,
and in places they stretch for hundreds of miles, where
trading parties have worn them in the search for ivory, or

in the old days when
raising or purchas-
ing slaves. The trails
made by the men are
made much as the
beasts make theirs.
They are generally
longer and better de-
fined, although I have
seen hippo tracks
more deeply marked
than any made by
savage man. But they
are made simply by
men following in one
another's footsteps,
and they are never
quite straight. They
bend now a little to
one side, now a little
to the other, and sud-
den loops mark the
spot where some van-
ished obstacle once

A tribe of the Wakamba with their chief (in khaki with
a golf cap) that came to present Mr. Roosevelt with
a sheep near Kilimakiu

From a photograph by Kermit Roosevelt

stood; around it the first trail-makers went, and their suc-
cessors have ever trodden in their footsteps, even though
the need for so doing has long passed away.

Our camp at Kilimakiu was by a grove of shady trees,
and from it at sunset we looked across the vast plain and
saw the far-off mountains grow umber and purple as the
light waned.   Back of the camp, and of the farm-house

near which we were, rose Kilimakiu Mountain, beautifully
studded with groves of trees of many kinds. On its farther
side lived a tribe of the Wakamba. Their chief with all the
leading men of his village came in state to call upon me,
and presented me with a fat hairy sheep, of the ordinary
kind found in this part of Africa, where the sheep very
wisely do not grow wool. The headman was dressed in
khaki, and showed me with pride an official document
which confirmed him in his position by direction of the
government, and required him to perform various acts,
chiefly in the way of preventing his tribes-people from
committing robbery or murder, and of helping to stamp
out cattle disease. Like all the Wakamba they had flocks
of goats and sheep, and herds of humped cattle; but they
were much in need of meat and hailed my advent. They
were wild savages with filed teeth, many of them stark
naked, though some of them carried a blanket. Their
heads were curiously shaved so that the hair tufts stood out
in odd patterns, and they carried small bows, and arrows
with poisoned heads.

The following morning I rode out with Captain Slatter.
We kept among the hills. The long drought was still unbroken. The little pools were dry and their bottoms baked
like iron, and there was not a drop in the watercourses.
Part of the land was open and part covered with a thin
forest or bush of scattered mimosa-trees. In the open
country were many zebras and hartebeests, and the latter
were found even in the thin bush. In the morning we found
a small herd of eland at which, after some stalking, I got a
long shot and missed. The eland is the largest of all the
horned creatures that are called antelope, being quite as
heavy as a fattened ox. The herd I approached consisted
of a dozen individuals, two of them huge bulls, their coats
having turned a slaty blue, their great dewlaps hanging
down, and the legs looking almost too small for the massive
bodies. The reddish-colored cows were of far lighter build.
Eland are beautiful creatures and ought to be domesticated.

As I crept toward them I was struck by their likeness to
great, clean, handsome cattle. They were grazing or resting, switching their long tails at the flies that hung in
attendance upon them and lit on their flanks, just as if they
were Jerseys in a field at home. My bullet fell short, their
size causing me to underestimate the distance, and away
they went at a run, one or two of the cows in the first hurry
and confusion skipping clean over the backs of others that
got in their way—a most unexpected example of agility in
such large and ponderous animals. After a few hundred
yards they settled down to the slashing trot which is their
natural gait, and disappeared over the brow of a hill.

The morning was a blank, but early in the afternoon
we saw the eland herd again. They were around a tree in
an open space, and we could not get near them. But instead of going straight away they struck off to the right and
described almost a semicircle, and though they were over
four hundred yards distant, they were such big creatures and
their gait was so steady that I felt warranted in shooting.
On the dry plain I could mark where my bullets fell, and
though I could not get a good chance at the bull I finally
downed a fine cow; and by pacing I found it to be a little
over a quarter of a mile from where I stood when shooting.

It was about nine miles from camp, and I dared not
leave the eland alone, so I stationed one of the gun-bearers
by the great carcass and sent a messenger in to Heller, on
whom we depended for preserving the skins of the big
game. Hardly had this been done when a Wakamba man
came running up to tell us that there was a rhinoceros on
the hill-side three-quarters of a mile away, and that he had
left a companion to watch it while he carried us the news.
Slatter and I immediately rode in the direction given, following our wild-looking guide; the other gun-bearer trotting
after us. In five minutes we had reached the opposite hill-
crest, where the watcher stood, and he at once pointed out
the rhino. The huge beast was standing in entirely open
country, although there were a few scattered trees of no

great size at some little distance from him. We left our
horses in a dip of the ground and began the approach;
I cannot say that we stalked him, for the approach was too
easy. The wind blew from him to us, and a rhino's eyesight
is dull. Thirty yards from where he stood was a bush four
or five feet high, and though it was so thin that we could

Skinning the eland
From a photograph by Edmund Heller

distinctly see him through the leaves, it shielded us from
the vision of his small, piglike eyes as we advanced toward
it, stooping and in single file, I leading. The big beast
stood like an uncouth statue, his hide black in the sunlight; he seemed what he was, a monster surviving over
from the world's past, from the days when the beasts of
the prime ran riot in their strength, before man grew so
cunning of brain and hand as to master them. So little
did he dream of our presence that when we were a hundred
yards off he actually lay down.

Walking lightly, and with every sense keyed up, we at last reached the bush, and I pushed forward the safety of the double-barrelled Holland rifle which I was now to use for the first time on big game. As I stepped to one side of the bush so as to get a clear aim, with Slatter following, the rhino saw me and jumped to his feet with the agility of a polo pony. As he rose I put in the right barrel, the bullet going through both lungs. At the same moment he wheeled, the blood spouting from his nostrils, and galloped full on us. Before he could get quite all the way round in his headlong rush to reach us, I struck him with my left-hand barrel, the bullet entering between the neck and shoulder and piercing his heart. At the same instant Captain Slatter fired, his bullet entering the neck vertebræ. Ploughing up the ground with horn and feet, the great bull rhino, still head toward us, dropped just thirteen paces from where we stood.

This was a wicked charge, for the rhino meant mischief and came on with the utmost determination. It is not safe to generalize from a few instances. Judging from what I have since seen, I am inclined to believe that both lion and buffalo are more dangerous game than rhino; yet the first two rhinos I met both charged, whereas we killed our first four lions and first four buffaloes without any of them charging, though two of each were stopped as they were on the point of charging. Moreover, our experience with this bull rhino illustrates what I have already said as to one animal being more dangerous under certain conditions, and another more dangerous under different conditions. If it had been a lion instead of a rhino, my first bullet would, I believe, have knocked all the charge out of it; but the vitality of the huge pachyderm was so great, its mere bulk counted for so much, that even such a hard-hitting rifle as my double Holland—than which I do not believe there exists a better weapon for heavy game—could not stop it outright, although either of the wounds inflicted would have been fatal in a few seconds.

Before he could get quite all the way round in his headlong rush to reach us, I struck him with my left-hand barrel

Drawn by Philip R. Goodwin from photographs and from descriptions furnished by Mr. Roosevelt

Leaving a couple of men with the dead rhino, to protect it from the Wakamba by day and the lions by night, we rode straight to camp, which we reached at sunset. It was necessary to get to work on the two dead beasts as soon as possible in order to be sure of preserving their skins. Heller was the man to be counted on for this task. He it was who handled all the skins, who, in other words, was making the expedition of permanent value so far as big game was concerned; and no work at any hour of the day or night ever came amiss to him. He had already trained eight Wakamba porters to act as skinners under his supervision. On hearing of our success, he at once said that we ought to march out to the game that night so as to get to work by daylight. Moreover, we were not comfortable at leaving only two men with each carcass, for lions were both bold and plentiful.

The moon rose at eight and we started as soon as she was above the horizon. We did not take the horses, because there was no water where we were going, and furthermore we did not like to expose them to a possible attack by lions. The march out by moonlight was good fun, for though I had been out all day, I had been riding, not walking, and so was not tired. A hundred porters went with us so as to enable us to do the work quickly and bring back to camp the skins and all the meat needed, and these porters carried water, food for breakfast, and what little was necessary for a one-night camp. We tramped along in single file under the moonlight, up and down the hills, and through the scattered thorn forest. Kermit and Medlicott went first, and struck such a pace that after an hour we had to halt them so as to let the tail end of the file of porters catch up. Then Captain Slatter and I set a more decorous pace, keeping the porters closed up in line behind us. In another hour we began to go down a long slope toward a pin-point of light in the distance which we knew was the fire by the rhinoceros. The porters, like the big children they were, felt in high feather, and began to chant to an accompaniment of whistling and horn-blowing as we tramped through the dry grass which was flooded with silver by the moon, now high in the heavens.

As soon as we reached the rhino, Heller with his Wakamba skinners pushed forward the three-quarters of a mile to the eland, returning after midnight with the skin and all the best parts of the meat.

Around the dead rhino the scene was lit up both by the moon and by the flicker of the fires. The porters made their camp under a small tree a dozen rods to one side of the carcass, building a low circular fence of branches on which they hung their bright-colored blankets, two or three big fires blazing to keep off possible lions. Half as far on the other side of the rhino a party of naked savages had established their camp, if camp it could be called, for really all they did was to squat down round a couple of fires with a few small bushes disposed round about. The rhino had been opened, and they had already taken out of the carcass what they regarded as titbits and what we certainly did not grudge them. Between the two camps lay the huge dead beast, his hide glistening in the moonlight. In each camp the men squatted around the fires chatting and laughing as they roasted strips of meat on long sticks, the fitful blaze playing over them, now leaving them in darkness, now bringing them out into a red relief. Our own tent was pitched under another tree a hundred yards off, and when I went to sleep, I could still hear the drumming and chanting of our feasting porters; the savages were less at ease, and their revel was quiet.

Early next morning I went back to camp, and soon after reaching there again started out for a hunt. In the afternoon I came on giraffes and got up near enough to shoot at them. But they are such enormous beasts that I thought them far nearer than they were. My bullet fell short, and they disappeared among the mimosas, at their strange leisurely looking gallop. Of all the beasts in an African landscape none is more striking than the giraffe. Usually

Percival on his way to Kapiti station with trophies
Kilima Theki in background
From a photograph by Edmund Heller

it is found in small parties or in herds of fifteen or twenty or more individuals. Although it will drink regularly if occasion offers, it is able to get along without water for months at a time, and frequents by choice the dry plains or else the stretches of open forest where the trees are scattered and ordinarily somewhat stunted. Like the rhinoceros— the ordinary or prehensile-lipped rhinoceros—the giraffe is a browsing and not a grazing animal. The leaves, buds, and twigs of the mimosas or thorn-trees form its customary food. Its extraordinary height enables it to bring into play to the best possible advantage its noteworthy powers of vision, and no animal is harder to approach unseen. Again and again I have made it out a mile off or rather have seen it a mile off when it was pointed out to me, and looking at it through my glasses, would see that it was gazing steadily at us. It is a striking-looking animal and handsome in its way, but its length of leg and neck and sloping back make it appear awkward even at rest. When alarmed it may go off at a long swinging pace or walk, but if really frightened it strikes into a peculiar gallop or canter. The tail is cocked and twisted, and the huge hind legs are thrown forward well to the outside of the forelegs. The movements seem deliberate and the giraffe does not appear to be going at a fast pace, but if it has any start a horse must gallop hard to overtake it. When it starts on this gait, the neck may be dropped forward at a sharp angle with the straight line of the deep chest, and the big head is thrust in advance. They are defenceless things and, though they may kick at a man who incautiously comes within reach, they are in no way dangerous.

The following day I again rode out with Captain Slatter. During the morning we saw nothing except the ordinary game, and we lunched on a hill-top, ten miles distant from camp, under a huge fig-tree with spreading branches and thick, deep-green foliage. Throughout the time we were taking lunch a herd of zebras watched us from near by, standing motionless with their ears pricked forward, their beautifully striped bodies showing finely in the sunlight. We scanned the country round about with our glasses, and made out first a herd of elands, a mile in our rear, and then three giraffes a mile and a half in our front. I wanted a bull eland, but I wanted a giraffe still more, and we mounted our horses and rode toward where the three tall beasts stood, on an open hill-side with trees thinly scattered over it. Half a mile from them we left the horses in a thick belt of timber beside a dry watercourse, and went forward on foot.

There was no use in trying a stalk, for that would merely have aroused the giraffe's suspicion. But we knew they were accustomed to the passing and repassing of Wakamba men and women, whom they did not fear if they kept at a reasonable distance, so we walked in single file diagonally in their direction;

Masai Elmoran, Machakos road station
From a photograph by Edmund Heller

that is, toward a tree which I judged to be about three hundred yards from them. I was carrying the Winchester loaded with full metal-patched bullets. I wished to get for the museum both a bull and a cow. One of the three giraffes was much larger than the other two, and as he was evidently a bull I thought the two others were cows.

As we reached the tree the giraffes showed symptoms of uneasiness. One of the smaller ones began to make off, and both the others shifted their positions slightly, curling their tails. I instantly dropped on my knee, and getting the bead just behind the big bull's shoulder, I fired with the three-hundred-yard sight. I heard the "pack" of the bullet as it struck just where I aimed; and away went all three giraffes at their queer rocking-horse canter. Running forward I emptied my magazine, firing at the big bull and also at one of his smaller companions, and then, slipping into the barrel what proved to be a soft-nosed bullet, I fired at the latter again. The giraffe was going straightaway and it was a long shot, at four or five hundred yards; but by good luck the bullet broke its back and down it came. The others were now getting over the crest of the hill, but the big one was evidently sick, and we called and beckoned to the two saises to hurry up with the horses. The moment they arrived we jumped on, and Captain Slatter cantered up a neighboring hill so as to mark the direction in which the giraffes went if I lost sight of them. Meanwhile I rode full speed after the giant quarry. I was on the tranquil sorrel, the horse I much preferred in riding down game of any kind, because he had a fair turn of speed, and yet was good about letting me get on and off. As soon as I reached the hill-crest I saw the giraffes ahead of me, not as far off as I had feared, and I raced toward them without regard to rotten ground and wart-hog holes. The wounded one lagged behind, but when I got near he put on a spurt, and as I thought I was close enough I leaped off, throwing the reins over the sorrel's head, and opened fire. Down went the big bull, and I thought my task was done. But as I went back to mount the sorrel he struggled to his feet again and disappeared after his companion among the trees, which were thicker here, as we had reached the bottom of the valley. So I tore after him again, and in a minute came to a dry watercourse. Scrambling into and out of this I saw the giraffes ahead of me just beginning the ascent of the opposite slope; and touching the horse with the spur we flew after the wounded bull. This time I made up my mind I would get up close enough; but Tranquillity did not quite like the look of the thing ahead of him.   He did not refuse to come up to the giraffe, but he evidently felt that, with such an object close by and evident in the landscape, it behooved him to be careful as to what

A young bull giraffe, shot by Mr. Roosevelt at Kilimakiu
From a photograph by Edmund Heller

might be hidden therein, and he shied so at each bush we passed that we progressed in series of loops.   So off I jumped, throwing the reins over his head, and opened fire once more; and this time the great bull went down for good.

Tranquillity recovered his nerve at once and grazed contentedly while I admired the huge proportions and beautiful coloring of my prize.   In a few minutes Captain Slatter loped up, and the gun-bearers and saises followed.

As if by magic, three or four Wakamba turned up immediately afterward, their eyes glistening at the thought of the
feast ahead for the whole tribe.   It was mid-afternoon,
and there was no time to waste.   My sais, Simba, an excellent long-distance runner, was sent straight to camp to get
Heller and pilot him back to the dead giraffes.   Beside
each of the latter, for they had fallen a mile apart, we left
a couple of men to build fires.   Then we rode toward camp.
To my regret, the smaller giraffe turned out to be a young
bull and not a cow.

At this very time, and utterly without our knowledge,
there was another giraffe hunt going on.   Sir Alfred had
taken out Kermit and Medlicott, and they came across a
herd of a dozen giraffes right out in the open plains.   Medlicott's horse was worn out and he could not keep up, but
both the others were fairly well mounted.   Both were light
men and hard riders, and although the giraffes had three-
quarters of a mile the start, it was not long before both
were at the heels of the herd.   They singled out the big bull,
which by the way turned out to be an even bigger bull than
mine, and fired at him as they galloped.   In such a headlong helter-skelter chase, however, it is no easy matter to
score a hit from horseback unless one is very close up; and
Sir Alfred made up his mind to try to drive out the bull
from the rest of the herd.   He succeeded; but at this moment his horse put a forefoot into a hole and turned a complete somersault, almost wrenching out his shoulder.   Sir
Alfred was hurled off head over heels, but even as he rolled
over, clutching his rifle, he twisted himself round to his
knees, and took one last shot at the flying giraffe.   This
left Kermit alone and he galloped hard on the giraffe's
heels, firing again and again with his Winchester.   Finally
his horse became completely done out and fell behind;
whereupon Kermit jumped off, and being an excellent
long-distance runner, ran after the giraffe on foot for more
than a mile.   But he did not need to shoot again.   The
great beast had been mortally wounded and it suddenly

Mr. Roosevelt, Captain Slatter, and rhino shot by Mr. Roosevelt at Kilimakiu

From a photograph by Edmund Heller

slowed down, halted, and fell over dead. As a matter of curiosity we kept the Winchester bullets both from Kermit's giraffe and from mine. I made a point of keeping as many as possible of the bullets with which the different animals were slain so as to see just what was done by the different types of rifles we had with us.

When I reached camp I found that Heller had already started. Next morning I rode down to see him and found him hard at work with the skins; but as it would take him two or three days to finish them and put them in condition for transport, we decided that the safari should march back to the Potha camp, and that from thence we would send Percival's ox wagon to bring back to the camp all the skins, Heller and his men accompanying him. The plan was carried out, and the following morning we shifted the big camp as proposed.

Heller, thus left behind, came near having an unpleasant adventure. He slept in his own tent, and his Wakamba skinners slept under the fly not far off. One night they let the fires die down and were roused at midnight by hearing the grunting of a hungry lion apparently not a dozen yards off in the darkness. Heller quickly lit his lantern and sat up with his shot-gun loaded with bird shot, the only weapon he had with him. The lion walked round and round the tent, grunting at intervals. Then, after some minutes of suspense, he drew off. While the grunting had been audible, not a sound came from the tent of the Wakambas, who all cowered under their blankets in perfect silence. But once he had gone there was a great chattering, and in a few minutes the fires were roaring, nor were they again suffered to die down.

Heller's skinners had grown to work very well when under his eye. He had encountered much difficulty in getting men who would do the work, and had tried the representatives of various tribes, but without success until he struck the Wakamba. These were real savages who filed their teeth and delighted in raw flesh, and Heller's

explanation of their doing well was that their taste for the
raw flesh kept them thoroughly interested in their job, so
that they learned without difficulty. The porters speedily
christened each of the white men by some title of their
own, using the ordinary Swahili title of Bwana (master) as
a prefix. Heller was the Bwana Who Skinned; Loring,
who collected the small mammals, was named, merely
descriptively, the Mouse Master, Bwana Pania. I was

The Percival family
From a photograph by Edmund Heller

always called Bwana Makuba, the chief or Great Master;
Kermit was first called Bwana Medogo, the young mas-
ter, and afterward was christened " the Dandy," Bwana
Merodadi.

From Potha the safari went in two days to McMillan's
place, Juja Farm, on the other side of the Athi. I stayed
behind, as I desired to visit the American Mission Station
at Machakos. Accordingly, Sir Alfred and I rode thither.
Machakos has long been a native town, for it was on the
route formerly taken by the Arab caravans that went from
the coast to the interior after slaves and ivory. Riding
toward it we passed herd after herd of cattle, sheep, and
goats, each guarded by two or three savage herdsmen.
The little town itself was both interesting and attractive.

Besides the natives there were a number of Indian traders and the English commissioner and assistant commissioner, with a small body of native soldiers. The latter not a long time before had been just such savages as those round about them, and the change for the better wrought in their physique and morale by the ordered discipline to which they had submitted themselves could hardly be exaggerated. When we arrived, the commissioner and his assistant were engaged in cross-examining some neighboring chiefs as to the cattle sickness. The English rule in Africa has been of incalculable benefit to Africans themselves, and indeed this is true of the rule of most European nations. Mistakes have been made, of course, but they have proceeded at least as often from an unwise effort to accomplish too much in the way of beneficence, as from a desire to exploit the natives. Each of the civilized nations that has taken possession of any part of Africa has had its own peculiar good qualities and its own peculiar defects. Some of them have done too much in supervising and ordering the lives of the natives, and in interfering with their practices and customs. The English error, like our own under similar conditions, has, if anything, been in the other direction. The effort has been to avoid wherever possible all interference with tribal customs, even when of an immoral and repulsive character, and to do no more than what is obviously necessary, such as insistence upon keeping the peace and preventing the spread of cattle disease. Excellent reasons can be advanced in favor of this policy, and it must always be remembered that a fussy and ill-considered benevolence is more sure to awaken resentment than cruelty itself; while the natives are apt to resent deeply even things that are obviously for their ultimate welfare. Yet I cannot help thinking that with caution and wisdom it would be possible to proceed somewhat farther than has yet been the case in the direction of pushing upward some at least of the East African tribes: and this though I recognize fully that many of these tribes are of a low and brutalized type. Having

said this much in the way of criticism, I wish to add my
tribute of unstinted admiration for the disinterested and
efficient work being done, alike in the interest of the white
man and the black, by the government officials whom I

Group of skin-laden mules passing by the Bondoni waterhole on
their way to the railroad
From a photograph by Kermit Roosevelt

met in East Africa. They are men in whom their country
has every reason to feel a just pride.

We lunched with the American missionaries. Mission
work among savages offers many difficulties, and often the
wisest and most earnest effort meets with dishearteningly
little reward; while lack of common-sense, and of course,
above all, lack of a firm and resolute disinterestedness, insures the worst kind of failure. There are missionaries who
do not do well, just as there are men in every conceivable
walk of life who do not do well; and excellent men who
are not missionaries, including both government officials

and settlers, are only too apt to jump at the chance of criti-
cising a missionary for every alleged sin of either omission
or commission. Finally, zealous missionaries, fervent in the
faith, do not always find it easy to remember that savages can only be raised by slow steps, that an empty adhe-
rence to forms and ceremonies amounts to nothing, that
industrial training is an essential in any permanent upward
movement, and that the gradual elevation of mind and
character is a prerequisite to the achievement of any kind
of Christianity which is worth calling such. Nevertheless,
after all this has been said, it remains true that the good
done by missionary effort in Africa has been incalculable.
There are parts of the great continent, and among them
I include many sections of East Africa, which can be made
a white man's country; and in these parts every effort
should be made to favor the growth of a large and prosperous
white population. But over most of Africa the problem for
the white man is to govern, with wisdom and firmness, and
when necessary with severity, but always with an eye single
to their own interests and development, the black and brown
races. To do this needs sympathy and devotion no less than
strength and wisdom, and in the task the part to be played
by the missionary and the part to be played by the official
are alike great, and the two should work hand in hand.

    After returning from Machakos, I spent the night at Sir
Alfred's, and next morning said good-by with most genuine regret to my host and his family. Then, followed by
my gun-bearers and sais, I rode off across the Athi Plains.
Through the bright white air the sun beat down mercilessly, and the heat haze wavered above the endless flats
of scorched grass. Hour after hour we went slowly forward, through the morning, and through the burning heat
of the equatorial noon, until in mid-afternoon we came to
the tangled tree growth which fringed the half-dried bed of
the Athi. Here I off-saddled for an hour; then, mounting,
I crossed the river-bed where it was waterless, and before
evening fell I rode up to Juja Farm.

CHAPTER V

JUJA FARM; HIPPO AND LEOPARD

At Juja Farm we were welcomed with the most generous hospitality by my fellow-countryman and his wife, Mr. and Mrs. W. N. McMillan. Selous had been staying with them, and one afternoon I had already ridden over from Sir Alfred's ranch to take tea with them at their other house, on the beautiful Mua hills.

Juja Farm lies on the edge of the Athi Plains, and the house stands near the junction of the Nairobi and Rewero Rivers. The house, like almost all East African houses, was of one story, a broad, vine-shaded veranda running around it. There were numerous out-buildings of every kind; there were flocks and herds, cornfields, a vegetable garden, and, immediately in front of the house, a very pretty flower garden, carefully tended by unsmiling Kikuyu savages. All day long these odd creatures worked at the grass and among the flower beds; according to the custom of their tribe their ears were slit so as to enable them to stretch the lobes to an almost unbelievable extent, and in these apertures they wore fantastically carved native ornaments. One of them had been attracted by the shining surface of an empty tobacco can, and he wore this in one ear to match the curiously carved wooden drum he carried in the other. Another, whose arms and legs were massive with copper and iron bracelets, had been given a blanket because he had no other garment; he got along quite well with the blanket excepting when he had to use the lawn mower, and then he would usually wrap the blanket around his neck and handle the lawn mower with the evident feeling that he had done all that the most exacting conventionalism could require.

The house boys and gun-bearers, and most of the boys
who took care of the horses, were Somalis, whereas the
cattle-keepers who tended the herds of cattle were Masai,
and the men and women who worked in the fields were
Kikuyus. The three races had nothing to do with one
another, and the few Indians had nothing to do with any of
them. The Kikuyus lived in their beehive huts scattered
in small groups; the Somalis all dwelt in their own little
village on one side of the farm; and half a mile off the
Masai dwelt in their village. Both the Somalis and Masai
were fine, daring fellows; the Somalis were Mohammedans
and horsemen; the Masai were cattle-herders, who did their
work as they did their fighting, on foot, and were wild
heathen of the most martial type. They looked carefully
after the cattle, and were delighted to join in the chase of
dangerous game, but regular work they thoroughly de-
spised. Sometimes when we had gathered a mass of Kikuyus or of our own porters together to do some job, two or
three Masai would stroll up to look on with curiosity, sword
in belt and great spear in hand; their features were well cut,
their hair curiously plaited, and they had the erect carriage
and fearless bearing that naturally go with a soldierly race.

Within the house, with its bedrooms and dining-room,
its library and drawing-room, and the cool, shaded veranda,
everything was so comfortable that it was hard to realize
that we were far in the interior of Africa and almost under
the equator. Our hostess was herself a good rider and
good shot, and had killed her lion; and both our host and
a friend who was staying with him, Mr. Bulpett, were not
merely mighty hunters who had bagged every important
variety of large and dangerous game, but were also explorers of note, whose travels had materially helped in
widening the area of our knowledge of what was once
the dark continent.

Many birds sang in the garden, bulbuls, thrushes, and
warblers; and from the narrow fringe of dense woodland
along the edges of the rivers other birds called loudly, some

The house at Juja Farm
From a photograph by J. Alden Loring

with harsh, some with musical voices. Here for the first
time we saw the honey-guide, the bird that insists upon
leading any man it sees to honey, so that he may rob the
hive and give it a share.

Game came right around the house. Hartebeests, wildebeests, and zebras grazed in sight on the open plain. The
hippopotami that lived close by in the river came out at
night into the garden. A couple of years before a rhino
had come down into the same garden in broad daylight,
and quite wantonly attacked one of the Kikuyu laborers,
tossing him and breaking his thigh. It had then passed
by the house out to the plain, where it saw an ox cart,
which it immediately attacked and upset, cannoning off
after its charge and passing up through the span of
oxen, breaking all the yokes but fortunately not killing an
animal. Then it met one of the men of the house on
horseback, immediately assailed him, and was killed for
its pains.

My host was about to go on safari for a couple of
months with Selous, and to manage their safari they had

one of the noted professional hunters of East Africa, Mr. H. Judd; and Judd was kind enough to take me out hunting almost every day that we were at Juja. We would breakfast at dawn and leave the farm about the time that it grew light enough to see: ordinarily our course was eastward, toward the Athi, a few miles distant. These morning rides were very beautiful. In our front was the mountain mass of Donyo Sabuk, and the sun rose behind it, flooding the heavens with gold and crimson. The morning air blew fresh in our faces, and the unshod feet of our horses made no sound as they trod the dew-drenched grass. On every side game stood to watch us, herds of hartebeests and zebras, and now and then a herd of wildebeests or a few straggling old wildebeest bulls. Sometimes the zebras and kongoni were very shy, and took fright when we were yet a long way off; at other times they would stand motionless and permit us to come within fair gunshot, and after we had passed we could still see them regarding us without their having moved. The wildebeests were warier; usually when we were yet a quarter of a mile or so distant, the herd, which had been standing with heads up, their short, shaggy necks and heavy withers giving the animals an unmistakable look, would take fright, and, with heavy curvets, and occasional running in semicircles, would make off, heads held down and long tails lashing the air.

In the open woods which marked the border between the barren plains and the forested valley of the Athi, Kermit and I shot waterbuck and impalla. The waterbuck is a stately antelope with long, coarse gray hair and fine carriage of the head and neck; the male alone carries horns. We found them usually in parties of ten or a dozen, both of bulls and cows; but sometimes a party of cows would go alone, or three or four bulls might be found together. In spite of its name, we did not find it much given to going in the water, although it would cross the river fearlessly whenever it desired; it was, however, always found not very far from water. It liked the woods and did not go many miles from the streams, yet we frequently saw it on the open plains a mile or two from trees, feeding in the vicinity of the zebra and the hartebeest. This was, however, usually quite early in the morning or quite late in the afternoon.

Masai warriors near McMillan's ranch on the Mua hills
From a photograph by Kermit Roosevelt

In the heat of the day it clearly preferred to be in the forest, along the stream's edge, or in the bush-clad ravines.

The impalla are found in exactly the same kind of country as the waterbuck, and often associate with them. To my mind they are among the most beautiful of all antelope. They are about the size of a white-tailed deer, their beautiful annulated horns making a single spiral, and their coat is like satin with its contrasting shades of red and white. They have the most graceful movements of any animal I know, and it is extraordinary to see a herd start off when frightened, both bucks and does bounding clear over the tops of the tall bushes, with a peculiar bird-like motion and lightness. Usually a single old buck will be found with a large company of does and fawns; the other bucks go singly or in small parties. It was in the middle of May, and we saw fawns of all ages. When in the open, where, like the waterbuck, it often went in the morning and evening, the impalla was very shy, but I did not find it particularly so among the woods. In connection with shooting two of the impalla, there occurred little incidents which are worthy of mention.

In one case I had just killed a waterbuck cow, hitting it at a considerable distance and by a lucky fluke, after a good deal of bad shooting. We started the porters in with the waterbuck, and then rode west through an open country, dotted here and there with trees and with occasional ant-hills. In a few minutes we saw an impalla buck, and I crept up behind an ant-hill and obtained a shot at about two hundred and fifty yards. The buck dropped, and as I was putting in another cartridge I said to Judd that I didn't like to see an animal drop like that, so instantaneously, as there was always the possibility that it might only be creased, and that if an animal so hurt got up, it always went off exactly as if unhurt. When we raised our eyes again to look for the impalla it had vanished. I was sure that we would never see it again, and Judd felt much the same way, but we walked in the direction toward which its head had been pointed, and Judd ascended an ant-hill to scan the surrounding country with his glasses. He did so, and after a minute remarked that he could not see the wounded impalla; when a sudden movement caused us to look down, and there it was, lying at our very feet, on the side of the ant-hill, unable to rise. I had been using a sharp-pointed bullet in the Springfield, and this makes a big hole. The bullet had gone too far back, in front of the hips. I should not have wondered at all if the animal had failed to get up after falling, but I did not understand why, as it recovered enough from the shock to be able to get up, it had not continued to travel, instead of falling after going one hundred yards. Indeed, I am inclined to think that a deer or prongbuck, hit in the same fashion, would have gone off and would have given a long chase before being overtaken. Judging from what others have said, I have no doubt that African game is very tough and succumbs less easily to wounds than is the case with animals of the northern temperate zone; but in my own experience, I several times saw African antelopes succumb to wounds quicker than the average northern animal would have succumbed to a similar wound. One was this impalla. Another was the cow eland I first shot; her hind leg was broken high up, and the wound, though crippling, was not such as would have prevented a moose or wapiti from

Head of a waterbuck bull shot by Kermit Roosevelt

From a photograph by Edmund Heller

hobbling away on three legs; yet in spite of hard struggles the eland was wholly unable to regain her feet.

The impalla thus shot, by the way, although in fine condition and the coat of glossy beauty, was infested by ticks; around the horns the horrid little insects were clustered in thick masses for a space of a diameter of some inches. It was to me marvellous that they had not set up inflammation or caused great sores, for they were so thick that at a distance of a few feet they gave the appearance of there being some big gland or bare place at the root of each horn.

The other impalla buck also showed an unexpected softness, succumbing to a wound which I do not believe would have given me either a white-tailed or a black-tailed deer. I had been vainly endeavoring to get a waterbuck bull, and as the day was growing hot I was riding homeward, scanning the edge of the plain where it merged into the trees that extended out from the steep bank that hemmed in one side of the river-bottom. From time to time we would see an impalla or a waterbuck making its way from the plain back to the river-bottom, to spend the day in the shade. One of these I stalked, and after a good deal of long-range shooting broke a hind leg high up. It got out of sight and we rode along the edge of the steep descent which led down into the river-bottom proper. In the bottom there were large, open, grassy places, while the trees made a thick fringe along the river course. We had given up the impalla and turned out toward the plain, when one of my gun-bearers whistled to us and said he had seen the wounded animal cross the bottom and go into the fringe of trees bounding a deep pool in which we knew there were both hippos and crocodiles. We were off our horses at once, and, leaving them at the top, scrambled down the descent and crossed the bottom to the spot indicated. The impalla had lain down as soon as it reached cover, and as we entered the fringe of wood I caught a glimpse of it getting up and making off. Yet fifty yards farther it stopped again, standing right on the brink of the pool, so close that when I shot it, it fell over into the water.

When, after arranging for this impalla to be carried back to the farm, we returned to where our horses had been left, the boys told us with much excitement that there was a large snake near by; and sure enough a few yards off, coiled up in the long grass under a small tree, was a python. I could not see it distinctly, and using a solid bullet I just missed the backbone, the bullet going through

the body about its middle. Immediately the snake lashed
at me with open jaws, and then, uncoiling, came gliding
rapidly in our direction. I do not think it was charging;
I think it was merely trying to escape. But Judd, who
was utterly unmoved by lion, leopard, or rhino, evidently
held this snake in respect, and yelled to me to get out of
the way. Accordingly, I jumped back a few feet, and the

The python
From a photograph by W. N. McMillan

snake came over the ground where I had stood; its evil
genius then made it halt for a moment and raise its head
to a height of perhaps three feet, and I killed it by a shot
through the neck. The porters were much wrought up
about the snake, and did not at all like my touching it and
taking it up, first by the tail and then by the head. It was
only twelve feet long. We tied it to a long stick and sent
it in by two porters.

Another day we beat for lions, but without success.
We rode to a spot a few miles off, where we were joined by
three Boer farmers. They were big, upstanding men,

looking just as Boer farmers ought to look who had been through a war and had ever since led the adventurous life of frontier farmers in wild regions. They were accompanied by a pack of big, rough-looking dogs, but were on foot, walking with long and easy strides. The dogs looked a rough-and-ready lot, but on this particular morning showed themselves of little use; at any rate they put up nothing.

But Kermit had a bit of deserved good luck. While the main body of us went down the river-bed, he and Mc-Millan, with a few natives, beat up a side ravine, down the middle of which ran the usual dry watercourse fringed with patches of brush. In one of these they put up a leopard, and saw it slinking forward ahead of them through the bushes. Then they lost sight of it, and came to the conclusion that it was in a large thicket. So Kermit went on one side of it and McMillan on the other, and the beaters approached to try and get the leopard out. Of course none of the beaters had guns; their function was merely to make a disturbance and rouse the game, and they were cautioned on no account to get into danger. But the leopard did not wait to be driven. Without any warning, out he came and charged straight at Kermit, who stopped him when he was but six yards off with a bullet in the forepart of the body; the leopard turned, and as he galloped back Kermit hit him again, crippling him in the hips. The wounds were fatal, and they would have knocked the fight out of any animal less plucky and savage than the leopard; but not even in Africa is there a beast of more unflinching courage than this spotted cat. The beaters were much excited by the sight of the charge and the way in which it was stopped, and they pressed jubilantly forward, too heedlessly; one of them, who was on McMillan's side of the thicket, went too near it, and out came the wounded leopard at him. It was badly crippled or it would have got the beater at once; as it was, it was slowly overtaking him as he ran through the tall grass, when McMillan, standing on an ant-heap, shot it again. Yet, in spite of having this third bullet in it, it ran down the beater and seized him, worrying him with teeth and claws; but it was weak because of its wounds, and the powerful savage wrenched himself free, while McMillan fired into the beast again; and back it went through the long grass into the thicket.   There was a

Kermit Roosevelt and the leopard
From a photograph by W. N. McMillan

pause, and the wounded beater was removed to a place of safety, while a messenger was sent on to us to bring up the Boer dogs.   But while they were waiting, the leopard, on its own initiative, brought matters to a crisis, for out it came again straight at Kermit, and this time it dropped dead to Kermit's bullet.   No animal could have shown a more fearless and resolute temper.   It was an old female, but small, its weight being a little short of seventy pounds. The smallest female cougar I ever killed was heavier than this, and one very big male cougar which I killed in Colorado was three times the weight. Yet I have never heard of any cougar which displayed anything like the spirit and ferocity of this little leopard, or which in any way approached it as a dangerous foe. It was sent back to camp in company with the wounded beater, after the wounds of the latter had been dressed; they were not serious, and he was speedily as well as ever.

Native boy carrying in a leopard shot by Kermit Roosevelt near Juja Ranch

From a photograph by Kermit Roosevelt

The rivers that bounded Juja Farm, not only the Athi, but the Nairobi and Rewero, contained hippopotami and crocodiles in the deep pools. I was particularly anxious to get one of the former, and early one morning Judd and I rode off across the plains, through the herds of grazing game seen dimly in the dawn, to the Athi. We reached the river, and, leaving our horses, went down into the wooded bottom, soon after sunrise. Judd had with him a Masai, a keen-eyed hunter, and I my two gun-bearers. We advanced with the utmost caution toward the brink of a great pool; on our way we saw a bushbuck, but of course did not dare to shoot at it, for hippopotami are wary, except in very unfrequented regions, and any noise will disturb them. As we crept noiselessly up to the steep bank which edged the pool, the sight was typically African. On the still water floated a crocodile, nothing but his eyes and nostrils visible. The bank was covered with a dense growth of trees, festooned with vines; among the branches sat herons; a little cormorant dived into the water; and a very small and brilliantly colored kingfisher, with a red beak and large turquoise

Without any warning, out he came and charged straight at Kermit, who stopped him when he was but six yards off

Drawn by Philip R. Goodwin from photographs and from descriptions furnished by Mr. Roosevelt

crest, perched unheedingly within a few feet of us. Here
and there a dense growth of the tall and singularly graceful papyrus rose out of the water, the feathery heads, which
crowned the long smooth green stems, waving gently to
and fro.

We scanned the waters carefully, and could see no sign
of hippos, and, still proceeding with the utmost caution, we

Judd permanganating the beater who was mauled by the leopard
From a photograph by W. N. McMillan

moved a hundred yards farther down to another lookout.
Here the Masai detected a hippo head a long way off on
the other side of the pool; and we again drew back and
started cautiously forward to reach the point opposite which
he had seen the head.

But we were not destined to get that hippo. Just as
we had about reached the point at which we had intended
to turn in toward the pool, there was a succession of snorts
in our front and the sound of the trampling of heavy feet

and of a big body being shoved through a dense mass of tropical bush. My companions called to me in loud whispers that it was a rhinoceros coming at us, and to "Shoot, shoot." In another moment the rhinoceros appeared, twitching its tail and tossing and twisting its head from side to side as it came toward us. It did not seem to have very good horns, and I would much rather not have killed it; but there hardly seemed any alternative, for it certainly showed every symptom of being bent on mischief. My first shot, at under forty yards, produced no effect whatever, except to hasten its approach. I was using the Winchester, with full-jacketed bullets; my second bullet went in between the neck and shoulder, bringing it to a halt. I fired into the shoulder again, and as it turned toward the bush I fired into its flank both the bullets still remaining in my magazine.

For a moment or two after it disappeared we heard the branches crash, and then there was silence. In such cover a wounded rhino requires cautious handling, and as quietly as possible we walked through the open forest along the edge of the dense thicket into which the animal had returned. The thicket was a tangle of thorn-bushes, reeds, and small, low-branching trees; it was impossible to see ten feet through it, and a man could only penetrate it with the utmost slowness and difficulty, whereas the movements of the rhino were very little impeded. At the far end of the thicket we examined the grass to see if the rhino had passed out, and sure enough there was the spoor, with so much blood along both sides that it was evident the animal was badly hit. It led across this space and into another thicket of the same character as the first; and again we stole cautiously along the edge some ten yards out. I had taken the heavy Holland double-barrel, and with the safety catch pressed forward under my thumb, I trod gingerly through the grass, peering into the thicket and expectant of developments. In a minute there was a furious snorting and crashing directly opposite us in the thicket, and I brought up my rifle; but the rhino did not quite place us, and broke out of the cover in front, some thirty yards away; and I put both barrels into and behind the shoulder. The terrific striking force of the heavy gun told at once, and the rhino wheeled, and struggled back into the thicket, and we heard it fall. With the utmost

The second rhino
From a photograph by J. Alden Loring

caution, bending and creeping under the branches, we made our way in, and saw the beast lying with its head toward us. We thought it was dead, but would take no chances; and I put in another, but as it proved needless, heavy bullet.

It was an old female, considerably smaller than the bull I had already shot, with the front horn measuring fourteen inches as against his nineteen inches; as always with rhinos, it was covered with ticks, which clustered thickly in the folds and creases of the skin, around and in the ears,

and in all the tender places. McMillan sent out an ox
wagon and brought it in to the house, where we weighed it.
It was a little over two thousand two hundred pounds.
It had evidently been in the neighborhood in which we
found it for a considerable time, for a few hundred yards
away we found its stamping ground, a circular spot where
the earth had been all trampled up and kicked about, according to the custom of rhinoceroses; they return day
after day to such places to deposit their dung, which is then
kicked about with the hind feet. As with all our other
specimens, the skin was taken off and sent back to the
National Museum. The stomach was filled with leaves
and twigs, this kind of rhinoceros browsing on the tips of
the branches by means of its hooked, prehensile upper lip.

Now I did not want to kill this rhinoceros, and I am
not certain that it really intended to charge us. It may
very well be that if we had stood firm it would, after much
threatening and snorting, have turned and made off; veteran hunters like Selous could, I doubt not, have afforded
to wait and see what happened. But I let it get within forty
yards, and it still showed every symptom of meaning mischief, and at a shorter range I could not have been sure of
stopping it in time. Often under such circumstances the
rhino does not mean to charge at all, and is acting in a
spirit of truculent and dull curiosity; but often, when its
motions and actions are indistinguishable from those of an
animal which does not mean mischief, it turns out that a
given rhino does mean mischief. A year before I arrived
in East Africa a surveyor was charged by a rhinoceros
entirely without provocation; he was caught and killed.
Chanler's companion on his long expedition, the Austrian
Von Höhnel, was very severely wounded by a rhino and
nearly died; the animal charged through the line of march
of the safari, and then deliberately turned, hunted down
Von Höhnel, and tossed him. Again and again there have
been such experiences, and again and again hunters who
did not wish to kill rhinos have been forced to do so in

order to prevent mischief. Under such circumstances it is not to be expected that men will take too many chances when face to face with a creature whose actions are threatening and whose intentions it is absolutely impossible to divine. In fact, I do not see how the rhinoceros can be permanently preserved, save in very out-of-the-way places or in regular game reserves. There is enough interest and excitement in the pursuit to attract every eager young hunter, and, indeed, very many eager old hunters; and the beast's stupidity, curiosity, and truculence make up a combination of qualities which inevitably tend to insure its destruction.

As we brought home the whole body of this rhinoceros, and as I had put into it eight bullets, five from the Winchester and three from the Holland, I was able to make a tolerably fair comparison between the two. With the full-jacketed bullets of the Winchester I had mortally wounded the animal; it would have died in a short time, and it was groggy when it came out of the brush in its final charge; but they inflicted no such smashing blow as the heavy bullets of the Holland. Moreover, when they struck the heavy bones they tended to break into fragments, while the big Holland bullets ploughed through. The Winchester and the Springfield were the weapons one of which I always carried in my own hand, and for any ordinary game I much preferred them to any other rifles. The Winchester did admirably with lions, giraffes, elands, and smaller game, and, as will be seen, with hippos. For heavy game like rhinoceroses and buffaloes, I found that for me personally the heavy Holland was unquestionably the proper weapon. But in writing this I wish most distinctly to assert my full knowledge of the fact that the choice of a rifle is almost as much a matter of personal idiosyncrasy as the choice of a friend. The above must be taken as merely the expression of my personal preferences. It will doubtless arouse as much objection among the ultra-champions of one type of gun as among the ultra-champions of another. The truth is that any good modern rifle is good enough. The determining factor is the man behind the gun.

In the afternoon of the day on which we killed the rhino Judd took me out again to try for hippos, this time in the Rewero, which ran close by the house. We rode upstream a couple of miles. Then we sent back our horses and walked down the river bank as quietly as possible, Judd scanning the pools, and the eddies in the running stream, from every point of vantage. Once we aroused a crocodile, which plunged into the water. The stream was full of fish, some of considerable size; and in the meadow-land on our side we saw a gang of big, black wild-geese feeding. But we got within half a mile of McMillan's house without seeing a hippo, and the light was rapidly fading. Judd announced that we would go home, but took one last look around the next bend, and instantly sank to his knees, beckoning to me. I crept forward on all-fours, and he pointed out to me an object in the stream, fifty yards off, under the overhanging branch of a tree, which jutted out from the steep bank opposite. In that light I should not myself have recognized it as a hippo head; but it was one, looking toward us, with the ears up and the nostrils, eyes, and forehead above water. I aimed for the centre; the sound told that the bullet had struck somewhere on the head, and the animal disappeared without a splash. Judd was sure I had killed, but I was by no means so confident myself, and there was no way of telling until next morning, for the hippo always sinks when shot and does not rise to the surface for several hours. Accordingly, back we walked to the house.

At sunrise next morning Cuninghame, Judd, and I, with a crowd of porters, were down at the spot. There was a very leaky boat in which Cuninghame, Judd, and I embarked, intending to drift and paddle downstream while the porters walked along the bank. We did not have far to go, for as we rounded the first point we heard the porters break into guttural exclamations of delight, and there

Towing the hippo shot by Mr. Roosevelt
From a photograph by W. N. McMillan

Landing the hippo
From a photograph by W. N. McMillan

ahead of us, by a little island of papyrus, was the dead
hippo. With the help of the boat it was towed to a convenient landing-place, and then the porters dragged it
ashore. It was a cow, of good size for one dwelling in a
small river, where they never approach the dimensions
of those making their homes in a great lake like the Victoria Nyanza. This one weighed nearly two thousand eight
hundred pounds, and I could well believe that a big lake
bull would weigh between three and four tons.

In wild regions hippos rest on sandy bars, and even
come ashore to feed, by day; but wherever there are inhabitants they land to feed only at night. Those in the
Rewero continually entered McMillan's garden. Where
they are numerous they sometimes attack small boats and
kill the people in them; and where they are so plentiful
they do great damage to the plantations of the natives, so
much so that they then have to be taken off the list of
preserved game and their destruction encouraged. Their
enormous jaws sweep in quantities of plants, or lush grass,
or corn, or vegetables, at a mouthful, while their appetites
are as gigantic as their bodies. In spite of their short legs,
they go at a good gait on shore, but the water is their real
home, and they always seek it when alarmed. They
dive and float wonderfully, rising to the surface or sinking
to the bottom at will, and they gallop at speed along the
bottoms of lakes or rivers, with their bodies wholly sub-
merged; but as is natural enough, in view of their big bodies
and short legs, they are not fast swimmers for any length
of time. They make curious and unmistakable trails along
the banks of any stream in which they dwell; their short
legs are wide apart, and so when they tread out a path
they leave a ridge of high soil down the centre. Where
they have lived a long time, the rutted paths are worn
deep into the soil, but always carry this distinguishing
middle ridge.

The full-jacketed Winchester bullet had gone straight
into the brain; the jacket had lodged in the cranium, but

Mr. Roosevelt and Bwana Engozi (Judd)

From a photograph by W. N. McMillan

the lead went on, entering the neck and breaking the atlas vertebra.

At Juja Farm many animals were kept in cages. They included a fairly friendly leopard, and five lions, two of which were anything but friendly. There were three cheetahs, nearly full-grown; these were continually taken out on leashes, Mrs. McMillan strolling about with them and leading them to the summer-house. They were good-tempered, but they did not lead well. Cheetahs are interesting beasts; they are aberrant cats, standing very high on their legs, and with non-retractile claws like a dog. They are nearly the size of a leopard, but are not ordinarily anything like as ferocious, and prey on the smaller antelope, occasionally taking something as big as a half-grown kongoni. For a short run, up to say a quarter of a mile or even perhaps half a mile, they are the swiftest animals on earth, and with a good start easily overtake the fastest antelope; but their bolt is soon shot, and on the open plain they can readily be galloped down with a horse. When they sit on their haunches their attitude is that neither of a dog nor of a cat so much as of a big monkey. On the whole, they are much more easily domesticated than most other cats, but, as with all highly developed wild creatures, they show great individual variability of character and disposition. They have a very curious note, a birdlike chirp, in uttering which they twist the upper lip as if whistling. When I first heard it I was sure that it was uttered by some bird, and looked about quite a time before finding that it was the call of a cheetah.

Then there was a tame wart-hog, very friendly, indeed, which usually wandered loose, and was as comical as pigs generally are, with its sudden starts and grunts. Finally, there was a young tommy buck and a Grant's gazelle doe, both of which were on good terms with every one and needed astonishingly little looking after to prevent their straying. When I was returning to the house on the morning I killed the rhinoceros, I met the string of porters and the ox wagon just after they had left the gate on their way to the carcass. The Grant doe had been attracted by the departure, and was following immediately behind the last porter; a wild-looking Masai warrior, to whom, as I learned, the especial care of the gazelle had been intrusted for that day, was running as hard as he could after her from the gate; when he overtook her he ran in between her and the

Mrs. McMillan and cheetah
From a photograph by W. N. McMillan

rearmost porter, and headed her for the farm gate, uttering what sounded like wild war-cries and brandishing his spear. They formed a really absurd couple, the little doe slowly and decorously walking back to the farm, quite unmoved by the clamor and threats, while her guardian, the very image of what a savage warrior should look when on the war-path, walked close behind, waving his spear and uttering deep-toned shouts, with what seemed a ludicrous disproportion of effort to the result needed.

Antelopes speedily become very tame and recognize

clearly their friends. Leslie Tarlton's brother was keeping
a couple of young kongoni and a partly grown Grant on
his farm just outside Nairobi. (The game comes right to
the outskirts of Nairobi; one morning Kermit walked out
from the McMillans' town-house, where we were staying,
in company with Percival, the game ranger, and got photographs of zebras, kongoni, and Kavirondo cranes; and a
leopard sometimes came up through the garden on to the
veranda of the house itself.) Tarlton's young antelopes
went freely into the country round about, but never fled
with the wild herds; and they were not only great friends
with Tarlton's dogs, but recognized them as protectors.
Hyenas and other beasts frequently came round the farm
after nightfall, and at their approach the antelopes fled
at speed to where the dogs were, and then could not be
persuaded to leave them.

   We spent a delightful week at Juja Farm, and then
moved to Kamiti Ranch, the neighboring farm, owned by
Mr. Hugh H. Heatley, who had asked me to visit him for
a buffalo hunt. While in the highlands of British East
Africa it is utterly impossible for a stranger to realize that
he is under the equator; the climate is delightful and healthy.
It is a white man's country, a country which should be filled
with white settlers; and no place could be more attractive for visitors. There is no more danger to health incident to an ordinary trip to East Africa than there is to an
ordinary trip to the Riviera. Of course, if one goes on a
hunting trip there is always a certain amount of risk, including the risk of fever, just as there would be if a man
camped out in some of the Italian marshes. But the ordinary visitor need have no more fear of his health than if
he were travelling in Italy, and it is hard to imagine a trip
better worth making than the trip from Mombasa to Nairobi
and on to the Victoria Nyanza.

CHAPTER VI

A BUFFALO HUNT BY THE KAMITI

HEATLEY'S RANCH comprises twenty thousand acres lying between the Rewero and Kamiti Rivers. It is seventeen miles long, and four across at the widest place. It includes some as beautiful bits of natural scenery as can well be imagined, and though Heatley—a thorough farmer, and the son and grandson of farmers—was making it a successful farm, with large herds of cattle, much improved stock, hundreds of acres under cultivation, a fine dairy, and the like, yet it was also a game reserve such as could not be matched either in Europe or America. From Juja Farm we marched a dozen miles and pitched our tent close beside the Kamiti. The Kamiti is a queer little stream, running for

Heatley with two leopard cubs he caught
From a photograph by Kermit Roosevelt

most of its course through a broad swamp of tall papyrus. Such a swamp is almost impenetrable. The papyrus grows to a height of over twenty feet, and the stems are so close together that in most places it is impossible to see anything at a distance of six feet. Ten yards from the edge, when within the swamp, I was wholly unable to tell in which direction the open ground lay, and could get out only by

either following my back track or listening for voices.
Underfoot, the mud and water are hip-deep. This swamp
was the home of a herd of buffalo numbering perhaps
a hundred individuals. They are semi-aquatic beasts, and
their enormous strength enables them to plough through
the mud and water and burst their way among the papyrus stems without the slightest difficulty, whereas a man
is nearly helpless when once he has entered the reedbeds.
They had made paths hither and thither across the swamp,
these paths being three feet deep in ooze and black water.
There were little islands in the swamp on which they could
rest. Toward its lower end, where it ran into the Nairobi,
the Kamiti emerged from the papyrus swamp and became
a rapid brown stream of water with only here and there a
papyrus cluster along its banks.

The Nairobi, which cut across the lower end of the
farm, and the Rewero, which bounded it on the other side
from the Kamiti, were as different as possible from the
latter. Both were rapid streams broken by riffle and water-
fall, and running at the bottom of tree-clad valleys. The
Nairobi Falls, which were on Heatley's Ranch, were singularly beautiful. Heatley and I visited them one evening
after sunset, coming home from a day's hunt. It was
a ride I shall long remember. We left our men, and
let the horses gallop. As the sun set behind us, the long
lights changed the look of the country and gave it a beauty
that had in it an element of the mysterious and the unreal.
The mountains loomed both larger and more vague than
they had been in the bright sunlight, and the plains lost
their look of parched desolation as the afterglow came and
went. We were galloping through a world of dim shade
and dying color; and, in this world, our horses suddenly
halted on the brink of a deep ravine from out of which
came the thunder of a cataract. We reined up on a jutting
point. The snowy masses of the fall foamed over a ledge
on our right, and below at our feet was a great pool of
swirling water. Thick-foliaged trees, of strange shape

and festooned with creepers, climbed the sheer sides of the
ravine.   A black-and-white eagle perched in a blasted

Falls on the Rewero River
From a photograph by Edmund Heller

tree top in front; and the bleached skull of a long-dead
rhinoceros glimmered white near the brink to one side.
On another occasion we took our lunch at the foot of

Rewero Falls. These are not as high as the falls of the Nairobi, but they are almost as beautiful. We clambered down into the ravine a little distance below and made our way toward them, beside the brawling, rock-choked torrent. Great trees towered overhead, and among their tops the monkeys chattered and screeched. The fall itself was broken in two parts like a miniature Niagara, and the spray curtain shifted to and fro as the wind blew.

The lower part of the farm, between the Kamiti and Rewero and on both sides of the Nairobi, consisted of immense rolling plains, and on these the game swarmed in almost incredible numbers. There were Grant's and Thomson's gazelles, of which we shot one or two for the table. There was a small herd of blue wildebeest, and among them one unusually large bull with an unusually fine head; Kermit finally killed him. There were plenty of wart-hogs, which were to be found feeding right out in the open, both in the morning and the evening. One day Kermit got a really noteworthy sow with tusks much longer than those of the average boar. He ran into her on horseback after a sharp chase of a mile or two, and shot her from the saddle as he galloped nearly alongside, holding his rifle as the old buffalo-runners used to hold theirs, that is, not bringing it to his shoulder. I killed two or three half-grown pigs for the table, but I am sorry to say that I missed several chances at good boars. Finally one day I got up to just two hundred and fifty yards from a good boar as he stood broadside to me; firing with the little Springfield I put the bullet through both shoulders, and he was dead when we came up.

But of course the swarms of game consisted of zebra and hartebeest. At no time, when riding in any direction across these plains, were we ever out of sight of them. Sometimes they would act warily and take the alarm when we were a long distance off. At other times herds would stand and gaze at us while we passed within a couple of hundred yards. One afternoon we needed meat for the

safari, and Cuninghame and I rode out to get it. Within
half a mile we came upon big herds both of hartebeest and
zebra. They stood to give me long-range shots at about
three hundred yards. I wounded a zebra, after which
Cuninghame rode. While he was off, I killed first a zebra

Wildebeest bull shot by Kermit Roosevelt at Kamiti
From a photograph by Kermit Roosevelt

and then a hartebeest, and shortly afterward a cloud of dust
announced that Cuninghame was bringing a herd of game
toward me. I knelt motionless, and the long files of red-
coated hartebeest and brilliantly striped zebra came galloping past. They were quite a distance off, but I had time
for several shots at each animal I selected, and I dropped
one more zebra and one more hartebeest, in addition, I

regret to add, to wounding another hartebeest. The four hartebeest and zebra lay within a space of a quarter of a mile; and half a mile further I bagged a tommy at two hundred yards—his meat was for our own table, the kongoni and the zebra being for the safari.

On another day, when Heatley and I were out together, he stationed me among some thin thorn-bushes on a little knoll, and drove the game by me, hoping to get me a shot at some wildebeest. The scattered thorn-bushes were only four or five feet high, and so thin that there was no difficulty in looking through them and marking every movement of the game as it approached. The wildebeest took the wrong direction and never came near me—though they certainly fared as badly as if they had done so, for they passed by Kermit, and it was on this occasion that he killed the big bull. A fine cock ostrich passed me and I much wished to shoot at him, but did not like to do so, because ostrich-farming is one of the staple industries of the region, and it is not well to have even the wild birds shot. The kongoni and the zebra streamed by me, herd after herd, hundreds and hundreds of them, many passing within fifty yards of my shelter, now on one side, now on the other; they went at an easy lope, and I was interested to see that many of the kongoni ran with their mouths open. This is an attitude which we usually associate with exhaustion, but such cannot have been the case with the kongoni—they had merely cantered for a mile or so. The zebra were, as usual, noisy, a number of them uttering their barking neigh as they passed. I do not know how it is ordinarily, but these particular zebra, all stallions by the way, kept their mouths open throughout the time they were neighing, and their ears pricked forward; they did not keep their mouths open while merely galloping, as did the kongoni. We had plenty of meat, and the naturalists had enough specimens; and I was glad that there was no need to harm the beautiful creatures. They passed so close that I could mark every slight movement, and the ripple of the muscles under the skin. The very young fawns of the kongoni seemed to have little fear of a horseman, if he approached while they were lying motionless on the ground; but they would run from a man on foot.

There were interesting birds, too. Close by the woods at the river's edge, we saw a big black ground hornbill walking about, on the lookout for its usual dinner of small snakes and lizards. Large flocks of the beautiful Kavirondo

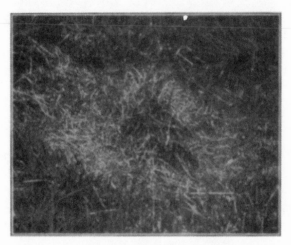

Whydah birds' dancing-ring
From a photograph by Kermit Roosevelt

cranes stalked over the plains and cultivated fields, or flew by with mournful, musical clangor. But the most interesting birds we saw were the black whydah finches. The female is a dull-colored, ordinary-looking bird, somewhat like a female bobolink. The male in his courtship dress is clad in a uniform dark glossy suit, and his tail-feathers are almost like some of those of a barn-yard rooster, being over twice as long as the rest of the bird, with a downward curve at the tips. The females were generally found in flocks, in which there would often be a goodly number of males also, and when the flocks put on speed the males tended to drop behind. The flocks were feeding in Heat-

ley's grain-fields, and he was threatening vengeance upon
them. I was sorry, for the male birds certainly have habits
of peculiar interest. They were not shy, although if we
approached too near them in their favorite haunts, the
grassland adjoining the papyrus beds, they would fly off
and perch on the tops of the papyrus stems. The long
tail hampers the bird in its flight, and it is often held at
rather an angle downward, giving the bird a peculiar and
almost insect-like appearance. But the marked and extraordinary peculiarity was the custom the cocks had of
dancing in artificially made dancing-rings. For a mile and
a half beyond our camp, down the course of the Kamiti,
the grassland at the edge of the papyrus was thickly strewn
with these dancing-rings. Each was about two feet in diameter, sometimes more, sometimes less. A tuft of growing grass perhaps a foot high was left in the centre. Over
the rest of the ring the grass was cut off close by the roots,
and the blades strewn evenly over the surface of the ring.
The cock bird would alight in the ring and hop to a
height of a couple of feet, wings spread and motionless, tail
drooping, and the head usually thrown back. As he came
down he might or might not give an extra couple of little
hops. After a few seconds he would repeat the motion,
sometimes remaining almost in the same place, at other
times going forward during and between the hops so as
finally to go completely round the ring. As there were
many scores of these dancing-places within a comparatively limited territory, the effect was rather striking when
a large number of birds were dancing at the same time. As
one walked along, the impression conveyed by the birds
continually popping above the grass and then immediately
sinking back, was somewhat as if a man was making peas
jump in a tin tray by tapping on it. The favorite dancing
times were in the early morning, and, to a less extent, in the
evening. We saw dancing-places of every age, some with the
cut grass which strewed the floor green and fresh, others with
the grass dried into hay and the bare earth showing through.

But the game we were after was the buffalo herd that haunted the papyrus swamp. As I have said before, the buffalo is by many hunters esteemed the most dangerous of African game. It is an enormously powerful beast with, in

Heatley and a buffalo path

Showing how the enormous strength of the buffalo enables him to burst his way among the papyrus stems which grow to a height of over twenty feet

From a photograph by Kermit Roosevelt

this country, a coat of black hair which becomes thin in the old bulls, and massive horns which rise into great bosses at the base, these bosses sometimes meeting in old age so as to cover the forehead with a frontlet of horn. Their habits vary much in different places. Where they are much persecuted, they lie in the densest cover, and only venture

out into the open to feed at night. But Heatley, though
he himself had killed a couple of bulls, and the Boer farmer
who was working for him another, had preserved the herd
from outside molestation, and their habits were doubtless
much what they would have been in regions where man is
a rare visitor.

The first day we were on Heatley's farm, we saw the
buffalo, to the number of seventy or eighty, grazing in the
open, some hundreds of yards from the papyrus swamp,
and this shortly after noon. For a mile from the papyrus
swamp the country was an absolutely flat plain, gradually
rising into a gentle slope, and it was an impossibility to
approach the buffalo across this plain save in one way to
be mentioned hereafter. Probably when the moon was
full the buffalo came out to graze by night. But while we
were on our hunt the moon was young, and the buffalo
evidently spent most of the night in the papyrus, and came
out to graze by day. Sometimes they came out in the early
morning, sometimes in the late evening, but quite as often
in the bright daylight. We saw herds come out to graze at
ten o'clock in the morning, and again at three in the afternoon. They usually remained out several hours, first grazing and then lying down. Flocks of the small white cow-
heron usually accompanied them, the birds stalking about
among them or perching on their backs; and occasionally
the whereabouts of the herd in the papyrus swamp could
be determined by seeing the flock of herons perched on the
papyrus tops. We did not see any of the red-billed tick-
birds on the buffalo; indeed, the only ones that we saw in
this neighborhood happened to be on domestic cattle—in
other places we found them very common on rhinoceros. At
night the buffalo sometimes came right into the cultivated
fields, and even into the garden close by the Boer farmer's
house; and once at night he had shot a bull. The bullet
went through the heart but the animal ran to the papyrus
swamp, and was found next day dead just within the edge.
Usually the main herd, of bulls, cows, and calves, kept to-

gether; but there were outlying bulls found singly or in
small parties.   Not only the natives but the whites were inclined to avoid the immediate neighborhood of the papyrus swamp, for there had been one or two narrow escapes
from unprovoked attacks by the buffalo.   The farmer told
us that a man who was coming to see him had been regularly followed by three bulls, who pursued him for quite a
distance.   There is no doubt that under certain circumstances buffalo, in addition to showing themselves exceedingly dangerous opponents when wounded by hunters, become truculent and inclined to take the offensive themselves.
There are places in East Africa where as regards at least
certain herds this seems to be the case; and in Uganda the
buffalo have caused such loss of life, and such damage to the
native plantations, that they are now ranked as vermin and
not as game, and their killing is encouraged in every possible way.   The list of white hunters that have been killed
by buffalo is very long, and includes a number of men of
note, while accidents to natives are of constant occurrence.

The morning after making our camp, we started at dawn
for the buffalo ground, Kermit and I, Cuninghame and
Heatley, and the Boer farmer with three big, powerful
dogs.   We walked near the edge of the swamp.   The whydah birds were continually bobbing up and down in front
of us as they rose and fell on their dancing-places, while
the Kavirondo cranes called mournfully all around.   Before we had gone two miles, buffalo were spied, well ahead,
feeding close to the papyrus.   The line of the papyrus
which marked the edge of the swamp was not straight, but
broken by projections and indentations; and by following it
closely and cutting cautiously across the points, the opportunity for stalking was good.   As there was not a tree of
any kind anywhere near, we had to rely purely on our
shooting to prevent damage from the buffalo.   Kermit and
I had our double-barrels, with the Winchesters as spare
guns, while Cuninghame carried a 577, and Heatley a
magazine rifle.

Cautiously threading our way along the edge of the swamp, we got within a hundred and fifty yards of the buffalo before we were perceived. There were four bulls, grazing close by the edge of the swamp, their black bodies glistening in the early sun-rays, their massive horns showing white, and the cow-herons perched on their backs. They stared sullenly at us with out-stretched heads from under their great frontlets of horn. The biggest of the four stood a little out from the other three, and at him I fired, the bullet telling with a smack on the tough hide and going through the lungs. We had been afraid they would at once turn into the papyrus, but instead of this they started straight across our front directly for the open country. This was a piece of huge good luck. Kermit put his first barrel into the second bull, and I my second barrel into one of the others, after which it became impossible to say which bullet struck which animal, as the firing became general. They ran a quarter of a mile into the open, and then the big bull I had first shot, and which had no other bullet in him, dropped dead, while the other three, all of which were wounded, halted beside him. We walked toward them, rather expecting a charge; but when we were still over two hundred yards away they started back for the swamp, and we began firing. The distance being long, I used my Winchester. Aiming well before one bull, he dropped to the shot as if pole-axed, falling straight on his back with his legs kicking; but in a moment he was up again and after the others. Later I found that the bullet, a full-metal patch, had struck him in the head but did not penetrate to the brain, and merely stunned him for the moment. All the time we kept running diagonally to their line of flight. They were all three badly wounded, and when they reached the tall rank grass, high as a man's head, which fringed the papyrus swamp, the two foremost lay down, while the last one, the one I had floored with the Winchester, turned, and with nose out-stretched began to come toward us. He was badly crippled, however, and with a soft-

Mr. Roosevelt and Kermit Roosevelt with the first buffalo

nosed bullet from my heavy Holland I knocked him down, this time for good. The other two then rose, and though each was again hit they reached the swamp, one of them to our right, the other to the left where the papyrus came out in a point.

We decided to go after the latter, and advancing very cautiously toward the edge of the swamp, put in the three big dogs. A moment after, they gave tongue within the papyrus; then we heard the savage grunt of the buffalo and saw its form just within the reeds; and as the rifles cracked, down it went. But it was not dead, for we heard it grunt savagely, and the dogs bayed as loudly as ever. Heatley now mounted his trained shooting-pony and rode toward the place, while we covered him with our rifles, his plan being to run right across our front if the bull charged. The bull was past charging, lying just within the reeds, but he was still able to do damage, for in another minute one of the dogs came out by us and ran straight back to the farm-house, where we found him dead on our return. He had been caught by the buffalo's horns when he went in too close. Heatley, a daring fellow, with great confidence in both his horse and his rifle, pushed forward as we came up, and saw the bull lying on the ground while the two other dogs bit and worried it; and he put a bullet through its head.

The remaining bull got off into the swamp, where a week later Heatley found his dead body. Fortunately the head proved to be in less good condition than any of the others, as one horn was broken off about half-way up; so that if any of the four had to escape, it was well that this should have been the one.

Our three bulls were fine trophies. The largest, with the largest horns, was the first killed, being the one that fell to my first bullet; yet it was the youngest of the three. The other two were old bulls. The second one killed had smaller horns than the other, but the bosses met in the middle of the forehead for a space of several inches, making a solid shield. I had just been reading a pamphlet by

a German specialist who had divided the African buffalo
into fifteen or twenty different species, based upon differences in various pairs of horns.   The worth of such fine

Cuninghame, Kermit, Mr. Roosevelt, Heller, and Heatley at buffalo camp

distinctions, when made on insufficient data, can be gathered from the fact that on the principles of specific divi-
sion adopted in the pamphlet in question, the three bulls we
had shot would have represented certainly two and possibly three different species.

Heller was soon on the ground with his skinning-tent and skinners, and the Boer farmer went back to fetch the ox wagon on which the skins and meat were brought in to camp. Laymen can hardly realize, and I certainly did not realize, what an immense amount of work is involved in preparing the skins of large animals such as buffalo, rhino, hippo, and above all elephant, in hot climates. On this first five weeks' trip we got over seventy skins, including twenty-two species ranging in size from a dikdik to a rhino, and all of these Heller prepared and sent to the Smithsonian. Mearns and Loring were just as busy shooting birds and trapping small mammals. Often while Heller would be off for a few days with Kermit and myself, Mearns and Loring would be camped elsewhere, in a region better suited for the things they were after. While at Juja Farm they went down the Nairobi in a boat to shoot water birds, and saw many more crocodiles and hippo than I did. Loring is a remarkably successful trapper of small mammals. I do not believe there is a better collector anywhere. Dr. Mearns, in addition to birds and plants, never let pass the opportunity to collect anything else from reptiles and fishes to land shells. Moreover, he was the best shot in our party. He killed two great bustards with the rifle, and occasionally shot birds like vultures on the wing with a rifle. I do not believe that three better men than Mearns, Heller, and Loring, for such an expedition as ours, could be found anywhere.

It was three days later before we were again successful with buffalo. On this occasion we started about eight in the morning, having come to the conclusion that the herd was more apt to leave the papyrus late than early. Our special object was to get a cow. We intended to take advantage of a small half-dried watercourse, an affluent of the Kamiti, which began a mile beyond where we had killed our bulls, and for three or four miles ran in a course generally parallel to the swamp, and at a distance which varied, but averaged perhaps a quarter of a mile. When we reached the beginning of this watercourse, we left our

It was not a nice country in which to be charged by the herd, and for a moment things trembled in the balance

Drawn by Philip R. Goodwin from photographs and from descriptions by Theodore Roosevelt

horses and walked along it. Like all such watercourses, it
wound in curves. The banks were four or five feet high,
the bottom was sometimes dry and sometimes contained
reedy pools, while at intervals there were clumps of papyrus. Heatley went ahead, and just as we had about concluded that the buffalo would not come out, he came back
to tell us that he had caught a glimpse of several, and believed that the main herd was with them. Cuninghame, a
veteran hunter and first-class shot, than whom there could be
no better man to have with one when after dangerous game,
took charge of our further movements. We crept up the
watercourse until about opposite the buffalo, which were
now lying down. Cuninghame peered cautiously at them,
saw there were two or three, and then led us on all-fours
toward them. There were patches where the grass was short,
and other places where it was three feet high, and after a good
deal of cautious crawling we had covered half the distance
toward them, when one of them made us out, and several
rose from their beds. They were still at least two hundred
yards off—a long range for heavy rifles; but any closer
approach was impossible, and we fired. Both the leading
bulls were hit, and at the shots there rose from the grass not
half a dozen buffalo, but seventy or eighty, and started at a
gallop parallel to the swamp and across our front. In the
rear were a number of cows and calves, and I at once singled out a cow and fired. She plunged forward at the shot
and turned toward the swamp, going slowly and dead lame,
for my bullet had struck the shoulder and had gone into the
cavity of the chest. But at this moment our attention was
distracted from the wounded cow by the conduct of the
herd, which, headed by the wounded bulls, turned in a
quarter-circle toward us, and drew up in a phalanx facing
us with out-stretched heads. It was not a nice country in
which to be charged by the herd, and for a moment things
trembled in the balance. There was a perceptible motion
of uneasiness among some of our followers. "Stand steady!
Don't run!" I called out. "And don't shoot!" called out

Cuninghame; for to do either would invite a charge. A few seconds passed, and then the unwounded mass of the herd resumed their flight, and after a little hesitation the wounded bulls followed. We now turned our attention to the wounded cow, which was close to the papyrus. She went down to our shots, but the reeds and marsh-grass were above our

Third buffalo bull shot in the swamp
From a photograph by Edmund Heller

heads when we drew close to the swamp. Once again Heatley went in with his white horse, as close as it was even reasonably safe, with the hope either of seeing the cow, or of getting her to charge him and so give us a fair chance at her. But nothing happened and we loosed the two dogs. They took up the trail and went some little distance into the papyrus, where we heard them give tongue, and immediately afterward there came the angry grunt of the wounded buffalo. It had risen and gone off thirty yards into the papyrus, although mortally wounded—the frothy blood from the lungs was actually coming out of my first bullet-

hole. Its anger now made it foolish, and it followed the
dogs to the edge of the papyrus. Here we caught a glimpse
of it. Down it went to our shots, and in a minute we heard
the moaning bellow which a wounded buffalo often gives before dying. Immediately afterward we could hear the dogs
worrying it, while it bellowed again. It was still living as I
came up, and though it evidently could not rise, there was a
chance of its damaging one of the dogs, so I finished it off
with a shot from the Winchester. Heller reached it that
afternoon, and the skin and meat were brought in by the
porters before nightfall.

Cuninghame remained with the body while the rest of
us rode off and killed several different animals we wanted.
In the afternoon I returned, having a vaguely uncomfort-
able feeling that as it grew dusk the buffalo might possibly make their appearance again. Sure enough, there they
were. A number of them were in the open plain, although
close to the swamp, a mile and a half beyond the point
where the work of cutting up the cow was just being finished, and the porters were preparing to start with their
loads. It seemed very strange that after their experience in
the morning any of the herd should be willing to come into
the open so soon. But there they were. They were grazing
to the number of about a dozen. Looking at them through
the glasses I could see that their attention was attracted to
us. They gazed at us for quite a time, and then walked
slowly in our direction for at least a couple of hundred yards.
For a moment I was even doubtful whether they did not
intend to come toward us and charge. But it was only
curiosity on their part, and after having gazed their fill, they
sauntered back to the swamp and disappeared. There
was no chance to get at them, and moreover darkness was
rapidly falling.

Next morning we broke camp. The porters, strapping
grown-up children that they were, felt as much pleasure
and excitement over breaking camp after a few days' rest
as over reaching camp after a fifteen-mile march. On this

occasion, after they had made up their loads, they danced in a ring for half an hour, two tin cans being beaten as tomtoms. Then off they strode in a long line with their burdens, following one another in Indian file, each greeting me with a smile and a deep "Yambo, Bwana!" as he passed. I had grown attached to them, and of course especially to my tent boys, gun-bearers, and saises, who quite touched me by their evident pleasure in coming to see me and greet me if I happened to be away from them for two or three days.

Kermit and I rode off with Heatley to pass the night at his house. This was at the other end of his farm, in a totally different kind of country, a country of wooded hills, with glades and dells and long green grass in the valleys. It did not in the least resemble what one would naturally expect in equatorial Africa. On the contrary it reminded me of the beautiful rolling wooded country of middle Wisconsin. But of course everything was really different. There were monkeys and leopards in the forests, and we saw whydah birds of a new kind, with red on the head and throat, and brilliantly colored woodpeckers, and black-and-gold weaver-birds. Indeed, the wealth of bird life was such that it cannot be described. Here, too, there were many birds with musical voices, to which we listened in the early morning. The best timber was yielded by the tall mahogo-tree, a kind of sandal-wood. This was the tree selected by the wild fig for its deadly embrace. The wild fig begins as a huge parasitic vine, and ends as one of the largest and most stately, and also one of the greenest and most shady, trees in this part of Africa. It grows up the mahogo as a vine and gradually, by branching, and by the spreading of the branches, completely envelops the trunk and also grows along each limb, and sends out great limbs of its own. Every stage can be seen, from that in which the big vine has begun to grow up along the still flourishing mahogo, through that in which the tree looks like a curious composite, the limbs and thick foliage of the fig branching

Porters dancing when breaking camp at Kamiti

From a photograph by Edmund Heller

out among the limbs and scanty foliage of the still living
mahogo, to the stage in which the mahogo is simply a dead
skeleton seen here and there through the trunk or the foliage

Heller preparing to send off game heads of the first five weeks' shooting
From a photograph by Kermit Roosevelt

of the fig.   Finally nothing remains but the fig, which grows
to be a huge tree.

Heatley's house was charming, with its vine-shaded
veranda, its summer-house and out-buildings, and the
great trees clustered round about.   He was fond of sport in
the right way, that is, he treated it as sport and not busi-

ness, and did not allow it to interfere with his prime work of being a successful farmer. He had big stock-yards for his cattle and swine, and he was growing all kinds of things of both the temperate and the tropic zones: wheat and apples, coffee and sugar-cane. The bread we ate and the coffee we drank were made from what he had grown on his own farm. There were roses in the garden and great bushes of heliotrope by the veranda, and the drive to his place was bordered by trees from Australia and beds of native flowers.

Next day we went into Nairobi, where we spent a most busy week, especially the three naturalists; for the task of getting into shape for shipment and then shipping the many hundreds of specimens—indeed, all told there were thousands of specimens—was of herculean proportions. Governor Jackson—a devoted ornithologist and probably the best living authority on East African birds, taking into account the stand-points of both the closet naturalist and the field naturalist—spent hours with Mearns, helping him to identify and arrange the species.

Nairobi is a very attractive town, and most interesting, with its large native quarter and its Indian colony. One of the streets consists of little except Indian shops and bazaars. Outside the business portion, the town is spread over much territory, the houses standing isolated, each by itself, and each usually bowered in trees, with vines shading the verandas, and pretty flower-gardens round about. Not only do I firmly believe in the future of East Africa for settlement as a white man's country, but I feel that it is an ideal playground alike for sportsmen, and for travellers who wish to live in health and comfort, and yet to see what is beautiful and unusual.

CHAPTER VII

TREKKING THROUGH THE THIRST TO THE SOTIK

On June 5th we started south from Kijabe to trek through the thirst, through the waterless country which lies across the way to the Sotik.

The preceding Sunday, at Nairobi, I had visited the excellent French Catholic Mission, had been most courteously received by the fathers, had gone over their plantations and the school in which they taught the children of the settlers (much to my surprise, among them were three Parsee children, who were evidently put on a totally different plane from the other Indians, even the Goanese), and had been keenly interested in their account of their work and of the obstacles with which they met.

At Kijabe I spent several exceedingly interesting hours at the American Industrial Mission. Its head, Mr. Hurlburt, had called on me in Washington at the White House, in the preceding October, and I had then made up my mind that if the chance occurred I must certainly visit his mission. It is an interdenominational mission, and is carried on in a spirit which combines to a marked degree broad sanity and common-sense with disinterested fervor. Of course, such work, under the conditions which necessarily obtain in East Africa, can only show gradual progress; but I am sure that missionary work of the Kijabe kind will be an indispensable factor in the slow uplifting of the natives. There is full recognition of the fact that industrial training is a foundation stone in the effort to raise ethical and moral standards. Industrial teaching must go hand in hand with moral teaching—and in both the mere force of example and the influence of firm, kindly sympathy and understanding, count immeasurably. There is further recognition of the

174

fact that in such a country the missionary should either
already know how to, or else at once learn how to, take the
lead himself in all kinds of industrial and mechanical work.
Finally the effort is made consistently to teach the native
how to live a more comfortable, useful, and physically and
morally cleanly life, not under white conditions, but under

Mr. Roosevelt after luncheon with the head missionary
From a photograph by Kermit Roosevelt

the conditions which he will actually have to face when he
goes back to his people, to live among them, and, if things
go well, to be in his turn a conscious or unconscious missionary for good.

At lunch, in addition to the missionaries and their wives
and children, there were half a dozen of the neighboring
settlers, with their families.   It is always a good thing to see
the missionary and the settler working shoulder to shoulder.
Many parts of East Africa can, and I believe will, be made
into a white man's country; and the process will be helped,

The safari
From a photograph

not hindered, by treating the black man well. At Kijabe, nearly under the equator, the beautiful scenery was almost northern in type; at night we needed blazing camp-fires and the days were as cool as September on Long Island or by the southern shores of the Great Lakes. It is a very healthy region; the chil-

Ulyate and eland calf brought in by Masai
From a photograph by Kermit Roosevelt

dren of the missionaries and settlers, of all ages, were bright and strong; those of Mr. and Mrs. Hurlburt had not been out of the country for eight years, and showed no ill effects whatever; on the contrary, I quite believed Mrs. Hurlburt when she said that she regarded the fertile wooded hills of Kijabe, with their forests and clear brooks, as forming a true health resort.

The northern look of the place was enhanced

on the march
by Edmund Heller

by the fact that the forests contained junipers; but they
also contained monkeys, a small green monkey, and the big
guerza, with its long silky hair and bold black-and-white
coloring.   Kermit, Heller, and Loring shot several.   There
were rhinoceros and buffalo in the   neighborhood.   A
few days previously some buffalo had
charged, unprovoked, a couple of the
native boys of the mission, who had
escaped only by their agility in tree-
climbing.   On one of his trips to an
outlying mission station, Mr. Hurlburt
had himself narrowly escaped a serious accident.   Quite wantonly, a cow
rhino, with a calf, charged the safari
almost before they knew of its presence.   It attacked Hurlburt's mule,
which fortunately he was not riding,
and tossed and killed it; it passed
through the line, and then turned and
again charged it, this time attacking
one of the porters.   The porter dodged
behind a tree, and the rhino hit the
tree, knocked off a huge flake of bark
and wood, and galloped away.

An askari on duty

*From a photograph by J. Aláen
Loring*

The trek across "the thirst," as any waterless country
is apt to be called by an Africander, is about sixty miles,
by the road. On our horses we could have ridden it in a
night; but on a serious trip of any kind loads must be
carried, and laden porters cannot go fast, and must rest at
intervals. We had rather more than our porters could
carry, and needed additional transportation for the water
for the safari; and we had hired four ox wagons. They
were under the lead of a fine young colonial Englishman
named Ulyate, whose great-grandfather had come to South
Africa in 1820, as part of the most important English emi-
gration that ever went thither. His father and sisters had
lunched with us at the missionaries' the day before; his wife's
baby was too young for her to come. It was the best kind
of pioneer family; all the members, with some of their fel-
low-colonials, had spent much of the preceding three years
in adventurous exploration of the country in their ox wagons,
the wives and daughters as valiant as the men; one of the
two daughters I met had driven one of the ox wagons on
the hardest and most dangerous trip they made, while her
younger sister led the oxen. It was on this trip that they
had pioneered the way across the waterless route I was to
take. For those who, like ourselves, followed the path they
had thus blazed, there was no danger to the men, and
merely discomfort to the oxen; but the first trip was a real
feat, for no one could tell what lay ahead, or what exact
route would be practicable. The family had now settled
on a big farm, but also carried on the business of "transport riding," as freighting with wagons is called in Africa;
and they did it admirably.

With Ulyate were three other white wagon-drivers, all
colonials; two of them English, the third Dutch, or Boer.
There was also a Cape boy, a Kaffir wagon-driver; utterly
different from any of the East African natives, and dressed
in ordinary clothes. In addition there were various
natives—primitive savages in dress and habit, but coming
from the cattle-owning tribes. Each ox-team was guided

by one of these savages, who led the first yoke by a leathern thong, while the wagon-driver, with his long whip, stalked to and fro beside the line of oxen, or rode in the wagon. The huge wagons, with their white tops or "sails," were larger than those our own settlers and freighters used. Except one small one, to which there were but eight oxen, each was drawn by a span of seven or eight yoke; they were all native humped cattle.

We had one hundred and ninety-six porters, in addition to the askaris, tent boys, gun-bearers, and saises. The management of such a safari is a work of difficulty; but no better man for the purpose than Cuninghame could be found anywhere, and he had chosen his headmen well. In the thirst, the march goes on by day and night. The longest halt is made in the day, for men and animals both travel better at night than under the blazing noon. We were fortunate in that it was just after the full of the moon, so that our night treks were made in good light. Of course, on such a march the porters must be spared as much as possible; camp is not pitched, and each white man uses for the trip only what he wears, or carries on his horse—and the horse also must be loaded as lightly as possible. I took nothing but my army overcoat, rifle and cartridges, and three canteens of water. Kermit did the same.

The wagons broke camp about ten, to trek to the water, a mile and a half off, where the oxen would be outspanned to take the last drink for three days; stock will not drink early in the morning nearly as freely as if the march is begun later. We, riding our horses, followed by the long line of burdened porters, left at half-past twelve, and in a couple of hours overtook the wagons. The porters were in high spirits. In the morning, before the start, they twice held regular dances, the chief musician being one of their own number who carried an extraordinary kind of native harp; and after their loads were allotted they marched out of camp singing and blowing their horns and whistles. Three askaris brought up the rear to look after

The ox wagons trekking through the scrub
From a photograph by R. J. Cuninghame

laggards, and see that no weak or sick man fell out without our knowing or being able to give him help.

The trail led first through open brush, or low, dry forest, and then out on the vast plains, where the withered grass was dotted here and there with low, scantily leaved thorntrees, from three to eight feet high. Hour after hour we drew slowly ahead under the shimmering sunlight. The horsemen walked first, with the gun-bearers, saises, and

usually a few very energetic and powerful porters; then came the safari in single file; and then the lumbering white-topped wagons, the patient oxen walking easily, each team led by a half-naked savage with frizzed hair and a spear or throwing-stick in his hand, while at intervals the long whips of the drivers cracked like rifles. The dust rose in

The porter-harper and his native harp
From a photograph by J. Alden Loring

clouds from the dry earth, and soon covered all of us; in the distance herds of zebra and hartebeest gazed at us as we passed, and we saw the old spoor of rhino, beasts we hoped to avoid, as they often charge such a caravan.

Slowly the shadows lengthened; the light waned, the glare of the white, dusty plain was softened, and the bold outlines of the distant mountains grew dim. Just before nightfall we halted on the further side of a dry watercourse. The safari came up singing and whistling, and the men put down their loads, lit fires, and with chatter and laughter prepared their food. The crossing was not good, the sides of the watercourse being steep; and each wagon was brought through by a double span, the whips cracking lustily as an accompaniment to the shouts of the drivers, as the thirty oxen threw their weight into the yokes by which they were attached to the long trek tow. The horses were fed. We had tea, with bread and cold meat—and a most delicious meal it was—and then lay dozing or talking beside the bush-fires. At half-past eight, the moon having risen, we were off again. The safari was still in high spirits, and started with the usual chanting and drumming.

We pushed steadily onward across the plain, the dust rising in clouds under the spectral moonlight. Sometimes we rode, sometimes we walked to ease our horses. The Southern Cross was directly ahead, not far above the horizon. Higher and higher rose the moon, and brighter grew the flood of her light. At intervals the barking call of zebras was heard on either hand. It was after midnight when we again halted. The porters were tired, and did not sing as they came up; the air was cool, almost nipping, and they at once huddled down in their blankets, some of them building fires. We, the white men, after seeing our horses staked out, each lay down in his overcoat or jacket and slicker, with his head on his saddle, and his rifle beside him, and had a little over two hours' sleep. At three we were off again, the shivering porters making no sound as they started; but once under way the more irrepressible

spirits speedily began a kind of intermittent chant, and
most of the rest by degrees joined in the occasional grunt
or hum that served as chorus.

For four hours we travelled steadily, first through the
moonlight, and then through the reddening dawn. Jackals
shrieked, and the plains plover wailed and scolded as they
circled round us. When the sun was well up, we halted;
the desolate flats stretched far and wide on every side and
rose into lofty hills ahead of us. The porters received their
water and food, and lay down to sleep, some directly in the
open, others rigging little sun shelters under the scattering
thorn-bushes. The horses were fed, were given half a
pail of water apiece, and were turned loose to graze with
the oxen; this was the last time the oxen would feed freely,
unless there was rain; and this was to be our longest halt.
We had an excellent breakfast, like our supper the night
before, and then slept as well as we could.

Noon came, and soon afterward we again started. The
country grew hilly, and brushy. It was too dry for much
game, but we saw a small herd of giraffe, which are independent of water. Now riding our horses, now leading
them, we travelled until nearly sunset, when we halted at
the foot of a steep divide, beyond which our course lay
across slopes that gradually fell to the stream for which
we were heading. Here the porters had all the food and
water they wished, and so did the horses; and, each with
a double span of oxen, the wagons were driven up the
slope, the weary cattle straining hard in the yokes.

Black clouds had risen and thickened in the west,
boding rain. Three-fourths of our journey was over; and
it was safe to start the safari and then leave it to come on
by itself, while the ox wagons followed later. At nine, before the moon struggled above the hill-crests to our left, we
were off. Soon we passed the wagons, drawn up abreast,
a lantern high on a pole, while the tired oxen lay in their
yokes, attached to the trek tow. An hour afterward we
left the safari behind, and rode ahead, with only our saises

and gun-bearers. Gusts of rain blew in our faces, and gradually settled into a steady, gentle downpour. Our horses
began to slip in the greasy soil; we knew the rain would
refresh the cattle, but would make the going harder.

At one we halted, in the rain, for a couple of hours' rest.
Just before this we heard two lions roaring, or rather grunting, not far in front of us; they were after prey. Lions

A halt
From a photograph by R. J. Cuninghame

are bold on rainy nights, and we did not wish to lose any
of our horses; so a watch was organized, and we kept ready
for immediate action, but the lions did not come. The
native boys built fires, and lay close to them, relieving one
another, and us, as sentinels. Kermit and I had our army
overcoats, which are warm and practically water-proof;
the others had coats almost as good. We lay down in the
rain, on the drenched grass, with our saddle-cloths over
our feet, and our heads on our saddles, and slept comfortably for two hours.

At three we mounted and were off again, the rain still falling. There were steep ravines to cross, slippery from the wet; but we made good time, and soon after six off-saddled on the farther side of a steep drift or ford in the little Suavi River. It is a rapid stream flowing between high, well-wooded banks; it was an attractive camp site, and, as we afterward found, the nights were so cool as to make great camp-fires

Every one rested under the fly-tent at noon in the trek through the thirst

From a photograph by Kermit Roosevelt

welcome. At half-past ten the safari appeared, in excellent spirits, the flag waving, to an accompaniment of chanting and horn-blowing; and, to their loudly expressed satisfaction, the porters were told that they should have an extra day's rations, as well as a day's rest. Camp was soon pitched; and all, of every rank, slept soundly that night, though the lions moaned near by. The wagons did not get in until ten the following morning. By that time the oxen had been nearly three days without water, so, by dawn, they were unyoked and driven down to drink before the drift was attempted, the wagons being left a mile or two back. The approaches to the drift were steep and difficult, and, with two spans to each, the wagons swayed and plunged, over the twisted bowlder-choked trails down into the river-bed, crossed it, and, with lurching and straining, men shouting and whips cracking, drew slowly up the opposite bank.

After a day's rest, we pushed on, in two days' easy travelling, to the Guaso Nyero of the south. Our camps were pleasant, by running streams of swift water; one was really beautiful, in a grassy bend of a rapid little river, by huge African yew-trees, with wooded cliffs in front. It was cool, rainy weather, with overcast skies and misty mornings, so that it seemed strangely unlike the tropics. The country was alive with herds of Masai cattle, sheep, and

Watering the oxen.   Taking their last drink for three days
From a photograph by Kermit Roosevelt

donkeys. The Masai, herdsmen by profession and warriors by preference, with their great spears and ox-hide shields, were stalwart savages, and showed the mixture of types common to this part of Africa, which is the edge of an ethnic whirlpool. Some of them were of seemingly pure negro type; others except in their black skin had little negro about them, their features being as clear-cut as those of ebony Nilotic Arabs. They were dignified, but friendly and civil, shaking hands as soon as they came up to us.

On the Guaso Nyero was a settler from South Africa, with his family; and we met another settler travelling with a big flock of sheep which he had bought for trading purposes. The latter, while journeying over our route with cattle, a month before, had been attacked by lions one night. They seized his cook as he lay by the fire, but fortunately grabbed his red blanket, which they carried off, and the terrified man escaped; and they killed a cow and a calf. Ulyate's brother-in-law, Smith, had been rendered a hopeless cripple for life, six months previously, by a lioness he had wounded. Another settler while at one of our camping-places lost two of his horses, which were killed although within a boma. One night lions came within threatening neighborhood of our ox wagons; and we often heard them moaning in the early part of the night, roaring when full fed toward morning; but we were not molested.

The safari was in high feather, for the days were cool, the work easy, and we shot enough game to give them meat. When we broke camp after breakfast, the porters would all stand ranged by their loads; then Tarlton would whistle, and a chorus of whistles, horns, and tomtoms would answer, as each porter lifted and adjusted his burden, fell into his place, and then joined in some shrill or guttural chorus as the long line swung off at its marching pace. After nightfall the camp-fires blazed in the cool air, and as we stood or sat around them each man had tales to tell: Cuninghame and Tarlton of elephant hunting in the Congo, and of perilous adventures hunting lion and buffalo; Mearns of long hikes and fierce fighting in the steaming Philippine forests; Loring and Heller of hunting and collecting in Alaska, in the Rockies, and among the deserts of the Mexican border; and always our talk came back to strange experiences with birds and beasts, both great and small, and to the ways of the great game. The three naturalists revelled in the teeming bird life, with its wealth

bil's and
e weave :-
drinking

Young
dikdik

courser

Tame serval
kitten

ephant
shrew

A banded
mongoose

pring-
haas

Colobus
monkey

of beauty and color—nor was the beauty only of color and shape, for at dawn the bird songs made real music. The naturalists trapped many small mammals: big-eared mice looking like our white-footed mice, mice with spiny fur, mice that lived in trees, rats striped like our chipmunks, rats that jumped like jerboas, big cane-rats, dormice, and tiny shrews. Meercats, things akin to a small mongoose, lived out in the open plains, burrowing in com-

A wounded wildebeest
From a photograph by Kermit Roosevelt

panies like prairie dogs, very spry and active, and looking like picket pins when they stood up on end to survey us. I killed a nine-foot python which had swallowed a rabbit. Game was not plentiful, but we killed enough for the table. I shot a wildebeest bull one day, having edged up to it on foot, after missing it standing; I broke it down with a bullet through the hips as it galloped across my front at three hundred yards. Kermit killed our first topi, a bull; a beautiful animal, the size of a hartebeest, its glossy coat with a satin sheen, varying from brown to silver and purple.

By the Guaso Nyero we halted for several days; and we arranged to leave Mearns and Loring in a permanent camp, so that they might seriously study and collect the birds and small mammals while the rest of us pushed wherever we wished after the big game. The tents were pitched, and the ox wagons drawn up on the southern side of the muddy river, by the edge of a wide plain, on which we could see the game grazing as we walked around camp. The alluvial flats bordering the river, and some of the higher plains, were covered with an open forest growth, the most common tree looking exactly like a giant sage-brush, thirty feet high; and there were tall aloes and cactus and flat-topped mimosa. We found a wee hedgehog, with much white about it. He would cuddle up in my hand snuffing busily with his funny little nose. We did not have the heart to turn the tame, friendly little fellow over to the naturalists, and so we let him go. Birds abounded. One kind of cuckoo called like a whippoorwill in the early morning and late evening,

A Colobus monkey

From a photograph by J. Alden Loring

and after nightfall. Among our friendly visitors were the pretty, rather strikingly colored little chats—Livingstone's wheatear—which showed real curiosity in coming into camp. They were nesting in burrows on the open plains round about. Mearns got a white egg and a nest at the end of a little burrow two feet long; wounded, the birds ran into holes or burrows. They sang attractively on the wing, often at night. The plover-like coursers, very pretty birds, continually circled round us with querulous clamor. Gorgeously colored, diminutive sunbirds, of many different kinds, were abundant; they had an especial fondness for the gaudy flowers of the tall mint which grew close to the river. We got a small cobra, less than eighteen inches long; it had swallowed another snake almost as big as itself; unfortunately the head of the swallowed snake was digested, but the body looked like that of a young puff adder.

The day after reaching this camp I rode off for a hunt, accompanied by my two gun-bearers and with a dozen porters following, to handle whatever I killed. One of my original gun-bearers, Mahomet, though a good man in the field, had proved in other respects so unsatisfactory that he had been replaced by another, a Wakamba heathen named Gouvimali—I could never remember his name until, as a mnemonic aid, Kermit suggested that I think of Gouverneur Morris, the old Federalist statesman, whose life I had once studied. He was a capital man for the work.

Half a mile from camp I saw a buck tommy with a good head, and as we needed his delicious venison for our own table, I dismounted and after a little care killed him as he faced me at two hundred and ten yards. Sending him back by one of the porters, I rode on toward two topi we saw far in front. But there were zebra, hartebeest, and wildebeest in between, all of which ran; and the topi proved wary. I was still walking after them when we made out two eland bulls ahead and to our left. The ground was too open to admit of the possibility of a stalk; but leaving my horse and the porters to follow slowly, the gun-bearers and I walked quartering toward them. They hesitated about going, and when I had come as close as I dared, I motioned to the two gun-bearers to continue walking and dropped on one knee. I had the little Springfield, and was anxious to test the new sharp-pointed military bullet on some large animal. The biggest bull was half facing me, just two hundred and eighty yards off; I fired a little bit high and a trifle to the left; but the tiny ball broke his back and the splendid beast, heavy as a prize steer, came plunging and struggling to the ground. The other bull started to run off but after I had walked a hundred yards forward he actually trotted back toward his companion; then halted, turned, and galloped across my front at a distance of a hundred and eighty yards; and him too I

brought down with
a single shot. The
little full-jacketed,
sharp-pointed bullet
made a terrific rend-
ing compared with
the heavier, ordina-
ry-shaped bullet of
the same composi-
tion.
I was much
pleased with my
two prizes, for the
National Museum
particularly desired

A wounded tommy

From a photograph by Kermit Roosevelt

a good group of eland. They were splendid animals, like
beautiful heavy cattle; and I could not sufficiently admire
their sleek, handsome, striped coats, their shapely heads,
fine horns, and massive bodies. The big bull, an old one,
looked blue at a distance; he was very heavy and his dewlap
hung down just as with cattle. His companion, although
much less heavy, was a full-grown bull in his prime, with
longer horns; for the big one's horns had begun to wear
down at the tips. In their stomachs were grass blades and,
rather to my surprise, aloe leaves.

We had two canvas cloths with us, which Heller had

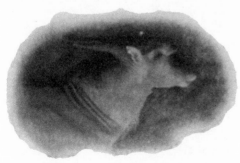

Head of the old bull eland

From a photograph by Edmund Heller

instructed me to put
over anything I shot,
in order to protect it
from the sun; so,
covering both bulls,
I left a porter with
them, and sent in
another to notify
Heller—who came
out with an ox wag-
on to bring in the

skins and meat. I had killed these two eland bulls, as well
as the buck gazelle (bringing down each with a single bullet)
within three-quarters of an hour after leaving camp.

I wanted a topi, and continued the hunt. The country swarmed with the herds and flocks of the Masai, who
own a wealth of live stock. Each herd of cattle and donkeys or flock of sheep was guarded by its herdsmen; bands
of stalwart, picturesque warriors, with their huge spears
and ox-hide shields, occasionally strolled by us; and we
passed many bomas, the kraals where the stock is gathered
at night, with the mud huts of the owners ringing them. Yet
there was much game in the country also, chiefly zebra and
hartebeest; the latter, according to their custom, continually jumping up on ant-hills to get a clearer view of me,
and sometimes standing on them motionless for a considerable time, as sentries to scan the country around.

At last we spied a herd of topi, distinguishable from
the hartebeest at a very long distance by their dark coloring,
the purples and browns giving the coat a heavy shading
which when far off, in certain lights, looks almost black.
Topi, hartebeest, and wildebeest belong to the same group,
and are specialized, and their peculiar physical and mental traits developed, in the order named. The wildebeest
is the least normal and most grotesque and odd-looking of
the three, and his idiosyncrasies of temper are also the
most marked. The hartebeest comes next, with his very
high withers, long face, and queerly shaped horns; while
the topi, although with a general hartebeest look, has the
features of shape and horn less pronounced, and bears a
greater resemblance to his more ordinary kinsfolk. In the
same way, though it will now and then buck and plunge
when it begins to run after being startled, its demeanor is less
pronounced in this respect. The topi's power of leaping is
great; I have seen one when frightened bound clear over a
companion, and immediately afterward over a high ant-hill.

The herd of topi we saw was more shy than the neighboring zebra and hartebeest. There was no cover and I

spent an hour trying to walk up to them by manœuvring in one way and another. They did not run clear away, but kept standing and letting me approach to distances varying from four hundred and fifty to six hundred yards; tempting me to shoot, while nevertheless I could not estimate the range accurately, and was not certain whether I was over or under shooting. So I fired more times than I care to mention before I finally got my topi—at just five hundred and twenty yards. It was a handsome cow, weighing two hundred and sixty pounds; for topi are somewhat smaller than kongoni. The beauty of its coat, in texture and coloring, struck me afresh as I looked at the sleek creature stretched out on the grass. Like the eland, it was

Giant Masai warriors and an average-sized porter

From a photograph by J. Alden Loring

free from ticks; for the hideous pests do not frequent this part of the country in any great numbers.

I reached camp early in the afternoon, and sat down at the mouth of my tent to enjoy myself. It was on such occasions that the Pigskin Library proved itself indeed a blessing. In addition to the original books we had picked up one or two old favorites on the way: Alice's Adventures, for instance, and Fitzgerald—I say Fitzgerald, because reading other versions of Omar Khayyam always leaves

me with the feeling that Fitzgerald is the major partner in
the book we really like. Then there was a book I had
not read, Dumas's "Louves de Machecoul." This was
presented to me at Port Said by M. Jusserand, the brother
of an old and valued friend, the French ambassador at
Washington—the vice-president of the "Tennis Cabinet."
We had been speaking of Balzac, and I mentioned regret-
fully that I did not at heart care for his longer novels ex-
cepting the "Chou-
ans"; and, as John
Hay once told me,
in the eye of all
true Balzacians to
like the "Chouans"
merely aggravates
the offence of not
liking the novels
which they deem

Topi (shot by Kermit)

From a photograph by Kermit Roosevelt

really great. M. Jusserand thereupon asked me if I knew
Dumas's Vendean novel; being a fairly good Dumas man,
I was rather ashamed to admit that I did not; whereupon
he sent it to me, and I enjoyed it to the full.

The next day was Kermit's red-letter day. We were
each out until after dark; I merely got some of the ordinary
game, taking the skins for the naturalists, the flesh for our
following; he killed two cheetahs, and a fine maned lion,
finer than any previously killed. There were three cheetahs together. Kermit, who was with Tarlton, galloped
the big male, and, although it had a mile's start, ran into it
in three miles, and shot it as it lay under a bush. He
afterward shot another, a female, who was lying on a
stone koppie. Neither made any attempt to charge; the
male had been eating a tommy. The lion was with a
lioness, which wheeled to one side as the horsemen galloped after her maned mate. He turned to bay after a run
of less than a mile, and started to charge from a distance
of two hundred yards; but Kermit's first bullets mortally

wounded him and crippled him so that he could not come at any pace and was easily stopped before covering half the distance. Although nearly a foot longer than the biggest of the lions I had already killed, he was so gaunt—whereas they were very fat—that he weighed but little more, only four hundred and twelve pounds.

The following day I was out by myself, after impalla and Roberts' gazelle; and the day after I went out with

The big lion shot by Kermit
From a photograph by Kermit Roosevelt

Tarlton to try for lion. We were away from camp for over fifteen hours. Each was followed by his sais and gun-bearers, and we took a dozen porters also. The day may be worth describing, as a sample of the days when we did not start before dawn for a morning's hunt.

We left camp at seven, steering for a high, rocky hill, four miles off. We passed zebra and hartebeest, and on the hill came upon Chanler's reedbuck; but we wanted none of these. Continually, Tarlton stopped to examine some distant object with his glasses, and from the hill we scanned

the country far and wide; but we saw nothing we desired
and continued on our course. The day was windy and
cool, and the sky often overcast. Slowly we walked across

Tarlton, and cheetah shot by Kermit Roosevelt

From a photograph by Kermit Roosevelt

the stretches of brown grassland, sometimes treeless, sometimes scantily covered with an open growth of thorn-trees,
each branch armed with long spikes, needle-sharp; and

among the thorns here and there stood the huge cactus-like euphorbias, shaped like candelabra, groups of tall aloes, and gnarled wild olives of great age, with hoary trunks and twisted branches. Now and then there would be a dry watercourse, with flat-topped acacias bordering it, and perhaps some one pool of thick greenish water. There was game always in view, and about noon we sighted three rhinos, a bull, a cow, and a big calf, nearly a mile ahead of us. We were travelling down wind, and they scented us, but did not charge, making off in a semicircle and halting when abreast of us. We examined them carefully through the glasses. The cow was bigger than the bull, and had fair horns, but nothing extraordinary; and as we were twelve miles from camp, so that Heller would have had to come out for the night if we shot her, we decided to leave her alone. Then our attention was attracted by seeing the game all gazing in one direction, and we made out a hyena; I got a shot at it, at three hundred yards, but missed. Soon afterward we saw another rhino, but on approaching it proved to be about two-thirds grown, with a stubby horn. We did not wish to shoot it, and therefore desired to avoid a charge; and so we passed three or four hundred yards to leeward, trusting to its bad eyesight. Just opposite it, when it was on our right, we saw another hyena on our left, about as far off as the rhino. I decided to take a shot, and run the chance of disturbing the rhino. So I knelt down and aimed with the little Springfield, keeping the Holland by me to be ready for events. I never left camp, on foot or on horseback, for any distance, no matter how short, without carrying one of the repeating rifles; and when on a hunt my two gun-bearers carried, one the other magazine rifle, and one the double-barrelled Holland.

Tarlton, whose eye for distance was good, told me the hyena was over three hundred yards off; it was walking slowly to the left. I put up the three-hundred-yard sight, and drew a rather coarse bead; and down went the hyena with its throat cut; the little sharp-pointed, full-jacketed bullet makes a slashing wound. The distance was just three hundred and fifty long paces. As soon as I had pulled trigger I wheeled to watch the rhino. It started round at the shot and gazed toward us with its ears cocked forward, but made no movement to advance. While a couple of porters were dressing the hyena, I could not help laughing at finding that we were the centre of a thoroughly African circle of deeply interested spectators.

A wart-hog shot by Kermit Roosevelt
From a photograph by Edmund Heller

We were in the middle of a vast plain, covered with sun-scorched grass and here and there a stunted thorn; in the background were isolated barren hills, and the mirage wavered in the distance. Vultures wheeled overhead. The rhino, less than half a mile away, stared steadily at us. Wildebeest—their heavy forequarters and the carriage of their heads making them look like bison—and hartebeest were somewhat nearer, in a ring all round us, intent upon our proceedings. Four topi became so much interested that they approached within two hundred and fifty yards and stood motionless. A buck tommy came even closer, and a zebra trotted by at about the same distance, uttering its queer bark or neigh. It continued its course past the rhino, and started a new train of ideas in the latter's muddled reptilian brain; round it wheeled, gazed after the zebra, and then evidently concluded that everything was normal, for it lay down to sleep.

On we went, past a wildebeest herd lying down; at a distance they looked exactly like bison as they used to lie out on the prairie in the old days. We halted for an hour and a half to rest the men and horses, and took our lunch under a thick-trunked olive-tree that must have been a couple of centuries old. Again we went on, ever scanning through the glasses every distant object which we thought might possibly be a lion, and ever being disappointed. A serval cat jumped up ahead of us in the tall grass, but I missed it. Then, trotting on foot, I got ahead of two warthog boars, and killed the biggest; making a bad initial miss and then emptying my magazine at it as it ran. We sent it in to camp, and went on, following a donga, or small watercourse, fringed with big acacias. The afternoon was wearing away, and it was time for lions to be abroad.

The sun was near the horizon when Tarlton thought he saw something tawny in the watercourse ahead of us, behind a grassy ant-hill, toward which we walked after dismounting. Some buck were grazing peacefully beyond it, and for a moment we supposed that this was what he had seen. But as we stood, one of the porters behind called out "Simba"; and we caught a glimpse of a big lioness galloping down beside the trees, just beyond the donga; she was out of sight in an instant. Mounting our horses, we crossed the donga; she was not to be seen, and we loped at a smart pace parallel with the line of trees, hoping to see her in the open. But, as it turned out, as soon as she saw us pass, she crouched in the bed of the donga; we had gone by her a quarter of a mile when a shout from one of our followers announced that he had seen her, and back we galloped, threw ourselves from our horses, and walked

toward where the man was pointing. Tarlton took his big
double-barrel and advised me to take mine, as the sun
had just set and it was likely to be close work; but I shook
my head, for the Winchester .405 is, at least for me personally, the "medicine gun" for lions. In another moment up she jumped, and galloped slowly down the other
side of the donga, switching her tail and growling; I scrambled across the donga, and just before she went round a
clump of trees, eighty yards off, I fired. The bullet hit
her fair, and going forward
injured her spine. Over she
rolled, growling savagely, and
dragged herself into the watercourse; and running forward
I finished
her with two
bullets be-
hind the
shoulder.
She was a
big, fat lion-
ess, very old,
with two

Extreme form of Roberts' gazelle
From a photograph by Edmund Heller

cubs inside her; her lower canines were much worn and
injured. She was very heavy, and probably weighed considerably over three hundred pounds.

The light was growing dim, and camp was eight or
ten miles away. The porters—they are always much excited over the death of a lion—wished to carry the body
whole to camp, and I let them try. While they were lashing
it to a pole another lion began to moan hungrily half a
mile away. Then we started; there was no moon, but the
night was clear and we could guide ourselves by the stars.
The porters staggered under their heavy load, and we
made slow progress; most of the time Tarlton and I walked,
with our double-barrels in our hands, for it was a dangerous neighborhood. Again and again we heard lions, and

twice one accompanied us for some distance, grunting occasionally, while we kept the men closed. Once the porters were thrown into a panic by a succession of steam-engine-like snorts on our left, which announced the immediate proximity of a rhino. They halted in a huddle while Tarlton and I ran forward and crouched to try to catch the great beast's loom against the sky-line; but it moved off. Four miles from camp was a Masai kraal, and we went toward this when we caught the gleam of the fires; for the porters were getting exhausted.

Masai with stretching-stone in ear

From a photograph by J. Alden Loring

The kraal was in shape a big oval, with a thick wall of thorn-bushes, eight feet high, the low huts standing just within this wall, while the cattle and sheep were crowded into small bomas in the centre. The fires gleamed here and there within, and as we approached we heard the talking and laughing of men and women, and the lowing and bleating of the pent-up herds and flocks. We hailed loudly, explaining our needs. At first they were very suspicious. They told us we could not bring the lion within, because it would frighten the cattle, but after some parley consented to our building a fire outside, and skinning the animal. They passed two brands over the thorn fence, and our men speedily kindled a blaze, and drew the lioness beside it.

A Masai woman and toto

From a photograph by Kermit Roosevelt

By this time the Masai were reassured, and a score of their warriors, followed soon by half a dozen women, came out through a small opening in the fence, and crowded close around the fire, with boisterous, noisy good-humor. They showed a tendency to chaff our porters. One, the humorist of the crowd, excited much merriment by describing, with pantomimic accompaniment of gestures, how when the white man shot a lion it might bite a Swahili, who thereupon would call for his mother. But they were entirely friendly, and offered me calabashes of milk. The men were tall, finely shaped savages, their hair plastered with red mud, and drawn out into longish ringlets; they were naked except for a blanket worn, not round the loins, but over the shoulders; their ears were slit, and from them hung bone and wooden ornaments; they wore metal bracelets and anklets, and chains which passed around their necks, or else over one side of the neck and under the opposite arm. The women had pleasant faces, and were laden with metal ornaments—chiefly wire anklets, bracelets, and necklaces—of many pounds weight. The features of the men were bold and clear-cut, and their bearing warlike and self-reliant; as the flame of the fire glanced over them, and brought their faces and bronze figures into lurid relief against the darkness, the likeness was striking, not to the West Coast negroes, but to the engravings on the tombs, temples, and palaces of ancient Egypt; they might have been soldiers in the armies of Thothmes or Rameses. They stood resting on their long staffs, and looked at me as I leaned on my rifle; and they laughed and jested with their women, who felt the lion's teeth and claws and laughed back at the men; our gun-bearers worked at the skinning, and answered the jests of their warlike friends with the freedom of men who themselves followed a dangerous trade; the two horses stood quiet just outside the circle; and over all the firelight played and leaped.

It was after ten when we reached camp, and I enjoyed

a hot bath and a shave before sitting down to a supper of eland venison and broiled spurfowl; and surely no supper ever tasted more delicious.

Next day we broke camp. My bag for the five days illustrates ordinary African shooting in this part of the continent. Of course I could have killed many other things; but I shot nothing that was not absolutely needed, both for scientific purposes and for food; the skin of every animal I shot was preserved for the National Museum. The bag included fourteen animals, of ten different species: one lioness, one hyena, one wart-hog boar, two zebra, two eland, one wildebeest, two topi, two impalla, one Roberts' gazelle, one Thomson's gazelle. Except the lioness and one impalla (both of which I shot running), all were shot at rather long ranges; seven were shot standing, two walking, five running. The average distance at which they were shot was a little over two hundred and twenty yards. I used sixty-five cartridges, an amount which will seem excessive chiefly to those who are not accustomed actually to count the cartridges they expend, to measure the distances at which they fire, and to estimate for themselves the range, on animals in the field when they are standing or running a good way off. Only one wounded animal got away; and eight of the animals I shot had to be finished with one bullet —two in the case of the lioness—as they lay on the ground. Many of the cartridges expended really represented range-finding.

CHAPTER VIII

HUNTING IN THE SOTIK

OUR next camp was in the middle of the vast plains, by some limestone springs, at one end of a line of dark acacias. There were rocky koppies two or three miles off on either hand. From the tents, and white-topped wagons, we could see the game grazing on the open flats, or among the scattered wizened thorns. The skies were overcast, and the nights cool; in the evenings the camp-fires blazed in front of the tents, and after supper we gathered round them, talking, or sitting silently, or listening to Kermit strumming on his mandolin.

The day after reaching this camp we rode out, hoping to get either rhino or giraffe; we needed additional specimens of both for the naturalists, who especially wanted cow giraffes. It was cloudy and cool, and the common game was shy; though we needed meat, I could not get within fair range of the wildebeest, hartebeest, topi, or big gazelle; however I killed a couple of tommies, one by a good shot, the other running, after I had missed him in rather scandalous fashion while he was standing.

An hour or two after leaving the tents we made out on the sky-line a couple of miles to our left some objects which scrutiny showed to be giraffe. After coming within a mile the others halted and I rode ahead on the tranquil sorrel, heading for a point toward which the giraffe were walking; stalking was an impossibility, and I was prepared either to manœuvre for a shot on foot, or to ride them, as circumstances might determine. I carried the little Springfield, being desirous of testing the small, solid, sharp-pointed army bullet on the big beasts. As I rode, a wildebeest bull played around me within two hundred yards, prancing, flourishing his tail, tossing his head and uttering his grunting bellow; it almost seemed as if he knew I would not shoot at him, or as if for the moment he had been infected with the absurd tameness which the giraffe showed.

There were seven giraffes, a medium-sized bull, four cows, and two young ones; and, funnily enough, the young ones were by far the shyest and most suspicious. I did not want to kill a bull unless it was exceptionally large; whereas I did want two cows and a young one, for the museum. When quarter of a mile away I dismounted, threw the reins over Tranquillity's head—whereat the good placid old fellow at once began grazing—and walked diagonally toward the biggest cow, which was ahead of the others. The tall, handsome, ungainly creatures were nothing like as shy as the smaller game had shown themselves that morning, and of course they offered such big targets that three hundred yards was a fair range for them. At two hundred and sixty yards I fired at the big cow as she stood almost facing me, twisting and curling her tail. The bullet struck fair and she was off at a hurried, clumsy gallop. I gave her another bullet, but it was not necessary, and down she went. The second cow, a fine young heifer, was now cantering across my front, and with two more shots I got her; the sharp-pointed bullets penetrating well, and not splitting into fragments, but seeming to cause a rending shock.

I met with much more difficulty in trying to kill the young one I needed. I walked and trotted a mile after the herd. The old ones showed little alarm, standing again and again to look at me. Finally I shot one of the two young ones, at four hundred and ten long paces, while a cow stood much nearer, and the bull only three hundred yards off. But this was not all. The four survivors did not leave even after such an experience, but stayed in the plain, not far off, for several hours, and thereby gave Kermit a chance to do something much better worth while than shooting them. His shoulder was sore, and he did not wish to use a rifle, and so was devoting himself to his camera, which one of his men always carried. With this, after the exercise of much patience, he finally managed to take a number of pictures of the giraffe, getting within fifty yards of the bull.

Nor were the giraffe the only animals that showed a tameness bordering on stupidity. Soon afterward we made out three rhino, a mile away. They were out in the bare plain, alternately grazing and enjoying a noontide rest; the bull by himself, the cow with her calf a quarter of a mile off. There was not a scrap of cover, but we walked up wind to within a hundred and fifty yards of the bull. Even then he did not seem to see us, but the tick-birds, which were clinging to his back and sides, gave the alarm, and he trotted to and fro, uncertain as to the cause of the disturbance. If Heller had not had his hands full with the giraffes I might have shot the bull rhino; but his horn and bulk of body, though fair, were not remarkable, and I did not molest him. He went toward the cow, which left her calf and advanced toward him in distinctly bellicose style; then she recognized him, her calf trotted up, and the three animals stood together, tossing their heads, and evidently trying to make out what was near them. But we were down wind, and they do not see well, with their little twinkling pig's eyes. We were anxious not to be charged by the cow and calf, as her horn was very poor, and it would have been unpleasant to be obliged to shoot her, and so we drew off.

Next day, when Kermit and I were out alone with our gun-bearers we saw another rhino, a bull, with a stubby horn. This rhino, like the others of the neighborhood, was enjoying his noonday rest in the open, miles from cover; "Look at him," said Kermit, "standing there in the middle of the African plain, deep in prehistoric thought." Indeed the rhinoceros does seem like a survival from the elder world that has vanished; he was in place in the pliocene; he would not have been out of place in the miocene; but

The safari fording a stream

From a photograph by Edmund Heller

nowadays he can only exist at all in regions that have lagged behind, while the rest of the world, for good or for evil, has gone forward. Like other beasts, rhinos differ in habits in different places. This prehensile-lipped species is everywhere a browser, feeding on the twigs and leaves of the bushes and low trees; but in their stomachs I have found long grass stems mixed with the twig tips and leaves of stunted bush. In some regions they live entirely in rather thick bush; whereas on the plains over which we were hunting the animals haunted the open by preference, feeding through thin bush, where they were visible miles away, and usually taking their rest, either standing or lying, out on the absolutely bare plains. They drank at the small shallow rain pools, seemingly once every twenty-four hours; and I saw one going to water at noon, and others just at dark; and their hours for feeding and resting were also irregular, though they were apt to lie down or stand motionless during the middle of the day. Doubtless in very hot weather they prefer to rest under a tree; but we were hunting in cool weather, during which they paid no heed whatever to the sun. Their sight is very bad, their scent and hearing acute.

On this day Kermit was shooting from his left shoulder, and did very well, killing a fine Roberts' gazelle, and three topi; I also shot a topi bull, as Heller wished a good series for the National Museum. The topi and wildebeest I shot were all killed at long range, the average distance for the first shot being over three hundred and fifty yards; and in the Sotik, where hunters were few, the game seemed if anything shyer than on the Athi Plains, where hunters were many. But there were wide and inexplicable differences in this respect among the animals of the same species. One day I wished to get a doe tommy for the museum; I saw scores, but they were all too shy to let me approach within shot; yet four times I passed within eighty yards of bucks of the same species which paid hardly any heed to me. Another time I walked for five minutes alongside a big

A rhino family. Tick-birds can be seen on the male's back (on the left)

From a photograph by Kermit Roosevelt

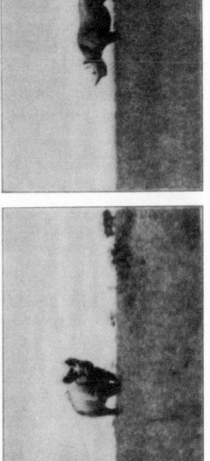

"In the middle of the African plain, deep in prehistoric thought"

From a photograph by Kermit Roosevelt

Rhino surveying the safari

From a photograph by Kermit Roosevelt

party of Roberts' gazelles, within a hundred and fifty yards, trying in vain to pick out a buck worth shooting; half an hour afterward I came on another party which contained such a buck, but they would not let me get within a quarter of a mile.

Wildebeest are usually the shyest of all game. Each herd has its own recognized beat, to which it ordinarily keeps. Near this camp, there was a herd almost always to be found somewhere near the southern end of a big hill two miles east of us; while a solitary bull was invariably seen around the base of a small hill a couple of miles southwest of us. The latter was usually in the company of a mixed herd of Roberts' and Thomson's gazelles. Here, as everywhere, we found the different species of game associating freely with one another. One little party interested us much. It consisted of two Roberts' bucks, two Roberts' does, and one Thomson's doe, which was evidently a *maîtresse femme*, of strongly individualized character. The four big gazelles had completely surrendered their judgment to that of the little tommy doe. She was the acknowledged leader; when she started they started and followed in whatever direction she led; when she stopped they stopped; if she found a given piece of pasture good, upon it they grazed contentedly. Around this camp the topi were as common as hartebeest; they might be found singly, or in small parties, perhaps merely of a bull, a cow, and a calf; or they might be mixed with zebra, wildebeest, and hartebeest. Like the hartebeest, but less frequently, they would mount ant-hills to get a better look over the country. The wildebeest were extraordinarily tenacious of life, and the hartebeest and topi only less so. After wounded individuals of all three kinds I more than once had sharp runs on horseback. On one occasion I wounded a wildebeest bull a couple of miles from camp; I was riding my zebra-shaped brown pony, who galloped well; and after a sharp run through the bush I overhauled the wildebeest; but when I jumped off, the pony bolted for camp, and as he

Giraffe at home

From photographs by Kermit Roosevelt

disappeared in one direction my game disappeared in the other.

At last a day came when I saw a rhino with a big body and a good horn. We had been riding for a couple of hours;

Bluffs near one of our camping-places
From a photograph by Edmund Heller

the game was all around us. Two giraffes stared at us with silly curiosity rather than alarm; twice I was within range of the bigger one. At last Bakhari, the gunbearer, pointed to a gray mass on the plain, and a glance through the glasses showed that it was a rhino lying asleep with his legs doubled under him. He proved to be a big bull, with a front horn nearly twenty-six inches long. I was anxious to try the sharp-pointed bullets of the little Springfield rifle on him; and Cuninghame and I, treading cautiously, walked up wind straight toward him, our horses following a hundred yards behind. He was waked by the tick-birds, and twisted his head to and fro, but at first did not seem to hear us, although looking in our direction. When we were a hundred yards off he rose and faced us, huge and threatening,

head up and tail erect. But he lacked heart after all. I
fired into his throat, and instead of charging, he whipped
round and was off at a gallop, immediately disappearing
over a slight rise. We ran back to our horses, mounted,
and galloped after him. He had a long start, and, though
evidently feeling his wound, was going strong; and it was
some time before we overtook him. I tried to gallop
alongside, but he kept
swerving; so jumping
off (fortunately, I was
riding Tranquillity) I
emptied the magazine
at his quarters and
flank. Rapid galloping
does not tend to pro-
mote accuracy of aim;
the rhino went on; and,
remounting, I followed,
overtook him, and re-
peated the perform-
ance. This time he
wheeled and faced
round, evidently with
the intention of charg-
ing, but a bullet straight
into his chest took all
the fight out of him, and

Striped hyena trapped by Heller
From a photograph by Edmund Heller

he continued his flight. But his race was evidently run,
and when I next overtook him I brought him down. I
had put nine bullets into him; and though they had done
their work well, and I was pleased to have killed the huge
brute with the little sharp-pointed bullets of the Springfield,
I was confirmed in my judgment that for me personally the
big Holland rifle was the best weapon for heavy game,
although I did not care as much for it against lighter-
bodied beasts like lions. In all we galloped four miles after
this wounded rhino bull.

We sent a porter to bring out Heller, and an ox wagon on which to take the skin to camp. While waiting for them I killed a topi bull, at two hundred and sixty yards, with one bullet, and a wildebeest bull with a dozen; I crippled him with my first shot at three hundred and sixty yards, and then walked and trotted after him a couple of miles, getting running and standing shots at from three hundred to five hundred yards. I hit him several times. As with everything else I shot, the topi and wildebeest were preserved as specimens for the museum, and their flesh used for food. Our porters had much to do, and they did it well, partly because they were fed well. We killed no game of which we did not make the fullest use. It would be hard to convey to those who have not seen it on the ground an accurate idea of its abundance. When I was walking up to this rhino there were in sight two giraffes, several wildebeest bulls, and herds of hartebeest, topi, zebra, and the big and little gazelles.

In addition to being a mighty hunter, and an adept in the by no means easy work of handling a large safari in the wilderness, Cuninghame was also a good field naturalist and taxidermist; and at this camp we got so many specimens that he was obliged to spend most of his time helping Heller; and they pressed into the work at times even Tarlton. Accordingly Kermit and I generally went off by ourselves, either together or separately. Once, however, Kermit went with Tarlton, and was as usual lucky with cheetahs, killing two. Tarlton was an accomplished elephant, buffalo, and rhino hunter, but he preferred the chase of the lion to all other kinds of sport; and if lions were not to be found he liked to follow anything else he could gallop on horseback. Kermit was also a good and hard rider. On this occasion they found a herd of eland, and galloped into it. The big bull they overhauled at once, but saw that his horns were poor and left him. Then they followed a fine cow with an unusually good head. She started at a rattling pace, and once leaped clear over another cow that got in her way; but they rode into her after a mile's smart gallop

—not a racing gallop by any means—and after that she was as manageable as a tame ox. Cantering and trotting within thirty yards of her on either quarter they drove her toward camp; but when it was still three-quarters of a mile distant they put up a cheetah, and tore after it; and they overtook and killed it just before it reached cover. A cheetah with a good start can only be overtaken by hard running. This one behaved just as did the others they ran down. For quarter of a mile no animal in the world has a cheetah's speed; but he cannot last. When chased the cheetahs did not sprint, but contented themselves with galloping ahead of the horses; at first they could easily keep their distance, but after a mile or two their strength and wind gave out, and then they always crouched flat to the earth, and were shot without their making any attempt to charge. But a wart-hog boar which Kermit ran down the same day and shot with his revolver did charge, and wickedly.

While running one of his cheetahs Kermit put up two old wildebeest bulls, and they joined in the procession, looking as if they too were pursuing the cheetah; the cheetah ran first, the two bulls, bounding and switching their tails, came next, and Kermit, racing in the rear, gained steadily. Wildebeest are the oddest in nature and conduct, and in many ways the most interesting, of all antelopes. There is in their temper something queer, fiery, eccentric, and their actions are abrupt and violent. A single bull will stand motionless with head raised to stare at an intruder until the latter is quarter of a mile off; then down goes his head, his tail is lashed up and around, and off he gallops, plunging, kicking, and shaking his head. He may go straight away, he may circle round, or even approach nearer to, the intruder; and then he halts again to stare motionless, and perhaps to utter his grunt of alarm and defiance. A herd when approached, after fixed staring will move off, perhaps at a canter. Soon the leaders make a half wheel, and lead their followers in a semicircle; suddenly a couple of old bulls leave the rest, and at a tearing gallop describe a semicircle in exactly the opposite direction, racing by their comrades as these canter the other way. With one accord the whole troop may then halt and stare again at the object they suspect; then off they all go at a headlong run, kicking and bucking, tearing at full speed in one direction, then suddenly wheeling in semicircles so abrupt as to be almost

Mr. Roosevelt, rhino, and bustard shot from rhino
From a photograph by Kermit Roosevelt

zigzags, the dust flying in clouds; and two bulls may suddenly drop to their knees and for a moment or two fight furiously in their own peculiar fashion. By careful stalking Kermit got some good pictures of the wildebeest in spite of their wariness. Like other game they seem most apt to lie down during the heat of the day; but they may lie down at night too; at any rate, I noticed one herd of hartebeest which after feeding through the late afternoon lay down at nightfall.

After getting the bull rhino, Heller needed a cow and calf to complete the group; and Kermit and I got him what he needed, one day when we were out alone with our gun-bearers. About the middle of the forenoon we made out the huge gray bulk of the rhino, standing in the bare plain, with not so much as a bush two feet high within miles; and we soon also made out her calf beside her. Getting the wind right we rode up within a quarter of a mile, and then dismounted and walked slowly toward her. It seemed impossible that on that bare plain we could escape even her dull vision, for she stood with her head in our direction; yet she did not see us, and actually lay down as we walked toward her. Careful examination through the glasses showed that she was an unusually big cow, with thick horns of fair length—twenty-three inches and thirteen inches respectively. Accordingly we proceeded, making as little noise as possible. At fifty yards she made us out, and jumped to her feet with unwieldy agility. Kneeling I sent the bullet from the heavy Holland just in front of her right shoulder as she half faced me. It went through her vitals, lodging behind the opposite shoulder; and at once she began the curious death waltz which is often, though by no means always, the sign of immediate dissolution in a mortally wounded rhino. Kermit at once put a bullet from his Winchester behind her shoulder; for it is never safe to take chances with a rhino; and we shot the calf, which when dying uttered a screaming whistle, almost like that of a small steam-engine. In a few seconds both fell, and we walked up to them, examined them, and then continued our ride, sending in a messenger to bring Cuninghame, Heller, and an ox wagon to the carcasses.

The stomach of this rhino contained some grass stems and blades, some leaves and twig tips of bushes, but chiefly the thick, thorny, fleshy leaves of a kind of euphorbia. As the juice of the euphorbia's cactus-like leaves is acrid enough to blister—not to speak of the thorns—this suffices to show what a rhino's palate regards as agreeably stimulating. This species of rhino, by the way, affords a curious illustration of how blind many men who live much of their lives out-doors may be to facts which stare them in the face. For years most South African hunters, and most naturalists, believed in the existence of two species of pre-hensile-lipped, or so-called "black," rhinoceros: one with the front horn much the longer, one with the rear horn at least equal to the front. It was Selous, a singularly clear-sighted and keen observer, who first proved conclusively that the difference was purely imaginary. Now, the curi-ous thing is that these experienced hunters usually attrib-uted entirely different temperaments to these two imagi-nary species. The first kind, that with the long front horn, they described as a miracle of dangerous ferocity, and the second as comparatively mild and inoffensive; and these veterans (Drummond is an instance) persuaded themselves that this was true, although they were writing in each case of identically the same animal!

After leaving the dead rhinos we rode for several miles, over a plain dotted with game, and took our lunch at the foot of a big range of hills, by a rapid little brook, run-ning under a fringe of shady thorns. Then we rode back to camp. Lines of zebra filed past on the horizon. Os-triches fled while we were yet far off. Topi, hartebeest, wildebeest, and gazelle gazed at us as we rode by, the sun-light throwing their shapes and colors into bold relief against the parched brown grass. I had an hour to my-self after reaching camp, and spent it with Lowell's "Es-says." I doubt whether any man takes keener enjoyment in the wilderness than he who also keenly enjoys many other sides of life; just as no man can relish books more than some at least of those who also love horse and rifle and the winds that blow across lonely plains and through the gorges of the mountains.

Next morning a lion roared at dawn so near camp that we sallied forth after him. We did not find him, but we enjoyed our three hours' ride through the fresh air before breakfast, with the game as usual on every hand. Some of the game showed tameness, some wildness, the difference

Wildebeest at home

Two bulls may suddenly drop to their knees and for a moment or two fight furiously

From photographs by Kermit Roosevelt

being not between species and species, but between given individuals of almost every species. While we were absent two rhinos passed close by camp, and stopped to stare curiously at it; we saw them later as they trotted away, but their horns were not good enough to tempt us.

At a distance the sunlight plays pranks with the coloring of the animals. Cock ostriches always show jet black, and are visible at a greater distance than any of the common game; the neutral tint of the hens making them far less conspicuous. Both cocks and hens are very wary, sharp-sighted, and hard to approach. Next to the cock ostrich in conspicuousness comes the wildebeest, because it shows black in most lights; yet when headed away from the on-looker, the sun will often make the backs of a herd look whitish in the distance. Wildebeest are warier than most other game. Round this camp the topi were as tame as the hartebeest; they look very dark in most lights, only less dark than the wildebeest, and so are also conspicuous. The hartebeest change from a deep brown to a light foxy red, according to the way they stand toward the sun; and when a herd was feeding away from us, their white sterns showed when a very long way off. The zebra's stripes cease to be visible after he is three hundred yards off, but in many lights he glistens white in the far distance, and is then very conspicuous; on this day I came across a mixed herd of zebra and eland in thin bush, and when still a long way off the zebras caught the eye, while their larger companions were as yet hardly to be made out without field-glasses. The gazelles usually show as sandy-colored, and are therefore rather less conspicuous than the others when still; but they are constantly in motion, and in some lights show up as almost white. When they are far off the sun-rays may make any of these animals look very dark or very light. In fact all of them are conspicuous at long distances, and none of them make any effort to escape observation as do certain kinds that haunt dense bush and forest. But constant allowance must be made for the wide variations among individuals. Ordinarily tommies are the tamest of the game, with the big gazelle and the zebra next; but no two herds will behave alike; and I have seen a wildebeest bull look at me motionless within a hundred and fifty yards, while the zebras, tommies, and big gazelles which were his companions fled in panic; and I left him still standing, as I walked after the gazelles, to kill a buck for the table. The game is usually

Rhino and young
From a photograph by Kermit Roosevelt

sensitive to getting the hunter's wind; but on these plains I have again and again seen game stand looking at us within fairly close range to leeward, and yet on the same day seen the same kind of game flee in mad fright when twice the distance to windward. Sometimes there are inexplicable variations between the conduct of beasts in one locality and in another. In East Africa the hyenas seem only occasionally to crunch the long bones of the biggest dead animals; whereas Cuninghame, who pointed out this fact to me, stated that in South Africa the hyenas, of the same kind, always crunched up the big bones, eating both the marrow and fragments of the bone itself.

Now and then the game will choose a tree as a rubbing post, and if it is small will entirely destroy the tree; and I have seen them use for the same purpose an oddly shaped stone, one corner of which they had worn quite smooth. They have stamping grounds, small patches of bare earth from which they have removed even the roots of the grass and bushes by the trampling of their hoofs, leaving nothing but a pool of dust. One evening I watched some zebras stringing slowly along in a line which brought them past a couple of these stamping grounds. As they came in succession to each bare place half the herd, one after another, lay down and rolled to and fro, sending up spurts of dust so thick that the animal was hidden from sight; while perhaps a companion, which did not roll, stood near by, seemingly to enjoy the dust.

On this same evening we rode campward facing a wonderful sunset. The evening was lowering and overcast. The darkening plains stretched dim and vague into the far distance. The sun went down under a frowning sky, behind shining sheets of rain; and it turned their radiance to an angry splendor of gold and murky crimson.

At this camp the pretty little Livingstone's wheatears or chats were very familiar, flitting within a few yards of the tents. They were the earliest birds to sing. Just before our eyes could distinguish the first faint streak of dawn first one and then another of them would begin to sing, apparently either on the ground or in the air, until there was a chorus of their sweet music. Then they were silent again until the sun was about to rise. We always heard them when we made a very early start to hunt. By the way, with the game of the plains and the thin bush, we found that nothing was gained by getting out early in the morning; we were quite as apt to get what we wanted in the evening or indeed at high noon.

The last day at this camp Kermit, Tarlton, and I spent on a twelve hours' lion hunt. I opened the day inauspiciously, close to camp, by missing a zebra, which we wished for the porters. Then Kermit, by a good shot, killed a tommy buck with the best head we had yet gotten. Early in the afternoon we reached our objective, some high koppies, broken by cliffs and covered with brush. There were klipspringers on these koppies, little rock-loving antelopes, with tiny hoofs and queer brittle hair; they are marvellous jumpers and continually utter a bleating whistle. I broke the neck of one as it ran at a distance of a hundred and fifty yards; but the shot was a fluke, and did not make amends for the way I had missed the zebra in the morning. Among the thick brush on these hills were huge euphorbias, aloes bearing masses of orange flowers, and a cactus-like ground plant with pretty pink blossoms. All kinds of game from the plains, even rhino, had wandered over these hill-tops.

But what especially interested us was that we immediately found fresh beds of lions, and one regular lair. Again and again, as we beat cautiously through the bushes, the rank smell of the beasts smote our nostrils. At last, as we sat at the foot of one koppie, Kermit spied through his glasses a lion on the side of the koppie opposite, the last and biggest; and up it we climbed. On the very summit was a mass of cleft and broken bowlders, and while on these Kermit put up two lions from the bushes which crowded beneath them. I missed a running shot at the lioness, as she made off through the brush. He probably hit the lion, and, very cautiously, with rifles at the ready, we beat through the thick cover in hopes to find it; but in vain. Then we began a hunt for the lioness, as apparently she had not left the koppie. Soon one of the gun-bearers, who was standing on a big stone, peering under some thick bushes, beckoned excitedly to me; and when I jumped up beside him he pointed at the lioness. In a second I made her out. The sleek sinister creature lay not ten paces off, her sinuous body following the curves of the rock as she crouched flat looking straight at me. A stone covered the lower part, and the left of the upper part, of her head; but I saw her two unwinking green eyes looking into mine. As she could have reached me in two springs, perhaps in one, I wished to shoot straight; but I had to avoid the rock which covered the lower part of her face, and moreover I fired a little too much to the left. The bullet went through the side of her head, and in between the neck and shoulder, inflicting a mortal, but not immediately fatal, wound. However it knocked her off the little ledge on which she was lying, and instead of charging she rushed uphill. We promptly followed, and again clambered up the mass of bowlders at the top. Peering over the one on which I had climbed there was the lioness directly at its foot, not twelve feet away, lying flat on her belly; I could only see the aftermost third of her back. I at once fired into her spine; with appalling grunts she dragged herself a few paces downhill; and another bullet behind the shoulder finished her.

She was skinned as rapidly as possible; and just before sundown we left the koppie. At its foot was a deserted Masai cattle kraal and a mile from this was a shallow, muddy pool, fouled by the countless herds of game that drank thereat. Toward this we went, so that the thirsty horses and men might drink their full. As we came near we saw three rhinoceros leaving the pool. It was already too dusk for good shooting, and we were rather relieved when, after some inspection, they trotted off and stood at a little distance in the plain. Our men and horses drank, and then we began our ten miles' march through the darkness to camp. One of Kermit's gun-bearers saw a puff adder (among the most deadly of all snakes); with delightful nonchalance he stepped on its head, and then held it up for me to put my knife through its brain and neck. I slipped it into my saddle pocket, where its blood stained the pigskin cover of the little pocket Nibelungenlied which that day I happened to carry. Immediately afterward there was a fresh alarm from our friends the three rhinos; dismounting, and crouching down, we caught the loom of their bulky bodies against the horizon; but a shot in the ground seemed to make them hesitate, and they finally concluded not to charge. So, with the lion skin swinging behind between two porters, a moribund puff adder in my saddle pocket, and three rhinos threatening us in the dark-

A giant candelabra euphorbia by our camp

From a photograph by Edmund Heller

ness to one side, we marched campward through the African night.

Next day we shifted camp to a rush-fringed pool by a grove of tall, flat-topped acacias at the foot of a range of low, steep mountains. Before us the plain stretched, and in front of our tents it was dotted by huge candelabra euphorbias. I shot a buck for the table just as we pitched camp. There were Masai kraals and cattle herds near by, and tall warriors, pleasant and friendly, strolled among our tents, their huge razor-edged spears tipped with furry caps to protect the points. Kermit was off all day with Tarlton, and killed a magnificent lioness. In the morning, on some high hills, he obtained a good impalla ram, after persevering hours of climbing and running—for only one of the gun-bearers and none of the whites could keep up with him on foot when he went hard. In the afternoon at four he and Tarlton saw the lioness. She was followed by three three-parts grown young lions, doubtless her cubs, and, without any concealment, was walking across the open plain toward a pool by which lay the body of a wildebeest bull she had killed the preceding night. The smaller lions saw the hunters and shrank back, but the old lioness never noticed them until they were within a hundred and fifty yards. Then she ran back, but Kermit crumpled her up with his first bullet. He then put another bullet into her, and as she seemed disabled walked up within fifty yards, and took some photos. By this time she was recovering, and, switching her tail, she gathered her hind quarters under her for a charge; but he stopped her with another bullet and killed her outright with a fourth.

We heard that Mearns and Loring, whom we had left ten days before, had also killed a lioness. A Masai brought in word to them that he had marked her down taking her noonday rest near a kongoni she had killed; and they rode out, and Loring shot her. She charged him savagely; he shot her straight through the heart, and she fell literally at his feet. The three naturalists were all good shots, and were used to all the mishaps and adventures of life in the wilderness. Not only would it have been indeed difficult to find three better men for their particular work—Heller's work, for instance, with Cuninghame's help, gave the chief point to our big-game shooting—but it would have been equally difficult to find three better men for any emergency. I could not speak too highly of them; nor indeed of our two other companions, Cuninghame and Tarlton, whose mastery of their own field was as noteworthy as the pre-eminence of the naturalists in their field.

The following morning the headmen asked that we get the porters some meat; Tarlton, Kermit, and I sallied

The wounded lioness ready to charge
From a photograph by Kermit Roosevelt

The wounded lioness
From a photograph by Kermit Roosevelt

forth accordingly. The country was very dry, and the game in our immediate neighborhood was not plentiful and was rather shy. I killed three kongoni out of a herd, at from two hundred and fifty to three hundred and ninety paces; one topi at three hundred and thirty paces, and a Roberts' gazelle at two hundred and seventy. Meanwhile the other two had killed a kongoni and five of the big gazelles; wherever possible the game being hallalled in orthodox fashion by the Mahometans among our attendants, so as to fit it for use by their coreligionists among the porters. Then we saw some giraffes, and galloped them to see if there was a really big bull in the lot. They had a long start, but Kermit and Tarlton overtook them after a couple of miles, while I pounded along in the rear. However there was no really good bull, Kermit and Tarlton pulled up, and we jogged along toward the koppies where two days before I had shot the lioness. I killed a big bustard, a very handsome, striking-looking bird, larger than a turkey, by a rather good shot at two hundred and thirty yards.

It was now mid-day, and the heat waves quivered above the brown plain. The mirage hung in the middle distance, and beyond it the bold hills rose like mountains from a lake. In mid-afternoon we stopped at a little pool, to give the men and horses water; and here Kermit's horse suddenly went dead lame, and we started it back to camp with a couple of men, while Kermit went forward with us on foot, as we rode round the base of the first koppies. After we had gone a mile loud shouts called our attention to one of the men who had left with the lame horse. He was running back to tell us that they had just seen a big maned lion walking along in the open plain toward the body of a zebra he had killed the night before. Immediately Tarlton and I galloped in the direction indicated, while the heart-broken Kermit ran after us on foot, so as not to miss the fun; the gun-bearers and saises stringing out behind him. In a few minutes Tarlton pointed out the lion, a

He came on steadily—ears laid back and uttering terrific coughing grunts

Drawn by Philip R. Goodwin from photographs and from descriptions furnished by Mr. Roosevelt

splendid old fellow, a heavy male with a yellow-and-black mane; and after him we went. There was no need to go fast; he was too burly and too savage to run hard, and we were anxious that our hands should be reasonably steady when we shot; all told, the horses, galloping and cantering, did not take us two miles.

The lion stopped and lay down behind a bush; jumping off I took a shot at him at two hundred yards, but only wounded him slightly in one paw; and after a moment's sullen hesitation off he went, lashing his tail. We mounted our horses and went after him; Tarlton lost sight of him, but I marked him lying down behind a low grassy ant-hill. Again we dismounted at a distance of two hundred yards; Tarlton telling me that now he was sure to charge. In all East Africa there is no man, not even Cuninghame himself, whom I would rather have by me than Tarlton, if in difficulties with a charging lion; on this occasion, however, I am glad to say that his rifle was badly sighted, and shot altogether too low.

Again I knelt and fired; but the mass of hair on the lion made me think he was nearer than he was, and I undershot, inflicting a flesh wound that was neither crippling nor fatal. He was already grunting savagely and tossing his tail erect, with his head held low; and at the shot the great sinewy beast came toward us with the speed of a greyhound. Tarlton then, very properly, fired, for lion hunting is no child's play, and it is not good to run risks. Ordinarily it is a very mean thing to experience joy at a friend's miss; but this was not an ordinary case, and I felt keen delight when the bullet from the badly sighted rifle missed, striking the ground many yards short. I was sighting carefully, from my knee, and I knew I had the lion all right; for though he galloped at a great pace, he came on steadily— ears laid back, and uttering terrific coughing grunts—and there was now no question of making allowance for distance, nor, as he was out in the open, for the fact that he had not before been distinctly visible. The bead of my foresight was exactly on the centre of his chest as I pressed the trigger, and the bullet went as true as if the place had been plotted with dividers. The blow brought him up all standing, and he fell forward on his head. The soft-nosed Winchester bullet had gone straight through the chest cavity, smashing the lungs and the big blood-vessels of the heart. Painfully he recovered his feet, and tried to come on, his ferocious courage holding out to the last; but he staggered, and turned from side to side, unable to stand firmly, still less to advance at a faster pace than a walk. He had not ten seconds to live; but it is a sound principle to take no chances with lions. Tarlton hit him with his second bullet, probably in the shoulder; and with my next shot I broke his neck. I had stopped him when he was still a hundred yards away; and certainly no finer sight could be imagined than that of this great maned lion as he charged. Kermit gleefully joined us as we walked up to the body; only one of our followers had been able to keep up with him on his two-miles run. He had had a fine view of the charge, from one side, as he ran up, still three hundred yards distant; he could see all the muscles play as the lion galloped in, and then everything relax as he fell to the shock of my bullet.

The lion was a big old male, still in his prime. Between uprights his length was nine feet four inches, and his weight four hundred and ten pounds, for he was not fat. We skinned him and started for camp, which we reached after dark. There was a thunder-storm in the south-west, and in the red sunset that burned behind us the rain clouds turned to many gorgeous hues. Then daylight failed, the clouds cleared, and, as we made our way across the formless plain, the half moon hung high overhead, strange stars shone in the brilliant heavens, and the Southern Cross lay radiant above the sky-line.

Our next camp was pitched on a stony plain, by a winding stream-bed still containing an occasional rush-fringed pool of muddy water, fouled by the herds and flocks of the numerous Masai. Game was plentiful around this camp. We killed what we needed of the common kinds, and in addition each of us killed a big rhino. The two

Mr. Roosevelt, Tarlton, and the big lion shot by Mr. Roosevelt
From a photograph by Kermit Roosevelt

rhinos were almost exactly alike, and their horns were of the so-called "Keitloa" type; the fore horn twenty-two inches long, the rear over seventeen. The day I killed mine I used all three of my rifles. We all went out together, as Kermit was desirous of taking photos of my rhino, if I shot one;

he had not been able to get good ones of his on the previous day. We also took the small ox wagon, so as to bring into camp bodily the rhino—if we got it—and one or two zebras, of which we wanted the flesh for the safari, the skeletons for the museum. The night had been cool, but the day was sunny and hot. At first we rode through a broad valley, bounded by high, scrub-covered hills. The banks of the dry stream were fringed with deep green acacias, and here and there in relief against their dark foliage flamed the orange-red flowers of the tall aloe clumps. With the Springfield I shot a steinbuck and a lesser bustard. Then we came out on the vast rolling brown plains. With the Winchester I shot two zebra stallions, missing each standing, at long range, and then killing them as they ran; one after a two-miles hard gallop, on my brown pony, which had a good turn of speed. I killed a third zebra stallion with my Springfield, again missing it standing and killing it running. In mid-afternoon we spied our rhino, and getting near saw that it had good horns. It was in the middle of the absolutely bare plain, and we walked straight up to the dull-sighted, dull-witted beast; Kermit with his camera, I with the Holland double-barrel. The tick-birds warned it, but it did not make us out until we were well within a hundred yards, when it trotted toward us, head and tail up. At sixty yards I put the heavy bullet straight into its chest, and knocked it flat with the blow; as it tried to struggle to its feet I again knocked it flat, with the left-hand barrel; but it needed two more bullets before it died, screaming like an engine whistle. Before I fired my last shot I had walked up directly beside the rhino; and just then Tarlton pointed me out a greater bustard, stalking along with unmoved composure at a distance of a hundred and fifty yards; I took the Springfield, and kneeling down beside the rhino's hind quarters I knocked over the bustard, and then killed the rhino. We rode into camp by moonlight. Both these rhinos had their stomachs filled with the closely chewed leaves and twig tips of short brush

mixed with grass—rather thick-stemmed grass—and in one
case with the pulpy, spiny leaves of a low, ground-creeping
euphorbia.

At this camp we killed five poisonous snakes: a light-
colored tree snake, two puff adders, and two seven-foot
cobras. One of the latter three times "spat" or ejected its
poison at us, the poison coming out from the fangs like white

A rhino "coming on"
From a photograph by Kermit Roosevelt

films or threads, to a distance of several feet. A few years
ago the singular power of this snake, and perhaps of certain
other African species, thus to eject the poison at the face of
an assailant was denied by scientists; but it is now well
known. Selous had already told me of an instance which
came under his own observation; and Tarlton had once been
struck in the eyes and for the moment nearly blinded by the
poison. He found that to wash the eyes with milk was of
much relief. On the bigger puff adder, some four feet long,
were a dozen ticks, some swollen to the size of cherries; ap-

parently they were disregarded by their sluggish and deadly host. Heller trapped some jackals, of two species; and two striped hyenas, the first we had seen; apparently more timid and less noisy beasts than their bigger spotted brothers.

One day Kermit had our first characteristic experience with a honey bird; a smallish bird, with its beak like a grosbeak's and its toes like a woodpecker's, whose extraordinary habits as a honey-guide are known to all the natives of Africa throughout its range. Kermit had killed an eland bull, and while he was resting, his gun-bearers drew his attention to the calling of the honey bird in a tree near by. He got up, and as he approached the bird, it flew to another tree in front and again began its twitter. This was repeated again and again as Kermit walked after it. Finally the bird darted round behind his followers, in the direction from which they had come; and for a moment they thought it had played them false. But immediately afterward they saw that it had merely overshot its mark, and had now flown back a few rods to the honey-tree, round which it was flitting, occasionally twittering. When they came toward the tree it perched silent and motionless in another, and thus continued while they took some honey—a risky business, as the bees were vicious. They did not observe what the bird then did; but Cuninghame told me that in one instance where a honey bird led him to honey he carefully watched it and saw it picking up either bits of honey and comb, or else, more probably, the bee grubs out of the comb, he could not be certain which.

To my mind no more interesting incident occurred at this camp.

CHAPTER IX

TO LAKE NAIVASHA

FROM this camp we turned north toward Lake Naivasha.

The Sotik country through which we had hunted was sorely stricken by drought. The grass was short and withered and most of the water-holes were drying up, while both the game and the flocks and herds of the nomad Masai gathered round the watercourses in which there were still occasional muddy pools, and grazed their neighborhood bare of pasturage. It was an unceasing pleasure to watch the ways of the game and to study their varying habits. Where there was a river from which to drink, or where there were many pools, the different kinds of buck, and the zebra, often showed comparatively little timidity about drinking, and came boldly down to the water's edge, sometimes in broad daylight, sometimes

Masai guides on Sotik trip
From a photograph by Edmund Heller

in darkness; although even under those conditions they were very cautious if there was cover at the drinking-place. But where the pools were few they never approached one without feeling panic dread of their great enemy the lion, who, they knew well, might be lurking around their drinking-place. At such a pool I once saw a herd of zebras come to water at nightfall. They stood motionless some distance off; then they slowly approached, and twice on false alarms wheeled and fled at speed; at last the leaders ventured to the brink of the pool and at once the whole herd came jostling and crowding in behind them, the water gurgling down their thirsty throats; and immediately afterward off they went at a gallop, stopping to graze some hundreds of yards away. The ceaseless dread of the lion felt by all but the heaviest game is amply justified by his ravages among them. They are always in peril from him at the drinking-places; yet in my experience I found that in the great majority of cases they were killed while feeding or resting far from water, the lion getting them far more often by stalking than by lying in wait. A lion will eat a zebra (beginning at the hind quarters, by the way, and sometimes having, and sometimes not having, previously disembowelled the animal) or one of the bigger buck at least once a week—perhaps once every five days. The dozen lions we had killed would probably, if left alive, have accounted for seven or eight hundred buck, pig, and zebra within the next year. Our hunting was a net advantage to the harmless game.

The zebras were the noisiest of the game. After them came the wildebeest, which often uttered their queer grunt; sometimes a herd would stand and grunt at me for some minutes as I passed, a few hundred yards distant. The topi uttered only a kind of sneeze, and the hartebeest a somewhat similar sound. The so-called Roberts' gazelle was merely the Grant's gazelle of the Athi, with the lyrate shape of the horns tending to be carried to an extreme of spread and backward bend. The tommy bucks carried good horns; the horns of the does were usually aborted, and were never more than four or five inches long. The most notable feature about the tommies was the incessant switching of their tails, as if jerked by electricity. In the Sotik the topis all seemed to have calves of about the same age, as if born from four to six months earlier; the young of the other game were of every age. The males of all the antelope fought much among themselves. The gazelle bucks of both species would face one another, their heads between the forelegs and the horns level with the ground, and each would punch his opponent until the hair flew.

Watching the game, one was struck by the intensity and the evanescence of their emotions. Civilized man now usually passes his life under conditions which eliminate the intensity of terror felt by his ancestors when death by violence was their normal end, and threatened them during every hour of the day and night. It is only in nightmares that the average dweller in civilized countries now undergoes the hideous horror which was the regular and frequent portion of his ages-vanished forefathers, and which is still an every-day incident in the lives of most wild creatures. But the dread is short-lived, and its horror vanishes with instantaneous rapidity. In these wilds the game dreaded the lion and the other flesh-eating beasts rather than man. We saw innumerable kills of all the buck, and of zebra, the neck being usually dislocated, and it being evident that none of the lion's victims, not even the truculent wildebeest or huge eland, had been able to make any fight against him. The game is ever on the alert against this greatest of foes, and every herd, almost every individual, is in imminent and deadly peril every few days or nights, and of course suffers in addition from countless false alarms. But no sooner is the danger over than the animals resume their feeding, or love making, or their fighting among themselves. Two bucks will do battle the minute the herd has stopped running from the foe that has seized one of its number, and a buck will cover a doe in the brief interval between the first and the second alarm, from hunter or lion. Zebra will make much noise when one of their number has been

killed; but their fright has vanished when once they begin their barking calls.

Death by violence, death by cold, death by starvation—
these are the normal endings of the stately and beautiful
creatures of the wilderness. The sentimentalists who prattle
about the peaceful life of nature do not realize its utter

The rhino stood looking at us with his big ears cocked forward
From a photograph by Kermit Roosevelt

mercilessness; although all they would have to do would
be to look at the birds in the winter woods, or even at the
insects on a cold morning or cold evening. Life is hard
and cruel for all the lower creatures, and for man also
in what the sentimentalists call a "state of nature." The
savage of to-day shows us what the fancied age of gold of
our ancestors was really like; it was an age when hunger,
cold, violence, and iron cruelty were the ordinary accompaniments of life. If Matthew Arnold, when he expressed
the wish to know the thoughts of Earth's "vigorous, primi-

tive" tribes of the past, had really desired an answer to his
question, he would have done well to visit the homes of the
existing representatives of his "vigorous, primitive" ancestors, and to watch them feasting on blood and guts; while
as for the "pellucid and pure" feelings of his imaginary
primitive maiden, they were those of any meek, cowlike
creature who accepted marriage by purchase
or of convenience, as a matter of course.

It was to me a perpetual source of won-
derment to notice the difference in the behavior of different individuals of the same
species, and in
the behavior of
the same indi-
vidual at differ-
ent times; as, for
example, in the
matter of wari-
ness, of the
times for going
to water, of the
times for resting,
and, as regards
dangerous game,
in the matter of

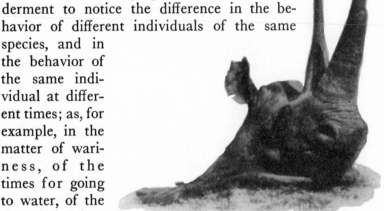

Rhino shot from Salt-marsh camp, of the Keitloa
type, with rear horn longer than front horn
From a photograph by Edmund Heller

ferocity. Their very looks changed. At one moment the
sun would turn the zebras of a mixed herd white, and
the hartebeest straw-colored, so that the former could be
seen much farther off than the latter; and again the conditions would be reversed when under the light the zebras
would show up gray, and the hartebeest as red as foxes.

I had now killed almost all the specimens of the common game that the museum needed. However, we kept
the skin or skeleton of whatever we shot for meat. Now
and then, after a good stalk, I would get a boar with
unusually fine tusks, a big gazelle with unusually long
and graceful horns, or a fine old wildebeest bull, its horns

thick and battered, its knees bare and calloused from its
habit of going down on them when fighting or threatening
fight.

On our march northward, we first made a long day's
journey to what was called a salt marsh. An hour or two
after starting we had a characteristic experience with a
rhino. It was a bull, with poor horns, standing in a plain
which was dotted by a few straggling thorn-trees and wild
olives. The safari's course would have taken it to windward
of the rhino, which then might have charged in sheer irri-
table bewilderment; so we turned off at right angles. The
long line of porters passed him two hundred yards away,
while we gun men stood between with our rifles ready;
except Kermit, who was busy taking photos. The rhino
saw us, but apparently indistinctly. He made little dashes
to and fro, and finally stood looking at us, with his big
ears cocked forward; but he did nothing more, and we left
him standing, plunged in meditation—probably it would
be more accurate to say, thinking of absolutely nothing,
as if he had been a huge turtle. After leaving him we
also passed by files of zebra and topi who gazed at us,
intent and curious, within two hundred yards, until we had
gone by and the danger was over; whereupon they fled
in fright.

The so-called salt marsh consisted of a dry watercourse,
with here and there a deep muddy pool. The ground
was impregnated with some saline substance, and the
game licked it, as well as coming to water. Our camp
was near two reedy pools, in which there were big yellow-
billed ducks, while queer brown herons, the hammerhead,
had built big nests of sticks in the tall acacias. Bush cuckoos
gurgled in the underbrush by night and day. Brilliant rollers flitted through the trees. There was much sweet bird
music in the morning. Funny little elephant shrews with
long snouts, and pretty zebra mice, evidently of diurnal
habit, scampered among the bushes or scuttled into their
burrows. Tiny dikdiks, antelopes no bigger than hares,

with swollen muzzles, and their little horns half hidden by tufts of hair, ran like rabbits through the grass; the females were at least as large as the males. Another seven-foot cobra was killed. There were brilliant masses of the red aloe flowers, and of yellow - blossomed vines. Around the pools the ground was bare, and the game trails leading to the water were deeply rutted by the hoofs of the wild creatures that had travelled them for countless generations.

The day after reaching this camp, Cuninghame and I hunted on the plains. Before noon we made out with our glasses two rhino lying down, a mile off. As usual with these sluggish creatures we made our preparations in leisurely style, and with scant regard to the animal itself. Moreover we did not intend to kill any rhino unless its horns were out of the common. I first stalked and shot a buck Roberts' gazelle with a good head. Then we off-saddied the horses and sat down to lunch under a huge thorn-tree, which stood by itself, lonely and beautiful, and offered a shelter from the blazing sun. The game was grazing on every side; and I kept thinking of all the life of the wilderness, and of its many tragedies, which the great tree must have witnessed during the centuries since it was a seedling.

Lunch over, I looked to the loading of the heavy rifle, and we started toward the rhinos, well to leeward. But the wind shifted every which way; and suddenly my gun-bearers called my attention to the rhinos, a quarter of a mile off, saying, "He charging, he charging." Sure enough, they had caught our wind, and were rushing toward us. I jumped off the horse and studied the oncoming beasts through my field-glass; but head on it was hard to tell about the horns. However, the wind shifted again, and when two hundred yards off they lost our scent, and turned to one side, tails in the air, heads tossing, evidently much wrought up. They were a large cow and a young heifer, nearly two-thirds grown. As they trotted sideways I could see the cow's horns, and her doom was sealed; for they were of good length, and the hind one (it proved to be two feet long) was slightly longer than the stouter front one; it was a specimen which the museum needed.

So after them we trudged over the brown plain. But they were uneasy, and kept trotting and walking. They never saw us with their dull eyes; but a herd of wildebeest galloping by renewed their alarm; it was curious to see them sweeping the ground with their long, ugly heads, endeavoring to catch the scent. A mile's rapid walk brought us within two hundred yards, and we dared not risk the effort for a closer approach lest they should break and run. The cow turned broadside to, and I hit her behind the shoulder; but I was not familiar with the heavy Holland rifle at that range, and my bullet went rather too low. I think the wound would eventually have proved fatal; but both beasts went off at a gallop, the cow now and then turning from side to side in high dudgeon, trying to catch the wind of her foe. We mounted our horses, and after a couple of miles' canter overhauled our quarry. Cuninghame took me well to leeward, and ahead, of the rhinos, which never saw us; and then we walked to within a hundred yards, and I killed the cow. But we were now much puzzled by the young one, which refused to leave; we did not wish to kill it, for it was big enough to shift for itself; but it was also big enough to kill either of us. We drew back, hoping it would go away; but it did not. So when the gun-bearers arrived we advanced and tried to frighten it; but this plan also failed. It threatened to charge, but could not quite make up its mind. Watching my chance I then creased its stern with a bullet from the little Springfield, and after some wild circular galloping it finally decided to leave.

Kermit, about this time, killed a heavy boar from horse-back after a three-miles run. The boar charged twice, causing the horse to buck and shy. Finally, just as he was going into his burrow backward, Kermit raced by and shot him, firing his rifle from the saddle after the manner of the old-time Western buffalo runners.

We now rejoined Mearns and Loring on the banks of the Guaso Nyero. They had collected hundreds of birds and small mammals, among them several new species. We had already heard that a Mr. Williams, whom we had met at McMillan's ranch, had been rather badly mauled by a lion, which he had mortally wounded, but which managed to charge home. Now we found that Dr. Mearns had been quite busily engaged in attending to cases of men who were hurt by lions. Loring nearly got in the category. He killed his lioness with a light automatic rifle, utterly unfit for use against African game. Though he actually put a bullet right through the beast's heart, the shock from the blow was so slight that she was not stopped even for a second; he hit her four times in all, each shot being mortal— for he was an excellent marksman,—and she died nearly at his feet, her charge carrying her several yards by him. Mearns had galloped into a herd of wildebeest and killed the big bull of the herd, after first running clean through a mob of zebras, which, as he passed, skinned their long yellow teeth threateningly at him, but made no attempt actually to attack him.

A settler had come down to trade with the Masai during our absence. He ran into a large party of lions, killed two, and wounded a lioness which escaped after mauling one of his gun-bearers. The gun-bearer rode into camp, and the Doctor treated his wounds. Next day Mearns was summoned to a Masai kraal sixteen miles off to treat the wounds of two of the Masai; it appeared that a body of them had followed and killed the wounded lioness, but that two of their number had been much maltreated in the fight. One, especially, had been fearfully bitten, the lioness having pulled the flesh loose from the bones with her fixed teeth. The Doctor attended to all three cases. The gun-bearer recovered; both the Masai died, although the Doctor did all in his power for the two gallant fellows. Their deaths did not hinder the Masai from sending to him all kinds of cases in which men or boys had met with accidents. He attended to them all, and gained a high reputation with the tribe; when the case was serious the patient's kinsfolk would usually present him with a sheep or war-spear, or something else of value. He took a great fancy to the Masai, as indeed all of us did. They are a fine, manly set of savages, bold and independent in their bearing. They never eat vegetables, subsisting exclusively on milk, blood, and flesh; and are remarkably hardy and enduring.

Kermit found a cave which had recently been the abode of a party of 'Ndorobo, the wild hunter-savages of the wilderness, who are more primitive in their ways of life than any other tribes of this region. They live on honey and the flesh of the wild beasts they kill; they are naked, with few and rude arms and utensils; and, in short, carry on existence as our own ancestors did at a very early period of palæolithic time. Around this cave were many bones. Within it were beds of grass, and a small roofed enclosure of thorn-bushes for the dogs. Fire sticks had been left on the walls, to be ready when the owners' wanderings again brought them back to the cave; and also very curious soup sticks, each a rod with one of the vertebræ of some animal stuck on the end, designed for use in stirring their boiled meat.

From our camp on the Guaso Nyero we trekked in a little over four days to a point on Lake Naivasha where we intended to spend some time. The first two days were easy travelling, the porters not being pressed and there being plenty of time in the afternoons to pitch camp comfortably; then the wagons left us with their loads of hides and skeletons and spare baggage. The third day we rose long before dawn, breakfasted, broke camp, and were off just at sunrise. There was no path; at one time we followed game trails, at another the trails made by the Masai sheep and cattle, and again we might make our own trail. We had two Masai guides, tireless runners, as graceful and sinewy as panthers; they helped us; but Cuninghame had to do most of the pathfinding himself. It was a diffi-cult country, passable only at certain points, which it was hard to place with exactness. We had seen that each porter had his water bottle full before starting; but, though will-ing, good-humored fellows, strong as bulls, in fore-thought they are of the grasshopper type; and all but a few exhausted their supply by mid-afternoon. At this time we were among bold mountain ridges, and here we struck the kraal of some Masai, who watered their cattle at some spring pools, three miles to one side, up a valley. It was too far for the heavily laden porters; but we cantered our horses thither and let them drink their fill; and then can-

A sick Masai boy and his father

The sheep is a present to Dr. Mearns for services

From a photograph by J. Alden Loring

tered along the trail left by the safari until we overtook the rear men just as they were going over the brink of the Mau escarpment. The scenery was wild and beautiful; in the open places the ground was starred with flowers of many colors; we rode under vine-tangled archways through forests of strange trees.

Down the steep mountain side went the safari, and at its foot struck off nearly parallel to the high ridge. On our left the tree-clad mountain side hung above us; ravines, with mimosas clustering in them, sundered the foot-hills, and wound until they joined into what looked like rivers; the thick grass grew waist high. It looked like a well-watered country; but it was of porous, volcanic nature, and the soil was a sieve. After nightfall we came to where we hoped to find water; but there was not a drop in the dried pools; and we had to make a waterless camp. A drizzling rain had set in, enough to wet everything, but not enough to give any water for drinking. It was eight o'clock before the last of the weary, thirsty burden-carriers stumbled through the black, bowlder-strewn ravine on whose farther side we were camped, and threw down his load among his fellows, who were already clustered around the little fires they had started in the tall grass. We slept as we were, and comfortably enough; indeed, there was no hardship for us white men, with our heavy overcoats, and our food and water—which we shared with our personal attendants; but I was uneasy for the porters, as there was another long and exhausting day's march ahead. Before sunrise we started; and four hours later, in the bottom of a deep ravine, Cuninghame found a pool of green water in a scooped-out cavity in the rock. It was a pleasant sight to see the thirsty porters drink. Then they sat down, built fires, and boiled their food; and went on in good heart.

Two or three times we crossed singularly beautiful ravines, the trail winding through narrow clefts that were almost tunnels, and along the brinks of sheer cliffs, while the green mat of trees and vines was spangled with many colored flowers. Then we came to barren ridges and bare, dusty plains; and at nightfall pitched camp near the shores of Lake Naivasha. It is a lovely sheet of water, surrounded by hills and mountains, the shores broken by rocky prom-ontories, and indented by papyrus-fringed bays. Next morn-ing we shifted camp four miles to a place on the farm, and near the house, of the Messrs. Attenborough, settlers on the shores of the lake, who treated us with the most generous courtesy and hospitality—as, indeed, did all the settlers we met. They were two brothers; one had lived twenty years on the Pacific Coast, mining in the Sierras, and the other had just retired from the British navy, with the rank of commander; they were able to turn their hands

The waterhole we struck after having made a dry camp on our trek to Naivasha
From a photograph by Kermit Roosevelt

to anything, and were just the men for work in a new country—for a new country is a poor place for the weak and incompetent, whether of body or mind. They had a steam launch and a big heavy row-boat, and they most kindly and generously put both at our disposal for hippo hunting.

At this camp I presented the porters with twenty-five sheep, as a recognition of their good conduct and hard work; whereupon they improvised long chants in my honor, and feasted royally.

We spent one entire day with the row-boat in a series of lagoons near camp, which marked an inlet of the lake. We did not get any hippo, but it was a most interesting

Camp at Lake Naivasha
From a photograph by Edmund Heller

day. A broad belt of papyrus fringed the lagoons and jutted out between them. The straight green stalks with their feathery heads rose high and close, forming a mass so dense that it was practically impenetrable save where the huge bulk of the hippos had made tunnels. Indeed, even for the hippos it was not readily penetrable. The green monotony of a papyrus swamp becomes wearisome after a while; yet it is very beautiful, for each reed is tall, slender, graceful, with its pale flowering crown; and they are typical of the tropics, and their mere sight suggests a vertical sun and hot, steaming swamps, where great marsh beasts feed and wallow and bellow, amidst a teeming reptilian life.

A fringe of papyrus here and there adds much to the beauty of a lake, and also to the beauty of the river pools, where clumps of them grow under the shade of the vine-tangled tropical trees.

The open waters of the lagoons were covered with water-lilies, bearing purple or sometimes pink flowers. Across the broad lily pads ran the curious "lily trotters," or jacanas,

Water-lilies, Lake Naivasha
From a photograph by Edmund Heller

richly colored birds, with toes so long and slender that the lily pads support them without sinking. They were not shy, and their varied coloring—a bright chestnut being the most conspicuous hue—and singular habits made them very conspicuous. There was a wealth of bird life in the lagoons. Small gulls, somewhat like our black-headed gull, but with their hoods gray, flew screaming around us. Black and white kingfishers, tiny red-billed kingfishers, with colors so brilliant that they flashed like jewels in the sun, and brilliant green bee-eaters with chestnut breasts perched among the reeds. Spur-winged plover clamored as they circled overhead near the edges of the water. Little rails and red-legged water-hens threaded the edges of the papyrus, and grebes dived in the open water.   A giant heron, the Goliath, flew up at our approach; and there were many smaller herons and egrets, white or parti-colored.   There were small, dark cormorants, and larger ones with white throats; and African ruddy ducks, and teal and big yellow-billed ducks, somewhat like mallards.   Among the many kinds of ducks was one which made a whistling noise with its wings as it flew.   Most plentiful of all were the coots, much resembling our common bald-pate coot, but with a pair of horns or papillæ at the hinder end of the bare frontal space.

There were a number of hippo in these lagoons.   One afternoon after four o'clock I saw two standing half out of water in a shallow, eating the water-lilies.   They seemed to spend the fore part of the day sleeping or resting in the papyrus or near its edge;   toward evening they splashed and waded among the water-lilies, tearing them up with their huge jaws;   and during the night they came ashore to feed on the grass and land plants.   In consequence those killed during the day, until the late afternoon, had their stomachs filled, not with water plants, but with grasses which they must have obtained in their night journeys on dry land.   At night I heard the bulls bellowing and roaring.   They fight savagely among themselves, and where they are not molested, and the natives are timid, they not only do great damage to the gardens and crops, trampling them down and shovelling basketfuls into their huge mouths, but also become dangerous to human beings, attacking boats or canoes in a spirit of wanton and ferocious mischief.   At this place, a few weeks before our arrival, a young bull, badly scarred, and evidently having been mishandled by some bigger bull, came ashore in the daytime and actually attacked the cattle, and was promptly shot in consequence.   They are astonishingly quick in their movements for such shapeless-looking, short-legged things.   Of course they cannot swim in deep water with anything like the speed of the real swimming mammals, nor move

What one has to shoot at when after hippo on water
From a photograph by Kermit Roosevelt

Mr. Roosevelt's hippo charging open-mouthed
From a photograph by Kermit Roosevelt

on shore with the agility and speed of the true denizens of the land; nevertheless, by sheer muscular power and in spite of their shape, they move at an unexpected rate of speed both on dry land and in deep water; and in shallow water, their true home, they gallop very fast on the bottom, under water. Ordinarily only their heads can be seen, and they must be shot in the brain. If they are found in a pool with little cover, and if the shots can be taken close by, from firm ground, there is no sport whatever in killing them. But the brain is small and the skull huge, and if they are any distance off, and especially if the shot has to be taken from an unsteady boat, there is ample opportunity to miss.

On the day we spent with the big row-boat in the lagoons both Kermit and I had shots; each of us hit, but neither of us got his game. My shot was at the head of a hippo facing me in a bay about a hundred yards off, so that I had to try to shoot very low between the eyes; the water was smooth, and I braced my legs well and fired off-hand. I hit him, but was confident that I had missed the brain, for he lifted slightly, and then went under, nose last; and when a hippo is shot in the brain the head usually goes under nose first. An exasperating feature of hippo shooting is that, save in exceptional circumstances, where the water is very shallow, the animal sinks at once when killed outright, and does not float for one or two or three hours; so that one has to wait that length of time before finding out whether the game has or has not been bagged. On this occasion we never saw a sign of the animal after I fired, and as it seemed impossible that in that situation the hippo could get off unobserved, my companions thought I had killed him; I thought not, and unfortunately my judgment proved to be correct.

Another day, in the launch, I did much the same thing. Again the hippo was a long distance off, only his head appearing, but unfortunately not in profile, much the best position for a shot; again I hit him; again he sank and,

Charged straight for the boat, with open jaws, bent on mischief

Drawn by Philip R. Goodwin from photographs and from descriptions furnished by Mr. Roosevelt

look as hard as we could, not a sign of him appeared, so that every one was sure he was dead; and again no body ever floated. But on this day Kermit got his hippo. He hit it first in the head, merely a flesh wound; but the startled creature then rose high in the water and he shot it in the lungs. It now found difficulty in staying under, and continually rose to the surface with a plunge like a porpoise, going as fast as it could toward the papyrus. After it we went, full speed, for once in the papyrus we could not have followed it; and Kermit finally killed it, just before it reached the edge of the swamp, and, luckily, where the water was so shallow that we did not have to wait for it to float, but fastened a rope to two of its turtle-like legs, and towed it back forthwith.

There were otters in the lake. One day we saw two playing together near the shore; and at first we were all of us certain that it was some big water snake. It was not until we were very close that we made out the supposed one big snake to be two otters; it was rather interesting, as giving one of the explanations of the stories that always appear about large water snakes, or similar monsters, existing in almost every lake of any size in a wild country. On another day I shot another near shore; he turned over and over, splashing and tumbling; but just as we were about to grasp him, he partially recovered and dived to safety in the reeds.

On the second day we went out in the launch I got my hippo. We steamed down the lake, not far from the shore, for over ten miles, dragging the big, clumsy rowboat, in which Cuninghame had put three of our porters who knew how to row. Then we spied a big hippo walking entirely out of water on the edge of the papyrus, at the farther end of a little bay which was filled with waterlilies. Thither we steamed, and when a few rods from the bay, Cuninghame, Kermit, and I got into the row-boat; Cuninghame steered, Kermit carried his camera, and I steadied myself in the bow with the little Springfield rifle.

The hippo was a self-confident, truculent beast; it went under water once or twice, but again came out to the papyrus and waded along the edge, its body out of water. We headed toward it, and thrust the boat in among the water-lilies, finding that the bay was shallow, from three to six feet deep. While still over a hundred yards from the hippo, I saw it turn as if to break into the papyrus, and at once fired into its shoulder, the tiny pointed bullet smashing the big bones. Round spun the great beast, plunged into the water, and with its huge jaws open came straight for the boat, floundering and splashing through the thick-growing water-lilies. I think that its chief object was to get to deep water; but we were between it and the deep water, and instead of trying to pass to one side it charged straight for the boat, with open jaws, bent on mischief. But I hit it again and again with the little sharp-pointed bullet. Once I struck it between neck and shoulder; once, as it rushed forward with its huge jaws stretched to their threatening utmost, I fired right between them, whereat it closed them with the clash of a sprung bear trap; and then, when under the punishment it swerved for a moment, I hit it at the base of the ear, a brain shot which dropped it in its tracks. Meanwhile Kermit was busily taking photos of it as it charged, and, as he mentioned afterward, until it was dead he never saw it except in the "finder" of his camera. The water was so shallow where I had killed the hippo that its body projected slightly above the surface. It was the hardest kind of work getting it out from among the water-lilies; then we towed it to camp behind the launch.

The engineer of the launch was an Indian Moslem. The fireman and the steersman were two half-naked and much-ornamented Kikuyus. The fireman wore a blue bead chain on one ankle, a brass armlet on the opposite arm, a belt of short steel chains, a dingy blanket (no loin cloth), and a skull-cap surmounted by a plume of ostrich feathers. The two Kikuyus were unconsciously entertaining com-

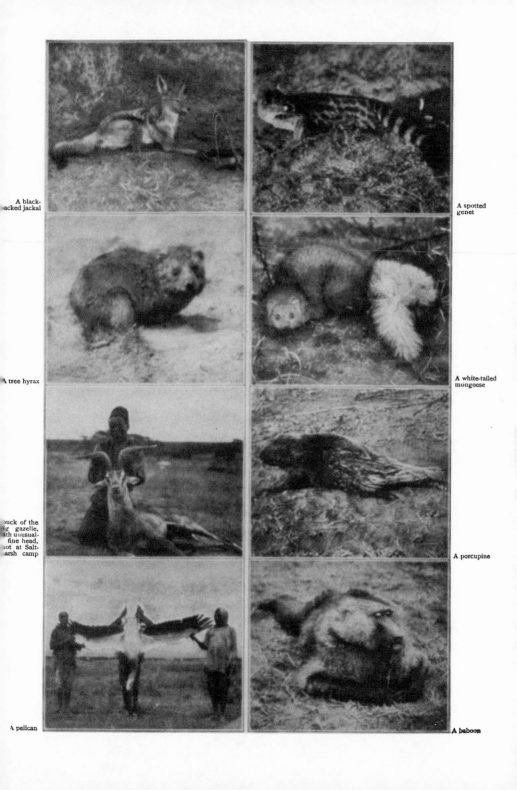

A black-backed jackal

A spotted genet

A tree hyrax

A white-tailed mongoose

buck of the big gazelle, with unusual fine head, shot at Salt-marsh camp

A porcupine

A pelican

A baboon

panions. Without any warning they would suddenly start a song or chant, usually an impromptu recitative of whatever at the moment interested them. They chanted for half an hour over the feat of the "Bwana Makuba" (great master or chief, my name) in killing the hippo; laying especial stress upon the quantity of excellent meat it would furnish, and how very good the eating would be. Usually one would improvise the chant, and the other join in the chorus. Sometimes they would solemnly sing complimentary songs to one another, each in turn chanting the manifold good qualities of his companion.

Around this camp were many birds. The most noteworthy was a handsome gray eagle owl, bigger than our great horned owl, to which it is closely akin. It did not hoot or scream, its voice being a kind of grunt, followed in a second or two by a succession of similar sounds, uttered more quickly and in a lower tone. These big owls frequently came round camp after dark, and at first their notes completely puzzled me, as I thought they must be made by some beast. The bulbuls sang well. Most of the birds were in no way like our home birds.

Loring trapped quantities of mice and rats, and it was curious to see how many of them had acquired characters which caused them superficially to resemble American animals with which they had no real kinship. The sand rats that burrowed in the dry plains were in shape, in color, eyes, tail, and paws strikingly like our pocket gophers, which have similar habits. So the long-tailed gerbilles, or gerbille-like rats, resembled our kangaroo rats; and there was a blunt-nosed, stubby-tailed little rat superficially hardly to be told from our rice rat. But the most characteristic rodent, the big long-tailed, jumping springhaas, resembled nothing of ours; and there were tree rats and spiny mice. There were gray monkeys in the trees around camp, which the naturalists shot.

Heller trapped various beasts; beautifully marked genets, and a big white-tailed mongoose which was very savage. But his most remarkable catch was a leopard. He had set a steel trap, fastened to a loose thorn-branch, for mongoose, civets, or jackals; it was a number two Blake, such as in America we use for coons, skunks, foxes, and perhaps bobcats and coyotes. In the morning he found it gone, and followed the trail of the thorn-branch until it led into a dense thicket, from which issued an ominous growl. His native boy shouted "simba"; but it was a leopard, not a lion. He could not see into the thicket; so he sent back to camp for his rifle, and when it came he climbed a tree and endeavored to catch a glimpse of the animal. He could see nothing, however; and finally fired into the thicket rather at random. The answer was a furious growl, and the leopard charged out to the foot of the tree, much hampered by the big thorn-branch. He put a bullet into it, and back it went, only to come out and to receive another bullet; and he killed it. It was an old male, in good condition, weighing one hundred and twenty-six pounds. The trap was not big enough to contain his whole paw, and he had been caught firmly by one toe. The thorn-bush acted as a drag, which prevented him from going far, and yet always yielded somewhat when he pulled. A bear thus caught would have chewed up the trap or else pulled his foot loose, even at the cost of sacrificing the toe; but the cats are more sensitive to pain. This leopard was smaller than any full-grown male cougar I have ever killed, and yet cougars often kill game rather heavier than leopards usually venture upon; yet very few cougars indeed would show anything like the pluck and ferocity shown by this leopard, and characteristic of its kind.

Kermit killed a waterbuck of a kind new to us, the singsing. He also killed two porcupines and two baboons. The porcupines are terrestrial animals, living in burrows to which they keep during the daytime. They are much heavier than, and in all their ways totally different from, our sluggish tree porcupines. The baboons were numerous around this camp, living both among the rocks and in

the tree tops. They are hideous creatures. They ravage
the crops and tear open new-born lambs to get at the milk
inside them; and where the natives are timid and unable
to harm them, they become wantonly savage and aggres-
sive and attack and even kill women and children. In
Uganda, Cuninghame had once been asked by a native
chief to come to his village and shoot the baboons, as they
had just killed two women, badly bitten several children,
and caused such a reign of terror that the village would be
abandoned if they were not killed or intimidated. He himself saw the torn and mutilated bodies of the dead women;
and he stayed in the village a week, shooting so many baboons that the remainder were thoroughly cowed. Baboons
and boars are the most formidable of all foes to the dogs
that hunt them—just as leopards are of all wild animals
those most apt to prey on dogs. A baboon's teeth and
hands are far more formidable weapons than those of any
dog, and only a very few wholly exceptional dogs of huge
size, and great courage and intelligence, can, single-handed,
contend with an old male. But we saw a settler whose three
big terriers could themselves kill a full-grown wart-hog boar;
an almost unheard-of feat. They backed up one another
with equal courage and adroitness, their aim being for
two to seize the hind legs; then the third, watching his
chance, would get one foreleg, when the boar was speedily
thrown, and, when weakened, killed by bites in his stomach.
    Hitherto we had not obtained a bull hippo, and I made
up my mind to devote myself to getting one, as otherwise
the group for the museum would be incomplete. Save in
exceptional cases I do not think hippo hunting, after the
first one has been obtained, a very attractive sport, because
usually one has to wait an hour before it is possible to tell
whether or not a shot has been successful, and also because, a portion of the head being all that is usually visible,
it is exceedingly difficult to say whether the animal seen
is a bull or a cow. As the time allowed for a shot is very
short, and any hesitation probably insures the animal's

escape, this means that two or three hippo may be killed, quite unavoidably, before the right specimen is secured. Still there may be interesting and exciting incidents in a

Mr. Roosevelt and Cuninghame discussing the next few days' march over a wildebeest shot by Mr. Roosevelt
From a photograph by Kermit Roosevelt

hippo hunt. Cuninghame, the two Attenboroughs, and I started early in the launch, towing the big, clumsy row-boat, with as crew three of our porters who could row. We steamed down the lake some fifteen miles to a wide bay, indented by smaller bays, lagoons, and inlets, all fringed by a broad belt of impenetrable papyrus, while the beautiful purple lilies, with their leathery-tough stems and broad surface-floating leaves, filled the shallows. At the mouth of the main bay we passed a floating island, a mass of papyrus perhaps a hundred and fifty acres in extent, which had been broken off from the shore somewhere, and was floating over the lake as the winds happened to drive it.

In an opening in the dense papyrus masses we left the launch moored, and Cuninghame and I started in the rowboat to coast the green wall of tall, thick-growing, feather-topped reeds. Under the bright sunshine the shallow flats were alive with bird life. Gulls, both the gray-hooded and the black-backed, screamed harshly overhead. The chestnut-colored lily trotters tripped daintily over the lily pads, and when they flew, held their long legs straight behind them, so that they looked as if they had tails like pheasants. Sacred ibis, white with naked black head and neck, stalked along the edge of the water, and on the bent papyrus small cormorants and herons perched. Everywhere there were coots and ducks, and crested grebes, big and little. Huge white pelicans floated on the water. Once we saw a string of flamingoes fly by, their plumage a wonderful red.

Immediately after leaving the launch we heard a hippo, hidden in the green fastness on our right, uttering a meditative soliloquy, consisting of a succession of squealing grunts. Then we turned a point, and in a little bay saw six or eight hippo, floating with their heads above water. There were two much bigger than the others, and Cuninghame, while of course unable to be certain, thought these were probably males. The smaller ones, including a cow and her calf, were not much alarmed, and floated quietly, looking at us, as we cautiously paddled and drifted nearer; but the bigger ones dove and began to work their way past us toward deep water. We could trace their course by the twisting of the lily pads. Motionless the rowers lay on their oars; the line of moving lily pads showed that one

Bringing the big bull hippo to shore
From a photograph by Edmund Heller

of the big hippo was about to pass the boat; suddenly the waters opened close at hand and a monstrous head appeared. "Shoot," said Cuninghame; and I fired into the back of the head just as it disappeared. It sank out of sight without a splash, almost without a ripple, the lily pads ceased twisting; a few bubbles of air rose to the surface; evidently the hippo lay dead underneath. Poling to the spot, we at once felt the huge body with our oar blades. But, alas, when the launch came round, and we raised the body, it proved to be that of a big cow.

So I left Cuninghame to cut off the head for the museum. and started off by myself in the boat with two rowers, neither of whom spoke a word of English. For an hour we saw only the teeming bird life. Then, in a broad, shallow lagoon, we made out a dozen hippo, two or three very big. Cautiously we approached them, and when seventy yards off I fired at the base of the ear of one of the largest. Down went every head, and utter calm succeeded. I had marked the spot where the one at which I shot had disappeared, and thither we rowed. When we reached the place, I told one of the rowers to thrust a pole down and see if he could touch the dead body. He thrust according, and at once shouted that he had found the hippo; in another moment his face altered, and he shouted much more loudly that the hippo was alive. Sure enough, bump went the hippo against the bottom of the boat, the jar causing us all to sit suddenly down—for we were standing. Another bump showed that we had again been struck; and the shallow, muddy water boiled, as the huge beasts, above and below the surface, scattered every which way. Their eyes starting, the two rowers began to back water out of the dangerous neighborhood, while I shot at an animal whose head appeared to my left, as it made off with frantic haste; for I took it for granted that the hippo at which I had first fired (and which was really dead) had escaped. This one disappeared as usual, and I had not the slightest idea whether or not I had killed it. I had small opportunity to ponder the subject, for twenty feet away the water bubbled and a huge head shot out facing me, the jaws wide open. There was no time to guess at its intentions, and I fired on the instant. Down went the head, and I felt the boat quiver as the hippo passed underneath. Just here the lily pads were thick; so I marked its course, fired as it rose, and down it went. But on the other quarter of the boat a beast, evidently of great size—it proved to be a big bull—now appeared, well above water; and I put a bullet into its brain.

I did not wish to shoot again unless I had to, and stood motionless, with the little Springfield at the ready. A head burst up twenty yards off, with a lily pad plastered over one eye, giving the hippo an absurd resemblance to a discomfited prize-fighter, and then disappeared with great agitation. Two half-grown beasts stupid from fright appeared, and stayed up for a minute or two at a time, not knowing what to do. Other heads popped up, getting farther and farther away. By degrees everything vanished, the water grew calm, and we rowed over to the papyrus, moored ourselves by catching hold of a couple of stems, and awaited events. Within an hour four dead hippos appeared: a very big bull and three big cows. Of course, I would not have shot the latter if it could have been avoided; but under the circumstances I do not see how it was possible to help it. The meat was not wasted; on the contrary it was a godsend, not only to our own porters, but to the natives round about, many of whom were on short commons on account of the drought.

Bringing over the launch we worked until after dark to get the bull out of the difficult position in which he lay. It was nearly seven o'clock before we had him fixed for towing on one quarter, the row-boat towing on the other, by which time two hippos were snorting and blowing within a few yards of us, their curiosity much excited as to what was going on. The night was overcast; there were drenching rain squalls, and a rather heavy sea was running, and I

did not get back to camp until after three. Next day the
launch fetched in the rest of the hippo meat.

From this camp we went into Naivasha, on the line of
the railway. In many places the road was beautiful, leading among the huge yellow trunks of giant thorn-trees, the

Mr. Roosevelt's big bull hippo
From a photograph by Kermit Roosevelt

ground rising sheer on our left as we cantered along the
edge of the lake. We passed impalla, tommies, zebra, and
wart-hog; and in one place saw three waterbuck cows feeding just outside the papyrus at high noon. They belonged
to a herd that lived in the papyrus and fed on the grassy
flats outside; and their feeding in the open exactly at noon
was another proof of the fact that the custom of feeding
in the early morning and late evening is with most game
entirely artificial and the result of fear of man. Birds

abounded. Parties of the dark-colored ant-eating wheat-ear sang sweetly from trees and bushes, and even from the roofs of the settlers' houses. The tricolored starlings —black, white, and chestnut—sang in the air, as well as when perched on twigs. Stopping at the government farm (which is most interesting; the results obtained in improving the native sheep, goats, and cattle by the use of imported thoroughbred bulls and rams have been astonishingly successful) we saw the little long-tailed, red-billed, black and white whydahs flitting around the out-buildings as familiarly as sparrows. Water birds of all kinds thronged the meadows bordering the papyrus, and swam and waded among the water-lilies; sacred ibis, herons, beautiful white spoonbills, darters, cormorants, Egyptian geese, ducks, coots, and water-hens. I got up within rifle range of a flock of the queer ibis stork, black and white birds with curved yellow bills, naked red faces, and wonderful purple tints on the edges and the insides of the wings; with the little Springfield I shot one on the ground and another on the wing, after the flock had risen.

That night Kermit and Dr. Mearns went out with lanterns and shot-guns, and each killed one of the spring-haas, the jumping hares, which abounded in the neighborhood. These big, burrowing animals, which progress by jumping like kangaroos, are strictly nocturnal, and their eyes shine in the glare of the lanterns.

Next day I took the Fox gun, which had already on ducks, guinea-fowl, and francolin shown itself an exceptionally hard-hitting and close-shooting weapon, and collected various water birds for the naturalists; among others, a couple of Egyptian geese. I also shot a white pelican with the Springfield rifle; there was a beautiful rosy flush on the breast.

Here we again got news of the outside world. While on safari the only newspaper which any of us ever saw was the *Owego Gazette*, which Loring, in a fine spirit of neighborhood loyalty, always had sent to him in his mail. To the Doctor, by the way, I had become knit in a bond of close intellectual sympathy ever since a chance allusion to "William Henry's Letters to His Grandmother" had disclosed the fact that each of us, ever since the days of his youth, had preserved the bound volumes of "Our Young Folks," and moreover firmly believed that there never had been its equal as a magazine, whether for old or young; even though the Plancus of our golden consulship was the not wholly happy Andrew Johnson.

CHAPTER X

ELEPHANT HUNTING ON MOUNT KENIA

On July 24th, in order to ship our fresh accumulations of specimens and trophies, we once more went into Nairobi. It was a pleasure again to see its tree-bordered streets and

Meru porters carrying trophy ivory
From a photograph by Edmund Heller

charming houses bowered in vines and bushes, and to meet once more the men and women who dwelt in the houses. I wish it were in my power to thank individually the members of the many East African households of which I shall always cherish warm memories of friendship and regard.

At Nairobi I saw Sclous, who had just returned from a two months' safari with McMillan, Williams, and Judd. Their experience shows how large the element of luck is in lion hunting. Selous was particularly anxious to kill a good lion; there is nowhere to be found a more skilful or more hard-working hunter; yet he never even got a shot.

271

Williams, on the other hand, came across three. Two he killed easily. The third charged him. He was carrying a double-barrelled .450, but failed to stop the beast; it seized him by the leg, and his life was saved by his Swahili gun-bearer, who gave the lion a fatal shot as it stood over him. He came within an ace of dying; but when I saw him, at the hospital, he was well on the road to recovery. One day Selous while on horseback saw a couple of lion-esses, and galloped after them, followed by, Judd, seventy or eighty yards behind. One lioness stopped and crouched under a bush, let Selous pass, and then charged Judd. She was right alongside him, and he fired from the hip; the bullet went into her eye; his horse jumped and swerved at the shot, throwing him off, and he found himself sitting on the ground, not three yards from the dead lioness. Nothing more was seen of the other.

Continually I met men with experiences in their past lives which showed how close the country was to those primitive conditions in which warfare with wild beasts was one of the main features of man's existence. At one dinner my host and two of my fellow-guests had been within a year or eighteen months severely mauled by lions. All three, by the way, informed me that the actual biting caused them at the moment no pain whatever; the pain came later. On meeting Harold Hill, my companion on one of my Kapiti Plains lion hunts, I found that since I had seen him he had been roughly handled by a dying leopard. The government had just been obliged to close one of the trade routes to native caravans because of the ravages of a man-eating lion, which carried men away from the camps. A safari which had come in from the north had been charged by a rhino, and one of the porters tossed and killed, the horn being driven clean through his loins. At Heatley's farm three buffalo (belonging to the same herd from which we had shot five) rushed out of the papyrus one afternoon at a passing buggy, which just managed to escape by a breakneck run across the level plain, the beasts chasing it

for a mile. One afternoon, at Government House, I met
a government official who had once succeeded in driving
into a corral seventy zebras, including more stallions than
mares; their misfortune in no way abated their savagery
toward one another, and as the limited space forbade the
escape of the weaker, the stallions fought to the death with
teeth and hoofs during the first night, and no less than
twenty were killed outright or died of their wounds.

Most of the time in Nairobi we were the guests of ever-
hospitable McMillan, in his low, cool house, with its broad,
vine-shaded veranda, running around all four sides, and its
garden, fragrant and brilliant with innumerable flowers.
Birds abounded, singing beautifully; the bulbuls were the
most noticeable singers, but there were many others. The
dark ant-eating chats haunted the dusky roads on the outskirts of the town, and were interesting birds; they were
usually found in parties, flirted their tails up and down
as they sat on bushes or roofs or wires, sang freely in chorus
until after dusk, and then retired to holes in the ground for
the night. A tiny owl with a queer little voice called continually not only after nightfall, but in the bright afternoons.
Shrikes spitted insects on the spines of the imported cactus
in the gardens.

It was race week, and the races, in some of which Kermit
rode, were capital fun. The white people—army officers,
government officials, farmers from the country roundabout,
and their wives—rode to the races on ponies or even on
camels, or drove up in rickshaws, in gharries, in bullock
tongas, occasionally in automobiles, most often in two-
wheel carts or rickety hacks drawn by mules and driven by
a turbaned Indian or a native in a cotton shirt. There
were Parsees, and Goanese dressed just like the Europeans.
There were many other Indians, their picturesque women-
kind gaudy in crimson, blue, and saffron. The constabulary, Indian and native, were in neat uniforms and well
set up, though often barefooted. Straight, slender Somalis
with clear-cut features were in attendance on the horses.

Native negroes, of many different tribes, flocked to the
race-course and its neighborhood. The Swahilis, and those
among the others who aspired toward civilization, were well
clad, the men in half European costume, the women in
flowing, parti-colored robes. But most of them were clad,
or unclad, just as they always had been. Wakamba, with
filed teeth, crouched in circles on the ground. Kikuyu
passed, the men each with a blanket hung round the shoulders, and girdles of chains, and armlets and anklets of
solid metal; the older women bent under burdens they
carried on the back, half of them in addition with babies
slung somewhere round them, while now and then an un-
married girl would have her face painted with ochre and
vermilion. A small party of Masai warriors kept close
together, each clutching his shining, long-bladed war spear,
their hair daubed red and twisted into strings. A large
band of Kavirondo, stark naked, with shield and spear and
head-dress of nodding plumes, held a dance near the race-
track. As for the races themselves, they were carried on in
the most sporting spirit, and only the Australian poet Patterson could adequately write of them.

On August 4th I returned to Lake Naivasha, stopping
on the way at Kijabe to lay the corner-stone of the new
mission building. Mearns and Loring had stayed at Naivasha and had collected many birds and small mammals.
That night they took me out on a springhaas hunt. Thanks
to Kermit we had discovered that the way to get this curious and purely nocturnal animal was by "shining" it with
a lantern at night, just as in our own country deer, coons,
owls, and other creatures can be killed. Springhaas live
in big burrows, a number of them dwelling together in one
community, the holes close to one another, and making
what in the West we would call a "town" in speaking of
prairie dogs. At night they come out to feed on the grass.
They are as heavy as a big jack-rabbit, with short forelegs,
and long hind legs and tail, so that they look and on occasion
move like miniature kangaroos, although, in addition to

making long hops or jumps, they often run almost like an ordinary rat or rabbit. They are pretty creatures, fawn-colored above, and white beneath, with the terminal half of the tail very dark. In hunting them we simply walked over the flats for a couple of hours, flashing the bull's-eye lantern on all sides, until we saw the light reflected back by a springhaas's eyes. Then I would approach to within range, and hold the lantern in my left hand so as to shine both on the sight and on the eyes in front, resting my gun on my left wrist. The number 3 shot, in the Fox double-barrel, would always do the business, if I

A waterbuck

From a photograph by Kermit Roosevelt

held straight enough. There was nothing but the gleam of the eyes to shoot at; and this might suddenly be raised or lowered as the intently watching animal crouched on all-fours or raised itself on its hind legs. I shot half a dozen, all that the naturalists wanted. Then I tried to shoot a fox; but the moon had risen from behind a cloud bank; I had to take a long shot and missed; but my companions killed several, and found that they were a new species of the peculiar African long-eared fox.

While waiting for the safari to get ready, Kermit went off on a camping trip and shot two bushbuck, while I spent a couple of days trying for singsing waterbuck on the edge of the papyrus. I missed a bull, and wounded another which I did not get. This was all the more exasperating because interspersed with the misses were some good shots: I killed a fine waterbuck cow at a hundred yards, and a buck tommy for the table at two hundred and fifty; and, after missing a handsome black and white, red-billed and red-legged jabiru, or saddle-billed stork, at a hundred and fifty yards, as he stalked through the meadow after frogs, I cut him down on the wing at a hundred and eighty, with the

Creek on slopes of Kenia near first elephant camp

From a photograph by Edmund Heller

little Springfield rifle. The waterbuck spent the daytime outside, but near the edge of, the papyrus; I found them grazing or resting, in the open, at all times between early morning and late afternoon. Some of them spent most of the day in the papyrus, keeping to the watery trails made by the hippos and by themselves; but this was not the general habit, unless they had been persecuted. When frightened they often ran into the papyrus, smashing the dead reeds and splashing the water in their rush. They are noble-looking antelope, with long, shaggy hair, and their chosen haunts beside the lake were very attractive. Clumps of thorn-trees and flowering bushes grew at the edge of the tall papyrus here and there, and often formed a matted jungle, the trees laced together by creepers, many of them brilliant in their bloom. The climbing morning-glories sometimes completely covered a tree with their pale-purple flowers; and other blossoming vines spangled the green over which their sprays were flung with masses of bright yellow.

Four days' march from Naivasha, where we again left Mearns and Loring, took us to Neri. Our line of march lay across the high plateaus and mountain chains of the Aberdare range. The steep, twisting trail was slippery with mud. Our last camp, at an altitude of about ten thousand feet, was so cold that the water froze in the basins, and the shivering porters slept in numbed discomfort. There was constant fog and rain, and on the highest plateau the bleak landscape, shrouded in driving mist, was northern to all the senses. The ground was rolling, and through the deep valleys ran brawling brooks of clear water; one little foaming stream, suddenly tearing down a hill-side, might have been that which Childe Roland crossed before he came to the dark tower.

There was not much game, and it generally moved abroad by night. One frosty evening we killed a duiker by shining its eyes. We saw old elephant tracks. The high, wet levels swarmed with mice and shrews, just as our arctic and alpine meadows swarm with them. The species were really widely different from ours, but many of them showed curious analogies in form and habits; there was a short-tailed shrew much like our mole shrew, and a long-haired, short-tailed rat like a very big meadow mouse. They were so plentiful that we frequently saw them, and the grass was cut up by their runways. They were abroad during the day, probably finding the nights too cold, and in an hour Heller trapped a dozen or two individuals belonging to seven species and five different genera. There were not many birds so high up. There were deer ferns; and Spanish moss hung from the trees and even from the bamboos. The flowers included utterly strange forms, as for instance giant lobelias ten feet high. Others we know in our gardens; geraniums and red-hot pokers, which in places turned the glades to a fire color. Yet others either were like, or looked like, our own wild flowers: orange lady-slippers, red gladiolus on stalks six feet high, pansy-like violets, and blackberries and yellow raspberries. There were stretches of bushes bearing masses of small red or large white flowers shaped somewhat like columbines, or like the garden balsam; the red flower bushes were under the bamboos, the white at a lower level. The crests and upper slopes of the mountains were clothed in the green uniformity of the bamboo forest, the trail winding dim under its dark archway of tall, close-growing stems. Lower down were junipers and yews, and then many other trees, with among them tree ferns and strange dragon-trees with lily-like frondage. Zone succeeded zone from top to bottom, each marked by a different plant life.

In this part of Africa, where flowers bloom and birds sing all the year round, there is no such burst of bloom and song as in the northern spring and early summer. There is nothing like the mass of blossoms which carpet the meadows of the high mountain valleys and far northern meadows, during their brief high tide of life, when one short joyous burst of teeming and vital beauty atones for the long death of the iron fall and winter. So it is with the bird songs. Many of them are beautiful, though to my ears none quite as beautiful as the best of our own bird songs. At any rate there is nothing that quite corresponds to the chorus that during May and June moves northward from the Gulf States and southern California to Maine, Minnesota, and Oregon, to Ontario and Saskatchewan; when there comes the great vernal burst of bloom and song; when the may-flower, bloodroot, wake-robin, anemone, adder's tongue, liverwort, shadblow, dogwood, redbud, gladden the woods; when mocking-birds and cardinals sing in the magnolia groves of the South, and hermit thrushes, winter wrens, and sweetheart sparrows in the spruce and hemlock forests of the North; when bobolinks in the East and meadow-

Kikuyu Ngama, Neri

From a photograph by Edmund Heller

larks East and West sing in the fields; and water ousels by
the cold streams of the Rockies, and canyon wrens in their
sheer gorges; when from the Atlantic seaboard to the
Pacific wood thrushes, veeries, rufous-backed thrushes,
robins, bluebirds, orioles, thrashers, cat-birds, house finches,
song sparrows—some in the East, some in the West, some
both East and West—and many, many other singers thrill
the gardens at sunrise; until the long days begin to shorten,
and tawny lilies burn by the roadside, and the indigo bunt-
ings trill from the tops of little trees throughout the hot
afternoons.

We were in the Kikuyu country. On our march we met
several parties of natives. I had been much inclined to
pity the porters, who had but one blanket apiece; but
when I saw the Kikuyus, each with nothing but a smaller
blanket, and without the other clothing and the tents of
the porters, I realized how much better off the latter were
simply because they were on a white man's safari. At
Neri boma we were greeted with the warmest hospitality
by the district commissioner, Mr. Browne. Among other
things, he arranged a great Kikuyu dance in our honor.
Two thousand warriors, and many women, came in; as
well as a small party of Masai moran. The warriors were
naked, or half-naked; some carried gaudy blankets, others
girdles of leopard skin; their ox-hide shields were colored
in bold patterns, their long-bladed spears quivered and
gleamed. Their faces and legs were painted red and yellow;
the faces of the young men who were about to undergo the
rite of circumcision were stained a ghastly white, and their
bodies fantastically painted. The warriors wore bead necklaces and waist belts and armlets of brass and steel, and
spurred anklets of monkey skin. Some wore head-dresses
made out of a lion's mane or from the long black and white
fur of the Colobus monkey; others had plumes stuck in
their red-daubed hair. They chanted in unison a deep-
toned chorus, and danced rhythmically in rings, while the
drums throbbed and the horns blared; and they danced

by us in column, springing and chanting. The women shrilled applause, and danced in groups by themselves. The Masai circled and swung in a panther-like dance of their own, and the measure, and their own fierce singing and calling, maddened them until two of their number, their eyes staring, their faces working, went into fits of ber-serker frenzy, and were disarmed at once to prevent mischief. Some of the tribesmen held wilder dances still in the evening, by the light of fires that blazed in a grove where their thatched huts stood.

The second day after reaching Neri the clouds lifted and we dried our damp clothes and blankets. Through the bright sunlight we saw in front of us the high rock peaks of Kenia, and shining among them the fields of ever-lasting snow which feed her glaciers; for beautiful, lofty Kenia is one of the glacier-bearing mountains of the equator. Here Kermit and Tarlton went northward on a safari of their own, while Cuninghame, Heller, and I headed for Kenia itself. For two days we travelled through a well-peopled country. The fields of corn—always called mealies in Africa—of beans, and sweet-potatoes, with occasional plantations of bananas, touched one another in almost uninterrupted succession. In most of them we saw the Kikuyu women at work with their native hoes; for among the Kikuyus, as among other savages, the woman is the drudge and beast of burden. Our trail led by clear, rushing streams, which formed the head-waters of the Tana; among the trees fringing their banks were graceful palms, and there were groves of tree ferns here and there on the sides of the gorges.

On the afternoon of the second day we struck upward among the steep foot-hills of the mountain, riven by deep ravines. We pitched camp in an open glade, surrounded by the green wall of tangled forest, the forest of the tropical mountain sides.

The trees, strange of kind and endless in variety, grew tall and close, laced together by vine and creeper, while underbrush crowded the space between their mossy trunks, and covered the leafy mould beneath. Toward dusk crested ibis flew overhead with harsh clamor, to seek their night roosts; parrots chattered, and a curiously home-like touch was given by the presence of a thrush in color and shape almost exactly like our robin. Monkeys called in the depths

Kikuyu village near first elephant camp
From a photograph by Edmund Heller

of the forest, and after dark tree-frogs piped and croaked, and the tree hyraxes uttered their wailing cries.

Elephants dwelt permanently in this mountainous region of heavy woodland. On our march thither we had already seen their traces in the "shambas," as the cultivated fields of the natives are termed; for the great beasts are fond of raiding the crops at night, and their inroads often do serious damage. In this neighborhood their habit is to live high up in the mountains, in the bamboos, while the weather is dry; the cows and calves keeping closer to the bamboos than the bulls. A spell of wet weather, such as we had fortunately been having drives them down in the dense forest which covers the lower slopes. Here they may either pass all their time, or at night they may go still further down, into the open valley where the shambas lie; or they may occasionally still do what they habitually did in the days before the white hunters came, and wander far away, making migrations that are sometimes seasonal, and sometimes irregular and unaccountable.

No other animal, not the lion himself, is so constant a theme of talk, and a subject of such unflagging interest round the camp-fires of African hunters and in the native villages of the African wilderness, as the elephant. Indeed the elephant has always profoundly impressed the imagination of mankind. It is, not only to hunters, but to naturalists, and to all people who possess any curiosity about wild creatures and the wild life of nature, the most interesting of all animals. Its huge bulk, its singular form, the value of its ivory, its great intelligence—in which it is only matched, if at all, by the highest apes, and possibly by one or two of the highest carnivores—and its varied habits, all combine to give it an interest such as attaches to no other living creature below the rank of man. In line of descent and in physical formation it stands by itself, wholly apart from all the other great land beasts, and differing from them even more widely than they differ from one another. The two existing species—the African, which is the larger and finer animal, and the Asiatic—differ from one another as much as they do from the mammoth and similar extinct forms which were the contemporaries of early man in Europe and North America. The carvings of our palæolithic forefathers, etched on bone by cavern dwellers, from whom we are sundered by ages which stretch into an immemorial past, show that in their lives the hairy elephant of the north played the same part that his remote collateral descendant now plays in the lives of the savages who dwell under a vertical sun beside the tepid waters of the Nile and the Congo.

In the first dawn of history, the sculptured records of the kings of Egypt, Babylon, and Nineveh show the immense importance which attached in the eyes of the mightiest monarchs of the then world to the chase and the trophies of this great strange beast. The ancient civilization of India boasts as one of its achievements the taming of the elephant; and in the ancient lore of that civilization the elephant plays a distinguished part.

The elephant is unique among the beasts of great bulk in the fact that his growth in size has been accompanied by growth in brain power. With other beasts growth in bulk of body has not been accompanied by similar growth of mind. Indeed sometimes there seems to have been mental retrogression. The rhinoceros, in several different forms, is found in the same regions as the elephant, and in one of its forms it is in point of size second only to the elephant among terrestrial animals. Seemingly the ancestors of the two creatures, in that period, separated from us by un- counted hundreds of thousands of years, which we may con- veniently designate as late miocene or early pliocene, were substantially equal in brain development. But in one case increase in bulk seems to have induced lethargy and atrophy of brain power, while in the other case brain and body have both grown. At any rate the elephant is now one of the wisest and the rhinoceros one of the stupidest of big mam- mals. In consequence the elephant outlasts the rhino, although he is the largest, carries infinitely more valuable spoils, and is far more eagerly and persistently hunted. Both animals wandered freely over the open country of East Africa thirty years ago. But the elephant learns by ex- perience infinitely more readily than the rhinoceros. As a rule, the former no longer lives in the open plains, and in many places now even crosses them if possible only at night. But those rhinoceros which formerly dwelt in the plains for the most part continued to dwell there until killed out. So it is at the present day. Not the most foolish elephant would under similar conditions behave as the rhinos that we studied and hunted by Kilimakiu and in the Sotik behaved. No elephant, in regions where they have been much persecuted by hunters, would habitually spend its days lying or standing in the open plain; nor would it, in such places, repeatedly, and in fact uniformly, permit men to walk boldly up to it without heeding them until in its immediate neighborhood. The elephant's sight is bad, as is that of the rhinoceros; but a comparatively brief experience with rifle-bearing man

West side of Kenia's peak, taken at an altitude of 15,000 feet
From a photograph by J. Alden Loring

usually makes the former take refuge in regions where scent and hearing count for more than sight; while no experience has any such effect on the rhino. The rhinos that now live in the bush are the descendants of those which always lived in the bush; and it is in the bush that the species will linger long after it has vanished from the open; and it is in the bush that it is most formidable.

Elephant and rhino differ as much in their habits as in their intelligence. The former is very gregarious, herds of

several hundred being sometimes found, and is of a restless, wandering temper, often shifting his abode and sometimes making long migrations. The rhinoceros is a lover of
solitude; it is usually found alone, or a bull and cow, or
cow and calf may be in company; very rarely are as many
as half a dozen found together. Moreover, it is comparatively stationary in its habits, and as a general thing stays
permanently in one neighborhood, not shifting its position
for very many miles unless for grave reasons.

The African elephant has recently been divided into a
number of sub-species; but as within a century its range
was continuous over nearly the whole continent south of the
Sahara, and as it was given to such extensive occasional
wanderings, it is probable that the examination of a sufficient series of specimens would show that on their confines
these races grade into one another. In its essentials the
beast is almost everywhere the same, although, of course,
there must be variation of habits with any animal which
exists throughout so wide and diversified a range of territory; for in one place it is found in high mountains, in another in a dry desert, in another in low-lying marshes or
wet and dense forests.

In East Africa the old bulls are usually found singly
or in small parties by themselves. These have the biggest
tusks; the bulls in the prime of life, the herd bulls or breeding bulls, which keep in herds with the cows and calves,
usually have smaller ivory. Sometimes, however, very
old but vigorous bulls are found with the cows; and I am
inclined to think that the ordinary herd bulls at times also
keep by themselves, or at least in company with only a few
cows, for at certain seasons, generally immediately after
the rains, cows, most of them with calves, appear in great
numbers at certain places, where only a few bulls are ever
found. Where undisturbed elephant rest, and wander
about at all times of the day and night, and feed without
much regard to fixed hours. Morning or evening, noon or
midnight, the herd may be on the move, or its members

may be resting; yet, during the hottest hours of noon they seldom feed, and ordinarily stand almost still, resting—for elephant very rarely lie down unless sick. Where they are afraid of man, their only enemy, they come out to feed in thinly forested plains, or cultivated fields, when they do so at all, only at night, and before daybreak move back into the forest to rest. Elsewhere they sometimes spend the day in the open, in grass or low bush. Where we were, at this time, on Kenia, the elephants sometimes moved down at night to feed in the shambas, at the expense of the crops of the natives, and sometimes stayed in the forest, feeding by day or night on the branches they tore off the trees, or, occasionally, on the roots they grubbed up with their tusks. They work vast havoc among the young or small growth of a forest, and the readiness with which they uproot, overturn, or break off medium-sized trees conveys a striking impression of their enormous strength. I have seen a tree a foot in diameter thus uprooted and over-turned.

The African elephant has never, like his Indian kins-man, been trained to man's use. There is still hope that the feat may be performed; but hitherto its probable eco-nomic usefulness has for various reasons seemed so ques-tionable that there has been scant encouragement to un-dergo the necessary expense and labor. Up to the present time the African elephant has yielded only his ivory as an asset of value. This, however, has been of such great value as wellnigh to bring about the mighty beast's utter extermi-nation. Ivory hunters and ivory traders have penetrated Africa to the haunts of the elephant since centuries before our era, and the elephant's boundaries have been slowly receding throughout historic time; but during the century just past its process has been immensely accelerated, until now there are but one or two out-of-the-way nooks of the Dark Continent to the neighborhood of which hunter and trader have not penetrated. Fortunately the civilized pow-ers which now divide dominion over Africa have waked

up in time, and there is at present no danger of the extermination of the lord of all four-footed creatures. Large
reserves have been established on which various herds of

Falls on slope of Kenia near first elephant camp
From a photograph by Edmund Heller

elephants now live what is, at least for the time being, an entire-ly safe life. Fur-thermore, over great tracts of territory outside the reserves reg-ulations have been promul-gated which, if enforced as they a r e   n o w en-forced, will pre-vent any exces-sive diminution of the herds. In British East Africa, for in-stance, no cows are allowed to be shot save for special pur-poses, as for preservation in a museum, or to safeguard life and property; and no bulls
with tusks weighing less than thirty pounds apiece. This
renders safe almost all the females and an ample supply of
breeding males. Too much praise cannot be given the
governments and the individuals who have brought about

this happy result; the credit belongs especially to England and to various Englishmen. It would be a veritable and most tragic calamity if the lordly elephant, the giant among existing four-footed creatures, should be permitted to vanish from the face of the earth.

But of course protection is not permanently possible over the greater part of that country which is well fitted for settlement ; nor anywhere, if the herds grow too numerous. It would be not merely silly, but worse than silly, to try to stop all killing of elephants. The unchecked increase of any big and formidable wild beast, even though not a flesh-eater, is incompatible with the existence of man when he has emerged from the stage of lowest savagery.

Elephant trail in bamboo
From a photograph by J. Alden Loring

This is not a matter of theory, but of proved fact. In place after place in Africa where protection has been extended to hippopotamus or buffalo, rhinoceros or elephant, it has been found necessary to withdraw it because the protected animals did such damage to property, or became such menaces to human life. Among all four species cows with calves often attack men without provocation, and old bulls are at any time likely to become infected by a spirit of wanton and ferocious mischief and apt to become man-killers. I know settlers who tried to preserve the rhinoceros which they found living on their big farms, and who were obliged to abandon the attempt, and themselves to kill the rhinos because of repeated and wanton attacks on human beings by the latter. Where we were by Neri, a year or two before our visit, the rhinos had become so dangerous, killing one white man and several natives, that the district commissioner who preceded Mr. Browne was forced to undertake a crusade against them, killing fifteen. Both in South Africa and on the Nile protection extended to hippopotamus has in places been wholly withdrawn because of the damage done by the beasts to the crops of the natives, or because of their unprovoked assaults on canoes and boats. In one instance a last surviving hippo was protected for years, but finally grew bold because of immunity, killed a boy in sheer wantonness, and had to be himself slain. In Uganda the buffalo were for years protected, and grew so bold, killed so many natives, and ruined so many villages, that they are now classed as vermin and their destruction in every way encouraged. In the very neighborhood where I was hunting at Kenia, but six weeks before my coming, a cow buffalo had wandered down into the plains and run amuck, had attacked two villages, had killed a man and a boy, and had then been mobbed to death by the spearmen. Elephant, when in numbers, and when not possessed of the fear of man, are more impossible neighbors than hippo, rhino, or buffalo; but they are so eagerly sought after by ivory hunters that it is only rarely that they get the chance to become really dangerous to life, although in many places their ravages among the crops are severely felt by the unfortunate natives who live near them.

The chase of the elephant, if persistently followed, entails more fatigue and hardship than any other kind of African hunting. As regards risk, it is hard to say whether it is more or less dangerous than the chase of the lion and the buffalo. Both Cuninghame and Tarlton, men of wide experience, ranked elephant hunting, in point of danger,

Camping after death of the first bull

The porters exult over the death of the bull

From photographs by Edmund Heller

as nearly on the level with lion hunting, and as more dangerous than buffalo hunting; and all three kinds as far more dangerous than the chase of the rhino. Personally, I believe the actual conflict with a lion, where the conditions are the same, to be normally the more dangerous sport; though far greater demands are made by elephant hunting on the qualities of personal endurance and hardihood and resolute perseverance in the face of disappointment and difficulty. Buffalo, seemingly, do not charge as freely as elephant, but are more dangerous when they do charge. Rhino when hunted, though at times ugly customers, seem to me certainly less dangerous than the other three; but from sheer stupid truculence they are themselves apt to take the offensive in unexpected fashion, being far more prone to such aggression than are any of the others—man-eating lions always excepted.

Very few of the native tribes in Africa hunt the elephant systematically. But the 'Ndorobo, the wild bush people of East Africa, sometimes catch young elephants in the pits they dig with slow labor, and very rarely they kill one with a kind of harpoon. The 'Ndorobo are doubtless in part descended from some primitive bush people, but in part also derive their blood from the more advanced tribes near which their wandering families happen to live; and they grade into the latter, by speech and through individuals who seem to stand half-way between. Thus we had with us two Masai 'Ndorobo, true wild people, who spoke a bastard Masai; who had formerly hunted with Cuninghame, and who came to us because of their ancient friendship with him. These shy woods creatures were afraid to come to Neri by daylight, when we were camped there, but after dark crept to Cuninghame's tent. Cuninghame gave them two fine red blankets, and put them to sleep in a little tent, keeping their spears in his own tent, as a measure of precaution to prevent their running away. The elder of the two, he informed me, would certainly have a fit of hysterics when we killed our elephant! Cuninghame was also joined by other old friends of former hunts, Kikuyu 'Ndorobo these, who spoke Kikuyu like the people who cultivated the fields that covered the river-bottoms and hill-sides of the adjoining open country, and who were, indeed, merely outlying, forest-dwelling members of the lowland tribes. In the deep woods we met one old Dorobo, who had no connection with any more advanced tribe, whose sole belongings were his spear, skin cloak, and fire stick, and who lived purely on honey and game; unlike the bastard 'Ndorobo, he was ornamented with neither paint nor grease. But the 'Ndorobo who were our guides stood farther up in the social scale. The men passed most of their time in the forest, but up the mountain sides they had squalid huts on little clearings, with shambas, where their wives raised scanty crops. To the 'Ndorobo, and to them alone, the vast, thick forest was an open book; without their aid as guides both Cuninghame and our own gun-bearers were at fault, and found their way around with great difficulty and slowness. The bush people had nothing in the way of clothing save a blanket over the shoulders, but wore the usual paint and grease and ornaments; each carried a spear which might have a long and narrow, or short and broad blade; two of them wore head-dresses *of tripe*—skull-caps made from the inside of a sheep's stomach.

The 'Ndorobo who had hysterics on the elephant

From a photograph by Edmund Heller

For two days after reaching our camp in the open glade on the mountain side it rained. We were glad of this, because it meant that the elephants would not be in the bamboos, and Cuninghame and the 'Ndorobo went off to hunt for fresh signs. Cuninghame is as skilful an elephant hunter as can be found in Africa, and is one of the very few white men able to help even the wild bushmen at their work. By the afternoon of the second day they were fairly well satisfied as to the whereabouts of the quarry.

The following morning a fine rain was still falling when Cuninghame, Heller, and I started on our hunt; but by noon it had stopped. Of course we went in single file and on foot; not even a bear hunter from the cane-brakes of the lower Mississippi could ride through that forest. We left our home camp standing, taking blankets and a coat and change of underclothing for each of us, and two small Whymper tents, with enough food for three days; I also took my wash kit and a book from the Pigskin Library. First marched the 'Ndorobo guides, each with his spear, his blanket round his shoulders, and a little bundle of corn and sweet-potato. Then came Cuninghame, followed by his gun-bearer. Then I came, clad in khaki-colored flannel shirt and khaki trousers buttoning down the legs, with hobnailed shoes and a thick slouch hat; I had intended to wear rubber-soled shoes, but the soaked ground was too slippery. My two gun-bearers followed, carrying the Holland and the Springfield. Then came Heller, at the head of a dozen porters and skinners; he and they were to fall behind when we actually struck fresh elephant spoor, but to follow our trail by the help of a Dorobo who was left with them.

For three hours our route lay along the edge of the woods. We climbed into and out of deep ravines in which groves of tree-ferns clustered. We waded through streams of swift water, whose course was broken by cataract and rapid. We passed through shambas, and by the doors of little hamlets of thatched beehive huts. We met flocks of goats and hairy, fat-tailed sheep guarded by boys; strings of burden-bearing women stood meekly to one side to let us pass; parties of young men sauntered by, spear in hand.

Then we struck into the great forest, and in an instant the sun was shut from sight by the thick screen of wet foliage. It was a riot of twisted vines, interlacing the trees and bushes. Only the elephant paths, which, of every age, crossed and recrossed it hither and thither, made it passable. One of the chief difficulties in hunting elephants in the forest is that it is impossible to travel, except very slowly and with much noise, off these trails, so that it is sometimes very difficult to take advantage of the wind; and although the sight of the elephant is dull, both its sense of hearing and its sense of smell are exceedingly acute.

Hour after hour we worked our way onward through tangled forest and matted jungle. There was little sign of bird or animal life. A troop of long-haired black-and-white monkeys bounded away among the tree tops. Here and there brilliant flowers lightened the gloom. We ducked under vines and climbed over fallen timber. Poisonous nettles stung our hands. We were drenched by the wet boughs which we brushed aside. Mosses and ferns grew rank and close. The trees were of strange kinds. There were huge trees with little leaves, and small trees with big leaves. There were trees with bare, fleshy limbs, that writhed out through the neighboring branches, bearing sparse clusters of large frondage. In places the forest was low, the trees thirty or forty feet high, the bushes that choked the ground between, fifteen or twenty feet high. In other places mighty monarchs of the wood, straight and tall, towered aloft to an immense height; among them were trees whose smooth, round boles were spotted like sycamores, while far above our heads their gracefully spreading branches were hung with vines like mistletoe and draped with Spanish moss; trees whose surfaces were corrugated and knotted as if they were made of bundles of great creepers; and giants whose buttressed trunks were four times a man's length across.

Twice we got on elephant spoor, once of a single bull, once of a party of three. Then Cuninghame and the 'Ndorobo redoubled their caution. They would minutely examine the fresh dung; and above all they continually tested the wind, scanning the tree tops, and lighting matches to see from the smoke what the eddies were near the ground. Each time after an hour's stealthy stepping and crawling along the twisted trail a slight shift of the wind in the almost still air gave our scent to the game, and away it went before we could catch a glimpse of it; and we resumed our walk. The elephant paths led up hill and down—for the beasts are wonderful climbers—and wound in and out in every direction. They were marked by broken branches and the splintered and shattered trunks of the smaller trees, especially where the elephant had stood and fed, trampling down the bushes for many yards around. Where they had crossed the marshy valleys they had punched big round holes, three feet deep, in the sticky mud.

As evening fell we pitched camp by the side of a little brook at the bottom of a ravine, and dined ravenously on bread, mutton, and tea. The air was keen, and under our blankets we slept in comfort until dawn. Breakfast was soon over and camp struck; and once more we began our cautious progress through the dim, cool archways of the mountain forest.

The chief who acted as guide through shambas country near first elephant camp

From a photograph by Edmund Heller

Two hours after leaving camp we came across the fresh trail of a small herd of perhaps ten or fifteen elephant cows and calves, but including two big herd bulls. At once we took up the trail. Cuninghame and his bush people consulted again and again, scanning every track and mark with minute attention. The sign showed that the elephants had fed in the shambas early in the night, had then returned to the mountain, and stood in one place resting for several hours, and had left this sleeping ground some time before we reached it. After we had followed the trail a short while we made the experiment of trying to force our own way through the jungle, so as to get the wind more favorable; but our progress was too slow and noisy, and we returned to the path the elephants had beaten. Then the 'Ndorobo went ahead, travelling noiselessly and at speed. One of them was clad in a white blanket, and another in a red one, which were conspicuous; but they were too silent and cautious to let the beasts see them, and could tell exactly where they were and what they were doing by the sounds. When these trackers waited for us they would appear before us like ghosts; once one of them dropped down from the branches above, having climbed a tree with monkey-like agility to get a glimpse of the great game.

At last we could hear the elephants, and under Cuninghame's lead we walked more cautiously than ever. The wind was right, and the trail of one elephant led close alongside that of the rest of the herd, and parallel thereto. It was about noon. The elephants moved slowly, and we listened to the boughs crack, and now and then to the curious internal rumblings of the great beasts. Carefully, every sense on the alert, we kept pace with them. My double-barrel was in my hands, and wherever possible, as I followed the trail, I stepped in the huge footprints of the elephant, for where such a weight had pressed there were no sticks left to crack under my feet. It made our veins thrill thus for half an hour to creep stealthily along, but a few rods from the herd, never able to see it, because of the extreme denseness of the cover, but always hearing first one and then another of its members, and always trying to guess what each one might do, and keeping ceaselessly ready for whatever might befall. A flock of hornbills flew up with noisy clamor, but the elephants did not heed them.

At last we came in sight of the mighty game. The trail took a twist to one side, and there, thirty yards in front of us, we made out part of the gray and massive head of an elephant resting his tusks on the branches of a young tree. A couple of minutes passed before, by cautious scrutiny, we were able to tell whether the animal was a cow or a bull, and whether, if a bull, it carried heavy enough tusks. Then we saw that it was a big bull with good ivory. It turned its head in my direction and I saw its eye; and I fired a little to one side of the eye, at a spot which I thought would lead to the brain. I struck exactly where I aimed, but the head of an elephant is enormous and the brain small, and the bullet missed it. However, the shock momentarily stunned the beast. He stumbled forward, half falling, and as he recovered I fired with the second barrel, again aiming for the brain. This time the bullet sped true, and as I lowered the rifle from my shoulder, I saw the great lord of the forest come crashing to the ground.

But at that very instant, before there was a moment's time in which to reload, the thick bushes parted immediately on my left front, and through them surged the vast bulk of a charging bull elephant, the matted mass of tough creepers snapping like packthread before his rush. He was so close that he could have touched me with his trunk. I leaped to one side and dodged behind a tree trunk, opening the rifle, throwing out the empty shells, and slipping in two cartridges. Meanwhile Cuninghame fired right and left, at the same time throwing himself into the bushes on the other side. Both his bullets went home, and the bull stopped short in his charge, wheeled, and immediately disappeared in the thick cover. We ran forward, but the forest had closed over his wake. We heard him trumpet shrilly, and then all sounds ceased.

The 'Ndorobo, who had quite properly disappeared when this second bull charged, now went forward and soon returned with the report that he had fled at speed, but was evidently hard hit, as there was much blood on the spoor.

If we had been only after ivory we should have followed him at once; but there was no telling how long a chase he might lead us; and as we desired to save the skin of the dead elephant entire, there was no time whatever to spare.

It is a formidable task, occupying many days, to preserve an elephant for mounting in a museum, and if the skin is to be properly saved, it must be taken off without an hour's unnecessary delay.

So back we turned to where the dead tusker lay, and I felt proud indeed as I stood by the immense bulk of the slain monster and put my hand on the ivory. The tusks weighed a hundred and thirty pounds the pair. There was the usual scene of joyful excitement among the gun-bearers—who had behaved excellently—and among the wild bush people who had done

Tree-ferns on slopes of Kenia near first elephant camp

From a photograph by Edmund Heller

the tracking for us; and, as Cuninghame had predicted, the old Masai Dorobo, from pure delight, proceeded to have hysterics on the body of the dead elephant. The scene was repeated when Heller and the porters appeared half an hour later. Then, chattering like monkeys, and as happy as possible, all, porters, gun-bearers, and 'Ndorobo alike, began the work of skinning and cutting up the quarry, under the leadership and supervision of Heller and Cuninghame, and soon they were all splashed with blood

from head to foot. One of the trackers took off his blanket and squatted stark naked inside the carcass the better to use his knife. Each laborer rewarded himself by cutting off strips of meat for his private store, and hung them in red festoons from the branches round about. There was no let up in the work until it was stopped by darkness.

Our tents were pitched in a small open glade a hundred yards from the dead elephant. The night was clear, the stars shone brightly, and in the west the young moon hung just above the line of tall tree tops. Fires were speedily kindled and the men sat around them, feasting and singing in a strange minor tone until late in the night. The flickering light left them at one moment in black obscurity, and the next brought into bold relief their sinewy crouching figures, their dark faces,

Suliman Na Meru, one of the elephant guides

From a photograph by Kermit Roosevelt

gleaming eyes, and flashing teeth. When they did sleep, two of the 'Ndorobo slept so close to the fire as to burn themselves; an accident to which they are prone, judging from the many scars of old burns on their legs. I toasted slices of elephant's heart on a pronged stick before the fire, and found it delicious; for I was hungry, and the night was cold. We talked of our success and exulted over it, and made our plans for the morrow; and then we turned in under our blankets for another night's sleep.

Next morning some of the 'Ndorobo went off on the trail of Cuninghame's elephant to see if it had fallen, but found that it had travelled steadily, though its wounds were probably mortal. There was no object in my staying, for Heller and Cuninghame would be busy for the next ten days, and would ultimately have to use all the porters in taking off and curing the skin, and transporting it to Neri; so I made up my mind to go down to the plains for a hunt by myself. Taking one porter to carry my bedding, and with my gun-bearers, and a Dorobo as guide, I struck off through the forest for the main camp, reaching it early in the afternoon. Thence I bundled off a safari to Cuninghame and Heller, with food for a week, and tents and clothing; and then enjoyed the luxury of a shave and a warm bath. Next day was spent in writing and making preparations for my own trip. A Kikuyu chief, clad in a cloak of hyrax skins, and carrying his war spear, came to congratulate me on killing the elephant and to present me with a sheep. Early the following morning everything was in readiness; the bull-necked porters lifted their loads, I stepped out in front, followed by my led horse, and in ten hours' march we reached Neri boma, with its neat buildings, its trees, and its well-kept flower beds.

My hunting and travelling during the following fortnight will be told in the next chapter. On the evening of September 6th we were all together again at Meru boma, on the north-eastern slopes of Kenia—Kermit, Tarlton, Cuninghame, Heller, and I. Thanks to the unfailing kindness of the commissioner, Mr. Horne, we were given full information of the elephant in the neighborhood. He had no 'Ndorobo, but among the Wa-Meru, a wild martial tribe, who lived close around him, there were a number of hunters, or at least of men who knew the forest and the game, and these had been instructed to bring in any news.

We had, of course, no idea that elephant would be found close at hand. But next morning, about eleven,

Horne came to our camp with four of his black scouts, who reported that three elephants were in a patch of thick jungle beside the shambas, not three miles away. Horne said that the elephants were cows, that they had been in the neighborhood some days, devastating the shambas, and were bold and fierce, having charged some men who sought to drive them away from the cultivated fields; it is curious to see how little heed these elephants pay to the natives. I wished a cow for the museum, and also another bull. So off we started at once, Kermit carrying his camera. I slipped on my rubber-soled shoes, and had my gun-bearers accompany me barefooted, with the Holland and the Springfield rifles. We followed foot-paths among the fields until we reached the edge of the jungle in which the elephants stood.

This jungle lay beside the forest, and at this point separated it from the fields. It consisted of a mass of rank-growing bushes, allied to the cotton-plant, ten or twelve feet high, with only here and there a tree. It was not good ground in which to hunt elephant, for the tangle was practically impenetrable to a hunter save along the elephant trails, whereas the elephants themselves could move in any direction at will, with no more difficulty than a man would have in a hay-field. The bushes in most places rose just above their backs, so that they were completely hid from the hunter even a few feet away. Yet the cover afforded no shade to the mighty beasts, and it seemed strange that elephants should stand in it at mid-day with the sun out. There they were, however, for, looking cautiously into the cover from behind the bushes on a slight hill-crest quarter of a mile off, we could just make out a huge ear now and then as it lazily flapped.

On account of the wind we had to go well to one side before entering the jungle. Then in we went in single file, Cuninghame and Tarlton leading, with a couple of our naked guides. The latter showed no great desire to get too close, explaining that the elephants were "very fierce."

Once in the jungle, we trod as quietly as possible, threading our way along the elephant trails, which crossed and recrossed one another. Evidently it was a favorite haunt, for the sign was abundant, both old and new. In the impenetrable cover it was quite impossible to tell just where the elephants were, and twice we sent one of the savages up

Trunk of giant fig-tree in Kenia forest
From a photograph by Edmund Heller

a tree to locate the game. The last time the watcher, who stayed in the tree, indicated by signs that the elephant were not far off; and his companions wished to lead us round to where the cover was a little lower and thinner. But to do so would have given them our wind, and Cuninghame refused, taking into his own hands the management of the stalk. I kept my heavy rifle at the ready, and on we went, in watchful silence, prepared at any moment for a charge. We could not tell at what second we might catch our first glimpse at very close quarters of "the beast that hath between his eyes the serpent for a hand," and when thus surprised the temper of "the huge earth-shaking beast" is sometimes of the shortest.

Cuninghame and Tarlton stopped for a moment to consult; Cuninghame stooped, and Tarlton mounted his shoulders and stood upright, steadying himself by my hand. Down he came and told us that he had seen a small tree shake seventy yards distant; although upright on Cuninghame's shoulders he could not see the elephant itself. Forward we stole for a few yards, and then a piece of good luck befell us, for we came on the trunk of a great fallen tree, and scrambling up, we found ourselves perched in a row six feet above the ground. The highest part of the trunk was near the root, farthest from where the elephants were; and though it offered precarious footing, it also offered the best lookout. Thither I balanced, and looking over the heads of my companions I at once made out the elephant. At first I could see nothing but the shaking branches, and one huge ear occasionally flapping. Then I made out the ear of another beast, and then the trunk of a third was uncurled, lifted, and curled again; it showered its back with earth. The watcher we had left behind in the tree top coughed; the elephants stood motionless, and up went the biggest elephant's trunk, feeling for the wind; the watcher coughed again, and then the bushes and saplings swayed and parted as three black bulks came toward us. The cover was so high that we could not see their tusks, only the tops of their heads and their backs being visible. The leader was the biggest, and at it I fired when it was sixty yards away, and nearly broadside on, but heading slightly toward me. I had previously warned every one to kneel. The recoil of the heavy rifle made me rock, as I stood unsteadily on my perch, and I failed to hit the brain. But the bullet, only missing the brain by an inch or two, brought the elephant to its knees; as it rose I floored it with the second barrel. The blast of the big rifle, by the way, was none too pleasant for the other men on the log and made Cuninghame's nose bleed. Reloading, I fired twice at the next animal, which was now turning. It stumbled and nearly fell, but at the same

The charging bull elephant

"He could have touched me with his trunk"

Drawn by Philip R. Goodwin from photographs and from descriptions furnished by Mr. Roosevelt

moment the first one rose again, and I fired both barrels into its head, bringing it once more to the ground. Once again it rose—an elephant's brain is not an easy mark to hit under such conditions—but as it moved slowly off, half stunned, I snatched the little Springfield rifle, and this time shot true, sending the bullet into its brain. As it fell I took another shot at the wounded elephant, now disappearing in the forest, but without effect.

On walking up to our prize it proved to be not a cow, but a good-sized adult (but not old) herd bull, with thick, short tusks, weighing about forty pounds apiece. Ordinarily, of course, a bull, and not a cow, is what one desires, although on this occasion I needed a cow to complete the group for the National Museum. However, Heller and Cuninghame spent the next few days in preserving the skin, which I afterward gave to the University of California; and I was too much pleased with our luck to feel inclined to grumble. We were back in camp five hours after leaving it. Our gun-bearers usually felt it incumbent on them to keep a dignified bearing while in our company. But the death of an elephant is always a great event; and one of the gun-bearers, as they walked ahead of us campward, soon began to improvise a song, reciting the success of the hunt, the death of the elephant, and the power of the rifles; and gradually, as they got farther ahead, the more light-hearted among them began to give way to their spirits and they came into camp frolicking, gambolling, and dancing as if they were still the naked savages that they had been before they became the white man's followers.

Two days later Kermit got his bull. He and Tarlton had camped about ten miles off in a magnificent forest, and late the first afternoon received news that a herd of elephants was in the neighborhood. They were off by dawn, and in a few hours came on the herd. It consisted chiefly of cows and calves, but there was one big master bull, with fair tusks. It was open forest with long grass. By careful

stalking they got within thirty yards of the bull, behind
whom was a line of cows. Kermit put both barrels of his
heavy double .450 into the tusker's head, but without even
staggering him; and as he walked off Tarlton also fired
both barrels into him, with no more effect; then, as he
slowly turned, Kermit killed him with a shot in the brain
from the .405 Winchester. Immediately the cows lifted
their ears, and began trumpeting and threatening; if they
had come on in a body at that distance, there was not
much chance of turning them or of escaping from them:
and after standing stock still for a minute or two, Kermit
and Tarlton stole quietly off for a hundred yards, and
waited until the anger of the cows cooled and they had
moved away, before going up to the dead bull. Then they
followed the herd again, and Kermit got some photos
which, as far as I know, are better than any that have
ever before been taken of wild elephant. He took them
close up, at imminent risk of a charge.

The following day the two hunters rode back to Meru,
making a long circle. The elephants they saw were not
worth shooting, but they killed the finest rhinoceros we had
yet seen. They saw it in an open space of tall grass, surrounded by lantana brush, a flowering shrub with close-
growing stems, perhaps twenty feet high and no thicker
than a man's thumb; it forms a favorite cover for elephants
and rhinoceros, and is wellnigh impenetrable to hunters.
Fortunately this particular rhino was outside it, and Kermit and Tarlton got up to about twenty-five yards from
him. Kermit then put one bullet behind his shoulder,
and as he whipped round to charge, another bullet on the
point of his shoulder; although mortally wounded, he
showed no signs whatever of being hurt, and came at the
hunters with great speed and savage desire to do harm.
Then an extraordinary thing happened. Tarlton fired,
inflicting merely a flesh wound in one shoulder, and the
big, fearsome brute, which had utterly disregarded the two
fatal shots, on receiving this flesh wound, wheeled and ran.

The first bull elephant

From a photograph by R. J. Cuninghame

Both firing, they killed him before he had gone many yards. He was a bull, with a thirty-inch horn.

By this time Cuninghame and Heller had finished the skin and skeleton of the bull they were preserving. Near the carcass Heller trapped an old male leopard, a savage beast; its skin was in fine shape, but it was not fat, and weighed just one hundred pounds. Now we all joined, and shifted camp to a point eight or nine miles distant from Meru boma, and fifteen hundred feet lower among the foot-hills. It was much hotter at this lower level; palms were among the trees that bordered the streams. On the day we shifted camp Tarlton and I rode in advance to look for elephants, followed by our gun-bearers and half a dozen wild Meru hunters, each carrying a spear or a bow and arrows. When we reached the hunting grounds, open country with groves of trees and patches of jungle, the Meru went off in every direction to find elephant. We waited their return under a tree, by a big stretch of culti- vated ground. The region was well peopled, and all the way down the path had led between fields, which the Meru women were tilling with their adze-like hoes, and banana plantations, where among the bananas other trees had been planted, and the yam vines trained up their trunks. These cool, shady banana plantations, fenced in with tall hedges and bordered by rapid brooks, were really very attractive. Among them were scattered villages of conical thatched huts, and level places plastered with cow dung on which the grain was threshed; it was then stored in huts raised on posts. There were herds of cattle, and flocks of sheep and goats; and among the burdens the women bore we often saw huge bottles of milk. In the shambas there were platforms, and sometimes regular thatched huts, placed in the trees; these were for the watchers, who were to keep the elephants out of the shambas at night. Some of the natives wore girdles of banana leaves, looking, as Kermit said, much like the pictures of savages in Sun- day-school books.

1

IX

K. R.

a herd of elephant in an open forest of high timber; taken by Kermit from the a distance of about 25 yards; he was on the dead limb of a tree some about 5 or 6 feet from the ground.

[This, and the next two pictures, 2 & 3, are the best pictures of wild elephant ever taken; they should be copyrighted, & put both in the Magazine & the book]

Mr. Roosevelt's description of one of the elephant pictures—written on the back of it

Early in the afternoon some of the scouts returned with news that three bull elephants were in a piece of forest a couple of miles distant, and thither we went. It was an open grove of heavy thorn timber beside a strip of swamp; among the trees the grass grew tall, and there were many thickets of arbutilon, a flowering shrub a dozen feet high. On this the elephant were feeding. Tarlton's favorite sport was lion hunting, but he was also a first-class elephant hunter, and he brought me up to these bulls in fine style. Although only three hundred yards away, it took us two hours to get close to them. Tarlton and the "shenzis"—wild natives, called in Swahili (a kind of African chinook) "wa-shenzi"—who were with us, climbed tree after tree, first to place the elephants, and then to see if they carried ivory heavy enough to warrant my shooting them. At last Tarlton brought me to within fifty yards

A herd of elephant in an open forest of high timber

Taken by Kermit from a distance of about twenty-five yards; he was on the dead limb of a tree five or six feet from the ground

From a photograph, copyright, by Kermit Roosevelt

The herd getting uneasy

From a pho ograph, copyright, by Kermit Roosevelt

The same herd on the eve of charging

Immediately after taking this picture, Kermit had to quietly make his escape, slipping off among the trees to avoid the charge; he did not wish to shoot any of the herd if it could be avoided

From a photograph, copyright, by Kermit Roosevelt

of them. Two were feeding in bush which hid them from
view, and the third stood between, facing us. We could
only see the top of his head and back, and not his tusks, and
could not tell whether he was worth shooting. Much puzzled we stood where we were, peering anxiously at the huge
half-hidden game. Suddenly there was a slight eddy in
the wind, up went the elephant's trunk, twisting to and fro
in the air; evidently he could not catch a clear scent; but
in another moment we saw the three great dark forms
moving gently off through the bush. As rapidly as possible, following the trails already tramped by the elephants,
we walked forward, and after a hundred yards Tarlton
pointed to a big bull with good tusks standing motionless
behind some small trees seventy yards distant. As I aimed
at his head he started to move off; the first bullet from the
heavy Holland brought him to his knees, and as he rose I
knocked him flat with the second. He struggled to rise;
but, both firing, we kept him down; and I finished him
with a bullet in the brain from the little Springfield. Although rather younger than either of the bulls I had already
shot, it was even larger. In its stomach were beans from
the shambas, abutilon tips, and bark, and especially the
twigs, leaves, and white blossoms of a smaller shrub. The
tusks weighed a little over a hundred pounds the pair.

We still needed a cow for the museum; and a couple
of days later, at noon, a party of natives brought in word
that they had seen two cows in a spot five miles away.
Piloted by a naked spearman, whose hair was done into a
cue, we rode toward the place. For most of the distance
we followed old elephant trails, in some places mere tracks
beaten down through stiff grass which stood above the
head of a man on horseback, in other places paths rutted
deep into the earth. We crossed a river, where monkeys
chattered among the tree tops. On an open plain we saw
a rhinoceros cow trotting off with her calf. At last we came
to a hill-top with, on the summit, a noble fig-tree, whose
giant limbs were stretched over the palms that clustered

beneath. Here we left our horses and went forward on foot, crossing a palm-fringed stream in a little valley. From the next rise we saw the backs of the elephants as they stood in a slight valley, where the rank grass grew ten or twelve feet high. It was some time before we could see the ivory so as to be sure of exactly what we were shooting. Then the biggest cow began to move slowly forward, and we walked nearly parallel to her, along an elephant trail, until from a slight knoll I got a clear view of her at a distance of eighty yards. As she walked leisurely along, almost broadside to me, I fired the right barrel of the Holland into her head, knocking her flat down with the shock; and when she rose I put a bullet from the left barrel through her heart, again knocking her completely off her feet; and this time she fell permanently. She was a very old cow, and her ivory was rather better than in the average of her sex in this neighborhood, the tusks weighing about eighteen pounds apiece. She had been ravaging the shambas overnight—which accounted in part for the natives being so eager to show her to me—and in addition to leaves and grass, her stomach contained quantities of beans. There was a young one—just out of calfhood, and quite able to take care of itself—with her; it ran off as soon as the mother fell.

Early next morning Cuninghame and Heller shifted part of the safari to the stream near where the dead elephant lay, intending to spend the following three days in taking off and preparing the skin. Meanwhile Tarlton, Kermit, and I were to try our luck in a short hunt on the other side of Meru boma, at a little crater lake called Lake Ingouga. We could not get an early start, and reached Meru too late to push on to the lake the same day.

The following morning we marched to the lake in two hours and a half. We spent an hour in crossing a broad tongue of woodland that stretched down from the wonderful mountain forest lying higher on the slopes. The trail was blind in many places because elephant paths of every

age continually led along and across it, some of them being much better marked than the trail itself, as it twisted
through the sun-flecked shadows underneath the great trees.
Then we came out on high downs, covered with tall grass
and littered with volcanic stones; and broken by ravines
which were choked with dense underbrush.   There were
high hills, and to the left of the downs, toward Kenia, these
were clad in forest.   We pitched our tents on a steep cliff
overlooking the crater lake—or pond, as it might more
properly be called.   It was bordered with sedge, and through
the water-lilies on its surface we saw the reflection of the
new moon after nightfall.   Here and there thick forest came
down to the brink, and through this, on opposite sides of
the pond, deeply worn elephant paths, evidently travelled
for ages, wound down to the water.

That evening we hunted for bushbuck, but saw none.
While sitting on a hillock at dusk, watching for game, a
rhino trotted up to inspect us, with ears cocked forward
and tail erect.   A rhino always has something comic about
it, like a pig, formidable though it at times is.   This one
carried a poor horn, and therefore we were pleased when at
last it trotted off without obliging us to shoot it.   We saw
new kinds of whydah birds, one with a yellow breast, one
with white in its tail; at this altitude the cocks were still
in full plumage, although it was just past the middle of
September; whereas at Naivasha they had begun to lose
their long tail feathers nearly two months previously.

On returning to camp we received a note from Cuninghame saying that Heller had been taken seriously sick, and
Tarlton had to go to them.   This left Kermit and me to
take our two days' hunt together.

One day we got nothing.   We saw game on the open
downs, but it was too wary, and though we got within twenty-
five yards of eland in thick cover, we could only make out
a cow, and she took fright and ran without our ever getting
a glimpse of the bull that was with her.   Late in the afternoon we saw an elephant a mile and a half away, crossing

a corner of the open downs. We followed its trail until the light grew too dim for shooting, but never overtook it, although at the last we could hear it ahead of us breaking the branches; and we made our way back to camp through the darkness.

The other day made amends. It was Kermit's turn to shoot an elephant, and mine to shoot a rhinoceros; and each of us was to act as the backing gun for the other. In the forenoon, we saw a bull rhino with a good horn walking over the open downs. A convenient hill enabled us to cut him off without difficulty, and from its summit we killed him at the base, fifty or sixty yards off. His

A watch-tower in Meru shambas
From a photograph by Edmund Heller

front horn was nearly twenty-nine inches long; but though he was an old bull, his total length, from tip of nose to tip of tail, was only twelve feet, and he was, I should guess, not more than two-thirds the bulk of the big bull I killed in the Sotik.

We rested for an hour or two at noon, under the shade of a very old tree with glossy leaves, and orchids growing on its gnarled, hoary limbs, while the unsaddled horses grazed, and the gun-bearers slept near by, the cool moun-

Mr. Roosevelt's and Kermit's camp near which they got the rhino and elephant
From a photograph by Kermit Roosevelt

tain air, although this was mid-day under the equator, making them prefer the sunlight to the shade. When we moved on it was through a sea of bush ten or fifteen feet high, dotted here and there with trees; and riddled in every direction by the trails of elephant, rhinoceros, and buffalo. Each of these animals frequents certain kinds of country to which the other two rarely or never penetrate; but here they all three found ground to their liking. Except along their winding trails, which were tunnels where the jungle was tall, it would have been practically impossible to traverse the thick and matted cover in which they had made their abode.

We could not tell what moment we might find ourselves face to face with some big beast at such close quarters

A cow elephant

From a photograph by R. J. Cuninghame

as to insure a charge, and we moved in cautious silence, our rifles in our hands. Rhinoceros were especially plentiful, and we continually came across not only their tracks, but the dusty wallows in which they rolled, and where they came to deposit their dung. The fresh sign of elephant, however, distracted our attention from the lesser game, and we followed the big footprints eagerly, now losing the trail, now finding it again. At last near a clump of big trees we caught sight of three huge, dark bodies ahead of us. The wind was right, and we stole toward them, Kermit leading, and I immediately behind. Through the tangled branches their shapes loomed in vague outline; but we saw that one had a pair of long tusks, and our gun-bearers unanimously pronounced it a big bull, with good ivory. A few more steps gave Kermit a chance at its head, at about sixty yards, and with a bullet from his .405 Winchester he floored the mighty beast. It rose, and we both fired in unison, bringing it down again; but as we came up it struggled to get on its feet, roaring savagely, and once more we both fired together. This finished it. We were disappointed at finding that it was not a bull; but it was a large cow, with tusks over five feet long—a very unusual length for a cow—one weighing twenty-five, and the other twenty-two pounds.

Our experience had convinced us that both the Winchester .405, and the Springfield .300 would do good work with elephants; although I kept to my belief that, for such very heavy game, my Holland .500–.450 was an even better weapon.

Not far from where this elephant fell Tarlton had, the year before, witnessed an interesting incident. He was watching a small herd of elephants, cows and calves, which were in the open, when he saw them begin to grow uneasy. Then, with a shrill trumpet, a cow approached a bush, out of which bounded a big lion. Instantly all the cows charged him, and he fled as fast as his legs would carry him for the forest, two hundred yards distant. He just managed to reach the cover in safety; and then the infuriated cows, in their anger at his escape, demolished the forest for several rods in every direction.

CHAPTER XI

THE GUASO NYERO; A RIVER OF THE EQUATORIAL DESERT

WHEN I reached Neri, after coming down from killing my first elephant on Kenia, I was kept waiting two or three days before I could gather enough Kikuyu porters. As I could not speak a word of their language I got a couple of young Scotch settlers, very good fellows, to take charge of the safari out to where I intended to hunt. There was a party of the King's African Rifles camped at Neri; the powerful-looking enlisted men were from the south, chiefly from one of the northernmost tribes of Zulu blood, and their two officers were of the best Kipling-soldier type. Then there was another safari, that of Messrs. Kearton and Clark who were taking some really extraordinary photographs of birds and game. Finally, Governor and Mrs. Jackson arrived from a trip they had been making round Kenia; and I was much pleased to be able to tell the Governor, who had helped me in every way, about my bull elephant, and to discuss with him some of the birds we had seen and the mammals we had trapped. A great ingowa, a war-dance of the natives, was held in his honor, and the sight was, as always, one of interest and of a certain fascination. There was an Indian trader at Neri from whom we had obtained donkeys to carry to our elephant camp "posho," or food for the porters. He announced that they were all in readiness in a letter to Cuninghame, which was meant to be entirely respectful, but which sounded odd, as it was couched in characteristic Baboo English. The opening lines ran: "Dear K-ham, the donkeys are altogether deadly."

At last fifty Kikuyus assembled—they are not able to carry the loads of regular Swahili porters—and I started that moment, though it was too late in the afternoon to travel more than three or four miles. The Kikuyus were real savages, naked save for a dingy blanket, usually carried round the neck. They formed a picturesque safari; but it was difficult to make the grass-hopper-like creatures take even as much thought for the future as the ordinary happy-go-lucky porters take. At night if it rained they cowered under the bushes in drenched and shivering discomfort; and yet they had to be driven to make bough shelters for themselves. Once these shelters were up, and a little fire kindled at the entrance of each, the moping, spiritless wretches would speedily become transformed into beings who had lost all remembrance of ever having been wet or cold. After their posho had been distributed and eaten they would sit, huddled and cheerful, in their shelters, and sing steadily for a couple of hours.

Kikuyu warrior
From a photograph by Edmund Heller

Their songs were much wilder than those of the regular porters, and were often warlike. Occasionally, some "shanty man," as he would be called on shipboard, improvised or repeated a kind of story in short sentences or strophes; but the main feature of each song was the endless repetition of some refrain, musically chanted in chorus by the whole party. This repetition of a short sentence or refrain is a characteristic of many kinds of savage music; I have seen the Pawnees grow almost maddened by their triumph song, or victory song, which consisted of nothing whatever but the fierce, barking, wolf-like repetition of the words, "In the morning the wolves feasted."

Our first afternoon's march was uneventful; but I was amused at one of our porters and the "safari" ants. These safari ants are so called by the natives because they go on foraging expeditions in immense numbers. The big-headed warriors are able to inflict a really painful bite. In open spaces, as where crossing a path, the column makes a little sunken way through which it streams uninterruptedly. Whenever we came to such a safari ant column, in its sunken way, crossing our path, the porter in question laid two twigs on the ground as a peace-offering to the ants. He said that they were on safari, just as we were, and that it was wise to propitiate them.

That evening we camped in a glade in the forest. At nightfall dozens of the big black-and-white hornbill, croaking harshly, flew overhead, their bills giving them a curiously top-heavy look. They roosted in the trees near by.

Next day we came out on the plains, where there was no cultivation, and instead of the straggling thatch and wattle, unfenced villages of the soil-tilling Kikuyus, we found ourselves again among the purely pastoral Masai, whose temporary villages are arranged in a ring or oval, the cattle being each night herded in the middle, and the mud-daubed, cow-dung-plastered houses so placed that their backs form a nearly continuous circular wall, the spaces between being choked with thorn-bushes. I killed a steinbuck, missed a tommy, and at three hundred yards hit a Jackson's hartebeest too far back, and failed in an effort to ride it down.

The day after we were out on plains untenanted by human beings, and early in the afternoon struck water by

which to pitch our tents. There was not much game, and
it was shy; but I thought that I could kill enough to keep
the camp in meat so I sent back the two Scotchmen and
their Kikuyus, after having them build a thorn boma, or
fence, round the camp. One of the reasons why the Masai
had driven their herds and flocks off this plain was because a couple of lions had turned man-eaters, and had
killed a number of men and women. We saw no sign of
lions, and believed they had followed the Masai; but there
was no use in taking needless chances.

The camp was beside a cold, rapid stream, one of the
head-waters of the Guaso Nyero. It was heavily fringed
with thorn timber. To the east the crags and snow-
fields of Kenia rose from the slow swell of the mountain's
base. It should have been the dry season, but there were
continual heavy rains, which often turned into torrential
downpours. In the overcast mornings as I rode away from
camp, it was as cool as if I were riding through the fall
weather at home; at noon, if the sun came out, straight
overhead, the heat was blazing; and we generally returned
to camp at nightfall, drenched with the cold rain. The
first heavy storm, the evening we pitched camp, much excited all my followers. Ali came rushing into the tent to
tell me that there was "a big snake up high." This certainly seemed worth investigating, and I followed him outside where everybody was looking at the "snake," which
proved to be a huge, funnel-shaped, whirling cloud, career-
ing across the darkened sky. It was a kind of waterspout
or cyclone; fortunately it passed to one side of camp.

The first day I hunted I shot only a steinbuck for the
table. The country alternated between bare plains and
great stretches of sparse, stunted thorns. We saw zebra,
and two or three bands of oryx; big, handsome antelope
strongly built and boldly colored, with long, black, rapier-
like horns. They were very wary, much more so than the
zebra with which they associated, and we could not get
anywhere near them.

Next day I hunted along the edges of a big swamp. We saw waterbuck, but were unable to get within shot. However, near the farther end of the swamp, in an open swale, we found four eland feeding. The eland is the king of antelope; and not only did I desire meat for camp, but I wished the head of a good bull as a trophy for myself, the eland I had hitherto shot being for the National Museum. The little band included a big bull, a small bull, and two cows; at a distance the big bull looked slaty blue. The great, sleek, handsome creatures were feeding in the long

Two Kikuyu boys
From a photograph by Edmund Heller

grass just like cattle, switching their long tails at the flies. The country looked like a park, with clumps of thorn-trees scattered over the grassy sward. Carefully I crept on all-fours from tree clump to tree clump, trying always to move when the elands' heads were down grazing. At last I was within three hundred yards, when one of the cows caught a glimpse of me and alarmed the others. They were startled, but puzzled, and after trotting a few rods turned to stare at the half-seen object of their alarm. Rising to my knee I shot the big bull in the throat as with head erect he gazed in my direction. Off he went with a rush, the others bounding and leaping as they accompanied him, and we followed on the blood spoor. Bakhari and Gouvimali trotted fast on the trail, and in order to be fresh for the shot I mounted Tranquillity. Suddenly out bounced the wounded bull from some bushes close by, and the horse nearly had a fit; I could hardly get off in

From a photograph by Theodore Roosevelt

My boma where I was camped before

T. R.

time to empty my magazine at long range— fortunately with effect. It was a magnificent bull of the variety called Patterson's eland, with a fine head. Few prize oxen would be as heavy, and in spite of its great size, its finely moulded limbs and beautiful coat gave it a thoroughly game look.

Oryx were now what I especially wished, and we devoted all of the following day to their pursuit. We saw three bands,

two of them accompanying herds of zebra, after the manner of kongoni. Both species were found indifferently on
the bare, short-grass flats and among the thin, stunted
thorn-trees which covered much of the plains. After a
careful stalk, the latter part on all-fours, I got to within
about three hundred yards of a mixed herd, and put a
bullet into one oryx as it faced me, and hit another as it
ran. The first, from its position, I thought I would surely
kill if I hit it at all, and both of the wounded beasts were
well behind the herd when it halted a mile away on the other
side of the plain. But as we approached they all went off
together, and I can only hope the two I hit recovered; at
any rate, after we had followed them for miles, the tough
beasts were still running as strongly as ever.

All the morning I manœuvred and tramped hard, in
vain. At noon, I tried a stalk on a little band of six, who
were standing still, idly switching their tails, out in a big
flat. They saw me, and at four hundred yards I missed the
shot. By this time I felt rather desperate, and decided for
once to abandon legitimate proceedings and act on the
Ciceronian theory, that he who throws the javelin all day
must hit the mark some time. Accordingly I emptied the
magazines of both my rifles at the oryx, as they ran across
my front, and broke the neck of a fine cow, at four hundred
and fifty yards. Six or seven hundred yards off the survivors stopped, and the biggest bull, evidently much put
out, uttered loud bawling grunts and drove the others
round with his horns. Meanwhile I was admiring the
handsome dun gray coat of my prize, its long tail and long,
sharp, slender horns, and the bold black and white markings on its face. Hardly had we skinned the carcass before
the vultures lit on it; with them were two marabou storks,
one of which I shot with a hard bullet from the Springfield.

The oryx, like the roan and sable, and in striking contrast to the eland, is a bold and hard fighter, and when
cornered will charge a man or endeavor to stab a lion. If
wounded it must be approached with a certain amount of

caution. The eland, on the other hand, in spite of its huge size, is singularly mild and inoffensive, an old bull being as inferior to an oryx in the will and power to fight as it is in speed and endurance. "Antelope," as I have said, is a very loose term, meaning simply any hollow-horned ruminant that isn't an ox, a sheep, or a goat. The eland is one of the group of tragelaphs, which are as different from the true antelopes, such as the gazelles, as they are from the oxen. One of its kinsfolk is the handsome little bushbuck, about as big as a white-tail deer; a buck of which Kermit had killed two specimens. The bushbuck is a wicked fighter, no other buck of its size being as dangerous; which makes the helplessness and timidity of its huge relative all the more striking.

An oryx bull

From a photograph by Theodore Roosevelt

I had kept four Kikuyus with me to accompany me on my hunts and carry in the skins and meat. They were with me on this occasion; and it was amusing to see how my four regular attendants, Bakhari and Gouvimali the gunbearers, Simba the sais, and Kiboko the skinner, looked down on their wild and totally uncivilized brethren. They would not associate with the "shenzis," as they called them; that is, savages or bush people. But the "shenzis" always amused and interested me; and this was especially true on the afternoon in question. Soon after we had started campward with the skin and meat of the oryx, we encountered a succession of thunder-storms. The rain came down in a deluge, so that the water stood ankle deep on the flats, the lightning flashed continuously on every side, and the terrific peals of thunder made one continuous roll. At first it maddened my horse; but the uninterrupted blaze and roar, just because uninterrupted, ended by making him feel that there was nothing to be done, and he plodded stolidly forward through the driving storm. My regular attendants accepted it with an entire philosophy, which was finally copied by the Kikuyus, who at first felt frightened. One of them had an old umbrella which he shared with a crony. He himself was carrying the marabou stork; his crony had long strips of raw oryx meat wound in a swollen girdle about his waist; neither had a stitch on save the blankets which were wrapped round their throats; and they clasped each other in a tight embrace as they walked along under the battered old umbrella.

In this desolate and lonely land the majesty of the storms impressed on the beholder a sense of awe and solemn exaltation. Tossing their crests, and riven by lightning, they gathered in their wrath from every quarter of the heavens, and darkness was before and under them; then, in the lull of a moment, they might break apart, while the sun turned the rain to silver and the rainbows were set in the sky; but always they gathered again, menacing and mighty,—for the promise of the bow was never kept, and ever the clouds returned after the rain. Once as I rode facing Kenia the clouds tore asunder, to right and left, and the mountain towered between, while across its base was flung a radiant arch. But almost at once the many-colored glory was dimmed; for in splendor and terror the storm strode in front, and shrouded all things from sight in thunder-shattered sheets of rain.

These days alone in the wilderness went by very pleasantly, and, as it was for not too long, I thoroughly enjoyed
being entirely by myself, so far as white men were concerned.   By this time I had become really attached to my
native followers, who looked after my interest and comfort
in every way; and in return I kept them supplied with
plenty of food, saw that they were well clothed, and forced
them to gather enough firewood to keep their tents dry and
warm at night—for cold, rainy weather is always hard upon
them.

Ali, my faithful head tent boy, and Shemlani his assistant—poor Bill the Kikuyu had left because of an intricate row with his fellows—were both, as they proudly
informed me, Arabs.   On the East African coast the so-
called Arabs almost all have native blood in them and
speak Swahili; the curious, newly created language of the
descendants of the natives whom the Arabs originally en-
slaved, and who themselves may have in their veins a little
Arab blood; in fact, the dividing line between Swahili
and Arab becomes impracticable for an outsider to draw
where, as is generally the case, it is patent that the blood of
both races is mixed to a degree at which it is only possible
to guess.   Ali spoke some English; and he and Shemlani were devoted and efficient servitors.   Bakhari the gun-
bearer was a Swahili, quite fearless with dangerous game,
rather sullen, and unmoved by any emotion that I could
ever discover.   He spoke a little English, but it could not be
called idiomatic.   One day we saw two ostriches, a cock
and a hen, with their chicks, and Bakhari with some excitement said, "Look, sah! ostrich! bull, cow, and pups!"
The other gun-bearer, Gouvimali, in some ways an even
better hunter, and always good-tempered, knew but one
English phrase; regularly every afternoon or evening, after
cleaning the rifle he had carried, he would say, as he left
the tent, his face wreathed in smiles, "G-o-o-d-e-bye!"
Gouvimali was a Wakamba, as were Simba and my other
sais, M'nyassa, who had taken the place of Hamisi (Hamisi

had broken down in health, his legs, as he assured me, becoming "very sick"). The cook, Roberti, was a mission boy, a Christian; we had several Christians with the safari, one being a headman, and all did excellently. I mention this because one so often hears it said that mission boys turn out worthless. Most of our men were heathens; and of course many, both of the Christians and the Mohammedans, were rather thinly veneered with the religions they respectively professed.

When in the morning we started on our hunt my gunbearers and sais, and the skinners, if any were along, walked silently behind me, on the lookout for game. Returning, they were apt to get in front, to pilot me back to camp. If, as at this time was generally the case, we returned with our heads bent to the rushing rain, they trudged sturdily ahead in dripping silence. If the weather was clear the spirits of the stalwart fellows were sure to rise until they found some expression. The Wakamba might break into song; or they might all talk together in Swahili, recounting the adventures of the day, and chaffing one another with uproarious laughter about any small misadventure; a difference of opinion as to the direction of camp being always a subject, first for earnest discussion, and then for much mirth at the expense of whomever the event proved mistaken.

My two horses, when I did not use them, grazed contentedly throughout the day near the little thorn boma which surrounded our tents; and at nightfall the friendly things came within it of their own accord to be given their feed of corn and be put in their own tent. When the sun was hot they were tormented by biting flies; but their work was easy, and they were well treated and throve. In the daytime vultures, kites, and white-necked ravens came round camp, and after nightfall jackals wailed and hyenas uttered their weird cries as they prowled outside the thorn walls. Twice, at midnight, we heard the ominous sighing or moaning of a hungry lion, and I looked to my rifle, which

always stood, loaded, at the head of my bed. But on
neither occasion did he come near us. Every night a fire
was kept burning in the entrance to the boma, and the
three askaris watched in turn, with instructions to call me

Ivory-nut palms on the Guaso Nyero
From a photograph by Theodore Roosevelt

if there was any
need.

I easily kept the
camp in meat, as I
had guessed that I
could do. My men
feasted on oryx
and eland, while
I reserved the
tongues and ten-
derloins for myself.
Each day I hunted
for eight or ten
hours, something
of interest always
happening. I
would not shoot
at the gazelles;
and the game I
did want was so
shy that almost all
my shots were at
long range, and
consequently a
number of them
did not hit. However, I came on my best oryx in rather
thick bush, and killed it at a hundred and twenty-five yards,
as it turned with a kind of sneeze of alarm or curiosity, and
stood broadside to me, the sun glinting on its handsome
coat and polished black horns. One of my Kikuyu followers
packed the skin entire to camp. I had more trouble with
another oryx, wounding it one evening at three hundred
and fifty yards, and next morning following the trail and

after much hard work and a couple of misses killing it with a shot at three hundred yards. On September 2, I found two newly born oryx calves. The color of the oryx made them less visible than hartebeest when a long way off on the dry plains. I noticed that whenever we saw them mixed in a herd with zebra, it was the zebra that first struck our eyes. But in bright sunlight, in bush, I also noticed that the zebra themselves were hard to see.

One afternoon, while skirting the edge of a marsh teeming with waders and water-fowl, I came across four stately Kavirondo cranes, specimens of which bird the naturalists had been particularly anxious to secure. They were not very shy for cranes, but they would not keep still, and I missed a shot with the Springfield as they walked along about a hundred and fifty yards ahead of me. However, they were unwise enough to circle round me when they rose, still keeping the same distance, and all the time uttering their musical call, while their great wings flapped in measured beats. Wing shooting with the rifle, even at such large birds of such slow and regular flight, is never easy, and they were rather far off; but with the last cartridge in my magazine—the fifth—I brought one whirling down through the air, the bullet having pierced his body. It was a most beautiful bird, black, white, and chestnut, with an erect golden crest, and long, lanceolate gray feathers on the throat and breast.

There were waterbuck and impalla in this swamp. I tried to get a bull of the former but failed. Several times I was within fifty yards of doe impalla and cow waterbuck, with their young, and watched them as they fed and rested, quite unconscious of my presence. Twice I saw steinbuck, on catching sight of me, lie down, hoping to escape observation. The red coat of the steinbuck is rather conspicuous, much more so than the coat of the duiker; yet it often tries to hide from possible foes.

Late in the afternoon of September 3, Cuninghame and Heller, with the main safari, joined me, and I greeted them joyfully; while my men were equally pleased to see their fellows, each shaking hands with his especial friends. Next morning we started toward Meru, heading north-east, toward the foot-hills of Kenia. The vegetation changed its character as we rose. By the stream where we had camped grew the great thorn-trees with yellow-green trunks which we had become accustomed to associate with the presence of herds of game. Out on the dry flats were other thorns, weazened little trees, or mere scrawny bushes, with swellings like bulbs on the branches and twigs, and the long thorns far more conspicuous than the scanty foliage; though what there was of this foliage, now brilliant green, was exquisite in hue and form, the sprays of delicate little leaves being as fine as the daintiest lace. On the foot-hills all these thorn-trees vanished. We did not go as high as the forest belt proper (here narrow, while above it the bamboos covered the mountain side), but tongues of juniper forest stretched down along the valleys which we crossed, and there were large patches of coarse deer fern, while among many unknown flowers we saw blue lupins, ox-eye daisies, and clover. That night we camped so high that it was really cold, and we welcomed the roaring fires of juniper logs.

We rose at sunrise. It was a glorious morning, clear and cool, and as we sat at breakfast, the table spread in the open on the dew-drenched grass, we saw in the south-east the peak of Kenia, and through the high, transparent air the snow-fields seemed so close as almost to dazzle our eyes. To the north and west we looked far out over the wide, rolling plains to a wilderness of mountain ranges, barren and jagged. All that day and the next we journeyed eastward, almost on the equator. At noon the overhead sun burned with torrid heat; but with the twilight—short compared to the long northern twilights, but not nearly as short as tropical twilights are often depicted—came the cold, and each night the frost was heavy. The country was un-tenanted by man. In the afternoon of the third day we

began to go downhill, and hour by hour the flora changed.
At last we came to a broad belt of woodland, where the
strange trees of many kinds grew tall and thick. Among
them were camphor-trees, and trees with gouty branch
tips, bearing leaves
like those of the
black walnut, and
panicles of lilac
flowers, changing
into brown seed
vessels; and other
trees, with clusters
of purple flowers,
and the seeds or
nuts enclosed in
hard pods or seed
vessels like huge
sausages.

The Guaso Nyero
From a photograph by Theodore Roosevelt

On the other
side of the forest
we came suddenly
out on the culti-
vated fields of the
Wa-Meru, who,
like the Kikuyu,
till the soil; and
among them, far-
ther down, was
Meru boma, its
neat, picturesque buildings beautifully placed among green
groves and irrigated fields, and looking out from its cool
elevation over the hot valleys beneath. It is one of the
prettiest spots in East Africa. We were more than hospitably received by the commissioner, Mr. Horne, who
had been a cow-puncher in Wyoming for seven years—
so that naturally we had much in common. He had built
the station himself, and had tamed the wild tribes around

by mingled firmness and good treatment; and he was a
mighty hunter, and helped us in every way.

Here we met Kermit and Tarlton, and heard all about
their hunt. They had been away from us for three weeks
and a half, along the Guaso Nyero, and had enjoyed first-
rate luck. Kermit had been particularly interested in a
caravan they had met, consisting of wild spear-bearing
Borani, people like Somalis, who were bringing down scores
of camels and hundreds of small horses to sell at Nairobi.
They had come from the north, near the outlying Abyssinian lands, and the caravan was commanded by an Arab of
stately and courteous manners. Such an extensive caravan journey was rare in the old days before English rule;
but one of the results of the "Pax Europaica," wherever
it obtains in German, French, or English Africa, is a great
increase of intercourse, commercial and social, among the
different tribes, even where widely separated. This caravan had been followed by lions; and a day or two afterward Kermit and Tarlton ran into what were probably
these very lions. There were eleven of them: a male with a
heavy mane, three lionesses, and seven cubs, some of them
about half grown. As Kermit and Tarlton galloped after
them, the lion took the lead, the cubs coming in the middle,
while the three lionesses loped along in the rear, guarding
their young. The lion cared little for his wives and offspring, and gradually drew ahead of them, while the two
horsemen, riding at full speed, made a wide détour round
the others in order to reach him; so that at last they got
between him and the ten lionesses and cubs, the big lion
coming first, the horsemen next, and then the lesser lions,
all headed the same way. As the horse-hooves thundered
closer the lion turned to bay. Kermit—whose horse had
once fallen with him in the chase—and Tarlton leaped
off their horses, and Kermit hit the lion with his first shot,
and, as it started to charge, mortally wounded it with a
second bullet. It turned and tried to reach cover, and
Tarlton stopped it with a third shot; for there was no time

to lose, as they wished to tackle the other lions. After a sharp gallop they rounded up the lionesses and cubs. Kermit killed one large cub, which they mistook for a lioness; wounded a lioness which for the time being escaped; killed another with a single bullet from his 30-40 Winchester—for the others he used his .405 Winchester—and hit the third as she crouched facing him at two hundred

A Boran camp
From a photograph by Kermit Roosevelt

yards. She at once came in at full speed, making a most determined charge. Kermit and Tarlton were standing near their horses. The lioness came on with great bounds so that Kermit missed her twice, but broke her shoulder high up when she was but thirty yards off. She fell on her head and, on rising, galloped, not at the men, but at the horses, who, curiously enough, paid no heed to her. Tarlton stopped her with a bullet in the nick of time, just before she reached them, and with another bullet Kermit killed her. Two days later they came on the remaining cubs and the wounded lioness, and Kermit killed the latter; but they let the cubs go, feeling it unsportsmanlike to kill them—a feeling which I am by no means certain I share, for lions are scourges not only to both wild and tame animals, but to man himself.

Kermit also rode down and killed two cheetahs and a serval, and got a bad tumble while chasing a jackal, his horse turning a complete somersault through a thorny bush. This made seven cheetahs that he had killed, a record unequalled for any other East African trip of the same length; and the finding and galloping down of these cheetahs—going at breakneck speed over any and every kind of ground, and then shooting them either from foot or horseback— made one of the noteworthy features of our trip. One of these two cheetahs had just killed a steinbuck. The serval was with its mate, and Kermit watched them for some time through his glasses before following them. There was one curious feature of their conduct. One of them was playing about, now near the other, now leaving it; and near by was a bustard, which it several times pretended to stalk, crawling toward it a few yards, and then standing up and walking away. The bustard paid no heed to it; and, more singular still, two white-necked ravens lit close to it, within a few yards on either side; the serval sitting erect between them, seemingly quite unconcerned for a couple of minutes, and then strolling off without making any effort to molest them. I can give no explanation of the incident; it illustrates afresh the need of ample and well-recorded observations by trustworthy field naturalists, who shall go into the wilderness before the big game, the big birds, and the beasts of prey vanish. Those pages of the book of nature which are best worth reading can best be read far from the dwellings of civilized man; and for their full interpretation we need the services, not of one man, but of many men, who in addition to the gift of accurate observation shall if possible possess the power fully, accurately, and with vividness to write about what they have observed.

Kermit shot many other animals, among them three fine oryx, one of which he rode down on horseback, manœuvring so that at last it galloped fairly closely across his front, whereupon he leaped off his horse for the shot; an ardwolf (a miniature hyena with very weak teeth) which bolted from its hole at his approach; gerenuk, small antelope with necks relatively as long as giraffes', which are exceedingly shy and difficult to obtain; and the Grévy's zebra, as big as a small horse. Most of his hunting was done alone, either on foot or on horseback; on a long run or all-day tramp no other member of our outfit, black or white, could quite keep up with him. He and Tarlton found where a leopard had killed and partly eaten a nearly full-grown individual of this big zebra. He also shot a twelve-foot crocodile. The ugly, formidable brute had in its belly sticks, stones, the claws of a cheetah, the hoofs of an impalla, and the big bones of an eland, together with the shell plates of one of the large river-turtles; evidently it took toll indifferently from among its fellow-denizens of the river, and from among the creatures that came to drink, whether beasts of pasture or the flesh-eaters that preyed upon them.

He also shot three buffalo bulls, Tarlton helping him to finish them off, for they are tough animals, tenacious of life and among the most dangerous of African game. One turned to charge, but was disabled by the bullets of both of them before he could come on. Tarlton, whose experience in the hunting field against dangerous game had been large, always maintained that, although lion hunting was the most dangerous sport, because a hunted lion was far more apt to charge than any other animal, yet when a buffalo bull did charge he was more dangerous than a lion, because harder to kill or turn. Where zebra and other game are abundant, as on the Athi Plains, lion do not meddle with such formidable quarry as buffalo; on Heatley's farm lions sometimes made their lairs in the same papyrus swamp with the buffalo, but hardly ever molested them. In many places, however, the lion preys largely, and in some places chiefly, on the buffalo. The hunters of wide experience with whom I conversed, men like Tarlton, Cuninghame, and Horne, were a unit in stating that where a single lion killed a buffalo they had always found that the buffalo was a cow or immature bull, and that whenever they had found a full-grown bull thus killed, several lions had been engaged in the job. Horne had once found the carcass of a big bull which had been killed and eaten by lions, and near by lay a dead lioness with a great rip in her side, made by the buffalo's horn in the fight in which he succumbed. Even a buffalo cow, if fairly pitted against a single lion, would probably stand an even chance; but of course the fight never is fair, the lion's aim being to take his prey unawares and get a death grip at the outset; and then, unless his hold is broken, he cannot be seriously injured.

Twenty years ago the African buffalo were smitten with one of those overwhelming disasters which are ever occurring and recurring in the animal world. Africa is not only the land, beyond all others, subject to odious and terrible insect plagues of every conceivable kind, but is also peculiarly liable to cattle murrains. About the year 1889, or shortly before, a virulent form of rinderpest started among the domestic cattle and wild buffalo almost at the northern border of the buffalo's range, and within the next few years worked gradually southward to beyond the Zambesi. It wrought dreadful havoc among the cattle, and in consequence decimated by starvation many of the cattle-owning tribes; it killed many of the large bovine antelopes, and it wellnigh exterminated the buffalo. In many places the buffalo herds were absolutely wiped out, the species being utterly destroyed throughout great tracts of territory, notably in East Africa; in other places the few survivors did not represent the hundredth part of those that had died. For years the East African buffalo ceased to exist as a beast of the chase. But all the time it was slowly regaining the lost ground, and during the last decade its increase has been rapid. Unlike the slow-breeding elephant and rhinoceros, buffalo multiply apace, like domestic cattle, and in many places the herds have now become too numerous. Their rapid recovery from a calamity so terrific is interesting and instructive.* Doubtless for many years after man, in recognizably human form, appeared on this planet, he played but a small part in the destruction of big animals, compared to plague, to insect pests and

A domesticated young male eland at Meru
From a photograph by Edmund Heller

microbes, to drought, flood, earth upheaval, and change of temperature. But during the geological moment covering the few thousand years of recorded history man has been not merely the chief, but practically the sole factor in the extermination of big mammals and birds.

At and near Meru boma we spent a fortnight hunting elephant and rhinoceros, as described in the preceding chapter. While camped by the boma white-necked vultu-

*On our trip along the Guaso Nyero we heard that there had been a fresh outbreak of rinderpest among the buffalo; I hope it will not prove such a hideous disaster.

rine ravens and black and white crows came familiarly
around the tents. A young eland bull, quite as tame as a
domestic cow, was picketed, now here, now there, about us.
Horne was breaking it to drive in a cart.

During our stay another district commissioner, Mr.
Piggott, came over on a short visit; it was he who the preceding year, while at Neri, had been obliged to undertake
the crusade against the rhinos, because, quite unprovoked,
they had killed various natives. He told us that at the
same time a man-eating leopard made its appearance, and
killed seven children. It did not attack at night, but in the
daytime, its victims being the little boys who were watching
the flocks of goats; sometimes it took a boy and sometimes
a goat. Two old men killed it with spears on the occasion
of its taking the last victim. It was a big male, very old,
much emaciated, and the teeth worn to stumps. Horne
told us that a month or two before our arrival at Meru a
leopard had begun a career of woman-killing. It killed
one woman by a bite in the throat, and ate the body. It
sprang on and badly wounded another, but was driven off
in time to save her life. This was probably the leopard
Heller trapped and shot, in the very locality where it had
committed its ravages; it was an old male, but very thin,
with worn teeth. In these cases the reason for the beast's
action was plain: in each instance a big, savage male
had found his powers failing, and had been driven to prey
on the females and young of the most helpless of animals,
man. But another attack, of which Piggott told us, was
apparently due to the queer individual freakishness always
to be taken into account in dealing with wild beasts. A
Masai chief, with two or three followers, was sitting eating
under a bush, when, absolutely without warning, a leopard
sprang on him, clawed him on the head and hand, without
biting him, and as instantly disappeared. Piggott attended
to the wounded man.

In riding in the neighborhood, through the tall dry
grass, which would often rattle in the wind, I was amused

to find that if I suddenly heard the sound I was apt to stand alertly on guard, quite unconsciously and instinctively, because it suggested the presence of a rattlesnake. During the years I lived on a ranch in the West I was always hearing and killing rattlesnakes, and although I knew well that no African snake carries a rattle, my subconscious senses always threw me to attention if there was a sound resembling that made by a rattler. Tarlton, by the way, told me an interesting anecdote of a white-tailed mongoose and a snake. The mongoose was an inmate of the house where he dwelt with his brother and was quite tame. One day they brought in a rather small puff adder, less than two feet long, put it on the floor, and showed it to the mongoose. Instantly the latter sprang toward the snake, every hair in its body and tail on end, and halted five feet away, while the snake lay in curves like the thong of a whip, its head turned toward the mongoose. Both were motionless for a moment. Then suddenly the mongoose seemed to lose all its excitement; its hair smoothed down; and it trotted quietly up to the snake, seized it by the middle of the back— it always devoured its food with savage voracity—and settled comfortably down to its meal. Like lightning the snake's head whipped round. It drove its fangs deep into the snout or lip of the mongoose, hung on for a moment, and then repeated the blow. The mongoose paid not the least attention, but went on munching the snake's body, severed its backbone at once, and then ate it all up, head, fangs, poison, and everything; and it never showed a sign of having received any damage in the encounter. I had always understood that the mongoose owed its safety to its agility in avoiding the snake's stroke, and I can offer no explanation of this particular incident.

There were eland on the high downs not far from Meru, apparently as much at home in the wet, cold climate as on the hot plains. Their favorite gait is the trot. An elephant moves at a walk or rather rack; a giraffe has a very peculiar leisurely looking gallop, both hind legs coming forward nearly at the same time, outside the forelegs; rhino and buffalo trot and run. Eland when alarmed bound with astonishing agility for such large beasts—a trait not shown by other large antelope, like oryx—and then gallop for a short distance; but the big bulls speedily begin to trot, and the cows and younger bulls gradually also drop back into the trot. In fact, their gaits are in essence those of the wapiti, which also prefer the trot, although wapiti never make the bounds that eland do at the start. The moose, however, is more essentially a trotter than either eland or wapiti; a very old and heavy moose never, when at speed, goes at any other gait than a trot, except that under the pressure of great and sudden danger it may perhaps make a few bounds.*

While at Meru boma I received a cable, forwarded by native runners, telling me of Peary's wonderful feat in reaching the North Pole. Of course we were all overjoyed, and in particular we Americans could not but feel a special pride in the fact that it was a fellow-countryman who had performed the great and noteworthy achievement. A little more than a year had passed since I said good-by to Peary as he started on his Arctic quest; after leaving New York in the *Roosevelt*, he had put into Oyster Bay to see us, and we had gone aboard the *Roosevelt*, had examined with keen interest how she was fitted for the boreal seas and the boreal winter, and had then waved farewell to the tall, gaunt explorer, as he stood looking toward us over the side of the stout little ship.†

On September 21, Kermit and Tarlton started south-

---

*A perfectly trustworthy Maine hunter informed me that in the spring he had once seen in the snow where a bear had sprung at two big moose, and they had bounded for several rods before settling into the tremendous trot which is their normal gait when startled. I have myself seen signs that showed where a young moose had galloped for some rods under similar circumstances; and I have seen big moose calves, or half-grown moose, in captivity gallop a few yards in play, although rarely. But the normal, and under ordinary circumstances the only, gait of the moose is the trot.

† When I reached Neri I received from Peary the following cable: "Your farewell was a royal mascot. The Pole is ours.—PEARY."

west, toward Lake Hannington, and Cuninghame and I north toward the Guaso Nyero. Heller was under the weather, and we left him to spend a few days at Meru boma, and then to take in the elephant skins and other museum specimens to Nairobi.

As Cuninghame and I were to be nearly four weeks in

Helping a donkey across the stream
From a photograph by Kermit Roosevelt

a country with no food supplies, we took a small donkey safari to carry the extra food for our porters—for in these remote places the difficulty of taking in many hundred pounds of salt, as well as skin tents, and the difficulty of bringing out the skeletons and skins of the big animals collected, make such an expedition as ours, undertaken for scientific purposes, far more cumbersome and unwieldy than a mere hunting trip, or even than a voyage of exploration, and trebles the labor.

A long day's march brought us down to the hot country. That evening we pitched our tents by a rapid brook, bordered by palms, whose long, stiff fronds rustled ceaselessly in the wind. Monkeys swung in the tree tops. On the march I shot a Kavirondo crane on the wing with the little Springfield, almost exactly repeating my experience with the other crane which I had shot three weeks before, except that on this occasion I brought down the bird with my third bullet, and then wasted the last two cartridges in the magazine at his companions. At dusk the donkeys were driven to a fire within the camp, and they stood patiently round it in a circle throughout the night, safe from lions and hyenas.

Next day's march brought us to another small tributary of the Guaso Nyero, a little stream twisting rapidly through the plain, between sheer banks. Here and there it was edged with palms and beds of bulrushes. We pitched the tents close to half a dozen flat-topped thorn-trees. We spent several days at this camp. Many kites came around the tents, but neither vultures nor ravens. The country was a vast plain bounded on almost every hand by chains of far-off mountains. In the south-west, just beyond the equator, the snows of Kenia lifted toward the sky. To the north the barren ranges were grim with the grimness of the desert. The flats were covered with pale, bleached grass which waved all day long in the wind; for though there were sometimes calms, or changes in the wind, on most of the days we were out it never ceased blowing from some point in the south. In places the parched soil was crumbling and rotten; in other places it was thickly strewn with volcanic stones; there were but few tracts over which a horse could gallop at speed, although neither the rocks nor the rotten soil seemed to hamper the movements of the game. Here and there were treeless stretches. Elsewhere there were occasional palms; and trees thirty or forty feet high, seemingly cactus or aloes, which looked even more like candelabra than the euphorbia which is thus named; and a scattered growth of thorn-trees and bushes. The thorn-trees were of many kinds. One bore only a few leathery leaves, the place of foliage being taken by the mass of poisonous-looking, fleshy spines which, together with the ends of the branches, were bright green. The camel-thorn was completely armed with little, sharply hooked thorns which tore whatever they touched, whether flesh or clothes. Then there were the mimosas, with long, straight thorn spikes; they are so plentiful in certain places along the Guaso Nyero that almost all the lions have festering sores in their paws because of the spikes that have broken off in them. In these thorn-trees the weaver-birds had built multitudes of their straw nests, each with its bottle-shaped mouth toward the north, away from the direction of the prevailing wind.

Each morning we were up at dawn, and saw the heavens redden and the sun flame over the rim of the world. All day long we rode and walked across the endless flats, save that at noon, when the sky was like molten brass, we might rest under the thin half shade of some thorn-tree. As the shadows lengthened and the harsh, pitiless glare softened, we might turn campward; or we might hunt until the sun went down, and the mountains in the far-off west, and the sky above them, grew faint and dim with the hues of fairy-land. Then we would ride back through the soft, warm beauty of the tropic night, the stars blazing overhead and the silver moonlight flooding the reaches of dry grass; it was so bright that our shadows were almost as black and clear-cut as in the day. On reaching camp I would take a cup of tea with crackers or gingersnaps, and after a hot bath and a shave I was always eager for dinner.

Scattered over these flats were herds of zebra, oryx, and gazelle. The gazelle, the most plentiful and much the tamest of the game, were the northern form of the Grant's gazelle, with straighter horns which represented the opposite extreme when compared with the horns of the Roberts'

type which we got on the Sotik. They seemed to me somewhat less in size than the big gazelle of the Kapiti Plains.
One of the bucks I shot, an adult of average size (I was
not able to weigh my biggest one), weighed one hundred and
fifteen pounds; a very big true Grant's buck which I shot
on the Kapiti Plains weighed one hundred and seventy-one
pounds; doubtless there is complete intergradation, but
the Guaso Nyero form seemed slimmer and lighter, and
in some respects seemed to tend toward the Somaliland
gazelles. I marked no difference in the habits, except that
these northern gazelle switched their tails more jerkily,
more like tommies, than was customary with the true
Grant's gazelles. But the difference may have been in
my observation. At any rate, the gazelles in this neighborhood, like those elsewhere, went in small parties, or herds
of thirty or forty individuals, on the open plains or where
there were a few scattered bushes, and behaved like those
in the Sotik or on the Athi Plains. A near kinsman of
the gazelle, the gerenuk, a curious creature with a very
long neck, which the Swahilis call "little giraffe," was
scattered singly or in small parties through the brush, and
was as wild and wary as the common gazelle was tame.
It seemed to prefer browsing, while the common gazelle
grazes.

The handsome oryx, with their long horns carried by
both sexes, and their coloring of black, white, and dun
gray, came next to the gazelle in point of numbers. They
were generally found in herds of from half a dozen to fifty
individuals, often mixed with zebra herds. There were also
solitary bulls, probably turned out of the herds by more
vigorous rivals, and often one of these would be found with
a herd of zebras, more merciful to it than its own kinsfolk.
All this game of the plains is highly gregarious in habit,
and the species associate freely with one another. The
oryx cows were now generally accompanied by very young
calves, for, unlike what we found to be the case with the
hartebeest on the Athi, the oryx on the Guaso Nyero seem

to have a definite calving time—September.* I shot only
bulls (there was no meat, either for the porters or ourselves,
except what I got with the rifle), and they were so wary that
almost all those I killed were shot at ranges between three
hundred and five hundred yards; and at such ranges I
need hardly say that I did a good deal of missing. One
wounded bull which, the ground being favorable, I galloped down, turned to bay and threatened to charge the
horse. We weighed one bull; it tipped the scales at four
hundred pounds. The lion kills we found in this neighborhood were all oryx and zebra; and evidently the attack was
made in such fashion that the oryx had no more chance to
fight than the zebra.

The zebra were of both species, the smaller or Burchell's,
and the Grévy's, which the porters called kangani. Each
animal went in herds by itself, and almost as frequently
we found them in mixed herds containing both species.
But they never interbreed, and associate merely as each
does with the oryx. The kangani is a fine beast, much
bigger than its kinsman; it is as large as a polo pony. It is
less noisy than the common zebra, the "bonte quagga" of
the Boers, and its cry is totally different. Its gaits are a
free, slashing trot and gallop. When it stands facing one
the huge fringed ears make it instantly recognizable. The
stripes are much narrower and more numerous than those
on the small zebra, and in consequence cease to be distinguishable at a shorter distance; the animal then looks
gray, like a wild ass. When the two zebras are together
the coloring of the smaller kind is more conspicuous. In
scanning a herd with the glasses we often failed to make
out the species until we could catch the broad black and
white stripes on the rump of the common "bonte quagga."
There were many young foals with the kangani; I hap-

*Of course this represents only one man's experience. I wish there were many
such observations. On the Athi in May I found new-born wildebeest and hartebeest calves, and others several months old. In June in the Sotik I saw new-born
eland calves, and topi calves several months old. In September on the Guaso Nyero
all the oryx calves were new-born. The zebra foals were also very young.

pened not to see any with the Burchell's. I found the kangani even more wary and more difficult to shoot than the
oryx. The first one I killed was shot at a range of four
hundred yards; the next I wounded at that distance, and
had to ride it down, at the cost of a hard gallop over very
bad country and getting torn by the "wait-a-bit" thorns.

A mixed herd of Grévy's and Burchell's zebras
From a photograph by Kermit Roosevelt

There were a number of rhinos on the plains, dull of
wit and senses, as usual. Three times we saw cows with
calves trotting at their heels. Once, while my men were
skinning an oryx, I spied a rhino less than half a mile off.
Mounting my horse I cantered down, and examined it
within a hundred yards. It was an old bull with worn
horns, and never saw me. On another occasion, while we
were skinning a big zebra, there were three rhinoceros, all
in different places, in sight at the same time.

There were also ostriches. I saw a party of cocks, with

wings spread and necks curved backward, strutting and dancing. Their mincing, springy run is far faster than, when the bird is near by, it seems. The neck is held back in running, and when at speed the stride is twenty-one feet. No game is more wary or more difficult to approach. I killed both a cock and a hen—which I found the naturalists valued even more than a cock. We got them by stumbling on the nest, which contained eleven huge eggs, and was merely a bare spot in the sand, surrounded by grass two feet high; the bird lay crouched, with the neck flat on the ground. When we accidentally came across the nest the cock was on it, and I failed to get him as he ran. The next day we returned, and dismounted before we reached the near neighborhood of the nest. Then I advanced, cautiously, my rifle at the ready. It seemed impossible that so huge a bird could lie hidden in such scanty cover, but not a sign did we see until, when we were sixty yards off, the hen, which this time was on the nest, rose, and I killed her at sixty yards. Even this did not make the cock desert the nest; and on a subsequent day I returned, and after missing him badly, I killed him at eighty-five yards; and glad I was to see the huge black-and-white bird tumble in the dust. He weighed two hundred and sixty-three pounds and was in fine plumage. The hen weighed two hundred and forty pounds. Her stomach and gizzard, in addition to small, white quartz pebbles, contained a mass of vegetable substance; the bright-green leaves and twig tips of a shrub, a kind of rush with jointed stem and tuberous root, bean pods from different kinds of thorn-trees, and the leaves and especially the seed vessels of a bush, the seed vessels being enclosed in cases or pods so thorny that they pinched our fingers, and made us wonder at the bird's palate. Cock and hen brood the eggs alternately. We found the heart and liver of the ostrich excellent eating; the eggs were very good also. As the cock died it uttered a kind of loud, long-drawn grunting boom that was almost a roar. Its beautiful white wing plumes were almost unworn.

A full-grown wild ostrich is too wary to fall into the clutches of a lion or leopard, save by accident, and it will master any of the lesser carnivora; but the chicks are preyed on by jackals and wild-cats, and of course by the larger beasts of prey also; and the eggs are eagerly sought by furred and feathered foes alike. Seemingly trustworthy settlers have assured me that vultures break the tough shells with stones. The cock and hen will try to draw their more formidable foes away from the nest or the chicks by lingering so near as to lure them into pursuit; and anything up to the size of a hyena they will attack and drive away, or even kill. The terrific downward stroke of an ostrich's leg is as dangerous as the kick of a horse; the thump will break a rib or backbone of any ordinary animal, and in addition to the force of the blow itself the big nails may make a ghastly rip. Both cock and hen lead about the young brood and care for it. The two ostriches I shot were swarming with active parasitic flies, a little like those that were on the lions I shot in the Sotik. Later the porters brought us in several ostrich chicks. They also brought two genet kittens, which I tried to raise, but failed. They were much like ordinary kittens, with larger ears, sharper noses, and longer tails, and loved to perch on my shoulder or sit on my lap while I stroked them. They made dear little pets, and I was very sorry when they died.

On the day that I shot the cock ostrich I also shot a giraffe. The country in which we were hunting marks the southern limit of the "reticulated" giraffe, a form or species entirely distinct from the giraffe we had already obtained in the country south of Kenia. The southern giraffe is blotched with dark on a light ground, whereas this northern or north-eastern form is of a uniform dark color on the back and sides, with a net-work or reticulation of white lines placed in a large pattern on this dark background. The naturalists were very anxious to obtain a specimen of this form from its southern limit of distribution, to see if there was any intergradation with the south-

The old bull Athi giraffe

From a photograph by Edmund Heller

The reticulated giraffe

From a photograph by Theodore Roosevelt

ern form, of which we had already shot specimens near its northern, or at least north-eastern, limit. The distinction proved sharp.

On the day in question we breakfasted at six in the morning, and were off immediately afterward; and we did not eat anything again until supper at quarter to ten in the evening. In a hot climate a hunter does not need lunch; and though in a cold climate a simple lunch is permissible, anything like an elaborate or luxurious lunch is utterly out of place if the man is more than a parlor or drawing-room sportsman. We saw no sign of giraffe until late in the afternoon. Hour after hour we plodded across the plain, now walking, now riding, in the burning heat. The withered grass was as dry as a bone, for the country had been many months without rain; yet the oryx, zebra, and gazelle evidently throve on the harsh pasturage. There were innumerable game trails leading hither and thither, and, after the fashion of game trails, usually fading out after a few hundred yards. But there were certain trails which did not fade out. These were the ones which led to water. One such we followed. It led across stretches of grassland, through thin bush, thorny and almost leafless, over tracts of rotten soil, cracked and crumbling, and over other tracts where the unshod horses picked their way gingerly among the masses of sharp-edged volcanic stones. Other trails joined in, and it grew more deeply marked. At last it led to a bend in a little river, where flat shelves of limestone bordered a kind of pool in the current where there were beds of green rushes and a fringe of trees and thorn thickets. This was evidently a favorite drinking-place. Many trails converged toward it, and for a long distance round the ground was worn completely bare by the hoofs of the countless herds of thirsty game that had travelled thither from time immemorial. Sleek, handsome, long-horned oryx, with switching tails, were loitering in the vicinity, and at the waterhole itself we surprised a band of gazelles not fifty yards off; they fled panic-struck in every direction. Men and horses drank their fill; and we returned to the sunny plains and the endless reaches of withered, rustling grass.

At last, an hour or two before sunset, when the heat had begun a little to abate, we spied half a dozen giraffes scattered a mile and a half ahead of us, feeding on the tops of the few widely separated thorn-trees. Cuninghame and I started toward them on foot, but they saw us when we were a mile away, and after gazing a short while, turned and went off at their usual rocking-horse canter, twisting and screwing their tails. We mounted and rode after them. I was on my zebra-shaped brown horse, which was hardy and with a fair turn of speed, and which by this time I had trained to be a good hunting horse. On the right were two giraffe which eventually turned out to be a big cow followed by a nearly full-grown young one; but Cuninghame, scanning them through his glasses, and misled by the dark coloration, pronounced them a bull and cow; and after the big one I went. By good luck we were on one of the rare pieces of the country which was fitted for galloping. I rode at an angle to the giraffe's line of flight, thus gaining considerably; and when it finally turned and went straight away I followed it at a fast run, and before it was fully awake to the danger I was but a hundred yards behind. We were now getting into bad country, and jumping off I opened fire and crippled the great beast. Mounting, I overtook it again in a quarter of a mile and killed it.

In half an hour the skinners and porters came up—one of the troubles of hunting as a naturalist is that it necessitates the presence of a long tail of men to take off and carry in the big skins, in order that they may ultimately appear in museums. In an hour and a half the giraffe's skin, with the head and the leg bones, was slung on two poles; eight porters bore it, while the others took for their own use all the meat they could carry. They were in high good-humor, for an abundant supply of fresh meat always means a season of rejoicing, and they started campward singing loudly under their heavy burdens. While the giraffe was being skinned we had seen a rhinoceros feeding near our line of march campward, and had watched it until the light grew dim. By the time the skin was ready night had fallen, and we started under the brilliant moon. It lit up the entire landscape; but moonlight is not sunlight, and there was the chance of our stumbling on the rhino unawares, and of its charging; so I rode at the head of the column with full-jacketed bullets in my rifle. However, we never saw the rhino, nor had we any other adventure; and the ride through the moonlight, which softened all the harshness, and gave a touch of magic and mystery, to the landscape, was so pleasant that I was sorry when we caught the gleam of the camp-fires.

Next day we sent our porters to bring in the rest of the giraffe meat and the ostrich eggs. The giraffe's heart was good eating. There were many ticks on the giraffe, as on all the game hereabouts, and they annoyed us a little also, although very far from being the plague they were on the Athi Plain. Among the flies which at times tormented the horses and hung around the game, were big gadflies with long wings folded longitudinally down the back, not in the ordinary fly fashion; they were akin to the tsetse flies, one species of which is fatal to domestic animals, and another, the sleeping-sickness fly, to man himself. They produce death by means of the fatal microbes introduced into the blood by their bite; whereas another African fly, the seroot, found more to the north, in the Nile countries, is a scourge to man and beast merely because of its vicious bite, and where it swarms may drive the tribes that own herds entirely out of certain districts.

One afternoon, while leading my horse because the ground was a litter of sharp-edged stones, I came out on a plain which was crawling with zebra. In every direction there were herds of scores or of hundreds. They were all of the common or small kind, except three individuals of the big kangani, and were tame, letting me walk by within easy shot. Other game was mixed in with them. Soon, walking over a little ridge of rocks, we saw a rhino sixty yards off. To walk forward would give it our wind; I did not wish to kill it; and I was beginning to feel about rhino the way Alice did in Looking Glass country, when the elephants "did bother so." Having spied us the beast at once cocked its ears and tail, and assumed its usual absurd resemblance to a huge and exceedingly alert and interested pig. But with a rhino tragedy sometimes treads on the heels of comedy, and I watched it sharply, my rifle cocked, while I had all the men shout in unison to scare it away. The noise puzzled it much; with tail erect and head tossing and twisting, it made little rushes hither and thither, but finally drew off. Next day, in shifting camp, Cuninghame and I were twice obliged to dismount and keep guard over the safari while it marched by within a hundred yards of a highly puzzled rhino, which trotted to and fro in the bush, evidently uncertain whether or not to let its bewilderment turn into indignation.

The camp to which we thus shifted was on the banks of the Guaso Nyero, on the edge of an open glade in a shady grove of giant mimosas. It was a beautiful camp, and in the soft tropic nights I sat outside my tent and watched the full moon rising through and above the tree tops. There was absolutely no dew at night, by the way. The Guaso Nyero runs across and along the equator, through a desert country, eastward into the dismal Lorian swamp, where it disappears, save in very wet seasons, when it continues to the Tana. At our camp it was a broad, rapid, muddy stream infested with crocodiles. Along its banks grew groves of ivory-nut palms, their fronds fan-shaped, their tall trunks forked twenty or thirty feet from the ground, each stem again forking—something like the antlers of a black-tail buck. In the frond of a small palm of this kind we found a pale-colored, very long-tailed tree mouse, in its nest, which was a ball of chopped straw. Spurfowl and francolin abounded, their grating cries being heard everywhere; I shot a few as well as one or two sandgrouse;

and with the rifle I knocked off the heads of two guinea-fowls. The last feat sounds better in the narration than it was in the performance; for I wasted nearly a beltful of cartridges in achieving it, as the guineas were shy and ran rapidly through the tall grass. I also expended a large number of cartridges before securing a couple of gerenuk; the queer, long-legged, long-necked antelope were wary, and as soon as they caught a glimpse of me off they would go at a stealthy trot or canter through the bushes, with neck out-stretched. They had a curious habit of rising on their hind legs to browse among the bushes; I do not remember seeing any other antelope act in this manner. There were waterbuck along the river banks, and I shot a couple of good bulls; they belonged to the southern and eastern species, which has a light-colored ring around the rump; whereas the western form, which I saw at Naivasha, has the whole rump light-colored. They like the neighborhood of lakes and rivers. I have seen parties of them resting in the open plains during the day, under trees which yielded little more shade than telegraph poles. The handsome, shaggy-coated waterbuck has not the high withers which mark the oryx, wildebeest, and hartebeest, and he carries his head and neck more like a stag or a wapiti bull.

One day we went back from the river after giraffe. It must have been a year since any rain had fallen. The surface of the baked soil was bare and cracked, the sparse tussocks of grass were brittle straw, and the trees and bushes were leafless; but instead of leaves they almost all carried thorns, the worst being those of the wait-a-bit, which tore our clothes, hands, and faces. We found the giraffe three or four miles away from the river, in an absolutely waterless region, densely covered with these leafless wait-a-bit thorn-bushes. Hanging among the bare bushes, by the way, we roused two or three of the queer, diurnal, golden-winged, slate-colored bats; they flew freely in the glare of the sunlight, minding it as little as they did the furnace-like heat. We found the really dense wait-a-bit thorn thickets quite impenetrable, whereas the giraffe moved through them with utter unconcern. But the giraffe's indifference to thorns is commonplace compared to its indifference to water. These particular giraffe were not drinking either at the river or at the one or two streams which were run-ning into it; and in certain places giraffe will subsist for months without drinking at all. How the waste and evap-oration of moisture from their huge bodies is supplied is one of the riddles of biology.

We could not get a bull giraffe, and it was only a bull that I wanted. I was much interested, however, in coming up to a cow asleep. She stood with her neck drooping slightly forward, occasionally stamping or twitching an ear, like a horse when asleep standing. I saw her legs first, through the bushes, and finally walked directly up to her in the open, until I stood facing her at thirty yards. When she at last suddenly saw me, she came nearer to the execu-tion of a gambol than any other giraffe I have ever seen.

Another day we went after buffalo. We left camp be-fore sunrise, riding along parallel to the river to find the spoor of a herd which had drunk and was returning to the haunts, away from the river, in which they here habit-ually spent the day. Two or three hours passed before we found what we sought; and we at once began to follow the trail. It was in open thorn-bush, and the animals were evidently feeding. Before we had followed the spoor half an hour we ran across a rhinoceros. As the spoor led above wind, and as we did not wish to leave it for fear of losing it, Cuninghame stayed where he was, and I moved round to within fifty yards of the rhino, and, with my rifle ready, began shouting, trying to keep the just mean as regards noise, so as to scare him, and yet not yell so loudly as to reach the buffalo if they happened to be near by. At last I succeeded, and he trotted sullenly off, tacking and veer-ing, and not going far. On we went, and in another half-hour came on our quarry. I was the first to catch a glimpse of the line of bulky black forms, picked out with white where the sun glinted on the horn bosses. It was ten o'clock, a hot, windless morning on the equator, with the sun shining from a cloudless sky; yet these buffalo were feeding in the open, miles from water or dense cover. They were greedily cropping the few tufts of coarse herbage that grew among the sparse thorn-bushes, which here were not more than two feet high. In many places buffalo are purely nocturnal feeders, and do not come into the hot, bare plains in the scorching glare of daylight; and our experience with this herd illustrates afresh the need of caution in generalizing about the habits of game.

We crept toward them on all-fours, having left the porters hidden from sight. At last we were within rather long range—a buffalo's eyesight is good, and cannot be trifled with as if he were a rhino or elephant—and cautiously scrutinized the herd through our glasses. There were only cows and perhaps one or two young bulls with horns no bigger than those of cows. I would have liked another good bull's head for myself; but I also wished another cow for the museum. Before I could shoot, however, a loud yelling was heard from among the porters in our rear; and away went the buffalo. Full of wrath, we walked back to inquire. We found that one porter had lost his knife, and had started back to look for it, accompanied by two of his fellows, which was absolutely against orders. They had come across a rhino, probably the one I had frightened from our path, and had endeavored to avoid him; but he had charged them, whereupon they scattered. He overtook one and tossed him, goring him in the thigh; whereupon they came back, the two unwounded ones supporting the other, and all howling like lost souls. I had some crystals of permanganate, an antiseptic, and some cotton in my saddle pocket; Cuninghame tore some of the lining out of his sleeve for a bandage; and we fixed the man up and left him with one companion, while we sent another in to camp to fetch out a dozen men with a ground-sheet and some poles, to make a litter in which the wounded man could be

carried.   While we were engaged in this field surgery
another rhino was in sight half a mile off.

Then on we went on the trail of the herd.   It led straight
across the open, under the blazing sun; and the heat was

Dressing the porter who was tossed by the rhino
From a photograph by Theodore Roosevelt

now terrific.   At last, almost exactly at noon, Cuninghame,
who was leading, stopped short.   He had seen the buffalo,
which had halted, made a half-bend backward on their
tracks, and stood for their noonday rest among some scattered, stunted thorn-trees, leafless and yielding practically
no shade whatever.   A cautious stalk brought me to within
a hundred and fifty yards.   I merely wounded the one I

first shot at, but killed another as the herd started to run.
Leaving the skinners to take care of the dead animal, a fine
cow, Cuninghame and I started after the herd, to see if
the wounded one had fallen out. After a mile the trail led
into some scant cover. Here the first thing we did was to
run into another rhinoceros. It was about seventy yards
away, behind a thorn-tree, and began to move jerkily and
abruptly to and fro, gazing toward us. "Oh, you malev-
olent old idiot!" I muttered, facing it with rifle cocked;
then, as it did not charge, I added to Cuninghame, "Well,
I guess it will let us by, all right." And let us by it did.
We were anxious not to shoot it, both because in a country
with no settlers a rhino rarely does harm, and I object to
anything like needless butchery, and furthermore because we
desired to avoid alarming the buffalo. Half a mile farther
on we came on the latter, apparently past their fright. We
looked them carefully over with our glasses; the wounded
one was evidently not much hurt, and therefore I did not
wish to kill her, for I did not need another cow; and there
was no adult bull. So we did not molest them; and after
a while they got our wind and went off at a lumbering gallop. Returning to the dead cow, we found the skin ready
and marched back to camp, reaching it just as the moon
rose, at seven; we had been away thirteen hours, with
nothing to eat and only the tepid water in our canteens to
drink.

We were in the country of the Samburu, and several of
their old men and warriors visited us at this camp. They
are cattle-owning nomads like the Masai; but in addition
to cattle, sheep, and goats they own herds of camels, which
they milk but do not use as beasts of burden. In features
they are more like Somalis than negroes.

Near this camp was the remains of the boma or home
camp of Arthur Neuman, once the most famous elephant
hunter between the Tana and Lake Rudolf. Neuman,
whose native name was Nyama Yango, was a strange
moody man who died by his own hand. He was a mighty

hunter, of bold and adventure-loving temper. With whites he was unsocial, living in this far-off region exactly like a native, and all alone among the natives; living in some respects too much like a native. But, from the native standpoint, and without making any effort to turn the natives into anything except what they were, he did them good, and left a deep impression on their minds. They talked to us often about him, in many different places; they would not believe that he was dead; and when assured it was so they showed real grief. At Meru boma, when we saw the Meru tribesmen dance, one of the songs they sung was: "Since Nyama Yango came, our sheep graze untouched by the Samburu," and, rather curiously, the Samburu sing a similar song reciting how he saved them from the fear of having their herds raided by the nomads farther north.

After leaving this camp we journeyed up the Guaso Nyero for several days. The current was rapid and muddy, and there were beds of reeds and of the tall, graceful papyrus. The country round about was a mass of stony, broken hills, and the river wound down among these, occasionally cutting its way through deep gorges, and its course being continually broken by rapids. Whenever on our hunts we had to cross it, we shouted and splashed and even fired shots, to scare the crocodiles. I shot one on a sand bar in the river. The man the rhino had wounded was carried along on a litter with the safari.

Sometimes I left camp with my sais and gun-bearer before dawn, starting in the light of the waning moon, and riding four or five hours before halting to wait for the safari; on the way I had usually shot something for the table—a waterbuck, impalla, or gazelle. On other occasions Cuninghame and I would spend the day hunting in the waterless country back of the river, where the heat at mid-day was terrific. We might not reach camp until after nightfall. Once as we came to it in the dark it seemed as if ghostly arms stretched above it; for on this evening the tents had been pitched under trees up which huge rubber vines had climbed, and their massive dead-white trunks and branches glimmered pale and ghostly in the darkness.

Twice my gun-bearers tried to show me a cheetah; but my eyes were too slow to catch the animal before it bounded off in safety among the bushes. Another time after an excellent bit of tracking, the gun-bearers brought me up to a buffalo bull, standing for his noonday rest in the leafless thorns a mile from the river. I thought I held the heavy Holland straight for his shoulder, but I must have fired high; for though he fell to the shot he recovered at once. We followed the blood spoor for an hour, the last part of the time when the trail wandered among and through the heavy thickets under the trees on the river banks; here I walked beside the tracker with my rifle at full cock, for we could not tell what instant we might be charged. But his trail finally crossed the river, and as he was going stronger and stronger we had to abandon the chase. In the waterless country, away from the river, we found little except herds of zebra, of both kinds, occasional oryx and eland, and a few giraffe. A stallion of the big kangani zebra which I shot stood fourteen hands high at the withers and weighed about eight hundred and thirty pounds,* according to the Seton beam. I shot another kangani just at nightfall, a mile or so from camp, as it drank in a wild, tree-clad gorge of the river. I was alone, strolling quietly through the dusk, along the margin of the high banks by the stream, and saw a mixed herd of zebras coming down to a well-worn drinking-place, evidently much used by game, on the opposite side of the river. They were alert and nervous, evidently on the lookout for both lions and crocodiles. I singled out the largest, the leader of the troop, and shot it

* The aggregate of the weights of the different pieces was 778 pounds; the loss of blood and the drying of the pieces of flesh in the intense heat of the sun we thought certainly accounted for 50 pounds more. The stallion was not fat. At any rate it weighed between 800 and 850 pounds. Its testicles, though fully developed, had not come down out of the belly skin; one of those shot by Kermit showed the same peculiarity; Cuninghame says it is a common occurrence with this species. Moreover the stallions did not have their canine teeth developed.

across the stream; I have rarely taken a shot among more picturesque surroundings.

At our final camp on the river, before leaving it on our week's steady trek southward to Neri, we found a spot in which game abounded. It was about ten miles back from the river, a stretch of plain sparsely covered with thorn-trees, broken by koppies, and bounded by chains of low, jagged mountains, with an occasional bold, isolated peak. The crags and cliff walls were fantastically carved and channelled by the weathering of ages in that dry climate. It was a harsh, unlovely spot in the glare of the hot daylight; but at sunset it was very lovely, with a wild and stern beauty.

Here the game abounded, and was not wary. Before starting out on our week's steady marching I wished to give the safari a good feed; and one day I shot them five zebra and an oryx bull, together with a couple of gazelle for ourselves and our immediate attendants—enough of the game being hallalled to provide for the Mohammedans in the safari. I also shot an old bull giraffe of the northern form, after an uneventful stalk which culminated in a shot with the Winchester at a hundred and seventy yards. In most places this particular stretch of country was not suitable for galloping, the ground being rotten, filled with holes, and covered with tall, coarse grass. One evening we saw two lions half a mile away; I tried to ride them, but my horse fell twice in the first hundred and fifty yards and I could not even keep them in sight. Another day we got a glimpse of two lions, quarter of a mile off, gliding away among the thorns. They went straight to the river and swam across it. More surprising was the fact that a monkey, which lost its head when we surprised it in a tree by the river, actually sprang plump into the stream, and swam, easily and strongly, across it.

One day we had a most interesting experience with a cow giraffe. We saw her a long way off and stalked to within a couple of hundred yards before we could make out her sex. She was standing under some thorn-trees, occasionally shifting her position for a few yards, and then again standing motionless with her head thrust in among the branches. She was indulging in a series of noon naps. At last, when she stood and went to sleep again, I walked up to her, Cuninghame and our two gun-bearers, Bakhari and Kongoni, following a hundred yards behind. When I was within forty yards, in plain sight, away from cover, she opened her eyes and looked drowsily at me; but I stood motionless and she dozed off again. This time I walked up to within ten feet of her. Nearer I did not care to venture, as giraffe strike and kick very hard with their hooves, and, moreover, occasionally strike with the head, the blow seemingly not being delivered with the knobby, skin-covered horns, but with the front teeth of the lower jaw. She waked, looked at me, and then, rearing slightly, struck at me with her left foreleg, the blow falling short. I laughed and leaped back, and the other men ran up shouting. But the giraffe would not run away. She stood within twenty feet of us, looking at us peevishly, and occasionally pouting her lips at us, as if she were making a face. We kept close to the tree, so as to dodge round it, under the branches, if she came at us; for we would have been most reluctant to shoot her. I threw a stick at her, hitting her in the side, but she paid no attention; and when Bakhari came behind her with a stick she turned sharply on him and he made a prompt retreat. We were laughing and talking all the time. Then we pelted her with sticks and clods of earth, and, after having thus stood within twenty feet of us for three or four minutes, she cantered slowly off for fifty yards, and then walked away with leisurely unconcern. She was apparently in the best of health and in perfect condition. She did not get our wind; but her utter indifference to the close presence of four men is inexplicable.*

---

*After writing the above account I read it over to Mr. Cuninghame so as to be sure that it was accurate in all its details. All the game was tame in this locality,

On each of the two days we hunted this little district we left camp at sunrise, and did not return until eight or nine in the evening, fairly well tired, and not a little torn by the thorns into which we blundered during the final two hours' walk in the darkness. It was hot, and we neither had nor wished for food, and the tepid water in the canteens lasted us through. The day I shot the giraffe the porters carrying the skin fell behind, and never got in until next morning. Coming back in the late twilight a party of the big zebra, their forms shadowy and dim, trotted up to us, evidently attracted by the horses, and accompanied us for some rods; and a hedgehog, directly in our path, kept bleating loudly, like an antelope kid.

The day we spent in taking care of the giraffe skin we, of course, made no hunt. However, in the afternoon I sauntered upstream a couple of miles to look for crocodiles. I saw none, but I was much interested in some zebra and waterbuck. The zebra were on the opposite side of the river, standing among some thorns, and at three, mid-afternoon, they came down to drink; up to this time I had generally found zebra drinking in the evening or at night. Then I saw some waterbuck, also on the opposite bank, working their way toward the river, and seeing a well-marked drinking-place ahead I hastened toward it, and sat down in the middle of the broad game trail leading down to the water on my side. I sat perfectly still, and my clothes were just the color of the ground, and the waterbuck never noticed me, though I was in plain view when they drank, just opposite me, and only about fifty yards off. There were four cows and a bull. It was four o'clock in the afternoon. The cows came first, one by one, and were very alert and suspicious. Each continually stopped and stood motionless, or looked in every direction, and gave little false starts of alarm. When they reached the green

even the giraffe, but no other giraffe allowed us to get within two hundred yards, and most of them ran long before that distance was reached, even when we were stalking carefully.

grass by the water's edge each cropped a few mouthfuls, between times nervously raising its head and looking in every direction, nostrils and ears twitching. They were not looking for crocodiles, but for land foes, lions or leopards. Each in turn drank, skipping up to the top of the bank after a few mouthfuls, and then returning to the water. The bull followed with rather less caution, and before he had finished drinking the cows scurried hurriedly back to the thorn-trees and the open country. We had plenty of meat in camp, and I had completed my series of this species of waterbuck for the museum; and I was glad there was no need to molest them.

The porters were enjoying the rest and the abundance of meat. They were lying about camp or were scattered up and down stream fishing. When, walking back, I came to the outskirts of camp, I was attracted by the buzzing and twanging of the harp; there was the harper and two friends, all three singing to his accompaniment. I called "Yambo" (greeting), and they grinned and stood up, shouting "Yambo" in return. In camp a dozen men were still at work at the giraffe skin, and they were all singing loudly, under the lead of my gun-bearer, Gouvimali, who always acted as shanty man, or improvisatore, on such occasions.

For a week we now trekked steadily south across the equator, heel and toe marching, to Neri. Our first day's journey took us to a gorge riven in the dry mountain. Halfway up it, in a side pocket, was a deep pool, at the foot of a sloping sheet of rock, down which a broad, shallow dent showed where the torrents swept during the rains. In the trees around the pool black drongo shrikes called in bell-like tones, and pied hornbills flirted their long tails as they bleated and croaked. The water was foul; but in a dry country one grows gratefully to accept as water anything that is wet. Klipspringers and baboons were in the sheer hills around; and among the rocks were hyraxes (looking like our Rocky Mountain conies or Little Chief hares),

ck-and-
e crow,
*scapu-
latus*

Rusty rock-
rat

ow lark

Sand-rat

eatear
eating
chat)

African
hedgehog

strich
nest

"Mole-rat"

queer diurnal rats, and bright blue-green lizards with orange heads. Rhinos drank at this pool; we frequently saw
them on our journey, but always managed to avoid wounding their susceptibilities, and so escaped an encounter.
Each day we endeavored to camp a couple of hours before
sundown so as to give the men plenty of chance to get firewood, pitch the tents, and put everything in order. Sometimes we would make an early start; in which case we
would breakfast in the open, while in the east the crescent
of the dying moon hung over the glow that heralded the
sunrise.

As we reached the high, rolling downs the weather grew
cooler, and many flowers appeared; those of the aloes were
bright red, standing on high stalks above the clump of
fleshy, spined leaves, which were handsomely mottled, like
a snake's back. As I rode at the head of the safari I usually,
in the course of the day, shot a buck of some kind for the
table. I had not time to stalk, but simply took the shots
as they came, generally at long range. One day I shot
an eland, an old blue bull. We needed the skin for the
museum, and as there was water near by we camped where
we were; I had already shot a waterbuck that morning,
and this and the eland together gave the entire safari a feast
of meat.

On another occasion an eland herd afforded me fun,
although no profit. I was mounted on Brownie, the zebra-
shaped pony. Brownie would still occasionally run off
when I dismounted to shoot (a habit that had cost me an
eland bull); but he loved to gallop after game. We came
on a herd of eland in an open plain; they were directly
in our path. We were in the country where the ordinary
or Livingstone's eland grades into the Patterson's; and I
knew that the naturalists wished an additional bull's head
for the museum. So I galloped toward the herd; and for
the next fifteen or twenty minutes I felt as if I had renewed
my youth and was in the cow camps of the West, a quarter
of a century ago. Eland are no faster than range cattle.

Twice I rounded up the herd—just as once in the Yellowstone Park I rounded up a herd of wapiti for John Burroughs to look at—and three times I cut out of the herd a big animal, which, however, in each case, proved to be a cow. There were no big bulls, only cows and young stock; but I enjoyed the gallop.

From Neri we marched through mist and rain across the cold Aberdare table-lands, and in the forenoon of October 20 we saw from the top of the second Aberdare escarpment the blue waters of beautiful Lake Naivasha. On the next day we reached Nairobi.

CHAPTER XII

TO THE UASIN GISHU

AT Nairobi Kermit joined me, having enjoyed a notably successful hunt during the month since we had parted, killing both Neuman's hartebeest and koodoo. The great koodoo, with its spiral horns and striped coat, is the stateliest and handsomest antelope in the world. It is a shy creature, fond of bush and of rocky hills, and is hard to get.

After leaving me at Meru Kermit and Tarlton had travelled hard to Rumeruti. They had intended to go to Lake Hannington, but finding that this was in the reserve they went three days toward the north-west, stopping a score of miles east of Barengo. The country, which showed many traces of volcanic action, was rough, rocky, and dry; the hunting was exhausting, and Kermit was out from morning to night. Tarlton had been very sick on the Guaso Nyero, and although he was better he was in no shape to accompany Kermit, who therefore hunted only with his gun boys, taking them out alternately so as to spare them as much as possible. It took three days' steady work before he got his first koodoo. On the third day he hunted fruitlessly all the morning, came back to camp, picked up a fresh gun-bearer, Juma Yohari, and started out again. At four in the afternoon he came to the brink of a great hollow a mile across, perhaps an extinct crater, and looking from the rimrock, spied a koodoo bull in the bottom. The steep sides of the hollow were covered with a tangled growth of thorn scrub and cactus, traversed by rhinoceros paths. The bottom was more open, strewn with bushy mounds or hillocks, and on one of these stood a noble koodoo bull. He stood with his massive spiral horns thrown back, and they shifted slowly as he turned his head from side to side. Kermit stole down one of the rhino paths, save for which the scrub would have been practically impenetrable; it was alive with rhinos; Kermit heard several, and Juma who followed scme distance behind saw three. The stalk took time; and the sun was on the horizon and the light fading when, at over two hundred yards, Kermit took his shot. The first bullet missed, but as for a moment the bull paused and wheeled Kermit fired again and the second bullet went home. The wounded beast ran, Kermit, with Juma, hard on the trail; and he overtook and killed it just as darkness fell. Then back to camp they stumbled and plunged through the darkness, Kermit tearing the sole completely off one shoe. They reached camp at ten and Juma, who had only been working half the day, took out some porters to the dead bull, which they skinned, and then slept by until morning. Later, on his birthday, he killed a cow, which completed the group; the two koodoo cost him ten days' steady labor. The koodoo were always found on steep, rocky hills; their stomachs contained only grass, for both beasts when shot were grazing (I do not know whether or not they also browse). The mid-day hours, when the heat was most intense, they usually spent resting; but once Kermit came on two which were drinking in a stream exactly at noon.

From the koodoo camp the two hunters went to Lake Hannington, a lovely lake, with the mountains rising sheer from three of its sides. The water was saline, abounding with crocodiles and hippos; and there were myriads of flamingoes. They were to be seen swimming by thousands on the lake, and wading and standing in the shallows; and when they rose they looked like an enormous pink cloud; it was a glorious sight. They were tame; and Kermit had no difficulty in killing the specimens needed for the museum. Here Kermit also killed an impalla ram which had met with an extraordinary misadventure. It had been fighting with another ram, which had stabbed it in the chest with one horn.

The violent strain and shock, as the two vigorous beasts bounded together, broke off the horn, leaving the broken part, ten inches long, imbedded in the other buck's chest; about three inches of the point being fixed firmly in the body of the buck, while the rest stuck out like a picket pin. Yet the buck seemed well and strong.

Two days after leaving Lake Hannington they camped near the ostrich-farm of Mr. London, an American from Baltimore. He had been waging war on the lions and leopards, because they attacked his ostriches. He had killed at least a score of each, some with the rifle, some with poison or steel traps. The day following their arrival London went out hunting with Kermit and Tarlton. They saw nothing until evening, when Kermit's gun-bearer, Kassitura, spied a leopard coming from the carcass of a zebra which London had shot to use as bait for his traps. The leopard saw them a long way off and ran; Kermit ran after it and wounded it badly, twice; then Tarlton got a shot and hit it; and then London came across the dying beast at close quarters and killed it just as it was gathering itself to spring at him.

Thence they went to Nakuru, where Kermit killed two Neuman's hartebeest. They were scarce and wild, and Kermit obtained his two animals by long shots after following them for hours; following them until, as he expressed it, they got used to him, became a little less quick to leave, and gave him his chance.

While on this trip Kermit passed his twentieth birthday. While still nineteen he had killed all the kinds of African dangerous game—lion, leopard, elephant, buffalo, and rhino.

Heller also rejoined us, entirely recovered. He had visited Mearns and Loring at their camp high up on Mount Kenia, where they had made a thoroughly biological survey of the mountain. He had gone to the line of perpetual snow, where the rock peak rises abruptly from the swelling downs, and had camped near a little glacial lake whose waters froze every night. The zones of plant and animal life were

Juma Yohari with the impalla killed by Kermit Roosevelt at Lake Hannington

The broken horn of another ram imbedded in the buck's neck

From a photograph by Kermit Roosevelt

well marked; but there are some curious differences between the zones on these equatorial African snow mountains and those on similar mountains in the northern hemisphere, especially America. In the high mountains of North America the mammals are apt to be, at least in part, of totally different kinds from those found in the adjacent warm or hot plains, because they represent a fauna which was once spread over the land, but which has retreated northward, leaving faunal islands on the summits of the taller mountains. In this part of Africa, however, there has been no faunal retreat of this type, no survivals on the peaks of an ancient fauna which in the plains and valleys has been replaced by another fauna; here the mammals of the high mountains and table-lands are merely modified forms of the mammals of the adjacent lowlands, which have gradually crept up the slopes, changing in the process. High on Mount Kenia, for instance, are hyraxes, living among the snow-fields, much bigger than their brethren of the forests and rocky hills below; and light-colored mole rats, also much bigger than those of the lower country. Moreover, the lack of seasonal change is probably accountable for differences in the way that the tree zones are delimited. The mountain conifers of America are huge trees on the middle slopes, but higher up gradually dwindle into a thick, low scrub, composed of sprawling, dwarfed individuals of the same species. On Mount Kenia the tree zone ceases much more abruptly and with much less individual change among the different kinds of trees. Above this zone are the wet, cold downs and moors, with a very peculiar vegetation, plants which we know only as small flowering things having become trees. The giant groundsell, for instance, reaches a height of twenty feet, with very thick trunk and limbs which, though hollow, make good firewood; and this is only one example of the kind.

At Nairobi we learned, as usual, of incident after incident, which had happened among our friends and acquaintances, of exactly the type which would occur were it possible in North America or Europe suddenly to mix among existing conditions the men and animals that died out some hundreds of thousands of years ago. In a previous chapter I mentioned on one occasion meeting at dinner three men, all of whom had been mauled by lions; one being our host, Mr. F. A. Ward, who had served as a captain in the South African War, and was now one of the heads of the Boma Trading Company. Among our fellow-guests at this dinner was Captain Douglas Pennant of the British Army. When we went north to Kenia he went south to the Sotik. There he made a fine bag of lions; but having wounded a leopard and followed it into cover it suddenly sprang on him, apparently from a tree. His life was saved by his Somali gun-bearer who blew out the leopard's brains as it bore him to the ground, so that it had time to make only one bite; but this bite just missed crushing in the skull, broke the jaw, tore off one ear, and caused ghastly wreck. He spent some weeks in the hospital at Nairobi, and then went for further treatment to England; his place in the hospital being taken by another man who had been injured by a leopard.

There had been quite a plague of wild beasts in Nairobi itself. One family had been waked at midnight by a leopard springing on the roof of the house and thence to an adjacent shed; it finally spent a couple of hours on the veranda. A lion had repeatedly wandered at night through the outlying (the residential) portion of the town. Dr. Milne, the head of the Government Medical Department, had nearly run into it on his bicycle, and, as a measure of precaution, guests going out to dinner usually carried spears or rifles. One night I dined with the provincial commissioner, Mr. Hobley, and the next with the town clerk, Captain Sanderson. In each case the hostess, the host, and the house were all delightful, and the evening just like a very pleasant evening spent anywhere in civilization; the houses were only half a mile apart; and yet on the road between them a fortnight previously a lady on a bicycle, wheeling down to a rehearsal of "Trial by Jury," had been run into and upset by a herd of frightened zebras. One of my friends, Captain Smith, Director of Surveys in the Protectorate, had figured in another zebra incident to which only Mark Twain could do justice. Captain Smith lived on the outskirts of the town, and was much annoyed by the zebras tearing through his ground and trampling down his vegetables and flowers. So one night, by his direction, his Masai servant sallied out and speared a zebra which was tangled in a wire fence. But the magistrate, a rigid upholder of the letter of the law, fined the Masai for killing game without a license! (A touch quite worthy of comparison with Mark Twain's account of how, when he called for assistance while drowning, he was arrested for disturbing the peace.) Captain Smith decided that next time there should be no taint of illegality about his behavior, so he got ropes ready, and when the zebras returned he and his attendants again chased them toward the wire fences, and tied up one which got caught therein; and then with much difficulty he led it down town, *put it in the pound*, and notified Captain Sanderson, the town clerk, what he had done. This proceeding was entirely regular; and so was all that followed. For seven days the zebra was kept in the pound, while the authorities solemnly advertised for a highly improbable owner; then it was sold at auction, being brought to the sale, bucking, rolling, and fighting, securely held by ropes in the hands of various stalwart natives, and disposed of to the only bidder for five rupees. The court records are complete. The District Court criminal register, under date of February 1, 1909, contains the entry of the prosecution by the Crown through "Mutwa Wa. Najaka A.N." of the Masai for "killing zebra without a license (under section 4/35 Game Regulations of 15th April, 1906") and of the infliction of a fine of twenty rupees. The sequel appears in the Nairobi Municipality Pound Book under date of August 6, 1909. In the column headed "Description of

Animal" is the entry "1 zebra"; under the heading "By whom impounded" is the entry "Major Smith, R.E."; under the heading "Remarks" is the entry "Sold by Public Auctioneers Raphael & Coy on 24/8/09."

We had with us several recent books on East African big game; Chapman's "On Safari," dealing alike with the hunting and the natural history of big game; Powell Cotton's accounts of his noteworthy experiences both in hunting and in bold exploration; Stigand's capital studies of the spoor and habits of big game (it is to be regretted that he was too modest to narrate some of his own really extraordinary adventures in the chase of dangerous beasts); and Buxton's account of his two African trips.

Mr. Roosevelt in a bamboo forest
From a photograph by Kermit Roosevelt

Edward North Buxton's books ought to be in the hands of every hunter everywhere, and especially of every young hunter, because they teach just the right way in which to look at the sport. With Buxton big-game hunting is not a business but a pastime, not allowed to become a mania or in any way to interfere with the serious occupations of life, whether public or private; and yet as he has carried it on it is much more than a mere pastime, it is a craft, a pursuit of value in exercising and developing hardihood of body and the virile courage and resolution which necessarily lie at the base of every strong and manly character. He has not a touch of the game butcher in him; nor has he a touch of that craving for ease and luxury the indulgence in which turns any sport into a sham and a laughing-stock. Big-game hunting, pursued as he has pursued it, stands at the opposite pole from those so-called sports carried on primarily either as money-making exhibitions, or, what is quite as bad—though the two evils are usually found in different social strata—in a spirit of such luxurious self-indulgence as to render them at best harmless extravagances, and at worst forces which positively tend to the weakening of moral and physical fibre.

On October 26, Tarlton, Kermit, Heller, and I started from the railroad station of Londiani, for the Uasin Gishu plateau and the 'Nzoi River, which flows not far from the foot of Mount Elgon. This stretch of country has apparently received its fauna from the shores of Lake Victoria Nyanza, and contains several kinds of antelope, and a race or variety of giraffe, the five-horned, which are not found to the eastward, in the region where we had already hunted.

On the 27th we were marching hard, and I had no chance to hunt; I would have liked to take a hunt, because it was my birthday. The year before I had celebrated my fiftieth birthday by riding my jumping horse, Roswell, over all the jumps in Rock Creek Park, at Washington. Roswell is a safe and good jumper, and a very easy horse to sit at a jump; he took me, without hesitation or error, over everything, from the water-jump to the stone wall, the rails, and the bank, including a brush hurdle just over five feet and a half high.

For the first four days our route led among rolling hills and along valleys and ravines, the country being so high that the nights were actually cold, although we crossed and recrossed the equator. The landscape in its general effect called to mind southern Oregon and northern California rather than any tropical country. Some of the hills were bald, others wooded to the top; there were wet meadows, and hill-sides covered with tussocks of rank, thick-growing grass, alternating with stretches of forest; and the chief trees of the forest were stately cedars, yews, and tall laurel-leaved olives. All this was, at least in superficial aspect, northern enough; but now and then we came to patches of the thoroughly tropical bamboo, which in East Africa, however, one soon grows to associate with cold, rainy weather, for it only grows at high altitudes. In this country, high, cold, rainy, there were several kinds of buck, but none in any numbers. The most interesting were the roan antelope, which went in herds. Their trails led everywhere, across the high, rolling hill pastures of coarse grass, and through the tangled tree groves and the still, lifeless bamboo jungle. They were found in herds and lived in the open, feeding on the bare hill-sides and in the wet valleys at all hours; but they took cover freely, and when the merciless gales blew they sought shelter in woodland and jungle. Usually they grazed, but once I saw one browsing. Both on our way in and on our way back, through this hill country, we shot several roan, for, though their horns are poor, they form a distinct sub-species, peculiar to the region. The roan is a big antelope, nearly as tall, although by no means as bulky, as an eland, with curved scimitar-like horns, huge ears, and face markings as sharply defined as those of an oryx. It is found here and there, in isolated localities, throughout Africa south of the Sahara, and is of bold, fierce temper. One of those which Kermit shot was only crippled by the first bullet, and charged the gun-bearers, squealing savagely, in addition to using its horns; an angry roan, like a sable, is said sometimes to bite with its teeth. Kermit also killed a ratel or honey badger, in a bamboo thicket; an interesting beast; its back snow white and the rest of its body jet black.

As on the Aberdares and the slopes of Kenia, the nights among these mountains were cold; sometimes so cold that

I was glad to wear a mackinaw, a lumberman's jacket, which
had been given me by Jack Greenway, and which I certainly never expected to wear in Africa.

The porters always minded cold, especially if there was
rain, and I was glad to get them to the Uasin Gishu, where
the nights were merely cool enough to make one appreciate blankets,
while the days
were never op-
pressively hot.
Although the
Swahilis have
furnished the
model for all
East African
safari work,
and supply the
lingua franca
for the country,
they no longer
compose the

Kassitura with the roan antelope

From a photograph by Kermit Roosevelt

bulk of the porters. Of our porters at this time about two-
fifths were stalwart M'nuwezi from German East Africa,
two-fifths were Wakamba, and the remainder Swahilis with
half a dozen Kavirondos and Kikuyus. The M'nuwezi are
the strongest of all, and make excellent porters. They will
often be as much as two or three years away from their
homes; for safari work is very attractive to the best type
of natives, as they live much better than if travelling on
their own account, and as it offers almost the only way in
which they can earn money. The most severe punishment
that can be inflicted on a gun-bearer, tent boy, sais, or
porter is to dismiss him on such terms as to make it impossible for him again to be employed on a safari. In
camp the men of each tribe group themselves together in
parties, each man sharing any unwonted delicacy with his
cronies.

Very rarely did we have to take such long marches as to exhaust our strapping burden-bearers; usually they came into camp in high good-humor, singing and blowing antelope horns; and in the evening, after the posho had been distributed, cooked, and eaten, the different groups would gather each around its camp-fire, and the men would chant in unison while the flutes wailed and the buzzing harps twanged. Of course individuals were all the time meeting with accidents or falling sick, especially when they had the chance to gorge themselves on game that we had killed; and then Cuninghame or Tarlton—than whom two stancher and pleasanter friends, keener hunters, or better safari managers are not to be found in all Africa—would have to add the functions of a doctor to an already multifarious round of duties. Some of the men had to be watched lest they should malinger; others were always complaining of trifles; others never complained at all. Gosho, our excellent headman, came in the last category. On this Uasin Gishu trip we noticed him limping one evening; and inquiry developed the fact that the previous night, while in his tent, he had been bitten by a small poisonous snake. The leg was much swollen, and looked angry and inflamed; but Gosho never so much as mentioned the incident until we questioned him, and in a few days was as well as ever. Heller's chief feeling, by the way, when informed what had happened, was one of indignation because the offending snake, after paying the death penalty, had been thrown away instead of being given to him as a specimen.

The roans were calving in early November; whereas, when we went thirty miles on, at an elevation a thousand feet less, we at first saw no very young fawns accompanying the hartebeests, and no very young foals with the zebras. These hartebeests, which are named after their discoverer, Governor Jackson, are totally different from the hartebeests of the Athi and the Sotik countries, and are larger and finer in every way. One bull I shot weighed, in pieces, four hundred and seventy pounds. No allowance was made for the spilt blood, and inasmuch as he had been hallalled, I think his live weight would have been nearly four hundred and ninety pounds. He was a big, full-grown bull, but not of extraordinary size; later I killed much bigger ones, unusually fine specimens, which must have weighed well over five hundred pounds. The horns, which are sometimes two feet long, are set on great bony pedicels, so that the face seems long and homely even for a hartebeest. The first two or three of these hartebeests which I killed were shot at long range, for, like all game, they are sometimes exceedingly wary; but we soon found that normally they were as tame as they were plentiful. We frequently saw them close by the herds of the Boer settlers. They were the common game of the plains. At times of course they were difficult to approach; but again and again, usually when we were riding, we came upon not only individuals but herds, down wind and in plain view, which permitted us to approach to within a hundred yards before they definitely took flight. Their motions look ungainly until they get into their full speed stride. They utter no sound save the usual hartebeest sneeze.

There were bohor reedbuck also, pretty creatures, about the size of a white-tail deer, which lay close in the reedbeds, or in hollows among the tall grass, and usually offered rather difficult running shots or very long standing shots. Still prettier were the little oribi. These are grass antelopes, frequenting much the same places as the duiker and steinbuck and not much larger. Where the grass was long they would lie close, with neck flat along the ground, and dart off when nearly stepped on, with a pig-like rush like that of a reedbuck or duiker in similar thick cover. But where the grass was short, and especially where it was burned, they did not trust to lying down and hiding; on the contrary, in such places they were conspicuous little creatures, and trusted to their speed and alert vigilance for their safety. They run very fast, with great bounds, and when they stand—usually at a hundred and fifty or two hundred yards—they face the hunter, the forward-thrown ears being the most noticeable thing about them. We found that each oribi bagged cost us an unpleasantly large number of cartridges.

One day we found where a large party of hyenas had established their day lairs in the wet seclusion of some reed-

A hyena by flashlight

From a photograph by J. Alden Loring

beds. We beat through these reedbeds, and, in the words once used by an old plains friend in describing the behavior of a family of black bears under similar circumstances, the hyenas "came bilin' out." As they bolted Kermit shot one and I another; his bit savagely at a stick with which one of the gun-bearers poked it. It is difficult at first glance to tell the sex of a hyena, and our followers stoutly upheld the wide-spread African belief that they are bi-sexual, being male or female as they choose. A wounded or trapped hyena will of course bite if seized, but shows no sign of the ferocious courage which marks the leopard under such circumstances; for the hyena is as cowardly as it is savage, although its size and the tremendous power of its jaws ought to make it as formidable as the fierce spotted cat.

The day after this incident we came on a herd of giraffe. It was Kermit's turn for a giraffe; and just as the herd got under way he wounded the big bull. Away went the tall creatures, their tails twisting and curling, as they cantered along over the rough veldt and among the thorn-bushes, at that gait of theirs which looks so leisurely and which yet enables them to cover so much ground. After them we tore, Kermit and Tarlton in the lead; and a fine chase we had. It was not until we had gone two or three miles that the bull lagged behind the herd. I was riding the tranquil sorrel, not a speedy horse; and by this time my weight was telling on him. Kermit and his horse had already turned a somersault, having gone into an ant-bear hole, which the tall grass concealed; but they were up and off in an instant. All of Tranquillity's enthusiasm had vanished, and only by constant thumping with heels and gun butt could I keep him at a slow hand gallop, and in sight of the leaders. We came to a slight rise, where the rank grass grew high and thick; and Tranquillity put both his forelegs into an ant-bear hole, and with obvious relief rolled gently over on his side. It was not really a tumble; he hailed the ant-bear burrow as offering a way out of a chase in which he had grown to take less than no interest. Besides, he really was winded, and when we got up I could barely get him into a canter; and I saw no more of the run. Meanwhile Kermit and Tarlton raced alongside the wounded bull, one on each flank, and started him toward camp, which was about five miles from where the hunt began. Two or three times he came to a stand-still, and turned first toward one and then toward the other of his pursuers, almost as if he meditated a charge; but they shouted at him and he resumed his flight. They brought him within three hundred yards of camp, and then Kermit leaped off and finished him.

This bull was a fine specimen, colored almost exactly like the giraffes of the Athi and Sotik, but with much more horn development. I doubt whether this five-horned kind is more than a local race. The bulls have been described as very dark; but the one thus shot, a big and old master bull, was unusually light, and in the herd there were individuals of every shade, much the darkest being a rather small cow. Indeed, in none of the varieties of giraffe did we find that the old bulls were markedly darker than the others; many of them were dark, but some of the biggest were light-colored, and the darkest individuals in a herd were often cows. Giraffes, by the way, do sometimes lie down to sleep, but not often.*

In order that Heller might take care of the giraffe skin we had to spend a couple of days where we were then camped. The tents were pitched near a spring of good water, beside a slight valley in which there were marshy spots and reedbeds. The country was rolling, and covered with fine grass, unfortunately so tall as to afford secure cover for lions. There were stretches bare of trees, and other stretches with a sparse, scattered growth of low thorns or of the big, glossy-leaved bush which I have spoken of as the African jessamine because of the singularly sweet and jessamine-like fragrance of its flowers. Most of these bushes were in full bloom, as they had been six months before on the Athi and three months before near Kenia; some bore berries, of which it is said that the wild elephant herds are fond.

It is hard to lay down general rules as to the blossoming times of plants or breeding times of animals in equatorial

* This is just one of the points as to which no one observer should dogmatize or try to lay down general laws with no exceptions. Moreover, the personal equation of even the most honest observer must always be taken into account in considering not merely matters like this, but even such things as measurements. For example, Neuman, in his "Elephant Hunting," gives measurements of the height of both elephants and Grévy's zebra; our measurements made the elephants taller, and the big zebras less tall, than he found them. Measurements of the lengths of lions, made by different observers, are for this reason rarely of much value for purposes of comparison.

Africa. Before we left the Uasin Gishu table-land some of the hartebeest cows appeared with new-born calves. Some of the acacias had put forth their small, globular, yellow blossoms, just as the acacias on the Athi Plains were doing in the previous May. The blue lupins were flowering, for it is a cool, pleasant country.

Our camp here was attractive, and Kermit and I took advantage of our leisure to fill out the series of specimens of the big hartebeest and the oribi which Heller needed for the National Museum. The flesh of the oribis was reserved for our own table; that of the kongonis—which had been duly hallalled by the Moslems among our gun-bearers —was turned over to what might be called the officers' mess of the safari proper, the headmen, cooks, tent boys, gun-bearers, and saises; while of course the skinners and porters who happened to be out with us when any animal was slain got their share of the meat. We also killed two more hyenas; one, a dog, weighed one hundred and twenty pounds, being smaller than those Heller had trapped while skinning the first bull elephant I shot in the Kenia forest.

Good Ali, my tent boy, kept bowls of the sweet-scented jessamine on our dining-table; now that there were four of us together again we used the dining-tent, which I had discarded on the Guaso Nyero trip. Bakhari had been rather worn down by the work on the Guaso Nyero, and in his place I had taken Kongoni, a Wakamba with filed teeth, like my second gun-bearer, Gouvimali, but a Moslem —although his Moslemism did not go very deep. Kongoni was the best gun-bearer I had yet had, very willing, and excellent both at seeing and tracking game. Kermit's two gun-bearers were Juma Yohari, a coal-black Swahili Moslem, and Kassitura, a Christian negro from Uganda. Both of them were as eager to do everything for Kermit as mine were to render me any service great or small; and in addition they were capital men for their special work. Juma was always smiling and happy, and was a high favorite among his fellows; at lunch, when we had any, if

I gave my own followers some of the chocolate, or whatever else it was that I had put in my saddle pocket, I always noticed that they called up Yohari to share it. He it was who would receive the colored cards from my companions' tobacco pouches, or from the packages of chocolate, and after puzzling over them until he could himself identify the brilliantly colored ladies, gentlemen, little girls, and wild beasts, would volubly explain them to the others. Kassitura, quite as efficient and hardworking, was a huge, solemn black man, as faithful and uncomplaining a soul as I ever met. Kermit had picked him out from among the porters to carry his camera, and had then

Yohari with the waterbuck shot by Kermit Roosevelt
From a photograph by Kermit Roosevelt

promoted him to be gun-bearer. In his place he had taken as camera-bearer an equally powerful porter, a heathen M'nuwezi named Mali. His tent boy had gone crooked; and one evening some months later after a long and trying march he found Mali, whose performance of his new duties he had been closely watching, the only man up; and Mali, always willing, turned in of his own accord to help get Kermit's tent in shape; so Kermit suddenly told him he would promote him to be tent boy. At first Mali did not quite understand; then he pondered a moment or two, and suddenly leaped into the air exclaiming in Swahili, "Now I am a big man." And he faithfully strove to justify his promotion. In similar fashion Kermit picked out on the Nairobi race-track a Kikuyu sais named Magi, and brought him out with us. Magi turned out the best sais in the safari; and besides doing his own duty so well he was always exceedingly interested in everything that concerned his own Bwana, Kermit, or me—from the proper arrangement of our sunpads to the success of our shooting.

From the giraffe camp we went two days' journey to the 'Nzoi River. Until this Uasin Gishu trip we had been on waters which either vanished in the desert or else flowed into the Indian Ocean. Now we had crossed the divide, and were on the Nile side of the watershed. The 'Nzoi, a rapid muddy river, passing south of Mount Elgon, empties into the Victoria Nyanza. Our route to its bank led across a rolling country, covered by a dense growth of tall grass, and in most places by open thorn scrub, while here and there, in the shallow valleys or depressions, were swamps. There were lions, and at night we heard them; but in such long grass it was wellnigh hopeless to look for them. Evidently troops of elephants occasionally visited these plains, for the tops of the little thorn-trees were torn off and browsed down by the mighty brutes. How they can tear off and swallow such prickly dainties as these thorn branches, armored with needle-pointed spikes, is a mystery. Tarlton told me that he had seen an elephant, while feeding greedily on the young top of a thorn-tree, prick its trunk until it uttered a little scream or whine of pain; and it then in a fit of pettishness revenged itself by wrecking the thorn-tree.

Game abounded on the plains. We saw a couple of herds of giraffes. The hartebeests were the most plentiful and the least shy; time after time a small herd loitered until we were within a hundred yards before cantering away. Once or twice we saw topi among them; and often there were mixed herds of zebras and hartebeests. Oribi were common, and sometimes uttered a peculiar squealing whistle when they first saw us. The reedbuck also whistled, but their whistle was entirely distinct. It was astonishing how close the reedbuck lay. Again and again we put them up within a few feet of us from patches of reeds or hollows in the long grass. A much more singular habit is the way in which they share these retreats with dangerous wild beasts; a trait common also to the cover-loving bushbuck. From one of the patches of reeds in which Kermit and I shot two hyenas a reedbuck doe immediately afterward took flight. She had been reposing peacefully during the day within fifty yards of several hyenas! Tarlton had more than once found both reedbuck and bushbuck in comparatively small patches of cover which also held lions.

It is, by the way, a little difficult to know what names to use in distinguishing between the sexes of African game. The trouble is one which obtains in all new countries, where the settlers have to name new beasts; and is, of course, primarily due to the fact that the terms already found in the language originally applied only to domestic animals and to European beasts of the chase. Africanders, whether Dutch or English, speak of all antelope, of either sex, as "buck." Then they call the males and females of the larger kinds bulls and cows, just as Americans do when they speak of moose, wapiti, and caribou; and the males and females of the smaller kinds they usually speak of as rams and ewes.

While on safari to the 'Nzoi I was even more interested in honey birds which led us to honey than I was in the game. Before starting for Africa John Burroughs had especially charged me to look personally into this extraordinary habit of the honey bird; a habit so extraordinary that he was inclined to disbelieve the reality of its existence. But it unquestionably does exist. Every experienced hunter and every native who lives in the wilderness has again and again been an eye-witness of it. Kermit, in addition to his experience in the Sotik, had been

led by a honey bird to honey in a rock, near Lake Hannington. Once while I was tracking game a honey bird
made his appearance, chattering loudly and flying beside
us; I let two of the porters follow it, and it led them to
honey. On the morning of the day we reached the 'Nzoi,
a honey bird appeared beside the safari, behaving in the
same manner. Some of the men begged to be allowed to
follow it; while they were talking to me the honey bird
flew to a big tree fifty yards off, and called loudly as it
flitted to and fro
in the branches;
and sure enough
there was honey
in the tree. I let
some of the men
stay to get the
honey; but they
found little ex-
cept comb filled
with grubs.
Some of this was
put aside for the
bird, which ate
the grubs. The

Tarlton and singsing shot by Mr Roosevelt
From a photograph by Kermit Roosevelt

natives believe that misfortune will follow any failure on
their part to leave the honey bird its share of the booty.
They also insist that sometimes the honey bird will lead a
man to a serpent or wild beast; and sure enough Dr.
Mearns was once thus led up to a rhinoceros. While camped
on the 'Nzoi the honey birds were almost a nuisance; they
were very common, and were continually accompanying
us as we hunted, flying from tree to tree, and never ceasing
their harsh chatter. Several times we followed birds, which
in each case led us to bee-trees, and then perched quietly
by until the gun-bearers and porters (Gouvimali shone
on such occasions) got out the honey—which we found
excellent eating, by the way.

Our camp here was in a beautiful country, and game, for the most part Uganda kob and singsing waterbuck, often fed in sight of the tents. The kob is a small short-haired waterbuck, with slightly different horns. It is a chunky antelope, with a golden-red coat; I weighed one old buck which I shot and it tipped the beam at two hundred and twenty pounds; Kermit killed a bigger one, weighing two hundred and forty pounds, but its horns were poorer. In their habits the kob somewhat resemble impalla, the does being found in bands of twenty or thirty with a single master buck; and they sometimes make great impalla-like bounds. They fed, at all hours of the day, in the flats near the river, and along the edges of the swamps, and were not very wary. They never tried to hide, and were always easily seen; in utter contrast to the close-lying, skulking, bohor reedbuck, which lay like a rabbit in the long grass or reeds. The kob, on the contrary, were always anxious themselves to see round about, and, like waterbuck and hartebeest, frequently used the ant-heaps as lookout stations. It was a pretty sight to see a herd of the bright-red creatures clustered on a big ant-hill, all the necks outstretched and all the ears thrown forward. The females are hornless. By the middle of November we noticed an occasional new-born calf.

The handsome, shaggy-coated, singsing waterbuck had much the same habits as the kob. Like the kob they fed at all hours of the day; but they were more wary and more apt to be found in country where there were a good many bushes or small trees. Waterbuck and kob sometimes associated together.

The best singsing bull I got I owed to Tarlton's good eyesight and skill in tracking and stalking. The herd of which he was master bull were shy, and took the alarm just as we first saw them. Tarlton followed their trail for a couple of miles, and then stalked them to an inch, by the dextrous use of a couple of bushes and an ant-hill; the ant-hill being reached after a two hundred yards' crawl,

first on all-fours and then flat on the ground, which re-
sulted in my getting a good off-hand shot at a hundred and
eighty yards. At this time, about the middle of November,
some of the cows had new-born calves. One day I shot a
hartebeest bull, with horns twenty-four inches long, as it
stood on the top of an ant-heap. On going up to it we
noticed something behind a little bush, sixty yards off.
We were puzzled what it could be, but finally made out a
waterbuck cow; and a minute or two later away she bounded
to safety, followed by a wee calf. The porters much appreciated the flesh of the waterbuck. We did not. It is the
poorest eating of African antelope—and among the big
antelope only the eland is good as a steady diet.

One day we drove a big swamp, putting a hundred porters across it in line, while Kermit and I walked a little
ahead of them along the edges, he on one side and I on the
other. I shot a couple of bushbuck, a ewe and a young
ram; and after the drive was over he shot a female leopard
as she stood on the side of an ant-hill.

There were a number of both reedbuck and bushbuck
in the swamp. The reedbuck were all ewes, which we did
not want. There were one or two big bushbuck rams, but
they broke back through the beaters; and so did two
bushbuck ewes and one reedbuck ewe, one of the bushbuck
ewes actually knocking down a beater. They usually
either cleared out while the beaters were still half a mile
distant, or else waited until they were almost trodden on.
The bushbuck rams were very dark colored; the hornless
ewes, and the young, were a brilliant red, the belly, the
under side and edges of the conspicuous fluffy tail, and a
few dim spots on the cheeks and flanks, being white. Although these buck frequent thick cover, forest, or swamp,
and trust for their safety to hiding, and to eluding observation by their stealthy, skulking ways, their coloration has not
the smallest protective value, being on the contrary very
conspicuous in both sexes, but especially in the females and
young, who most need protection. Bushbuck utter a loud

bark. The hooves of those we shot were very long, as is often the case with water-loving, marsh-frequenting species. There is a curious collar-like space around the neck on which there is no hair. Although if anything smaller than our white-tail deer, the bushbuck is a vicious and redoubtable fighter, and will charge a man without hesitation.

The last day we were at the 'Nzoi the porters petitioned for one ample meal of meat; and we shot a dozen buck

Juma Yohari with Nilotic bushbuck
From a photograph by Kermit Roosevelt

for them—kongoni, kob, and singsing. One of the latter, a very fine bull, fairly charged Kermit and his gun-bearer when they got within a few yards of it, as it lay wounded. This bull grunted loudly as he charged; the grunt of an oryx under similar circumstances is almost a growl. On this day both Kermit and I were led to bee-trees by honey birds and took some of the honey for lunch. Kermit stayed after his boys had left the tree, so as to see exactly what the honey bird did. The boys had smoked out the bees, and when they left the tree was still smoking. Throughout the process the honey bird had stayed quietly in a neighboring tree, occasionally uttering a single bubbling cluck. As soon as the boys left, it flew straight for the smoking bee-tree, uttering a long trill, utterly different from the chattering noise made while trying to attract the attention of the men and lead them to the tree; and not only did it eat the grubs, but it also ate the bees that were stupefied by the smoke.

Next day we moved camp to the edge of a swamp about five miles from the river. Near the tents was one of the trees which, not knowing its real name, we called "sausage-tree"; the seeds or fruits are encased in a kind of hard gourd, the size of a giant sausage, which swings loosely at the end of a long tendril. The swamp was half or three-quarters of a mile across, with one or two ponds in the middle, from which we shot ducks. Francolins—delicious eating, as the ducks were also—uttered their grating calls near by; while oribi and hartebeest were usually to be seen from the tents. The hartebeest, by the way, in its three forms, is much the commonest game animal of East Africa.

A few miles beyond this swamp we suddenly came on a small herd of elephants in the open. There were eight cows and two calves, and they were moving slowly, feeding on the thorny tops of the scattered mimosas, and of other bushes which were thornless. The eyesight of elephants is very bad; I doubt whether they see more clearly than a rather near-sighted man; and we walked up to within seventy yards of these, slight though the cover was, so that Kermit could try to photograph them. We did not need to kill another cow for the National Museum, and so after we had looked at the huge, interesting creatures as long as we wished, we croaked and whistled, and they moved off with leisurely indifference. There is always a fascination about watching elephants; they are such giants, they are so intelligent—much more so than any other game, except perhaps the lion, whose intelligence has a very sinister bent—and they look so odd with their great ears flapping and their trunks lifting and curling. Elephants are rarely absolutely still for any length of time; now and then they flap an ear, or their bodies sway slightly, while at intervals they utter curious internal rumblings, or trumpet gently. These were feeding on saplings of the mimosas and other trees, apparently caring nothing for the thorns of the former; they would tear off branches, big or little, or snap a trunk short off if the whim seized them. They swallowed the leaves and twigs of these trees; but I have known them to merely chew and spit out the stems of certain bushes.

After leaving the elephants we were on our way back to camp when we saw a white man in the trail ahead; and on coming nearer whom should it prove to be but Carl Akeley, who was out on a trip for the American Museum of Natural History in New York. We went with him to his camp, where we found Mrs. Akeley, Clark, who was assisting him, and Messrs. McCutcheon and Stevenson who were along on a hunting trip. They were old friends and I was very glad to see them. McCutcheon, the cartoonist, had been at a farewell lunch given me by Robert Collier just before I left New York, and at the lunch we had been talking much of George Ade, and the first question I put to him was "*Where* is George Ade?" for if one unexpectedly meets an American cartoonist on a hunting trip in mid-Africa there seems no reason why one should not also see his crony, an American playwright. A year previously Mr. and Mrs. Akeley had lunched with me at the White House, and we had talked over our proposed African trips. Akeley, an old African wanderer, was going out with the especial purpose of getting a group of elephants for the American Museum, and was anxious that I should shoot one or two of them for him. I had told him that I certainly would if it were a possibility; and on learning that we had just seen a herd of cows he felt—as I did—that the chance had come for me to fulfil my promise. So we decided that he should camp with us that night, and that next morning we would

start with a light outfit to see whether we could not overtake the herd.

An amusing incident occurred that evening. After dark
some of the porters went through the reeds to get water from
the pond in the middle of the swamp. I was sitting in my
tent when a loud yelling and screaming rose from the swamp,
and in rushed Kongoni to say that one of the men, while
drawing water, had been seized by a lion. Snatching up
a rifle I was off at a run for the swamp, calling for lanterns;
Kermit and Tarlton joined me, the lanterns were brought,
and we reached the meadow of short marsh grass which
surrounded the high reeds in the middle. No sooner were
we on this meadow than there were loud snortings in the
darkness ahead of us, and then the sound of a heavy animal galloping across our front. It now developed that
there was no lion in the case at all, but that the porters had
been chased by a hippo. I should not have supposed that
a hippo would live in such a small, isolated swamp; but
there he was on the meadow in front of me, invisible, but
snorting, and galloping to and fro. Evidently he was much
interested in the lights, and we thought he might charge
us; but he did not, retreating slowly as we advanced, until
he plunged into the little pond. Hippos are sometimes
dangerous at night, and so we waded through the swamp
until we came to the pool at which the porters filled their
buckets, and stood guard over them until they were through;
while the hippo, unseen in the darkness, came closer to us,
snorting and plunging—possibly from wrath and insolence,
but more probably from mere curiosity.

Next morning Akeley, Tarlton, Kermit, and I started
on our elephant hunt. We were travelling light. I took
nothing but my bedding, wash kit, spare socks, and slippers,
all in a roll of waterproof canvas. We went to where we
had seen the herd and then took up the trail, Kongoni and
two or three other gun-bearers walking ahead as trackers.
They did their work well. The elephants had not been in
the least alarmed. Where they had walked in single file

it was easy to follow their trail; but the trackers had hard work puzzling it out where the animals had scattered out and loitered along feeding. The trail led up and down hills and through open thorn scrub, and it crossed and recrossed the wooded watercourses in the bottoms of the valleys. At last, after going some ten miles we came on sign where the elephants had fed that morning, and four or five miles further on we overtook them. That we did not scare them into flight was due to Tarlton. The trail went nearly across wind; the trackers were leading us swiftly along it, when suddenly Tarlton heard a low trumpet ahead and to the right hand. We at once doubled back, left the horses, and advanced toward where the noise indicated that the herd was standing.

In a couple of minutes we sighted them. It was just noon. There were six cows, and two well-grown calves— these last being quite big enough to shift for themselves or to be awkward antagonists for any man of whom they could get hold. They stood in a clump, each occasionally shifting its position or lazily flapping an ear; and now and then one would break off a branch with its trunk, tuck it into its mouth, and withdraw it stripped of its leaves. The wind blew fair, we were careful to make no noise, and with ordinary caution we had nothing to fear from their eyesight. The ground was neither forest nor bare plain; it was covered with long grass and a scattered open growth of small, scantily leaved trees, chiefly mimosas, but including some trees covered with gorgeous orange-red flowers. After careful scrutiny we advanced behind an ant-hill to within sixty yards, and I stepped forward for the shot.

Akeley wished two cows and a calf. Of the two best cows one had rather thick, worn tusks; those of the other were smaller, but better shaped. The latter stood half facing me, and I put the bullet from the right barrel of the Holland through her lungs, and fired the left barrel for the heart of the other. Tarlton, and then Akeley and Kermit, followed suit. At once the herd started diagonally past us, but half halted and faced toward us when only twenty-five yards distant, an unwounded cow beginning to advance with her great ears cocked at right angles to her head; and Tarlton called "Look out; they are coming for us." At such a distance a charge from half a dozen elephant is a serious thing; I put a bullet into the forehead of the advancing cow, causing her

to lurch heavily forward to her knees; and then we all fired. The heavy rifles were too much even for such big beasts, and round they spun and rushed off. As they turned I dropped the second cow I had wounded with a shot in the brain, and the cow that had started to charge also fell, though it needed two or three more shots to keep it down as it struggled to rise. The

Round the elephant

From a photograph by Kermit Roosevelt

cow at which I had first fired kept on with the rest of the herd, but fell dead before going a hundred yards. After we had turned the herd Kermit with his Winchester killed a bull calf, necessary to complete the museum group; we had been unable to kill it before because we were too busy stopping the charge of the cows. I was sorry to have to shoot the third cow, but with elephant starting to charge at twenty-five yards the risk is too great, and the need of instant action too imperative, to allow of any hesitation.

We pitched camp a hundred yards from the elephants, and Akeley, working like a demon, and assisted by Tarlton, had the skins off the two biggest cows and the calf by the time night fell; I walked out and shot an oribi for supper. Soon after dark the hyenas began to gather at the carcasses and to quarrel among themselves as they gorged. Toward

The hyena, which was swollen with elephant meat, had gotten inside the huge body

From a photograph by Carl Akeley

morning a lion came near and uttered a kind of booming, long-drawn moan, an ominous and menacing sound. The hyenas answered with an extraordinary chorus of yelling, howling, laughing, and chuckling, as weird a volume of noise as any to which I ever listened. At dawn we stole down to the carcasses in the faint hope of a shot at the lion. However, he was not there; but as we came toward one carcass a hyena raised its head seemingly from beside the elephant's belly, and I brained it with the little Springfield. On walking up it appeared that I need not have shot at all. The hyena, which was swollen with elephant meat, had gotten inside the huge body, and had then bitten a hole through the abdominal wall of tough muscle and thrust his head through. The wedge-shaped head had slipped through the hole all right, but the muscle had then contracted, and the hyena was fairly caught, with its body inside the elephant's belly, and its head thrust out through the hole. We took several photos of the beast in its queer trap.

After breakfast we rode back to our camp by the swamp. Akeley and Clark were working hard at the elephant skins; but Mrs. Akeley, Stevenson, and McCutcheon took lunch with us at our camp. They had been having a very successful hunt; Mrs. Akeley had to her credit a fine maned lion and a bull elephant with enormous tusks. This was the first safari we had met while we were out in the field; though in Nairobi, and once or twice at outlying bomas, we had met men about to start on, or returning from, expeditions; and as we marched into Meru we encountered the safari of an old friend, William Lord Smith—"Tiger" Smith—who, with Messrs. Brooks and Allen, were on a trip which was partly a hunting trip and partly a scientific trip undertaken on behalf of the Cambridge Museum.

From the 'Nzoi we made a couple days' march to Lake Sergoi, which we had passed on our way out; a reed-fringed pond, surrounded by rocky hills which marked about the limit to which the Boer and English settlers who were taking up the country had spread. All along our route we encountered herds of game; sometimes the herd would be of only one species; at other times we would come across a great mixed herd, the red hartebeest always predominating; while among them might be zebras, showing silvery white or dark gray in the distance, topis with beautifully colored coats, and even waterbuck. We shot what hartebeests, topis, and oribis were needed for food. All over the uplands we came on the remains of a race of which even the memory has long since vanished. These remains consist of large, nearly circular walls of stones, which are sometimes roughly squared. A few of these circular enclosures contain more than one chamber. Many of them, at least, are not cattle kraals, being too small, and built round hollows; the walls are so low that by themselves they could not serve for shelter or defence, and must probably have been used as supports for roofs of timber or skins. They were certainly built by people who were in some respects more advanced than the savage tribes who now dwell in the land; but the grass grows thick on the earth mounds into which the ancient stone walls are slowly crumbling, and not a trace of the builders remains. Barbarians they doubtless were; but they have been engulfed in the black oblivion of a lower barbarism, and not the smallest tradition lingers to tell of their craft or their cruelty, their industry or prowess, or to give us the least hint as to the race from which they sprang.

We had with us an ox wagon, with the regulation span of sixteen oxen, the driver being a young colonial Englishman from South Africa—for the Dutch and English Africanders are the best ox-wagon drivers in the world. On the way back to Sergoi he lost his oxen, which were probably run off by some savages from the mountains; so at Sergoi we had to hire another ox wagon, the South African who drove it being a Dutchman named Botha. Sergoi was as yet the limit of settlement; but it was evident that the whole Uasin Gishu country would soon be occupied. Already many Boers from South Africa, and a number of English Africanders, had come in; and no better pioneers exist to-day than these South Africans, both Dutch and English. Both are so good that I earnestly hope they will become indissolubly welded into one people; and the Dutch Boer has the supreme merit of preferring the country to the town and of bringing his wife and children—plenty of children—with him to settle on the land. The homemaker is the only type of settler of permanent value; and the cool, healthy, fertile Uasin Gishu region is an ideal land for the right kind of pioneer home-maker, whether he hopes to make his living by raising stock or by growing crops.

At Sergoi Lake there is a store kept by Mr. Kirke, a South African of Scotch blood. With a kind courtesy which I cannot too highly appreciate he, with the equally cordial help of another settler, Mr. Skally—also a South African, but of Irish birth—and of the district commissioner, Mr. Corbett, had arranged for a party of Nandi warriors to come over and show me how they hunted the lion. Two Dutch

Mr. Roosevelt and some of the Nandi warriors
From a photograph by Kermit Roosevelt

farmers, Boers, from the neighborhood, had also come; they were Messrs. Mouton and Jordaan, fine fellows both, the former having served with De Wet during the war. Mr. and Mrs. Corbett—who were hospitality itself—had also come to see the sport; and so had Captain Chapman, an English army officer who was taking a rest after several years' service in Northern Nigeria.

The Nandi are a warlike pastoral tribe, close kin to the Masai in blood and tongue, in weapons and in manner of life. They have long been accustomed to kill with the spear lions which become man-eaters or which molest their cattle overmuch; and the peace which British rule has imposed upon them—a peace so welcome to the weaker, so irksome to the predatory, tribes—has left lion killing one of the few pursuits in which glory can be won by a young warrior. When it was told them that if they wished they could come to hunt lions at Sergoi eight hundred warriors volunteered, and much heart-burning was caused in choosing the sixty or seventy who were allowed the privilege. They stipulated, however, that they should not be used merely as beaters, but should kill the lion themselves, and refused to come unless with this understanding.

The day before we reached Sergoi they had gone out, and had killed a lion and lioness; the beasts were put up from a small covert and despatched with the heavy throwing spears on the instant, before they offered, or indeed had the chance to offer, any resistance. The day after our arrival there was mist and cold rain, and we found no lions. Next day, November 20th, we were successful.

We started immediately after breakfast. Kirke, Skally, Mouton, Jordaan, Mr. and Mrs. Corbett, Captain Chapman, and our party, were on horseback; of course we carried our rifles, but our duty was merely to round up the lion and hold him, if he went off so far in advance that even the Nandi runners could not overtake him. We intended to beat the country toward some shallow, swampy valleys twelve miles distant.

In an hour we overtook the Nandi warriors, who were advancing across the rolling, grassy plains in a long line, with intervals of six or eight yards between the men. They were splendid savages, stark naked, lithe as panthers, the muscles rippling under their smooth dark skins; all their lives they had lived on nothing but animal food, milk, blood, and flesh, and they were fit for any fatigue or danger. Their faces were proud, cruel, fearless; as they ran they moved with long springy strides. Their head-dresses were fantastic; they carried ox-hide shields painted with strange devices; and each bore in his right hand the formidable war spear, used both for stabbing and for throwing at close quarters. The narrow spear heads of soft iron were burnished till they shone like silver; they were four feet long, and the point and edges were razor sharp. The wooden haft appeared for but a few inches; the long butt was also of iron, ending in a spike, so that the spear looked almost solid metal. Yet each sinewy warrior carried his heavy weapon as if it were a toy, twirling it till it glinted in the sun-rays. Herds of game, red hartebeests and striped zebra and wild swine, fled right and left before the advance of the line.

It was noon before we reached a wide, shallow valley, with beds of rushes here and there in the middle, and on either side high grass and dwarfed and scattered thorn-trees. Down this we beat for a couple of miles. Then, suddenly, a maned lion rose a quarter of a mile ahead of the line and galloped off through the high grass to the right; and all of us on horseback tore after him.

He was a magnificent beast, with a black and tawny mane; in his prime, teeth and claws perfect, with mighty thews, and savage heart. He was lying near a hartebeest on which he had been feasting; his life had been one unbroken career of rapine and violence; and now the maned master of the wilderness, the terror that stalked by night, the grim lord of slaughter, was to meet his doom at the hands of the only foes who dared molest him.

It was a mile before we brought him to bay. Then the Dutch farmer, Mouton, who had not even a rifle, but who rode foremost, was almost on him; he halted and turned under a low thorn-tree, and we galloped past him to the opposite side, to hold him until the spearmen could come. It was a sore temptation to shoot him; but of course we could not break faith with our Nandi friends. We were only some sixty yards from him, and we watched him with our rifles ready, lest he should charge either us, or the first two or three spearmen, before their companions arrived.

One by one the spearmen came up, at a run, and gradually began to form a ring round him. Each, when he came near enough, crouched behind his shield, his spear in his right hand, his fierce, eager face peering over the shield rim. As man followed man, the lion rose to his feet. His mane bristled, his tail lashed, he held his head low, the upper lip now drooping over the jaws, now drawn up so as to show the gleam of the long fangs. He faced first one way and then another, and never ceased to utter his murderous grunting roars. It was a wild sight; the ring of spearmen, intent, silent, bent on blood, and in the centre the great man-killing beast, his thunderous wrath growing ever more dangerous.

At last the tense ring was complete, and the spearmen rose and closed in. The lion looked quickly from side to side, saw where the line was thinnest, and charged at his topmost speed. The crowded moment began. With shields held steady, and quivering spears poised, the men in front braced themselves for the rush and the shock; and from either hand the warriors sprang forward to take their foe in flank. Bounding ahead of his fellows, the leader reached throwing distance; the long spear flickered and plunged; as the lion felt the wound he half turned, and then flung himself on the man in front. The warrior threw his spear; it drove deep into the life, for entering at one shoulder it came out of the opposite flank, near the thigh, a yard of steel through the great body. Rearing, the lion struck the man, bearing down the shield, his back arched; and for a moment he slaked his fury with fang and talon. But on the instant I saw another spear driven clear through his body from side to side; and as the lion turned again the bright spear blades darting toward him were flashes of white flame. The end had come. He seized another man, who stabbed him and wrenched loose. As he fell he gripped a spear-head in his jaws with such tremendous force that he bent it double. Then the warriors were round and over him, stabbing and shouting, wild with furious exultation.

From the moment when he charged until his death I doubt whether ten seconds had elapsed, perhaps less; but what a ten seconds! The first half-dozen spears had done the work. Three of the spear blades had gone clear through the body, the points projecting several inches; and these, and one or two others, including the one he had seized in his jaws, had been twisted out of shape in the terrible death struggle.

We at once attended to the two wounded men. Treating their wounds with antiseptic was painful, and so, while the operation was in progress, I told them, through Kirke, that I would give each a heifer. A Nandi prizes his cattle rather more than his wives; and each sufferer smiled broadly at the news, and forgot all about the pain of his wounds.

Then the warriors, raising their shields above their heads, and chanting the deep-toned victory song, marched with a slow, dancing step around the dead body of the lion; and this savage dance of triumph ended a scene of as fierce interest and excitement as I ever hope to see.

The Nandi marched back by themselves, carrying the two wounded men on their shields. We rode to camp by a roundabout way, on the chance that we might see another lion. The afternoon waned and we cast long shadows before us as we rode across the vast lonely plain. The game stared at us as we passed; a cold wind blew in our faces, and the tall grass waved ceaselessly; the sun set behind a sullen cloud bank; and then, just at nightfall, the tents glimmered white through the dusk.

Tarlton's partner, Newland—also an Australian, and as fine a fellow as Tarlton himself—once had a rather eerie adventure with a man-eating lion. He was camped near Kilimakiu, and after nightfall the alarm was raised that a lion was near by. He came out of his tent, more wood was thrown on the fire, and he heard footsteps re-

Rearing, the lion struck the man, bearing down the shield

Drawn by Philip R. Goodwin from photographs and from descriptions furnished by Mr. Roosevelt

treating, but could not make out whether they were those of a lion or a hyena. Going back to his tent he lay down on his bed with his face turned toward the tent wall. Just as he was falling to sleep the canvas was pushed almost into his face by the head of some creature outside; immediately afterward he heard the sound of a heavy animal galloping, and then the scream of one of his porters whom the lion had seized and was dragging off into the darkness. Rush-

The Nandi dance around the speared lion
From a photograph by Kermit Roosevelt

ing out with his rifle he fired toward the sounds, shooting high; the lion let go his hold and made off, and the man ultimately recovered.

It has been said that lions are monogamous and that they mate for life. If this were so they would almost always be found in pairs, a lion and a lioness. They are sometimes so found; but it is much more common to come across a lioness and her cubs, an old lion with several lionesses and their young (for they are often polygamous), a single lion or lioness, or a couple of lions or lionesses, or a small troop, either all lions or all lionesses, or of mixed sexes. These facts are not compatible with the romantic theory in question.

We tried to get the Nandi to stay with us for a few days
and beat for lions; but this they refused to do, unless they
were also to kill them; and I did not care to assist as a
mere spectator at any more lion hunts, no matter how exciting—though to do so once was well worth while. So we
moved on by ourselves, camping in likely places. In the
swamps, living among the reeds, were big handsome cuckoos, which ate mice. Our first camp was by a stream
bordered by trees like clove-trees; at evening multitudes
of yellow-billed pigeons flew up its course. They were
feeding on olives, and were good for the table; and so were
the yellow-billed mallards, which were found in the occasional pools. Everything we shot at this time went into
the pot—except a hyena. The stomachs of the reedbuck
and oribi contained nothing but grass; but the stomachs
of the duikers were filled with berries from a plant which
looked like the deadly nightshade. On the burned ground,
by the way, the oribi, which were very plentiful, behaved
precisely like tommies, except that they did not go in as
large troops; they made no effort to hide as they do in
thick grass; and as duikers, steinbucks, and reedbucks
always do. We saw, but could not get a shot at, one topi
with a white or blazed face, like a South African blesbok.
While beating one swamp a lion appeared for an instant
at its edge, a hundred and fifty yards off. I got a snap shot,
and ought to have hit him, but didn't. We tried our best
to get him out of the swamp, finally burning all of it that
was not too wet; but we never saw him again.

We recrossed the high hill country, through mists and
driving rains, and were back at Londiani on the last day
of November. Here, with genuine regret, we said good-
by to our safari; for we were about to leave East Africa,
and could only take a few of our personal attendants with
us into Uganda and the Nile Valley. I was really sorry to
see the last of the big, strong, good-natured porters. They
had been with us over seven months, and had always behaved well—though this, of course, was mainly owing to

Cuninghame's and Tarlton's management. We had not lost a single man by death. One had been tossed by a rhino, one clawed by a leopard, and several had been sent to hospital for dysentery, small-pox, or fever; but none had died. While on the Guaso Nyero trip we had run into a narrow belt of the dreaded tsetse fly, whose bite is fatal to

Mr. Roosevelt photographing the speared lion
From a photograph by Kermit Roosevelt

domestic animals. Five of our horses were bitten, and four of them died, two not until we were on the Uasin Gishu; the fifth, my zebra-shaped brown, although very sick, ultimately recovered, to the astonishment of the experts. Only three of our horses lasted in such shape that we could ride them in to Londiani; one of them being Tranquillity, and another Kermit's white pony, Huan Daw, who was always dancing and curvetting, and whom in consequence the saises had christened "merodadi," the dandy.

The first ten days of December I spent at Njoro, on the edge of the Mau escarpment, with Lord Delamere. It is a beautiful farming country; and Lord Delamere is a practical and successful farmer, and the most useful settler, from the stand-point of the all-round interests of the country, in British East Africa. Incidentally, the home ranch was most attractive—especially the library, the room containing Lady Delamere's books. Delamere had been himself a noted big-game hunter, his bag including fifty-two lions;

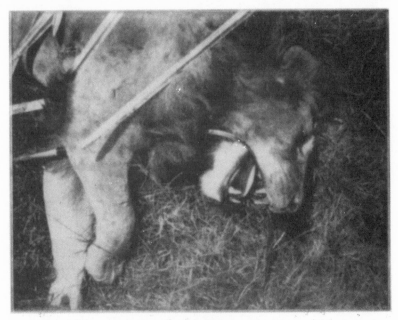

As he fell he gripped a spear-head in his jaws with such tremendous force
that he bent it double

From a photograph by Kermit Roosevelt

but instead of continuing to be a mere sportsman, he turned his attention to stock-raising and wheat-growing, and became a leader in the work of taming the wilderness, of conquering for civilization the world's waste spaces. No career can be better worth following.

During his hunting years Delamere had met with many strange adventures. One of the lions he shot mauled him, breaking his leg, and also mauling his two Somali gun-bearers. The lion then crawled off into some bushes fifty yards away, and camp was pitched where the wounded

men were lying. Soon after nightfall the hyenas assembled
in numbers and attacked, killed, and ate the mortally
wounded lion, the noise made by the combatants being
ear-rending. On another occasion he had heard a leopard
attack some baboons in the rocks, a tremendous row following as the big dog
baboons hastened to
the assistance of the
one who had been
seized and drove off the
leopard. That evening
a leopard, evidently the
same one, very thin and
hungry, came into camp
and was shot; it was
frightfully bitten, the
injuries being such as
only baboons inflict,
and would unquestion-
ably have died of its
wounds. The leopard
wherever possible takes
his kill up a tree,
showing extraordinary
strength in the perform-
ance of this feat. It is
undoubtedly due to fear
of interference from
hyenas. The 'Ndorobo
said that no single
hyena would meddle

The spears that did the trick
From a photograph by Edmund Heller

with a leopard, but that three or four would without
hesitation rob it of its prey. Some years before this
time, while hunting north of Kenia, Lord Delamere had
met a Dr. Kolb, who was killed by a rhino immediately
afterward. Dr. Kolb was fond of rhinoceros liver, and
killed scores of the animals for food; but finally a cow,

with a half-grown calf, which he had wounded charged him and thrust her horn right through the middle of his body.

We spent several days vainly hunting bongo in the dense mountain forests, with half a dozen 'Ndorobo. These were true 'Ndorobo, who never cultivate the ground, living in the deep forests on wild honey and game. It has been said that they hunt but little, and only elephant and rhino; but this is not correct as regards the 'Ndorobo in question. They were all clad in short cloaks of the skin of the tree hyrax; hyrax, monkey, bongo, and forest hog, the only game of the dense, cool, wet forest, were all habitually killed by them. They also occasionally killed rhino and buffalo, finding the former, because it must occasionally be attacked in the open, the more dangerous of the two; twice Delamere had come across small communities of 'Ndorobo literally starving because the strong man, the chief hunter, the breadwinner, had been killed by a rhino which he had attacked. The headman of those with us, who was named Mel-el-lek, had himself been fearfully injured by a wounded buffalo; and the father of another one who was with us had been killed by baboons which had rallied to the aid of one which he was trying to kill with his knobkerry. Usually they did not venture to meddle with the lions which they found on the edge of the forest, or with the leopards which occasionally dwelt in the deep woods; but once Mel-el-lek killed a leopard with a poisoned arrow from a tree, and once a whole party of them attacked and killed with their poisoned arrows a lion which had slain a cow buffalo near the forest. On another occasion a lion in its turn killed two of their hunters. In fact they were living just as palæolithic man lived in Europe, ages ago.

Their arms were bows and arrows, the arrows being carried in skin quivers, and the bows, which were strung with zebra gut, being swathed in strips of hide. When resting they often stood on one leg, like storks. Their eyesight was marvellous, and they were extremely skilful alike in tracking and in seeing game. They threaded their way through the forest noiselessly and at speed, and were extraordinary climbers. They were continually climbing trees to get at the hyrax, and once when a big black-and-white Colobus monkey which I had shot lodged in the top of a giant cedar one of them ascended and brought it down with matter-of-course indifference. He cut down a sapling, twenty-five feet long, with the stub of a stout branch left on as a hook, and for a rope used a section of vine which he broke and twisted into flexibility. Then, festooned with all his belongings, he made the ascent. There was a tall olive, sixty or eighty feet high, close to the cedar, and up this he went. From its topmost branches, where only a monkey or a 'Ndorobo could have felt at home, he reached his sapling over to the lowest limb of the giant cedar, and hooked it on; and then crawled across on this dizzy bridge. Up he went, got the monkey, recrossed the bridge, and climbed down again, quite unconcerned.

The big black-and-white monkeys ate nothing but leaves, and usually trusted for safety to ascending into the very tops of the tallest cedars. Occasionally they would come in a flying leap down to the ground, or to a neighboring tree; when on the ground they merely dashed toward another tree, being less agile than the ordinary monkeys, whether in the tree tops or on solid earth. They are strikingly handsome and conspicuous creatures. Their bold coloration has been spoken of as "protective"; but it is protective only to town-bred eyes. A non-expert finds any object, of no matter what color, difficult to make out when hidden among the branches at the top of a tall tree; but the black-and-white coloration of this monkey has not the slightest protective value of any kind. On the contrary, it is calculated at once to attract the eye. The 'Ndorobo were a unit in saying that these monkeys were much more easy to see than their less brightly colored kinsfolk who dwell in the same forests; and this was my own experience.

When camped in these high forests the woods after

nightfall were vocal with the croaking and wailing of the tree hyraxes. They are squat, woolly, funny things, and to my great amusement I found that most of the settlers called them "Teddy bears." They are purely arboreal and nocturnal creatures, living in hollows high up in the big trees, by preference in the cedars. At night they are very noisy, the call consisting of an opening series of batrachian-like croaks, followed by a succession of quavering wails—eerie sounds enough, as they come out of the black stillness of the midnight. They are preyed on now and then by big owls and by leopards, and the white-tailed mongoose is their especial foe, following them everywhere among the tree tops. This mongoose is both terrestrial and arboreal in habits, and is hated by the 'Ndorobo because it robs their honey buckets.

The bongo and the giant hog were the big game of these deep forests, where a tangle of undergrowth filled the spaces between the trunks of the cedar, the olive, and the yew or yellow-wood, while where the bamboos grew they usually choked out all other plants. Delamere had killed several giant hogs with his half-breed hounds; but on this occasion the hounds would not follow them. On three days we came across bongo; once a solitary bull, on both the other occasions herds. We never saw them, although we heard the solitary bull crash off through the bamboos; for they are very wary and elusive, being incessantly followed by the 'Ndorobo. They are as large as native bullocks, with handsomely striped skins, and both sexes carry horns. On each of the three days we followed them all day long, and it was interesting to trace so much as we could of their habits. Their trails are deeply beaten, and converge toward the watercourses, which run between the steep, forest-clad spurs of the mountains. They do not graze, but browse, cropping the leaves, flowers, and twigs of various shrubs, and eating thistles; they are said to eat bark, but this our 'Ndorobo denied. They are also said to be nocturnal, feeding at night, and lying up in the daytime; but this was

Sailinye, the Dorobo, who was with Kermit Roosevelt when he shot the bongo, holding up the bongo head

From a photograph by Kermit Roosevelt

certainly not the case with those we came across. Both of the herds, which we followed patiently and cautiously for hours without alarming them, were feeding as they moved slowly along. One herd lay down for a few hours at noon; the other kept feeding until mid-afternoon, when we alarmed it; and the animals then went straight up the mountain over the rimrock. It was cold rainy weather, and the dark of the moon, which may perhaps have had something to do with the bongo being on the move and feeding during the day; but the 'Ndorobo said that they never fed at night —I of course know nothing about this personally. Leopards catch the young bongo and giant hog, but dare not meddle with those that are full-grown. The forest which they frequent is so dense, so wellnigh impenetrable, that half the time no man can follow their trails save by bending and crawling, and cannot make out an object twenty yards ahead. It is extraordinary to see the places through which the bongo pass, and which are their chosen haunts.

While Lord Delamere and I were hunting in vain Kermit was more fortunate. He was the guest of Barclay Cole, Delamere's brother-in-law. They took eight porters and went into the forest accompanied by four 'Ndorobo. They marched straight up to the bamboo and yellow-wood forest near the top of the Mau escarpment. They spent five days hunting. The procedure was simply to find the trail of a herd, to follow it through the tangled woods as rapidly and noiselessly as possible until it was overtaken, and then to try to get a shot at the first patch of reddish hide of which they got a glimpse—for they never saw more than such a patch, and then only for a moment. The first day Kermit, firing at such a patch, knocked over the animal; but it rose and the tracks were so confused that even the keen eyes of the wild men could not pick out the right one. Next day they again got into a herd; this time Kermit was the first to see the game—all that was visible being a patch of reddish, the size of a man's two hands, with a white stripe across it. Firing he killed the animal;

but it proved to be only half grown. Even the 'Ndorobo
now thought it useless to follow the herd; but Kermit
took one of them and started in pursuit. After a couple
of hours' trailing the herd was again overtaken, and again
Kermit got a glimpse of the animals. He hit two; and
selecting the trail with most blood they followed it for three
or four miles, until Kermit overtook and finished off the
wounded bongo, a fine cow.

Kermit always found them lying up during the middle
of the day and feeding in the morning and afternoon; otherwise his observations of their habits coincided with mine.

The next ten days Kermit spent in a trip to the coast,
near Mombasa, for sable—the most beautiful antelope next
to the koodoo. The cows and bulls are red, the very old
bulls (of the typical form) jet black, all with white bellies;
like the roan, both sexes carry scimitar-shaped horns, but
longer than the roans. He was alone with his two gun-
bearers, and some Swahili porters; he acted as headman
himself. They marched from Mombasa, being ferried
across the harbor of Kilindini in a dhow, and then going
some fifteen miles south. Next day they marched about ten
miles to a Nyika village, where they arrived just in the middle of a funeral dance which was being held in honor of a
chief's son who had died. Kermit was much amused to find
that this death dance had more life and go to it than any
dance he had yet seen, and the music—the dirge music—had
such swing and vivacity that it almost reminded him of a
comic opera. The dancers wore tied round their legs queer
little wicker-work baskets, with beans inside, which rattled in
the rhythm of their dancing. Camp was pitched under a
huge baobab-tree, in sight of the Indian Ocean; but in the
middle of the night the ants swarmed in and drove everybody out; and next day, while Kermit was hunting, camp
was shifted on about an hour's march to a little grove of
trees by a brook. It was a well-watered country, very hilly,
with palm-bordered streams in each valley. These wild
palms bore ivory nuts, the fruit tasting something like an

Dance of boys of the Nyika tribe in honor of the chief's son who had just died

From a photograph by Kermit Roosevelt

apple. Each village had a grove of cocoanut palms, and Kermit found the cool cocoanut milk delicious after the return from a long day's hunting.

Each morning he was off before daylight, and rarely returned until after nightfall; and tired though he was he enjoyed to the full the walks campward in the bright moonlight among the palm groves beside the rushing streams, while the cicadas cried like katydids at home. The grass was long. The weather was very hot, and almost every day there were drenching thunder-storms, and the dews were exceedingly heavy, so that Kermit was wet almost all the time, although he kept in first-rate health. There were not many sable and they were shy. About nine or ten o'clock they would stop feeding, and leave their pasture grounds of long grass, taking refuge in some grove of trees and thick bushes, not coming out again until nearly five o'clock.

On the second day's hunting Juma spied a little band of sable just entering a grove. A long and careful stalk brought the hunters to the grove, but after reaching it they at first saw nothing of the game. Then Kermit caught a glimpse of a head, fired, and brought down the beast in its tracks. It proved to be a bull, just changing from the red to the black coat; the horns were fair—in this northern form they never reach the length of those borne by the sable bulls of South Africa. He also killed a cow, not fully grown. He therefore still needed a full-grown cow, which he obtained three days later; this animal when wounded was very savage, and tried to charge.

We now went to Nairobi, where Cuninghame, Tarlton, and the three naturalists were already preparing for the Uganda trip and shipping the stuff hitherto collected. Working like beavers we got everything ready—including additions to the Pigskin Library, which included, among others, Cervantes, Goethe's "Faust," Molière, Pascal, Montaigne, St. Simon, Darwin's "Voyage of the Beagle," and Huxley's "Essays"—and on December 18th started for Lake Victoria Nyanza.

CHAPTER XIII

UGANDA, AND THE GREAT NYANZA LAKES

When we left Nairobi it was with real regret that we said good-by to the many friends who had been so kind to us; officials, private citizens, almost every one we had met—including Sir Percy Girouard, the new governor. At Kijabe the men and women from the American Mission— and the children too—were down at the station to wish us good luck; and at Nakuru the settlers from the neighborhood gathered on the platform to give us a farewell cheer. The following morning we reached Kisu-

Kavirondos returning from market

From a photograph by Kermit Roosevelt

mu on Lake Victoria Nyanza. It is in the Kavirondo country, where the natives, both men and women, as a rule go absolutely naked, although they are peaceable and industrious. In the native market they had brought in baskets, iron spade heads, and food, to sell to the native and Indian traders who had their booths round about; the meat market, under the trees, was especially interesting.

At noon we embarked in a smart little steamer, to cross the lake. Twenty-four hours later we landed at Entebbe, the seat of the English Governor of Uganda. Throughout our passage the wind hardly ruffled the smooth surface of the lake. As we steamed away from the eastern shore the mountains behind us and on our right hand rose harsh and barren, yet with a kind of forbidding beauty. Dark clouds hung over the land we had left, and a rainbow stretched across their front. At nightfall, as the red sunset faded, the lonely waters of the vast in-

Kavirondos going down to fill their water-jars
From a photograph by Kermit Roosevelt

land sea stretched, ocean-like, west and south into a shoreless gloom. Then the darkness deepened, the tropic stars blazed overhead, and the light of the half moon drowned in silver the embers of the sunset.

Next morning we steamed along and across the equator; the last time we were to cross it, for thenceforth our course lay northward. We passed by many islands, green with meadow and forest, beautiful in the bright sunshine, but empty with the emptiness of death. A

Kavirondo bullock wagons
From a photograph by Kermit Roosevelt

decade previously these islands were thronged with tribes of fisher folk; their villages studded the shores, and their long canoes, planks held together with fibre, furrowed the surface of the lake.   Then, from out of the depths of the Congo forest came the dreadful scourge of the sleeping sickness, and smote the doomed peoples who dwelt beside the Victorian Nile, and on the coasts of the Nyanza Lakes and in the lands between.   Its agent was a biting fly, brother to the tsetse whose bite is fatal to domestic animals.   This fly dwells in forests, beside lakes and rivers; and wherever it dwells after the sleeping sickness came it was found that man could not live. In this country, between, and along the shores of, the great lakes, two hundred thousand people died in slow torment, before the hard-taxed wisdom and skill of medical science and governmental administration could work any betterment whatever in the situation.   Men still die by thousands, and the disease is slowly spreading into fresh districts.   But it has proved possible to keep it within limits in the regions already affected; yet only by absolutely abandoning certain districts, and by clearing all the forest and brush in tracts which serve as barriers to the fly, and which permit passage through the infected belts.   On the western shores of Victoria Nyanza, and in the islands adjacent thereto, the ravages of the pestilence were such, the mortality it caused was so appalling, that the government was finally forced to deport all the survivors inland, to forbid all residence beside or fishing in the lake, and with this end in view to destroy the villages and the fishing fleets of the people.   The teeming lake fish were formerly a main source of food supply to all who dwelt near by; but this has now been cut off, and the myriads of fish are left to themselves, to the hosts of water birds, and to the monstrous man-eating crocodiles of the lake, on whose blood the fly also feeds, and whence it is supposed by some that it draws the germs so deadly to humankind.

When we landed there was nothing in the hot, laughing, tropical beauty of the land to suggest the grisly horror that brooded so near.   In green luxuriance the earth lay under a cloudless sky, yielding her increase to the sun's burning caresses, and men and women were living their lives and doing their work well and gallantly.

At Entebbe we stayed with the acting-governor, Mr. Boyle, at Kampalla with the district commissioner, Mr. Knowles; both of them veteran administrators, and the latter

Entebbe, looking over lake

From a photograph by J. Alden Loring

also a mighty hunter; and both of them showed us every courtesy, and treated us with all possible kindness.   Entebbe is a pretty little town of English residents, chiefly officials; with well-kept roads, a golf course, tennis courts, and an attractive club-house.   The whole place is bowered in flowers, on tree, bush, and vine, of every hue—masses of lilac, purple, yellow, blue, and fiery crimson.   Kampalla is the native town, where the little King of Uganda, a boy, lives, and his chiefs of state, and where the native council meets; and it is the head-quarters of the missions, both Church of England and Roman Catholic.

Kampalla is an interesting place; and so is all Uganda. The first explorers who penetrated thither, half a century ago, found in this heathen state, of almost pure negroes, a veritable semi-civilization, or advanced barbarism, comparable to that of the little Arab-negro or Berber-negro sultanates strung along the southern edge of the Sahara, and contrasting sharply with the weltering savagery which surrounded it, and which stretched away without a break for many hundreds of miles in every direction. The people were industrious tillers of the soil, who owned sheep,

The Indian elephant at Entebbe

The only possession of the white man that really appalls the natives, as they know the wild elephant and cannot unders'and any one taming it and making it ob°y. Even the railroad fails to compare with it. The mahout is just mounting

From a photograph by Kermit Roosevelt

goats, and some cattle; they wore decent clothing, and hence were styled "womanish" by the savages of the Upper Nile region, who prided themselves on the nakedness of their men as a proof of manliness; they were unusually intelligent and ceremoniously courteous; and, most singular of all, although the monarch was a cruel despot, of the usual African (whether Mohammedan or heathen) type, there were certain excellent governmental customs, of binding observance, which in the aggregate might almost be called an unwritten constitution. Alone among the natives of tropical Africa the people of Uganda have proved very accessible to Christian teaching, so that the creed of Christianity is now dominant among them. For their good fortune, England has established a protectorate over them.

Most wisely the English Government officials, and as a rule the missionaries, have bent their energies to developing them along their own lines, in government, dress, and ways of life; constantly striving to better them and bring them forward, but not twisting them aside from their natural line of development, nor wrenching them loose from what was good in their past, by attempting the impossible task of turning an entire native population into black Englishmen at one stroke.

The problem set to the governing caste in Uganda is totally different from that which offers itself in British East Africa. The highlands of East Africa form a white man's country, and the prime need is to build up a large, healthy population of true white settlers, white homemakers, who shall take the land as an inheritance for their children's children. Uganda can never be this kind of white man's country; and although planters and merchants of the right type can undoubtedly do well there—to the advantage of the country as well as of themselves—it must remain essentially a black man's country, and the chief task of the officials of the intrusive and masterful race must be to bring forward the natives, to train them, and above all to help them train themselves, so that they may advance in industry, in learning, in morality, in capacity for self-government—for it is idle to talk of "giving" a people self-government; the gift of the forms, when the inward spirit is lacking, is mere folly; all that can be done is patiently to help a people acquire the necessary qualities —social, moral, intellectual, industrial, and lastly political —and meanwhile to exercise for their benefit, with justice, sympathy, and firmness, the governing ability which as yet they themselves lack. The widely spread rule of a strong European race in lands like Africa gives, as one incident thereof, the chance for nascent cultures, nascent semi-civilizations, to develop without fear of being overwhelmed in the surrounding gulfs of savagery; and this aside from the direct stimulus to development conferred by the con-

sciously and unconsciously exercised influence of the white
man, wherein there is much of evil, but much more of ultimate good. In any region of wide-spread savagery, the
chances for the growth of each self-produced civilization are
necessarily small, because each little centre of effort toward
this end is always exposed to destruction from the neighboring masses of pure savagery; and therefore progress is often
immensely accelerated by outside invasion and control. In
Africa the control and guidance is needed as much in the
things of the spirit as in the things of the body. Those who
complain of or rail at missionary work in Africa, and who
confine themselves to pointing out the undoubtedly too
numerous errors of the missionaries and shortcomings of
their flocks, would do well to consider that even if the
light which has been let in is but feeble and gray it has at
least dispelled a worse than Stygian darkness. As soon as
native African religions—practically none of which have
hitherto evolved any substantial ethical basis—develop beyond the most primitive stage they tend, notably in middle
and western Africa, to grow into malign creeds of unspeakable cruelty and immorality, with a bestial and revolting
ritual and ceremonial. Even a poorly taught and imperfectly understood Christianity, with its underlying foundation of justice and mercy, represents an immeasurable
advance on such a creed.

Where, as in Uganda, the people are intelligent and
the missionaries unite disinterestedness and zeal with common-sense, the result is astounding. The majority of
the people of Uganda are now Christian, Protestant or
Catholic; and many thousands among them are sincerely
Christian and show their Christianity in practical fashion by
putting conduct above ceremonial and dogma. Most fortunately, Protestant and Catholic seem now to be growing to
work in charity together, and to show rivalry only in healthy
effort against the common foe; there is certainly enough
evil in the world to offer a target at which all good men can
direct their shafts, without expending them on one another.

We visited the Church of England Mission, where we were received by Bishop Tucker, and the two Catholic Missions, where we were received by Bishops Hanlon and Streicher; we went through the churches and saw the

Colonel Roosevelt at Mother Paul's Mission
Mother Paul is standing between her two native women
From a photograph by Kermit Roosevelt

schools with the pupils actually at work. In all the missions we were received with American and British flags and listened to the children singing the "Star-spangled Banner." The Church of England Mission has been at work for a quarter of a century; what has been accomplished by Bishop Tucker and those associated with him makes one of the most interesting chapters in all recent missionary history.

I saw the high-school, where the sons of the chiefs are
being trained in large numbers for their future duties, and
I was especially struck by the admirable Medical Mission,
and by the handsome cathedral, built by the native Christians themselves without outside assistance in either money
or labor.   At dinner at Mr. Knowles's, Bishop Tucker gave
us exceedingly interesting details of his past experiences
in Uganda, and of the progress of the missionary work.
He had been much amused by an American missionary
who had urged him to visit America, saying that he would
"find the latch-string outside the door"; to an American
who knows the country districts well the expression seems
so natural that I had never even realized that it was an
Americanism.

At Bishop Hanlon's Mission, where I lunched with the
bishop, there was a friend, Mother Paul, an American;
before I left America I had promised that I would surely see
her, and look into the work which she, and the sisters associated with her, were doing.   It was delightful seeing her; she
not merely spoke my language but my neighborhood dialect.   She informed me that she had just received a message of good-will for me in a letter from two of "the finest"
—of course I felt at home when in mid-Africa, under the
equator, I received   in such fashion a message from two
of the men who had served under me in the New York
police.*   She had been teaching her pupils to sing some
lines of the "Star-spangled Banner," in English, in my
especial honor; and of course had been obliged, in writing it out, to use spelling far more purely phonetic than I
had ever dreamed of using.   The first lines ran as fol-

* For the benefit of those who do not live in the neighborhood of New York
I may explain that all good, or typical, New Yorkers invariably speak of their
police force as "the finest"; and if any one desires to know what a "good" or
"typical" New Yorker is, I shall add, on the authority of either Brander Mat-
thews or the late H. C. Bunner—I forget which—that when he isn't a Southerner
or of Irish or German descent he is usually a man born out West of New England
parentage.

lows: (Some of our word sounds have no equivalent in Uganda.)

"O se ka nyu si bai di mo nseli laiti
(O say can you see by the morn's* early light)

Wati so pulauli wi eli adi twayi laiti silasi giremi"
(What so proudly we hailed at the twilight's last gleaming.)

After having taught the children the first verse in this manner Mother Paul said that she stopped to avoid brain fever.

In addition to scholastic exercises Mother Paul and her associates were training their school children in all kinds of industrial work, taking especial pains to develop those industries that were natural to them and would be of use when they returned to their own homes. Both at Bishop Hanlon's Mission, and at Bishop Streicher's, the Mission of the White Fathers—originally a French organization, which has established churches and schools in almost all parts of Africa—the fathers were teaching the native men to cultivate coffee, and various fruits and vegetables.

I called on the little king, who is being well trained by his English tutor—few tutors perform more exacting or responsible duties—and whose comfortable house was furnished in English fashion. I met his native advisers, shrewd, powerful-looking men; and went into the Council Chamber, where I was greeted by the council, substantial-looking men, well dressed in the native fashion, and representing all the districts of the kingdom. When we visited the king it was after dark, and we were received by smart-looking black soldiers in ordinary khaki uniform, while accompanying them were other attendants dressed in the old-time native fashion; men with flaming torches, and others with the big Uganda drums which they beat to an accompaniment of wild cries. These drums are characteristic of Uganda; each chief has one, and beats upon

* sic.

it his own peculiar tattoo. The king, and all other people
of consequence, white, Indian, or native, went round in
rickshaws, one man pulling in the shafts and three others
pushing behind. The rickshaw men ran well, and sang
all the time, the man in the shafts serving as shanty-man,
while the three behind repeated in chorus every second
or two a kind of clanging note; and this went on without

Mother Paul's band composed of mission boys
From a photograph by Kermit Roosevelt

a break, hour
after hour.
The natives
looked well
and were
dressed well;
the men in
long flowing
garments of
white, the
women usually
in brown cloth
made in the old
native style out
of the bark of
the bark cloth
tree. The
clothes of the chiefs were tastefully ornamented. All the
people, gentle and simple, were very polite and ceremonious
both to one another and to strangers. Now and then we
met parties of Sikh soldiers, tall, bearded, fine-looking men
with turbans; and there were Indian and Swahili and
even Arab and Persian traders.

The houses had mud walls and thatched roofs. The
gardens were surrounded by braided cane fences. In the
gardens and along the streets were many trees; among them
bark cloth trees, from which the bark is stripped every
year for cloth; great incense-trees, the sweet-scented gum
oozing through wounds in the bark; and date-palms, in the
fronds of which hung the nests of the golden weaver-birds,

now breeding. White cow-herons, tamer than barn-yard fowls, accompanied the cattle, perching on their backs, or walking beside them. Beautiful Kavirondo cranes came familiarly round the houses. It was all strange and attractive. Birds sang everywhere. The air was heavy with the fragrance of flowers of many colors; the whole place was a riot of lush growing plants. Every day there

Colonel Roosevelt at the Mission of the White Fathers
From a photograph by Kermit Roosevelt

were terrific thunder-storms. At Kampalla three men had been killed by lightning within six weeks; a year or two before our host, Knowles, had been struck by lightning and knocked senseless, a huge zigzag mark being left across his body, and the links of his gold watch chain being fused; it was many months before he completely recovered.

Knowles arranged a situtunga hunt for us. The situtunga is closely related to the bushbuck but is bigger, with very long hoofs, and shaggy hair like a waterbuck. It is exclusively a beast of the marshes, making its home in the thick reedbeds, where the water is deep; and it is exceedingly shy, so that very few white men have shot, or even seen, it. Its long hoofs enable it to go over the most treacherous ground, and it swims well; in many of its haunts, in the thick papyrus, the water is waist deep on a man. Through the papyrus, and the reeds and marsh grass, it makes well-beaten paths. Where it is in any danger of molestation it is never seen abroad in the daytime, venturing from the safe cover of the high reeds only at night; but fifty miles inland, in the marsh grass on the edge of a big papyrus swamp, Kermit caught a glimpse of half a dozen feeding in the open, knee-deep in water, long after sunrise. On the hunt in question a patch of marsh was driven by a hundred natives, while the guns were strung along the likely passes which led to another patch of marsh. A fine situtunga buck came to Kermit's post, and he killed it as it bolted away. It had stolen up so quietly through the long marsh grass that he only saw it when it was directly on him. Its stomach contained not grass, but the leaves and twig tips of a shrub which grows in and alongside of the marshes.

The day after this hunt our safari started on its march north-westward to Lake Albert Nyanza. We had taken with us from East Africa our gun-bearers, tent boys, and the men whom the naturalists had trained as skinners. The porters were men of Uganda; the askaris were from the constabulary, and widely different races were represented among them, but all had been drilled into soldierly uniformity. The porters were well-clad, well-behaved, fine-looking men, and did their work better than the "shenzis," the wild Meru of Kikuyu tribesmen, whom we had occasionally employed in East Africa; but they were not the equals of the regular East African porters. I think this was largely because of their inferior food, for they ate chiefly yams and plantains; in other words inferior sweet-potatoes and bananas. They were quite as fond of singing as the East African porters, and in addition were cheered on the march by drum and fife; several men had fifes, and one carried nothing but one of the big Uganda drums, which he usually bore at the head of the safari, marching in company with the flag-bearer. Every hour or two the men would halt, often beside one of the queer little wicker-work booths in which native hucksters disposed of their wares by the roadside.

Along the road we often met wayfarers; once or twice bullock carts; more often men carrying rolls of hides or long bales of cotton on their heads; or a set of Bahima herdsmen, with clearcut features, guarding their herds of huge-horned Angola cattle.

All greeted us most courteously, frequently crouching or kneeling, as is their custom when they salute

The situtunga shot by Kermit Roosevelt at Kampalla
From a photograph by Edmund Heller

a superior; and we were scrupulous to acknowledge their salutes, and to return their greetings in the native fashion, with words of courtesy and long-drawn e-h-h-s and a-a-h-s. Along the line of march the chiefs had made preparations to receive us. Each afternoon, as we came to the spot where we were to camp for the night, we found a cleared space strewed with straw and surrounded by a plaited reed fence. Within this space cane houses, with thatched roofs of coarse grass, had been erected, some for our stores, one for a kitchen, one, which was always decked with flowers, as a rest-house for ourselves; the latter with open sides, the roof upheld by cane pillars, so that it was cool and comfortable, and afforded a welcome shelter, either from the burning sun if the weather was clear, or from the pelting, driving tropical storms if there was rain. The moon was almost full when we left Kampalla, and night after night it lent a half unearthly beauty to the tropical landscape.

Sometimes in the evenings the mosquitoes bothered us; more often they did not; but in any event we slept well under our nettings. Usually at each camp we found either the head chief of the district, or a sub-chief, with presents; eggs, chickens, sheep, once or twice a bullock, always pineapples and bananas. The chief was always well dressed in flowing robes, and usually welcomed us with dignity and courtesy (sometimes, however, permitting the courtesy to assume the form of servility); and we would have him in to tea, where he was sure to enjoy the bread and jam. Sometimes he came in a rickshaw, sometimes in a kind of wicker-work palanquin, sometimes on foot. When we left his territory we made him a return gift.

We avoided all old camping grounds, because of the spirillum tick. This dangerous fever tick is one of the insect scourges of Uganda, for its bite brings on a virulent spirillum fever which lasts intermittently for months, and may be accompanied by partial paralysis. It is common on old camping grounds and in native villages. The malarial mosquitoes also abound in places; and repeated attacks of malaria pave the way for black water fever, which is often fatal.

The first day's march from Kampalla led us through shambas, the fields of sweet-potatoes and plantations of bananas being separated by hedges or by cane fences. Then for two or three days we passed over low hills and through swampy valleys, the whole landscape covered by a sea of elephant grass, the close-growing, coarse blades more than twice the height of a man on horseback. Here and there it was dotted with groves of strange trees; in these groves monkeys of various kinds—some black, some red-tailed, some auburn—chattered as they raced away among the branches; there were brilliant rollers and bee-eaters; little

Road through banana shambas, Uganda
From a photograph by J. Alden Loring

green and yellow parrots, and gray parrots with red tails; and many colored butterflies. Once or twice we saw the handsome, fierce, short-tailed eagle, the bateleur eagle, and scared one from a reedbuck fawn it had killed. Among the common birds there were black drongos and musical bush shrikes; small black magpies with brown tails; white-headed kites and slate-colored sparrow-hawks; palm swifts, big hornbills; blue and mottled kingfishers, which never went near the water, and had their upper mandibles red and their under ones black; barbets, with swollen, saw-toothed bills, their plumage iridescent purple above and red below; bulbuls, also dark purple above and red below, which whistled and bubbled incessantly as they hopped among the thick bushes, behaving much like our own yellow-breasted chats; and a multitude of other birds, beautiful or fantastic. There were striped squirrels too, reminding us of the big Rocky Mountain chipmunk or Say's chipmunk, but with smaller ears and a longer tail.

Christmas day we passed on the march. There is not much use in trying to celebrate Christmas unless there are small folks to hang up their stockings on Christmas Eve, to rush gleefully in at dawn next morning to open the stockings, and after breakfast to wait in hopping expectancy until their elders throw open the doors of the room in which the big presents are arranged, those for each child on a separate table.

Forty miles from the coast the elephant grass began to disappear. The hills became somewhat higher, there were thorn-trees, and stately royal palms of great height, their stems swollen and bulging at the top, near the fronds. Parasitic ferns, with leaves as large as cabbage leaves, grew on the branches of the acacias. One kind of tree sent down from its branches to the ground roots which grew into thick trunks. There were wide, shallow marshes, and although the grass was tall it was no longer above a man's head. Kermit and I usually got two or three hours' hunting each day. We killed singsing waterbuck, bushbuck, and bohor reedbuck. The reedbuck differed slightly from those of East Africa; in places they were plentiful, and they were not wary. We also killed several hartebeests; a variety of the Jackson's hartebeest, being more highly colored, with black markings. I killed a very handsome harnessed bushbuck ram. It was rather bigger than a good-sized white-tail buck, its brilliant red coat beautifully marked with rows of white spots, its twisted black horns sharp and polished. It seemed to stand about half-way between the dark-colored bushbuck rams of East and South Africa and the beautifully marked harnessed antelope rams of the west coast forests. The ewes and young rams showed the harness markings even more plainly; and, as with all bushbuck, were of small size compared to the old rams. These bushbuck were found in tall grass, where the ground was wet, instead of in the thick bush where their East African kinsfolk spend the daytime.

At the bushbuck camp we met a number of porters returning from the Congo, where they had been with an elephant poacher named Busherri—at least that was as near the name as we could make out. He had gone into the Congo to get ivory, by shooting and trading; but the wild forest people had attacked him, and had killed him and seven of his followers, and the others were straggling homeward. In Kampalla we had met an elephant hunter named Quin who had recently lost his right arm in an encounter with a wounded tusker. Near one camp the head chief pointed out two places, now overgrown with jungle, where little villages had stood less than a year before. In each case elephants had taken to feeding at night in the shambas, and had steadily grown bolder and bolder until the natives, their crops ruined by the depredations and their lives in danger, had abandoned the struggle, and shifted to some new place in the wilderness.

We were soon to meet elephant ourselves. The morning of the 28th was rainy; we struck camp rather late, and the march was long, so that it was mid-afternoon when Kermit and I reached our new camping place. Soon afterward word was brought us that some elephants were near by; we were told that the beasts were in the habit of devastating the shambas, and were bold and truculent, having killed a man who had tried to interfere with them. Kermit and I at once started after them, just as the last of the safari came in, accompanied by Cuninghame, who could not go with us as he was recovering from a bout of fever.

In half an hour we came on fresh sign, and began to work cautiously along it. Our guide, a wild-looking savage with a blunt spear, went first, followed by my gun-bearer, Kongoni, who is excellent on spoor; then I came, followed by Kermit, and by the other gun-bearers. The country was covered with tall grass, and studded with numerous patches of jungle and small forest. In a few minutes we heard the elephants, four or five of them, feeding in thick jungle where the vines that hung in tangled masses from the trees and that draped the bushes made dark caves of greenery. It was difficult to find any space clear enough to see thirty yards ahead. Fortunately there was no wind whatever. We picked out the spoor of a big bull and for an hour and a half we followed it, Kongoni usually in the lead. Two or three times, as we threaded our way among the bushes, as noiselessly as possible, we caught glimpses of gray, shadowy bulks, but only for a second at a time, and never with sufficient distinctness to shoot. The elephants were feeding, tearing down the branches of a rather large-leafed tree with bark like that of a scrub-oak and big pods containing beans; evidently these beans were a favorite food. They fed in circles and zigzags, but toward camp, until they were not much more than half a mile from it, and the noise made by the porters in talking and gathering wood was plainly audible; but the elephants paid no heed to it, being evidently too much accustomed to the natives to have much fear of man. We continually heard them breaking branches, and making rumbling or squeaking sounds. They then fed slowly along in the opposite direction, and got into rather more open country; and we followed faster in the big footprints of the bull we had selected. Suddenly in an open glade Kongoni crouched and beckoned to me, and through a bush I caught the loom of the tusker. But at that instant he either heard us, saw us, or caught a whiff of our wind, and without a moment's hesitation he himself assumed the offensive. With his huge ears cocked at right angles to his head, and his trunk hanging down, he charged full tilt at us, coming steadily, silently, and at a great pace, his feet swishing through the long grass; and a formidable monster he looked. At forty yards I fired the right barrel of the Holland into his head, and though I missed the brain the shock dazed him and brought him to an instant halt. Immediately Kermit put a bullet from the Winchester into his head; as he wheeled I gave him the second barrel between the neck and shoulder, through his ear; and Kermit gave him three more shots before he slewed round and disappeared. There were not many minutes of daylight left, and we followed hard on his trail, Kongoni leading. At first there was only an occasional gout of dark blood; but soon we found splashes of red froth from the lungs; then we came to where he had fallen, and then we heard him crashing among the branches in thick jungle to the right. In we went after him, through the gathering gloom, Kongoni leading and I close behind, with the rifle ready for instant action; for though his strength was evidently fast failing, he was also evidently in a savage temper, anxious to wreak his vengeance before he died. On we went, following the bloody trail through dim, cavernous windings in the dark, vine-covered jungle; we heard him smash the branches but a few yards ahead, and fall and rise; and stealing forward Kermit and I slipped up to within a dozen feet of him as he stood on the other side of some small twisted trees, hung with a mat of creepers. I put a bullet into his heart, Kermit fired; each of us fired again on the instant; the mighty bull threw up his trunk, crashed over backward, and lay dead on his side among the bushes. A fine sight he was, a sight to gladden any hunter's heart, as he lay in the twilight, a giant in death.

At once we trotted back to camp, reaching it as darkness fell; and next morning all of us came out to the carcass. He was full grown, and was ten feet nine inches high. The tusks were rather short, but thick, and weighed a hundred and ten pounds the pair. Out of the trunk we made excellent soup.

Several times while following the trail of this big bull we could tell he was close by the strong elephant smell. Most game animals have a peculiar scent, often strong enough for the species to be readily recognizable before it is seen, if in forest or jungle. On the open plains, of course, one rarely gets close enough to an animal to smell it before seeing it; but I once smelled a herd of hartebeest, when the wind was blowing strongly from them, although

The dead tusker

From a photograph by J. Alden Loring

they were out of sight over a gentle rise. Waterbuck have a very strong smell. Buffalo smell very much like domestic cattle, but old bulls are rank. More than once, in forest, my nostrils have warned me before my eyes that I was getting near the quarry whose spoor I was on.

After leaving the elephant camp we journeyed through country for the most part covered with an open forest growth. The trees were chiefly acacias. Among them were interspersed huge candelabra euphorbias, all in bloom, and now and then one of the brilliant red flowering trees, which never seem to carry many leaves at the same time with their gaudy blossoms. At one place for miles the open forest was composed of the pod-bearing, thick-leafed trees on which we had found the elephants feeding; their bark and manner of growth gave them somewhat the look of jack-oaks; where they made up the forest, growing well apart from one another, it reminded us of the cross-timbers of Texas and Oklahoma. The grass was everywhere three or four feet high; here and there were patches of the cane-like elephant grass, fifteen feet high.

It was pleasant to stride along the road in the early mornings, followed by the safari, and we saw many a glorious sunrise. But as noon approached it grew very hot, under the glare of the brazen equatorial sun, and we were always glad when we approached our new camp, with its grass-strewn ground, its wicker-work fence, and cool, open rest-house. The local sub-chief and his elders were usually drawn up to receive me at the gate, bowing, clapping their hands, and uttering their long-drawn e-h-h-s; and often banana saplings or branches would be stuck in the ground to form avenues of approach, and the fence and rest-house might be decorated with flowers of many kinds. Sometimes we were met with music, on instruments of one string, of three strings, of ten strings—rudimentary fiddles and harps; and there was a much more complicated instrument, big and cumbrous, made of bars of wood placed on two banana stems, the bars being struck with a hammer, as if they were keys; its tones were deep and good. Along the road we did not see habitations or people; but continually there led away from it, twisting through the tall grass and the bush jungles, native paths, the earth beaten brown and hard by countless bare feet; and these, crossing and recrossing in a net-work, led to plantation after plantation of bananas and sweet-potatoes, and clusters of thatched huts.

In the afternoon, as the sun began to get well beyond the meridian, we usually sallied forth to hunt, under the guidance of some native who had come in to tell us where he had seen game that morning. The jungle was so thick in places and the grass was everywhere so long, that without such guidance there was little successful hunting to be done in only two or three hours. We might come back with a buck, or with two or three guinea-fowl, or with nothing.

There were a good many poisonous snakes; I killed a big puff adder with thirteen eggs inside it; and we also killed a squat, short-tailed viper, beautifully mottled, not eighteen inches long, but with a wide, flat head and a girth of body out of all proportion to its length; and another very poisonous and vicious snake, apparently of colubrine type, long and slender. The birds were an unceasing pleasure. White wagtails and yellow wagtails walked familiarly about us within a few feet, wherever we halted and when we were in camp. Long-tailed, crested colys, with all four of their red toes pointed forward, clung to the sides of the big fruits at which they picked. White-headed swallows caught flies and gnats by our heads. There were large plantain-eaters; and birds like small jays with yellow wattles round the eyes. There were boat-tailed birds, in color iridescent green and purple, which looked like our grakles, but were kin to the bulbuls; and another bird, related to the shrikes, with bristly feathers on the rump, which was colored like a red-winged blackbird, black with red shoulders. Vultures were not plentiful, but the yellow-billed kites, true camp scavengers, were common and tame, screaming as they circled overhead, and catching bits of meat which were thrown in the air for them. The shrews and mice which the naturalists trapped around each camping place were kin to the species we had already obtained in East Africa, but in most cases there was a fairly well-marked difference; the jerbilles for instance had shorter tails, more like ordinary rats. Frogs with queer voices abounded in the marshes. Among the ants was one arboreal kind which made huge nests, shaped like beehives or rather like big gray bells, in the trees. Near the lake, by the way, there were Goliath beetles, as large as small rats.

Ten days from Kampalla we crossed the little Kafu River, the black, smooth current twisting quickly along between beds of plumed papyrus. Beyond it we entered the native kingdom of Unyoro. It is part of the British protectorate of Uganda, but is separate from the native kingdom of Uganda, though its people in ethnic type and social development seem much the same. We halted for a day

Porters entering camp at Hoima
From a photograph by J. Alden Loring

at Hoima, a spread-out little native town, pleasantly situated among hills, and surrounded by plantations of cotton, plaintains, yams, millet, and beans. It is the capital of Unyoro, where the king lives, as well as three or four English officials, and Episcopalian and Roman Catholic missionaries. The king, accompanied by his prime-minister and by the English commissioner, called on me, and I gave him five-o'clock tea; he is a Christian, as are most of his chiefs and headmen, and they are sending their children to the mission schools.

A heron, about the size of our night heron but with a longer neck, and with a curiously crow-like voice, strolled about among the native houses at Hoima; and the kites almost brushed us with their wings as they swooped down for morsels of food. The cheerful, confiding little wagtails crossed the threshold of the rest-house in which we sat. Black-and-white crows and vultures came around camp; and handsome, dark hawks, with white on their wings and tails, and with long, conspicuous crests, perched upright on the trees. There were many kinds of doves; one

Cow-herons and Angola ox on the bank of Lake Victoria Nyanza

From a photograph by J. Alden Loring

pretty little fellow was but six inches long. At night the jackals wailed with shrill woe among the gardens.

From Hoima we entered a country covered with the tall, rank elephant grass. It was traversed by papyrus-bordered streams and broken by patches of forest. The date-palms grew tall, and among the trees were some with orange-red flowers like trumpet flowers growing in grape-shaped clusters; and both the flowers and the seed-pods into which they turned stood straight up in rows above the leafy tops of the trees that bore them.

The first evening, as we sat in the cool, open cane rest-house, word was brought us that an elephant was close at hand. We found him after ten minutes' walk; a young bull, with very small tusks, not worth shooting. For three-quarters of an hour we watched him, strolling about and feeding, just on the edge of a wall of high elephant grass. Although we were in plain sight, ninety yards off, and sometimes moved about, he never saw us; for an elephant's eyes are very bad. He was feeding on some thick, luscious grass, in the usual leisurely elephant fashion, plucking a big tuft, waving it nonchalantly about in his trunk, and finally tucking it into his mouth; pausing to rub his side against a tree, or to sway to and fro as he stood; and continually waving his tail and half cocking his ears.

At noon on January 5th, 1910, we reached Butiaba, a sandspit and marsh on the shores of Lake Albert Nyanza. We had marched about one hundred and sixty miles from Lake Victoria. We camped on the sandy beach by the edge of the beautiful lake, looking across its waters to the mountains that walled in the opposite shore. At mid-day the whole landscape trembled in the white, glaring heat; as the afternoon waned a wind blew off the lake, and the west kindled in ruddy splendor as the sun went down.

At Butiaba we took boats to go down the Nile to the Lado country. The head of the water transportation service in Uganda, Captain Hutchinson, R.N.R., met us, having most kindly decided to take charge of our flotilla himself. Captain Hutchinson was a mighty hunter, and had met with one most extraordinary experience while elephant hunting; in Uganda the number of hunters who have been killed or injured by elephants and buffaloes is large. He wounded a big bull in the head, and followed it for three days. The wound was serious and on the fourth day he overtook the elephant. It charged as soon as it saw him. He hit it twice in the head with his .450 double-barrel as it came on, but neither stopped nor turned it; his second rifle, a double 8 bore, failed to act; and the elephant seized him in its trunk. It brandished him to and fro in the air several times, and then planting him on the

Theodore. Roosevelt

Fac-simile of half of the last page of Chapter XIII of Mr. Roosevelt's manuscript—Page 453 ground knelt and stabbed at him with its tusks. Grasping one of its forelegs he pulled himself between them in time to avoid the blow; and as it rose he managed to seize a hind leg and clung to it. But the tusker reached round and plucked him off with its trunk, and once more brandished him high in the air, swinging him violently about. He fainted from pain and dizziness. When he came to he was lying on the ground; one of his attendants had stabbed the elephant with a spear, whereupon the animal had dropped the white man, vainly tried to catch its new assailant, and had then gone off for some three miles and died. Hutchinson was frightfully bruised and strained, and it was six months before he recovered.

CHAPTER XIV

THE GREAT RHINOCEROS OF THE LADO

"THE region of which I speak is a dreary region in Libya, by the borders of the river Zaire. And there is no quiet there nor silence. The waters of the river have a saffron hue, and for many miles on either side of the river's oozy bed is a pale desert of gigantic water-lilies . . . and I stood in the morass among the tall lilies and the lilies sighed one unto the other in the solemnity of their desolation. And all at once the moon arose through the thin ghastly mist, and was crimson in color. . . . And the man looked out upon the dreary river Zaire, and upon the yellow ghastly waters, and upon the pale legions of the water-lilies. . . . Then I went down into the recess of the morass, and waded afar in among the wilderness of the lilies, and called unto the hippopotami which dwelt among the fens in the recesses of the morass." I was reading Poe, on the banks of the Upper Nile; and surely his "fable" does deserve to rank with the "tales in the volumes of the Magi—in the ironbound, melancholy volumes of the Magi."

We had come down through the second of the great Nyanza lakes. As we sailed northward, its waters stretched behind us beyond the ken of vision, to where they were fed by streams from the Mountains of the Moon. On our left hand rose the frowning ranges on the other side of which the Congo forest lies like a shroud over the land. On our right we passed the mouth of the Victorian Nile, alive with monstrous crocodiles, and its banks barren of human life because of the swarms of the fly whose bite brings the torment which ends in death. As night fell we entered the White Nile, and steamed and drifted down the mighty stream.

The "white" rhino

Drawn by Philip R. Goodwin from photographs and from descriptions furnished by Mr. Roosevelt

Its current swirled in long curves between endless ranks of plumed papyrus. White and blue and red, the floating water-lilies covered the lagoons and the still inlets among the reeds; and here and there the lotus lifted its leaves and flowers stiffly above the surface. The brilliant tropic stars made lanes of light on the lapping water as we ran on through the night. The river horses roared from the reed-beds, and snorted and plunged beside the boat, and crocodiles slipped sullenly into the river as we glided by. Toward morning a mist arose and through it the crescent of the dying moon shone red and lurid. Then the sun flamed aloft and soon the African landscape, vast, lonely, mysterious, stretched on every side in a shimmering glare of heat and light; and ahead of us the great, strange river went twisting away into the distance.

At midnight we had stopped at the station of Koba, where we were warmly received by the district commissioner, and where we met half a dozen of the professional elephant hunters, who for the most part make their money, at hazard of their lives, by poaching ivory in the Congo. They are a hard-bit set, these elephant poachers; there are few careers more adventurous, or fraught with more peril, or which make heavier demands upon the daring, the endurance, and the physical hardihood of those who follow them. Elephant hunters face death at every turn, from fever, from the assaults of warlike native tribes, from their conflicts with their giant quarry; and the unending strain on their health and strength is tremendous.

At noon the following day we stopped at the deserted station of Wadelai, still in British territory. There have been outposts of white mastery on the Upper Nile for many years, but some of them are now abandoned, for as yet there has been no successful attempt at such development of the region as would alone mean permanency of occupation. The natives whom we saw offered a sharp contrast to those of Uganda; we were again back among wild savages. Near the landing at Wadelai was a group of

thatched huts surrounded by a fence; there were small
fields of mealies and beans, cultivated by the women,
and a few cattle and goats; while big wicker-work fish-
traps showed that the river also offered a means of livelihood.   Both men and women were practically naked;
some of the women entirely so except for a few beads.
Here we were joined by an elephant hunter, Quentin Grogan, who was to show us the haunts of the great square-

Sail-boat at Wadelai Landing
From a photograph by J. Alden Loring

mouthed rhinoceros, the so-called white rhinoceros, of the
Lado, the only kind of African heavy game which we
had not yet obtained.   We were allowed to hunt in the
Lado, owing to the considerate courtesy of the Belgian
Government, for which I was sincerely grateful.

After leaving Wadelai we again went downstream.   The
river flowed through immense beds of papyrus.   Beyond
these on either side were rolling plains gradually rising
in the distance into hills or low mountains.   The plains
were covered with high grass, dry and withered; and the

smoke here and there showed that the natives, according to their custom, were now burning it. There was no forest; but scattered over the plains were trees, generally thorns, but other kinds also, among them palms and euphorbias.

The following morning, forty-eight hours after leaving Butiaba, on Lake Albert Nyanza, we disembarked from

Rhino camp, Lado Enclave
From a photograph by Edmund Heller

the little flotilla which had carried us—a crazy little steam launch, two sail-boats, and two big row-boats. We made our camp close to the river's edge, on the Lado side, in a thin grove of scattered thorn-trees. The grass grew rank and tall all about us. Our tents were pitched, and the grass huts of the porters built, on a kind of promontory, the main stream running past one side, while on the other was a bay. The nights were hot and the days burning; the mosquitoes came with darkness, sometimes necessitating our putting on head nets and gloves in the evenings, and they would have made sleep impossible if we had not had mosquito biers. Nevertheless it was a very pleasant camp, and we thoroughly enjoyed it. It was a wild, lonely country, and we saw no human beings except an occasional party of naked savages armed with bows and poisoned arrows. Game was plentiful, and a hunter always enjoys a permanent camp in a good game country; for while the expedition is marching, his movements must largely be regulated by those of the safari, whereas at a permanent camp he is foot-loose.

There was an abundance of animal life, big and little, about our camp. In the reeds, and among the water-lilies of the bay, there were crocodiles, monitor lizards six feet long, and many water birds—herons, flocks of beautiful white egrets, clamorous spur-winged plover, sacred ibis, noisy purple ibis, saddle-billed storks, and lily trotters which ran lightly over the lily pads. There were cormorants and snake birds. Fish eagles screamed as they circled around; very handsome birds, the head, neck, tail, breast, and forepart of the back white, the rest of the plumage black and rich chestnut. There was a queer little eagle owl with inflamed red eyelids. The black and red bulbuls sang noisily. There were many kingfishers, some no larger than chippy sparrows, and many of them brilliantly colored; some had, and others had not, the regular kingfisher voice; and while some dwelt by the river bank and caught fish, others did not come near the water and lived on insects. There were paradise flycatchers with long, wavy white tails; and olive-green pigeons with yellow bellies. Red-headed, red-tailed lizards ran swiftly up and down the trees. The most extraordinary birds were the nightjars; the cocks carried in each wing one very long, waving plume, the pliable quill being twice the length of the bird's body and tail, and bare except for a patch of dark feather webbing at the end. The two big, dark plume tips were very conspicuous, trailing behind the bird as it flew, and so riveting the observer's attention as to make

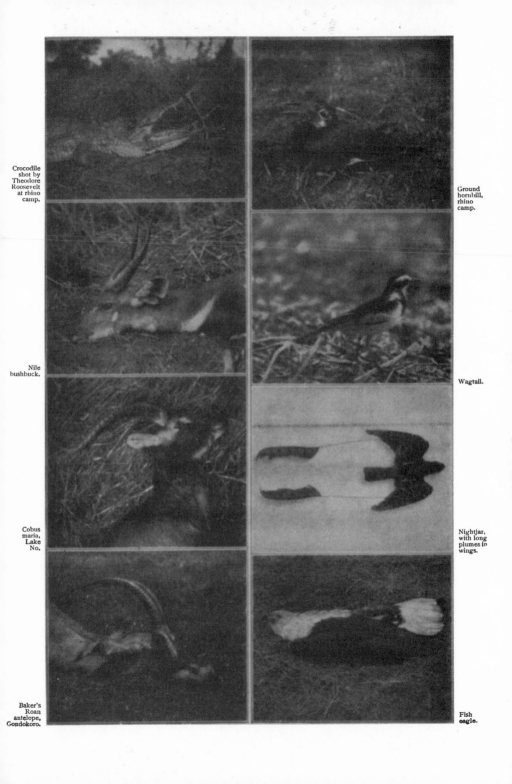

Crocodile shot by Theodore Roosevelt at rhino camp.

Ground hornbill, rhino camp.

Nile bushbuck.

Wagtail.

Cobus maria, Lake No.

Nightjar, with long plumes in wings.

Baker's Roan antelope, Gondokoro.

Fish eagle.

the bird itself almost escape notice. When seen flying, the first impression conveyed was of two large, dark moths or butterflies fluttering rapidly through the air; it was with a positive effort of the eye that I fixed the actual bird. The big slate and yellow bats were more interesting still. There were several kinds of bats at this camp; a small dark kind that appeared only when night had fallen and flew very near the ground all night long, and a somewhat larger one, lighter beneath, which appeared late in the evening and flew higher in the air. Both of these had the ordinary bat habits of continuous, swallow-like flight. But the habits of the slate and yellow bats were utterly different. They were very abundant, hanging in the thinly leaved acacias around the tents, and, as everywhere else, were crepuscular, indeed to a large extent actually diurnal, in habit. They saw well and flew well by daylight, passing the time hanging from twigs. They became active before sunset. In catching insects they behaved not like swallows but like flycatchers. Except that they perched upside down so to speak, that is, that they hung from the twigs instead of sitting on them, their conduct was precisely that of a phœbe bird or a wood peewee. Each bat hung from its twig until it espied a passing insect, when it swooped down upon it, and after a short flight returned with its booty to the same perch or went on to a new one close by; and it kept twitching its long ears as it hung head downward devouring its prey.

There were no native villages in our immediate neighborhood, and the game was not shy. There were many buck: waterbuck, kob, hartebeest, bushbuck, reedbuck, oribi, and duiker. Every day or two Kermit or I would shoot a buck for the camp. We generally went out together with our gun-bearers, Kermit striding along in front, with short trousers and leggings, his knees bare. Sometimes only one of us would go out. The kob and waterbuck were usually found in bands, and were perhaps the commonest of all. The buck seemed to have no settled time for feeding. Two oribi which I shot were feeding right in the open, just at noon, utterly indifferent to the heat. There were hippo both in the bay and in the river. All night long we could hear them splashing, snorting, and grunting; they were very noisy, sometimes uttering a strange, long-drawn bellow, a little like the exhaust of a giant steam-pipe, once or twice whinnying or neighing; but usually making a succession of grunts, or bubbling squeals through the nostrils. The long grass was traversed in all directions

Camp in the Lado
From a photograph by J. Alden Loring

by elephant trails, and there was much fresh sign of the huge beasts—their dung, and the wrecked trees on which they had been feeding; and there was sign of buffalo also. In middle Africa, thanks to wise legislation, and to the very limited size of the areas open to true settlement, there has been no such reckless, wholesale slaughter of big game as that which has brought the once wonderful big game fauna of South Africa to the verge of extinction. In certain small areas of middle Africa, of course, it has gone; but as a whole it has not much diminished, some species have actually increased, and none is in danger of immediate extinction, unless it be the white rhinoceros. During the last decade, for instance, the buffalo have been recovering their lost ground throughout the Lado, Uganda, and British East Africa, having multiplied many times over. During the same period, in the same region, the elephant have not greatly diminished in aggregate numbers, although the number of bulls carrying big ivory has been very much reduced; indeed the reproductive capacity of the herds has probably been very little impaired, the energies of the hunters having been almost exclusively directed to the killing of the bulls with tusks weighing over thirty pounds apiece; and the really big tuskers, which are most eagerly sought after, are almost always past their prime, and no longer associate with the herd.

But this does not apply to the great beast which was the object of our coming to the Lado, the square-mouthed, or, as it is sometimes miscalled, the white, rhinoceros. Africa is a huge continent, and many species of the big mammals inhabiting it are spread over a vast surface; and some of them offer strange problems for inquiry in the discontinuity of their distribution. The most extraordinary instance of this discontinuity is that offered by the distribution of the square-mouthed rhinoceros. It is almost as if our bison had never been known within historic times except in Texas and Ecuador. This great rhinoceros was formerly plentiful in South Africa south of the Zambesi, where it has been completely exterminated except for a score or so of individuals on a game reserve. North of the Zambesi it was and is utterly unknown, save that during the last ten years it has been found to exist in several localities on the left bank of the Upper Nile, close to the river, and covering a north and south extension of about two hundred miles. Even in this narrow ribbon of territory the square-mouthed rhinoceros is found only in certain localities, and although there has not hitherto been much slaughter of the mighty beast, it would certainly be well if all killing of it were prohibited until careful inquiry has been made as to its numbers and exact distribution. It is a curious animal, on the average distinctly larger than, and utterly different from, the ordinary African rhinoceros. The spinal processes of the dorsal vertebræ are so developed as to make a very prominent hump over the withers, while forward of this is a still higher and more prominent fleshy hump on the neck. The huge, misshapen head differs in all respects as

Veldt pool, rhino camp
From a photograph by Edmund Heller

widely from the head of the common or so-called black rhinoceros as the head of a moose differs from that of a wapiti.

The morning after making camp we started on a rhinoceros hunt. At this time in this neighborhood, the rhinoceros seemed to spend the heat of the day in sleep, and to feed in the morning and evening, and perhaps throughout the night; and to drink in the evening and morning, usually at some bay or inlet of the river. In the morning they walked away from the water for an hour or two, until they came to a place which suited them for the day's sleep. Unlike the ordinary rhinoceros, the square-mouthed rhinoceros feeds exclusively on grass. Its dung is very different; we only occasionally saw it deposited in heaps, according to the custom of its more common cousin. The big, sluggish beast seems fond of nosing the ant-hills of red earth, both with its horn and with its square muzzle; it may be that it licks them for some saline substance. It is apparently of less solitary nature than the prehensile-lipped rhino, frequently going in parties of four or five or half a dozen individuals.

We did not get an early start. Hour after hour we plodded on, under the burning sun, through the tall, tangled grass, which was often higher than our heads. Continually we crossed the trails of elephant and more rarely of rhinoceros, but the hard, sun-baked earth and stiff, tinder-dry long grass made it a matter of extreme difficulty to tell if a trail was fresh, or to follow it. Finally, Kermit and his gun-bearer, Kassitura, discovered some unquestionably fresh footprints which those of us who were in front had passed over. Immediately we took the trail, Kongoni and Kassitura acting as trackers, while Kermit and I followed at their heels. Once or twice the two trackers were puzzled, but they were never entirely at fault; and after half an hour Kassitura suddenly pointed toward a thorn-tree about sixty yards off. Mounting a low ant-hill I saw rather dimly through the long grass a big gray bulk, near the foot of the tree; it was a rhinoceros lying asleep on its side, looking like an enormous pig. It heard something and raised itself on its forelegs, in a sitting posture, the big ears thrown forward. I fired for the chest, and the heavy Holland bullet knocked it clean off its feet. Squealing loudly it rose again, but it was clearly done for, and it never got ten yards from where it had been lying.

At the shot four other rhino rose. One bolted to the right, two others ran to the left. Firing through the grass Kermit wounded a bull and followed it for a long distance, but could not overtake it; ten days later,* however, he found the carcass and saved the skull and horns. Meanwhile I killed a calf, which was needed for the museum;

---

* Kermit on this occasion was using the double-barrelled rifle which had been most kindly lent him for the trip by Mr. John Jay White, of New York.

the rhino I had already shot was a full-grown cow, doubtless the calf's mother. As the rhino rose I was struck by their likeness to the picture of the white rhino in Cornwallis Harris's folio of the big game of South Africa seventy years ago. They were totally different in look from the common rhino, seeming to stand higher and to be shorter in proportion to their height, while the hump and the huge, ungainly, square-mouthed head added to the dissimilarity. The common rhino is in color a very dark slate gray; these were a rather lighter slate gray; but this was probably a mere individual peculiarity, for the best observers say that they are of the same hue. The muzzle is broad and square, and the upper lip without a vestige of the curved, prehensile development which makes the upper lip of a common rhino look like the hook of a turtle's beak. The stomachs contained nothing but grass; it is a grazing, not a browsing animal.

There were some white egrets—not, as is usually the case with both rhinos and elephants, the cow-heron, but the slender, black-legged, yellow-toed egret—on the rhinos, and the bodies and heads of both the cow and calf looked as though they had been splashed with streaks of whitewash. One of the egrets returned after the shooting and perched on the dead body of the calf.

The heat was intense, and our gun-bearers at once began skinning the animals, lest they should spoil; and that afternoon Cuninghame and Heller came out from camp with tents, food, and water, and Heller cared for the skins on the spot, taking thirty-six hours for the job. The second night he was visited by a party of lions, which were after the rhinoceros meat and came within fifteen feet of the tents.

On the same night that Heller was visited by the lions we had to fight fire in the main camp. At noon we noticed two fires come toward us, and could soon hear their roaring. The tall, thick grass was like tinder; and if we let the fires reach camp we were certain to lose everything we had.

So Loring, Mearns, Kermit, and I, who were in camp, got out the porters and cut a lane around our tents and goods; and then started a back fire, section after section, from the other side of this lane. We kept every one ready, with branches and wet gunny-sacks, and lit each section in turn, so that we could readily beat out the flames at any point where they threatened. The air was still, and soon after nightfall our back fire had burnt fifty or a hundred yards away from camp, and the danger was practically over. Shortly afterward one of the fires against which we were guarding came over a low hill-crest into view, beyond the line of our back fire. It was a fine sight to see the long line of leaping, wavering flames advance toward one another. An hour or two passed before they met, half a mile from camp. Wherever they came together there would be a moment's spurt of roaring, crackling fire, and then it would vanish, leaving at that point a blank in the circle of flame. Gradually the blanks in the lines extended, until the fire thus burnt itself out, and darkness succeeded the bright red glare.

The fires continued to burn in our neighborhood for a couple of days. Finally one evening the great beds of papyrus across the bay caught fire. After nightfall it was splendid to see the line of flames, leaping fifty feet into the air as they worked across the serried masses of tall papyrus. When they came toward the water they kindled the surface of the bay into a ruddy glare, while above them the crimson smoke clouds drifted slowly to leeward. The fire did not die out until toward morning; and then, behind it, we heard the grand booming chorus of a party of lions. They were full fed, and roaring as they went to their day beds; each would utter a succession of roars which grew louder and louder until they fairly thundered, and then died gradually away, until they ended in a succession of sighs and grunts.

As the fires burned to and fro across the country birds of many kinds came to the edge of the flames to pick up the

The papyrus afire

From a photograph by J. Alden Loring

insects which were driven out. There were marabou storks, kites, hawks, ground hornbills, and flocks of beautiful egrets and cow-herons, which stalked sedately through the grass, and now and then turned a small tree nearly white by all perching in it. The little bank swallows came in myriads; exactly the same, by the way, as our familiar home friends, for the bank swallow is the most widely distributed of all birds. The most conspicuous attendants of the fires, however, were the bee-eaters, the largest and handsomest we had yet seen, their plumage every shade of blended red and rose, varied with brilliant blue and green. The fires seemed to bother the bigger animals hardly at all. The game did not shift their haunts, or do more than move in quite leisurely fashion out of the line of advance of the flames. I saw two oribi which had found a patch of short grass that split the fire, feeding thereon, entirely undisturbed, although the flames were crackling by some fifty yards on each side of them. Even the mice and shrews did not suffer much, probably because they went into holes. Shrews, by the way, were very plentiful, and Loring trapped four kinds, two of them new. It was always a surprise to me to find these tiny shrews swarming in Equatorial Africa just as they swarm in Arctic America.

In a little patch of country not far from this camp there were a few sleeping-sickness fly, and one or two of us were bitten, but, seemingly, the fly were not infected, although at this very time eight men were dying of sleeping sickness at Wadelai where we had stopped. There were also some ordinary tsetse fly, which caused us uneasiness about our mule. We had brought four little mules through Uganda, riding them occasionally on safari; and had taken one across into the Lado, while the other three, with the bulk of the porters, marched on the opposite bank of the Nile from Koba, and were to join us at Nimule.

It was Kermit's turn for the next rhino; and by good luck it was a bull, giving us a complete group of bull, cow, and calf for the National Museum. We got it as we had

gotten our first two. Marching through likely country—
burnt, this time—we came across the tracks of three rhino,
two big and one small, and followed them through the
black ashes. It was an intricate and difficult piece of
tracking, for the trail wound hither and thither and was
criss-crossed by others; but Kongoni and Kassitura gradually untangled the maze, found where the beasts had
drunk at a small pool that morning, and then led us to
where they were lying asleep under some thorn-trees. It
was about eleven o'clock. As the bull rose Kermit gave
him a fatal shot with his beloved Winchester. He galloped full speed toward us, not charging, but in a mad
panic of terror and bewilderment; and with a bullet from
the Holland I brought him down in his tracks only a few
yards away. The cow went off at a gallop. The calf,
a big creature, half grown, hung about for some time, and
came up quite close, but was finally frightened away by
shouting and hand-clapping. Some cow-herons were
round these rhino; and the head and body of the bull
looked as if it had been splashed with whitewash.

It was an old bull, with a short, stubby, worn-down
horn. It was probably no heavier than a big ordinary
rhino bull such as we had shot on the Sotik, and its horns
were no larger, and the front and rear ones were of the
same proportions relatively to each other. But the misshapen head was much larger, and the height seemed
greater because of the curious hump. This fleshy hump
is not over the high dorsal vertebræ, but just forward of
them, on the neck itself, and has no connection with the
spinal column. The square-mouthed rhinoceros of South
Africa is always described as being very much bigger than
the common prehensile-lipped African rhinoceros, and as
carrying much longer horns. But the square-mouthed
rhinos we saw and killed in the Lado did not differ from
the common kind in size and horn development as much
as we had been led to expect; although on an average they
were undoubtedly larger, and with bigger horns, yet there

was in both respects overlapping, the bigger prehensile-lipped rhinos equalling or surpassing the smaller individuals of the other kind. The huge, square-muzzled head, and

Cow square-nosed rhino of the Lado, shot by Mr. Roosevelt

From a photograph by Edmund Heller

the hump, gave the Lado rhino an utterly different look, however, and its habits are also in some important respects different. Our gun-bearers were all East Africans, who had never before been in the Lado. They had been very sceptical when told that the rhinos were different from those they knew, remarking that "all rhinos were the same"; and the first sight of the spoor merely confirmed them in their belief; but they at once recognized the dung as being

Rhino of the usual type, with prehensile lip, shot on the Sotik by Mr. Roosevelt

The differences of the two types are shown in the above photographs

From a photograph by Kermit Roosevelt

different; and when the first animal was down they examined it eagerly and proclaimed it as a rhinoceros with a hump, like their own native cattle, and with the mouth of a hippopotamus.

On the way to camp, after the death of this bull rhino, I shot a waterbuck bull with finer horns than any I had yet obtained. Herds of waterbuck and of kob stared tamely at me as I walked along; whereas a little party of harte-beest were wild and shy. On other occasions I have seen this conduct exactly reversed, the hartebeest being tame, and the waterbuck and kob shy. Heller, as usual, came out and camped by this rhino, to handle the skin and skeleton. In the middle of the night a leopard got caught in one of his small steel traps, which he had set out with a light drag. The beast made a terrific row and went off with the trap and drag. It was only caught by one toe; a hyena similarly caught would have wrenched itself loose; but the leopard, though a far braver and more dan-gerous beast, has less fortitude under pain than a hyena. Heller tracked it up in the morning, and shot it as, ham-pered by the trap and drag, it charged the porters.

On the ashes of the fresh burn the footprints of the game showed almost as distinctly as on snow. One morn-ing we saw where a herd of elephant, cows and calves, had come down the night before to drink at a big bay of the Nile, three or four miles north of our camp. Numerous hippo tracks showed that during the darkness these beasts wandered freely a mile or two inland. They often wan-dered back of our camp at night. Always beside these night trails we found withered remnants of water cabbage and other aquatic plants which they had carried inland with them; I suppose accidentally on their backs. On several occasions where we could only make out scrapes on the ground the hippo trails puzzled us, being so far inland that we thought they might be those of rhinos; until we would come on some patch of ashes or of soft soil where we could trace the four toe marks. The rhino has but three toes, the one in the middle being very big; it belongs, with the tapir and horse, to the group of ungulates which tends to develop one digit of each foot at the expense of all the others; a group which in a long-past geological age was the predominant ungulate group of the world. The hippo, on the contrary, belongs with such cloven-hoofed creatures as the cow and pig, in the group of ungulates which has developed equally two main digits in each foot; a group much more numerously represented than the other in the world of to-day.

As the hippos grew familiar with the camp they became bolder and more venturesome after nightfall. They grunted and brayed to one another throughout the night, splashed and wallowed among the reeds, and came close to the tents during their dry-land rambles in the darkness. One night, in addition to the hippo chorus, we heard the roaring of lions and the trumpeting of elephants. We were indeed in the heart of the African wilderness.

Early in the morning after this concert we started for a day's rhino hunt, Heller and Cuninghame having just finished the preparation, and transport to camp, of the skin of Kermit's bull. Loring, who had not hitherto seen either elephant or rhino alive, went with us; and by good luck he saw both.

A couple of miles from camp we were crossing a wide, flat, swampy valley in which the coarse grass grew as tall as our heads. Here and there were kob, which leaped up on the ant-hills to get a clear view of us. Suddenly our attention was attracted by the movements of a big flock of cow-herons in front of us, and then watching sharply we caught a glimpse of some elephants, about four hundred yards off. We now climbed an ant-hill ourselves, and inspected the elephants, to see if among them were any big-tusked bulls. There were no bulls, however; the little herd consisted of five cows and four calves, which were marching across a patch of burnt ground ahead of us, accompanied by about fifty white cow-herons. We stood where we were until they had passed; we did not wish to get too close, lest they might charge us and force us to shoot in self-defence. They walked in unhurried confidence, and yet were watchful, continually cocking their ears and raising and curling their trunks. One dropped behind and looked fixedly in our direction, probably having heard us talking; then with head aloft and tail stiffly erect it hastened after the others, presenting an absurd likeness to a baboon. The four calves played friskily about, especially a very comical little pink fellow which accompanied the leading cow. Meanwhile a few of the white herons rode on their backs, but most of the flock stalked sedately alongside through the burnt grass, catching the grasshoppers which were disturbed by the great feet. When, however, the herd reached the tall grass all the herons flew up and perched on the backs and heads of their friends; even the pink calf carried one. Half a mile inside the edge of the tall grass the elephants stopped for the day beside a clump of bushes; and there they stood, the white birds clustered on their dark bodies. At the time we could distinctly hear the Doctor's shot-gun, as he collected birds near camp; the reports did not disturb the elephants, and when we walked on we left them standing unconcernedly in the grass.

A couple of hours later, as we followed an elephant path, we came to where it was crossed by the spoor of two rhino. Our gun-bearers took up the trail, over the burnt ground, while Kermit and I followed immediately behind them. The trail wound about, and was not always easy to disentangle, but after a mile or two we saw the beasts. They were standing among bushes and patches of rank, unburned grass; it was just ten o'clock, and they were evidently preparing to lie down for the day. As they stood they kept twitching their big ears; both rhino and elephant are perpetually annoyed, as are most game, by biting flies, large and small. We got up very close, Kermit with his camera and I with the heavy rifle. Too little is known of these northern square-mouthed rhino for us to be sure that they are not lingering slowly toward extinction; and, lest this should be the case, we were not willing to kill any merely for trophies; while, on the other hand, we deemed it really important to get good groups for the National Museum in Washington and the American Museum in New York, and a head for the National Collection of Heads and Horns which was started by Mr. Hornaday, the director of the Bronx Zoological Park. Moreover Kermit and Loring desired to get some photos of the animals while they were alive.

Things did not go well this time, however. The rhinos saw us before either Kermit or Loring could get a good picture. As they wheeled I fired hastily into the chest of one, but not quite in the middle, and away they dashed— for they do not seem as truculent as the common rhino. We followed them. After an hour the trails separated; Cuninghame went on one, but failed to overtake the animal, and we did not see him until we reached camp late that afternoon.

Meanwhile our own gun-bearers followed the bloody spoor of the rhino I had hit, Kermit and I close behind, and Loring with us. The rhino had gone straight off at a gallop, and the trail offered little difficulty, so we walked fast. A couple of hours passed. The sun was now high and the heat intense as we walked over the burned ground. The scattered trees bore such scanty foliage as to cast hardly any shade. The rhino galloped strongly and without faltering; but there was a good deal of blood on the trail. At last, after we had gone seven or eight miles, Kiboko the skinner, who was acting as my gun-bearer, pointed toward a small thorn-tree; and beside it I saw the rhino standing with drooping head. It had been fatally hit, and if undisturbed would probably never have moved from where it was standing; and we finished it off forthwith. It was a cow, and before dying it ran round and round in a circle, in the manner of the common rhino.

Loring stayed to superintend the skinning and bringing in of the head and feet, and slabs of hide. Meanwhile Kermit and I, with our gun-bearers, went off with a

We walked up to within about twenty yards

From a photograph. copyright, by Kermit Roosevelt

"shenzi," a wild native who had just come in with the news that he knew where another rhino was lying, a few miles away. While bound thither we passed numbers of oribi, and went close to a herd of waterbuck which stared at us with stupid tameness; a single hartebeest was with them. When we reached the spot there was the rhino, sure enough, under a little tree, sleeping on his belly, his legs doubled up, and his head flat on the ground. Unfortunately the grass was long, so that it was almost impossible to photograph him. However, Kermit tried to get his picture from an ant-hill fifty yards distant, and then, Kermit with his camera and I with my rifle, we walked up to within about twenty yards. At this point we halted, and on the instant the rhino jumped to his feet with surprising agility and trotted a few yards out from under the tree. It was a huge bull, with a fair horn; much the biggest bull we had yet seen; and with head up and action high, the sun glinting on his slate hide and bringing out his enormous bulk, he was indeed a fine sight. I waited a moment for Kermit to snap him. Unfortunately the waving grass spoiled the picture. Then I fired right and left into his body, behind the shoulders, and down he went. In color he seemed of exactly the same shade as the common rhino, but he was taller and heavier, being six feet high. He carried a stout horn, a little over two feet long; the girth at the base was very great.

Leaving the gun-bearers (with all our water) to skin the mighty beast, Kermit and I started for camp; and as we were rather late Kermit struck out at a great pace in front, while I followed on the little ambling mule. On our way in we passed the elephants, still standing where we had left them in the morning, with the white cow-herons flying and walking around and over them. Heller and Cuninghame at once went out to camp by the skin and take care of it, and to bring back the skeleton. We had been out about eleven hours without food; we were very dirty from the ashes on the burnt ground; we had triumphed;

and we were thoroughly happy as we took our baths and ate our hearty dinner.

It was amusing to look at our three naturalists and compare them with the conventional pictures of men of science and learning—especially men of science and learning in the wilderness—drawn by the novelists a century ago. Nowadays the field naturalist—who is usually at all points superior to the mere closet naturalist—follows a profession as full of hazard and interest as that of the explorer

Marabous and vultures. The undertakers
From a photograph by J. Alden Loring

or of the big-game hunter in the remote wilderness. He penetrates to all the out-of-the-way nooks and corners of the earth; he is schooled to the performance of very hard work, to the endurance of fatigue and hardship, to encountering all kinds of risks, and to grappling with every conceivable emergency. In consequence he is exceedingly competent, resourceful, and self-reliant, and the man of all others to trust in a tight place.

Around this camp there were no ravens or crows; but multitudes of kites, almost as tame as sparrows, circled among the tents, uttering their wailing cries, and lit on the little trees near by or waddled about on the ground near the cook fires. Numerous vultures, many marabou storks, and a single fish eagle, came to the carcasses set for them outside the camp by Loring; and he took pictures of them. The handsome fish eagle looked altogether out of place among the foul carrion-feeding throng; on the ground the vultures made way for him respectfully enough, but they resented his presence, and now and then two or three would unite to mob him while on the wing.

We wished for another cow rhino, so as to have a bull and a cow both for the National Museum at Washington, and for the American Museum in New York; and Kermit was to shoot this. Accordingly he and I started off early one morning with Grogan—a man of about twenty-five, a good hunter and a capital fellow, with whom by this time we were great friends. It was much like our other hunts. We tramped through high grass across a big, swampy plain or broad valley between low rises of ground, until, on the opposite side, we struck a by-this-time familiar landmark, two tall royal palms, the only ones for some miles around. Here we turned into a broad elephant and rhinoceros path, worn deep and smooth by the generations of huge feet that had tramped it; for it led from the dry inland to a favorite drinking-place on the Nile. Along this we walked until Kassitura made out the trail of two rhino crossing it at right angles. They were evidently feeding and seeking a noonday resting-place; in this country the square-mouthed rhinoceros live on the grassy flats, sparsely covered with small thorn-trees, and only go into the high reeds on their way to drink. With Kassitura and Kongoni in the lead we followed the fresh trail for a mile or so, until we saw our quarry. The stupid beasts had smelt us, but were trotting to and fro in a state of indecision and excitement, tails twisting and ears cocked, uncertain what to do. At first we thought they were a bull and a small cow; but they proved to be a big cow with good horns, and a calf which was nearly full grown. The

wind and sun were both exactly wrong, so Kermit could
not take any photos; and accordingly he shot the cow
behind the shoulder. Away both animals went, Kermit
tearing along behind, while Grogan and I followed. After
a sharp run of a mile and a half Kermit overtook them,
and brought down
the cow. The
younger one then
trotted threaten-
ingly toward him.
He let it get with-
in ten yards, try-
ing to scare it; as
it kept coming
on, and could of
course easily kill
him, he then fired
into its face, to
one side, so as to
avoid inflicting a
serious injury,
and, turning, off it
went at a gallop.
When I came up
the cow had raised
itself on its fore-
legs, and he was
taking its picture.
It had been wal-
lowing, and its
whole body was

Mr. Roosevelt and Quentin Grogan
From a photograph by Kermit Roosevelt

covered with dry caked mud. It was exactly the color of
the common rhino, but a little larger than any cow of the
latter that we had killed. We at once sent for Heller—
who had been working without intermission since we struck
the Lado, and liked it—and waited by the body until he
appeared, in mid-afternoon.

Here in the Lado we were in a wild, uninhabited country, and for meat we depended entirely on our rifles; nor was there any difficulty in obtaining all we needed. We only shot for meat, or for museum specimens—all the museum specimens being used for food too—and as the naturalists were as busy as they well could be, we found that, except when we were after rhinoceros, it was not necessary to hunt for more than half a day or thereabouts. On one of these hunts, on which he shot a couple of buck, Kermit also killed a monitor lizard, and a crocodile ten feet long; it was a female, and contained fifty-two eggs, which, when scrambled, we ate and found good.

The morning after Kermit killed his cow rhino he and Grogan went off for the day to see if they could not get some live rhino photos. Cuninghame started to join Heller at the temporary camp which we had made beside the dead rhino, in order to help him with the skin and skeletons. Mearns and Loring were busy with birds, small beasts, and photographs. So, as we were out of fresh meat, I walked away from camp to get some, followed by my gunbearers, the little mule with its well-meaning and utterly ignorant shenzi sais, and a dozen porters.

We first went along the river brink to look for crocodiles. In most places the bank was high and steep. Wherever it was broken there was a drinking-place, with leading down to it trails deeply rutted in the soil by the herds of giant game that had travelled them for untold years. At this point the Nile was miles wide, and was divided into curving channels which here and there spread into lakelike expanses of still water. Along the edges of the river and between the winding channels and lagoons grew vast water-fields of papyrus, their sheets and bands of dark green breaking the burnished silver of the sunlit waters. Beyond the further bank rose steep, sharply peaked hills. The tricolored fish eagles, striking to the eye because of their snow-white heads and breasts, screamed continually, a wild eerie sound. Cormorants and snake birds were perched on trees overhanging the water, and flew away, or plunged like stones into the stream, as I approached; herons of many kinds rose from the marshy edges of the bays and inlets; wattled and spur-winged plovers circled overhead; and I saw a party of hippopotami in a shallow on the other side of the nearest channel, their lazy bulks raised above water as they basked asleep in the sun. The semi-diurnal slate-and-yellow bats flitted from one scantily leaved tree to another, as I disturbed them. At the foot of a steep bluff, several yards from the water, a crocodile lay. I broke its neck with a soft-nosed bullet from the little Springfield; for the plated skin of a crocodile offers no resistance to a modern rifle. We dragged the ugly man-eater up the bank, and sent one of the porters back to camp to bring out enough men to carry the brute in bodily. It was a female, containing thirty eggs. We did not find any crocodile's nest; but near camp, in digging a hole for the disposal of refuse, we came on a clutch of a dozen eggs of the monitor lizard. They were in sandy loam, two feet and a half beneath the surface, without the vestige of a burrow leading to them. When exposed to the sun, unlike the crocodile's eggs, they soon burst. Evidently the young are hatched in the cool earth and dig their way out.

We continued our walk and soon came on some kob. At two hundred yards I got a fine buck, though he went a quarter of a mile. Then, at a hundred and fifty yards, I dropped a straw-colored Nile hartebeest. Sending in the kob and hartebeest used up all our porters but two, and I mounted the little mule and turned toward camp, having been out three hours. Soon Gouvimali pointed out a big bustard, marching away through the grass a hundred yards off. I dismounted, shot him through the base of the neck, and remounted. Then Kongoni pointed out, some distance ahead, a bushbuck ram, of the harnessed kind found in this part of the Nile Valley. Hastily dismounting, and stealing rapidly from ant-heap to ant-heap, until I was not much over a hundred yards from him, I gave him a fatal shot; but the bullet was placed a little too far back, and he could still go a considerable distance. So far I had been shooting well; now, pride had a fall. Immediately after the shot a difficulty arose in the rear between the mule and

Mr. Roosevelt with kob, shot at rhino camp

From a photograph by Kermit Roosevelt

the shenzi sais; they parted company, and the mule joined the shooting party in front, at a gallop. The bushbuck, which had halted with its head down, started off and I trotted after it, while the mule pursued an uncertain course between us; and I don't know which it annoyed most. I emptied my magazine twice, and partly a third time, before I finally killed the buck and scared the mule so that it started for camp. The bushbuck in this part of the Nile Valley did not live in dense forest, like those of East Africa, but among the scattered bushes and acacias. Those that I shot in the Lado had in their stomachs leaves, twig tips, and pods; one that Kermit shot, a fine buck, had been eating grass also. On the Uasin Gishu, in addition to leaves and a little grass, they had been feeding on the wild olives.

Our porters were not as a rule by any means the equals of those we had in East Africa, and we had some trouble because, as we did not know their names and faces, those who wished to shirk would go off in the bushes while their more willing comrades would be told off for the needed work. So Cuninghame determined to make each readily identifiable; and one day I found him sitting, in Rhadamanthus mood, at his table before his tent, while all the porters filed by, each in turn being decorated with a tag, conspicuously numbered, which was hung round his neck —the tags, by the way, being Smithsonian label cards, contributed by Dr. Mearns.

At last Kermit succeeded in getting some good white rhino pictures. He was out with his gun-bearers and Grogan. They had hunted steadily for nearly two days without seeing a rhino; then Kermit made out a big cow with a calf lying under a large tree, on a bare plain of short grass. Accompanied by Grogan, and by a gun-bearer carrying his rifle, while he himself carried his "naturalist's graphlex" camera, he got up to within fifty or sixty yards of the dull-witted beasts, and spent an hour cautiously manœuvring and taking photos. He got several photos of the cow and calf lying under the tree. Then something, probably the click of the camera, rendered them uneasy and they stood up. Soon the calf lay down again, while the cow continued standing on the other side of the tree, her head held down, the muzzle almost touching the ground, according to the custom of this species. After taking one or two more pictures Kermit edged in, so as to get better ones. Gradually the cow grew alarmed. She raised her head, as these animals always do when interested or excited, twisted her tail into a tight knot, and walked out from under the tree, followed by the calf; she and the calf stood stern to stern for a few seconds, and Kermit took another photo. By this time the cow had become both puzzled and irritated. Even with her dim eyes she could make out the men and the camera, and once or twice she threatened a charge, but thought better of it. Then she began to move off; but suddenly wheeled and charged, this time bent on mischief. She came on at a slashing trot, gradually increasing her pace, the huge, square lips shaking from side to side. Hoping that she would turn Kermit shouted loudly and waited before firing until she was only ten yards off. Then, with the Winchester, he put a bullet in between her neck and shoulder, a mortal wound. She halted and half wheeled, and Grogan gave her right and left, Kermit putting in a couple of additional bullets as she went off. A couple of hundred yards away she fell, rose again, staggered, fell again, and died. The calf, which was old enough to shift for itself, refused to leave the body, although Kermit and Grogan pelted it with sticks and clods. Finally a shot through the flesh of the buttocks sent it off in frantic haste. Kermit had only killed the cow because it was absolutely necessary in order to avoid an accident, and he was sorry for the necessity; but I was not, for it was a very fine specimen, with the front horn thirty-one inches long; being longer than any other we had gotten. The second horn was compressed laterally, exactly as with many black rhinos (although it is sometimes stated that this does not occur in the case of the white rhino). We preserved the head-skin and skull for the National Museum.

The flesh of this rhino, especially the hump, proved excellent. It is a singular thing that scientific writers seem

The cow and calf square-nosed rhino under the tree after being disturbed
by the click of the camera

almost to have overlooked, and never lay any stress upon, the existence of this neck hump. It is on the neck, forward of the long dorsal vertebra, and is very conspicuous in the living animal; and I am inclined to think that some inches of the exceptional height measurements attributed to South African white rhinos may be due to measuring to the top of this hump. I am also puzzled by what seems

The calf, which was old enough to shift for itself, refused to leave the body
From a photograph, copyright, by Kermit Roosevelt

to be the great inferiority in horn development of these square-mouthed rhinos of the Lado to the square-mouthed or white rhinos of South Africa (and, by the way, I may mention that on the whole these Lado rhinos certainly looked lighter colored, when we came across them standing in the open, than did their prehensile-lipped East African brethren). We saw between thirty and forty square-mouthed rhinos in the Lado, and Kermit's cow had much the longest horn of any of them; and while they averaged much better horns than the black rhinos we had seen in East Africa, between one and two hundred in number, there were any number of exceptions on both sides. There are recorded measurements of white rhino horns from South Africa double as long as our longest from the Lado. Now this is, scientifically, a fact of some importance, but it is of no consequence whatever when compared with the question as to what, if any, the difference is between the average horns; and this last fact is very difficult to ascertain, largely because of the foolish obsession for "record" heads which seems to completely absorb so many hunters who write. What we need at the moment is more information about the average South African heads. There are to be found among most kinds of horn-bearing animals individuals with horns of wholly exceptional size, just as among all nations there are individuals of wholly exceptional height. But a comparison of these wholly exceptional horns, although it has a certain value, is, scientifically, much like a comparison of the giants of different nations. A good head is of course better than a poor one; and a special effort to secure an exceptional head is sportsmanlike and proper. But to let the desire for "record" heads, to the exclusion of all else, become a craze, is absurd. The making of such a collection is in itself not only proper but meritorious; all I object to is the loss of all sense of proportion in connection therewith. It is just as with philately, or heraldry, or collecting the signatures of famous men. The study of stamps, or of coats of arms, or the collecting of autographs, is an entirely legitimate amusement, and may be more than a mere amusement; it is only when the student or collector allows himself utterly to misestimate the importance of his pursuit that it becomes ridiculous.

Cuninghame, Grogan, Heller, Kermit, and I now went off on a week's safari inland, travelling as light as possible. The first day's march brought us to the kraal of a local chief named Sururu. There were a few banana-trees, and patches of scrawny cultivation, round the little cluster of huts, ringed with a thorn fence, through which led a low door; and the natives owned goats and chickens. Sururu himself wore a white sheet of cotton as a toga, and he owned a red fez and a pair of baggy blue breeches, which last he generally carried over his shoulder. His people were very scantily clad indeed, and a few of them, both men and women, wore absolutely nothing except a string of blue beads around the waist or neck. Their ears had not been pierced and stretched like so many East African savages, but their lower lips were pierced for wooden ornaments and quills. They brought us eggs and chickens, which we paid for with American cloth; this cloth, and some umbrellas, constituting our stock of trade goods, or gift goods, for the Nile.

The following day Sururu himself led us to our next camp, only a couple of hours away. It was a dry country of harsh grass, everywhere covered by a sparse growth of euphorbias and stunted thorns, which were never in sufficient numbers to make a forest, each little, wellnigh leafless tree, standing a dozen rods or so distant from its nearest fellow. Most of the grass had been burnt, and fires were still raging. Our camp was by a beautiful pond, covered with white and lilac water-lilies. We pitched our two tents on a bluff, under some large acacias that cast real shade. It was between two and three degrees north of the equator. The moon, the hot January moon of the mid-tropics, was at the full, and the nights were very lovely; the little sheet of water glimmered in the moon rays, and round about the dry landscape shone with a strange, spectral light.

Near the pond, just before camping, I shot a couple of young waterbuck bulls for food, and while we were pitching the tents a small herd of elephants—cows, young bulls, and calves, seemingly disturbed by a grass fire which was burning a little way off, came up within four hundred yards of us. At first we mistook one large cow for a bull, and running quickly from bush to bush, diagonally to its course, I got within sixty yards, and watched it pass at a quick shuffling walk, lifting and curling its trunk. The blindness of both elephant and rhino has never been sufficiently emphasized in books. Near camp was the bloody, broken skeleton of a young wart-hog boar, killed by a lion the previous night. There were a number of lions in the neighborhood, and they roared at intervals all night long. Next morning, after Grogan and I had started from camp, when the sun had been up an hour, we heard one roar loudly less than a mile away. Running toward the place we tried to find the lion; but near by a small river ran through beds of reeds, and the fires had left many patches of tall, yellow, half-burned grass, so that it had ample cover, and our search was fruitless.

Near the pond were green parrots and brilliant wood hoopoos, rollers, and sunbirds; and buck of the ordinary kinds drank at it. A duiker which I shot for the table had been feeding on grass tips and on the stems and leaves of a small, low-growing plant.

After giving up the quest for the lion Grogan and I, with our gun-bearers, spent the day walking over the great dry flats of burnt grass-land and sparse, withered forest. The heat grew intense as the sun rose higher and higher. Hour after hour we plodded on across vast level stretches, or up or down inclines so slight as hardly to be noticeable. The black dust of the burn rose in puffs beneath our feet; and now and then we saw dust devils, violent little whirlwinds, which darted right and left, raising to a height of many feet gray funnels of ashes and withered leaves. In places the coarse grass had half resisted the flames, and rose above our heads. Here and there bleached skulls of elephant and rhino, long dead, showed white against the charred surface of the soil. Everywhere, crossing and recrossing one another, were game trails, some slightly marked, others broad and hard, and beaten deep into the soil by the feet of the giant creatures that had trodden them for ages. The elephants had been the chief road makers; but the rhinoceros had travelled their trails, and also buffalo and buck.

There were elephant about, but only cows and calves, and an occasional bull with very small tusks. Of rhinoceros, all square-mouthed, we saw nine, none carrying horns which made them worth shooting. The first one I saw was in long grass. My attention was attracted by a row of white objects moving at some speed through the top of the grass. It took a second look before I made out that they were cow-herons perched on the back of a rhino. This proved to be a bull, which joined a cow and a calf. None had decent horns, and we plodded on. Soon we came to the trail of two others, and after a couple of miles' tracking Kongoni pointed to two gray bulks lying down under a tree. I walked cautiously to within thirty yards. They heard something, and up rose the two pig-like blinking creatures, who gradually became aware of my presence, and retreated a few steps at a time, dull curiosity continually overcoming an uneasiness which never grew into fear. Tossing their stumpy-horned heads, and twisting their tails into tight knots, they ambled briskly from side to side, and were ten minutes in getting to a distance of a hundred yards. Then our shenzi guide mentioned that there were other rhinos close by, and we walked off to inspect them. In three hundred yards we came on them, a cow and a well-grown calf. Sixty yards from them was an ant-hill with little trees on it. From this we looked at them until some sound or other must have made them uneasy, for up they got. The young one seemed to have rather keener suspicions, although no more sense, than its mother, and after a while grew so restless that it persuaded the cow to go off with it. But the still air gave no hint of our whereabouts, and they walked straight toward us. I did not wish to have to shoot one, and so when they were within thirty yards we raised a shout and away they cantered, heads tossing and tails twisting.

Three hours later we saw another cow and calf. By this time it was half-past three in the afternoon, and the two animals had risen from their noonday rest and were grazing busily, the great clumsy heads sweeping the ground. Watching them forty yards off it was some time before the cow raised her head high enough for me to see that her horns were not good. Then they became suspicious, and the cow stood motionless for several minutes, her head held low. We moved quietly back, and at last they either dimly saw us, or heard us, and stood looking toward us, their big ears cocked forward. At this moment we stumbled on a rhino skull, bleached, but in such good preservation that we knew Heller would like it; and we loaded it on the porters that had followed us. All the time we were thus engaged the two rhinos, only a hundred yards off, were intently gazing in our direction, with foolish and bewildered solemnity; and there we left them, survivors from a long-vanished world, standing alone in the parched desolation of the wilderness.

On another day Kermit saw ten rhino, none with more than ordinary horns. Five of them were in one party, and were much agitated by the approach of the men; they ran to and fro, their tails twisted into the usual pig-like curl, and from sheer nervous stupidity bade fair at one time to force the hunters to fire in self-defence. Finally, however, they all ran off. In the case of a couple of others a curious incident happened. When alarmed they failed to make out where the danger lay, and after running away a short distance they returned to a bush near by to look about. One remained standing, but the other deliberately sat down upon its haunches like a dog, staring ahead, Kermit meanwhile being busy with his camera. Two or three times I saw rhino, when roused from sleep, thus sit up on their haunches and look around before rising on all four legs; but this was the only time that any of us saw a rhino which was already standing assume such a position. No other kind of heavy game has this habit; and indeed, so

far as I know, only one other hoofed animal, the white goat
of the northern Rocky Mountains.   In the case of the
white goat, however, the attitude is far more often assumed,
and in more extreme form;   it is one of the characteristic

When alarmed they failed to make out where the danger lay
From a photograph, copyright, by Kermit Roosevelt

traits of the queer goat-antelope, so many of whose ways
and looks are peculiar to itself alone.

From the lily-pond camp we went back to our camp
outside Sururu's village.   This was a very pleasant camp
because while there, although the heat was intense in the
daytime, the nights were cool and there were no mosquitoes.
During our stay in the Lado it was generally necessary
to wear head nets and gloves in the evenings and to go to
bed at once after dinner, and then to lie under the mosquito
bar with practically nothing on through the long hot night,
sleeping or contentedly listening to the humming of the

One remained standing, but the other deliberately sat down upon its haunches like a dog

From a photograph, copyright, by Kermit Roosevelt

baffled myriads outside the net. At the Sururu camp, however, we could sit at a table in front of the tents, after supper—or dinner, whichever one chose to call it—and read by
lamplight, in the still, cool, pleasant air; or walk up and
down the hard, smooth elephant path which led by the
tents, looking at the large red moon just risen, as it
hung low over the horizon, or later, when, white and
clear, it rode high in the heavens and flooded the land
with its radiance.

There was a swamp close by, and we went through this
the first afternoon in search of buffalo. We found plenty of
sign; but the close-growing reeds were ten feet high, and
even along the winding buffalo trails by which alone they
could be penetrated it was impossible to see a dozen paces
ahead. Inside the reeds it was nearly impossible to get to
the buffalo, or at least to be sure to kill only a bull, which
was all I wanted; and at this time when the moon was just
past the full, these particular buffalo only came out into
the open to feed at night, or very early in the morning and
late in the evening. But Sururu said that there were other
buffalo which lived away from the reeds, among the thorn-
trees on the grassy flats and low hills; and he volunteered
to bring me information about them on the morrow. Sure
enough, shortly before eleven next morning, he turned
up with the news that he had found a solitary bull only
about five miles away. Grogan and I at once started back
with him, accompanied by our gun-bearers. The country
was just such as that in which we had hitherto found our
rhinos; and there was fresh sign of rhino as well as buffalo.
The thorny, scantily leaved trees were perhaps a little
closer together than in most places, and there were a good
many half-burned patches of tall grass. We passed a
couple of ponds which must have been permanent, as water-
lilies were growing in them; at one a buffalo had been
drinking. It was half-past twelve when we reached the
place where Sururu had seen the bull. We then advanced
with the utmost caution as the wind was shifty, and although

the cover was thin, it yet rendered it difficult to see a hundred yards in advance. At last we made out the bull, on his feet and feeding, although it was high noon. He was stern toward us, and while we were stealing toward him a puff of wind gave him our scent. At once he whipped around, gazed at us for a moment with out-stretched head, and galloped off. I could not get a shot through the bushes, and after him we ran, Kongoni leading, with me at his heels. It was hot work running, for at this time the thermometer registered 102° in the shade. Fortunately the bull had little fear of man, and being curious, and rather truculent, he halted two or three times to look round. Finally, after we had run a mile and a half, he halted once too often, and I got a shot at him at eighty yards. The heavy bullet went home; I fired twice again as rapidly as possible, and the bull never moved from where he had stood. He was an old bull, as big as an East African buffalo bull; but his worn horns were smaller and rather different. This had rendered Kongoni uncertain whether he might not be a cow; and when we came up to the body he exclaimed with delight that it was a "duck"—Kongoni's invariable method of pronouncing "buck," the term he used to describe anything male, from a lion or an elephant to a bustard or a crocodile; "cow" being his expression for the female of these and all other creatures. As Gouvimali came running up to shake hands, his face wreathed in smiles, he exclaimed "G-o-o-d-e morning"; a phrase which he had picked up under the impression that it was a species of congratulation.

As always when I have killed buffalo I was struck by the massive bulk of the great bull as he lay in death, and by the evident and tremendous muscular power of his big-boned frame. He looked what he was, a formidable beast. Thirty porters had to be sent out to bring to camp the head, hide, and meat. We found, by the way, that his meat made excellent soup, his kidneys a good stew, while his tongue was delicious.

Next morning Kermit and I with the bulk of the safari walked back to our main camp, on the Nile, leaving Cuninghame and Heller where they were for a day, to take care of the buffalo skin. Each of us struck off across the country by himself, with his gun-bearers. After walking five or six miles I saw a big rhino three-quarters of a mile off. At this point the country was flat, the acacias very thinly scattered, and the grass completely burnt off, the green young blades sprouting; and there was no difficulty in making out, at the distance we did, the vast gray bulk of the rhino as it stood inertly under a tree. Drawing nearer we saw that it had a good horn, although not as good as Kermit's best; and approaching quietly to within forty yards I shot the beast.

At the main camp we found that Mearns had made a fine collection of birds in our absence; while Loring had taken a variety of excellent photos, of marabou, vultures, and kites feeding, and, above all, of a monitor lizard plundering the nest of a crocodile. The monitors were quite plentiful near camp. They are amphibious, carnivorous lizards of large size; they frequent· the banks of the river, running well on the land, and sometimes even climbing trees, but taking to the water when alarmed. They feed on mice and rats, other lizards, eggs, and fish; the stomachs of those we caught generally contained fish, for they are expert swimmers. One morning Loring surprised a monitor which had just uncovered some crocodile eggs on a small sandy beach. The eggs, about thirty in number, were buried in rather shallow fashion, so that the monitor readily uncovered them. The monitor had one of the eggs transversely in its mouth, and, head erect, was marching off with it. As soon as it saw Loring it dropped the egg and scuttled into the reeds; in a few minutes it returned, took another egg, and walked off into the bushes, where it broke the shell, swallowed the yolk, and at once returned to the nest for another egg. Loring took me out to see the feat repeated, replenishing the rifled nest with

eggs taken from a crocodile the Doctor had shot; and I
was delighted to watch, from our hiding place, the big lizard
as he cautiously approached, seized an egg, and then retired to cover with his booty. Kermit came on a monitor
plundering a crocodile's nest at the top of a steep bank,
while, funnily enough, a large crocodile lay asleep at the
foot of the bank only a few yards distant. As soon as it

The monitor lizard robbing a crocodile's nest
From a photograph by J. Alden Loring

saw Kermit the monitor dropped the egg it was carrying,
ran up a slanting tree which overhung the river, and
dropped into the water like a snake bird.

There was always something interesting to do or to
see at this camp. One afternoon I spent in the boat. The
papyrus along the channel rose like a forest, thirty feet high,
the close-growing stems knit together by vines. As we
drifted down, the green wall was continually broken by
openings, through which side streams from the great river
rushed, swirling and winding, down narrow lanes and
under low archways, into the dim mysterious heart of
the vast reedbeds, where dwelt bird and reptile and water
beast. In a shallow bay we came on two hippo cows with
their calves, and a dozen crocodiles. I shot one of the

latter—as I always do, when I get a chance—and it turned
over and over, lashing with its tail as it sank. A half-grown
hippo came up close by the boat and leaped nearly clear of
the water; and in another place I saw a mother hippo
swimming, with the young one resting half on its back.

Another day Kermit came on some black-and-white
Colobus monkeys. Those we had shot east of the Rift
Valley had long mantles, and more white than black in
their coloring; west of the Rift Valley they had less white
and less of the very long hair; and here on the Nile the
change had gone still further in the same direction. On the
west coast this kind of monkey is said to be entirely black.
But we were not prepared for the complete change in habits. In East Africa the Colobus monkeys kept to the dense
cool mountain forests, dwelt in the tops of the big trees, and
rarely descended to the ground. Here, on the Nile, they
lived in exactly such country as that affected by the smaller
greenish-yellow monkeys, which we found along the Guaso
Nyero for instance; country into which the East African
Colobus never by any chance wandered. Moreover, instead
of living in the tall timber, and never going on the ground
except for a few yards, as in East Africa, here on the Nile
they sought to escape danger by flight over the ground, in
the scrub. Kermit found some in a grove of fairly big
acacias, but they instantly dropped to the earth and galloped off among the dry, scattered bushes and small thorn-
trees. Kermit also shot a twelve-foot crocodile in which
he found the remains of a big heron.

One morning we saw from camp a herd of elephants in
a piece of unburned swamp. It was a mile and a half
away in a straight line, although we had to walk three
miles to get there. There were between forty and fifty
of them, a few big cows with calves, the rest half-grown
and three-quarters-grown animals. Over a hundred white
herons accompanied them. From an ant-hill to leeward
we watched them standing by a mud hole in the swamp;
evidently they now and then got a whiff from our camp,

for they were continually lifting and curling their trunks. To see if by any chance there was a bull among them we moved them out of the swamp by shouting; the wind blew hard and as they moved they evidently smelled the camp strongly, for all their trunks went into the air; and off they went at a rapid pace, half of the herons riding on them, while the others hovered over and alongside, like a white cloud. Two days later the same herd again made its appearance.

Spur-winged plover were nesting near camp, and evidently distrusted the carrion feeders, for they attacked and drove off every kite or vulture that crossed what they considered the prohibited zone. They also harassed the marabous, but with more circumspection; for the big storks were short-tempered, and rather daunted the spurwings by the way they opened their enormous beaks at them. The fish eagles fed exclusively on fish, as far as we could tell, and there were piles of fish bones and heads under their favorite perches. Once I saw one plunge into the water, but it failed to catch anything. Another time, suddenly, and seemingly in mere mischief, one attacked a purple heron which was standing on a mud bank. The eagle swooped down from a tree and knocked over the heron; and when the astonished heron struggled to its feet and attempted to fly off, the eagle made another swoop and this time knocked it into the water. The heron then edged into the papyrus, and the eagle paid it no further attention.

In this camp we had to watch the white ants, which strove to devour everything. They are nocturnal, and work in the daytime only under the tunnels of earth which they build over the surface of the box, or whatever else it is, that they are devouring; they eat out everything, leaving this outside shell of earth. We also saw a long column of the dreaded driver ants. These are carnivorous; I have seen both red and black species; they kill every living thing in their path, and I have known them at night drive all the men in a camp out into the jungle to fight the mosquitoes unprotected until daylight. On another occasion, where a steamboat was moored close to a bank, an ant column entered the boat after nightfall, and kept complete possession of it for forty-eight hours. Fires, and boiling water, offer the only effectual means of resistance. The bees are at times as formidable; when their nests are disturbed they will attack every one in sight, driving all the crew of a boat overboard or scattering a safari, and not infrequently killing men and beasts of burden that are unable to reach some place of safety.

The last afternoon, when the flotilla had called to take us farther on our journey, we shot about a dozen buck, to give the porters and sailors a feast, which they had amply earned. All the meat did not get into camp until after dark—one of the sailors, unfortunately, falling out of a tree and breaking his neck on the way in—and it was picturesque to see the rows of big antelope—hartebeest, kob, waterbuck—stretched in front of the flaring fires, and the dark faces of the waiting negroes, each deputed by some particular group of gun-bearers, porters, or sailors to bring back its share.

Next morning we embarked, and steamed and drifted down the Nile; ourselves, our men, our belongings, and the spoils of the chase all huddled together under the torrid sun. Two or three times we grounded on sand bars; but no damage was done, and in twenty-six hours we reached Nimule. We were no longer in healthy East Africa. Kermit and I had been in robust health throughout the time we were in Uganda and the Lado; but all the other white men of the party had suffered more or less from dysentery, fever, and sun prostration while in the Lado; some of the gun-bearers had been down with fever, one of them dying while we were in Uganda; and four of the porters who had marched from Koba to Nimule had died of dysentery— they were burying one when we arrived.

At Nimule we were as usual greeted with hospitable heartiness by the English officials, as well as by two or

THE RHINOCEROS OF THE LADO 503

three elephant hunters. One of the latter, three days before, had been charged by an unwounded bull elephant. He fired both barrels into it as it came on, but it charged home, knocked him down, killed his gun-bearer, and made its escape into the forest. In the forlorn little graveyard at the station were the graves of two white men who had been killed by elephants. One of them, named Stoney, had been caught by a wounded bull, which stamped the life out of him and then literally dismembered him, tearing his arms from his body. In the African wilderness, when a man dies, his companion usually brings in something to show that he is dead, or some remnant of whatever it is that has destroyed him; the sailors whose companion was killed by falling out of the tree near our Lado camp, for instance, brought in the dead branch which had broken under his weight; and Stoney's gun-bearer marched back to Nimule carrying an arm of his dead master, and deposited his grewsome burden in the office of the district commissioner.

CHAPTER XV

DOWN THE NILE; THE GIANT ELAND

WE spent two or three days in Nimule, getting every-thing ready for the march north to Gondokoro.

By this time Kermit and I had grown really attached to our personal followers, whose devotion to us, and whose zeal for our success and welfare and comfort, had many times been made rather touchingly manifest; even their shortcomings were merely those of big, naughty children, and though they occasionally needed discipline, this was rare, whereas the amusement they gave us was unending. When we reached Nimule we were greeted with enthu-siasm by Magi, Kermit's Kikuyu sais, who had been in charge of the mules which we did not take into the Lado. Magi was now acting as sais for me as well as for Kermit; and he came to Kermit to discuss the new dual relation-ship. "Now I am the sais of the Bwana Makuba, as well as of you, the Bwana Merodadi" (the Dandy Master, as for some inscrutable reason all the men now called Kermit); "well, then, you'll both have to take care of me," concluded the rusé Magi.

Whenever we reached one of these little stations where there was an Indian trading store, we would see that those of our followers who had been specially devoted to us—and this always included all our immediate attendants—had a chance to obtain the few little comforts and luxuries, tea, sugar, or tobacco, for instance, which meant so much to them. Usually Kermit would take them to the store him-self, for they were less wily than the Indian trader, and, moreover, in the excitement of shopping occasionally pur-chased something for which they really had no use. Ker-mit would march his tail of followers into the store, give them time to look around, and then make the first purchase for the man who had least coming to him; this to avoid heartburnings, as the man was invariably too much interested in what he had received to scrutinize closely what the others were getting. The purchase might be an article of clothing or a knife, but usually took the form of tobacco, sugar, and tea; in tobacco the man was offered his choice between quality and quantity, that is, either a moderate quantity of good cigarettes or a large amount of trade tobacco. Funny little Juma Yohari, for instance, one of Kermit's gun-bearers, usually went in for quality, whereas his colleague Kassitura preferred quantity. Juma was a Zanzibari, a wiry merry little grig of a man, loyal, hardworking, fearless; Kassitura a huge Basoga negro, of guileless honesty and good faith, incapable of neglecting his duty. Juma was rather the wit of the gun-bearers' mess, and Kassitura the musician, having a little native harp on which for hours at a time he would strum queer little melancholy tunes, to which he hummed an accompaniment in undertone.

All the natives we met, and the men in our employ, were fond of singing, sometimes simply improvised chants, sometimes sentences of three or four words repeated over and over again. The Uganda porters who were with us after we left Kampalla did not sing nearly as freely as our East African safari, although they depended much on the man who beat the drum, at the head of the marching column. The East African porters did every kind of work to an accompaniment of chanting. When for instance, after camp was pitched, a detail of men was sent out for wood—the "wood safari"—the men as they came back to camp with their loads never did anything so commonplace as each merely to deposit his burden at the proper spot. The first comers waited in the middle of the camp until all had assembled, and then marched in order to where the fire was to be made, all singing vigorously and stepping in time together. The leader, or shanty man, would call

out "Kooni" (wood); and all the others would hum in
unison "Kooni telli" (plenty of wood). "Kooni," again
came the shout of the shanty man; and the answer would be
"Kooni." "Kooni," from the shanty man; and this time
all the rest would simply utter a long-drawn "Hum-m-m."
"Kooni," again; and the answer would be "Kooni telli,"
with strong emphasis on the "telli." Then, if they saw
me, the shanty man might vary by shouting that the wood
was for the Bwana Makuba; and so it would continue until
the loads were thrown down.

Often a man would improvise a song regarding any
small incident which had just happened to him, or a thought
which had occurred to him. Drifting down the Nile to
Nimule Kermit and the three naturalists and sixty porters were packed in sardine fashion on one of the sail-
boats. At nightfall one of the sailors, the helmsman, a
Swahili from Mombasa, began to plan how he would write
a letter to his people in Mombasa and give it to another
sailor, a friend of his, who intended shortly to return thither.
He crooned to himself as he crouched by the tiller, steering
the boat, and gradually, as the moon shone on the swift,
quiet water of the river, his crooning turned into a regular song. His voice was beautiful, and there was a wild
meaningless refrain to each verse; the verses reciting how
he intended to write this letter to those whom he had not
seen for two years; how a friend would take it to them, so
that the letter would be in Mombasa; but he, the man who
wrote it, would for two years more be in the far-off wilderness.

On February 17th the long line of our laden safari left
Nimule on its ten days' march to Gondokoro. We went
through a barren and thirsty land. Our first camp was
by a shallow, running river, with a shaded pool in which
we bathed. After that we never came on running water,
merely on dry watercourses with pools here and there,
some of the pools being crowded with fish. Tall half-
burnt grass, and scattered, wellnigh leafless thorn scrub

covered the monotonous landscape, although we could generally find some fairly leafy tree near which to pitch the tents. The heat was great; more than once the thermometer at noon rose to 112° in the shade—not real shade, however, but in a stifling tent, or beneath a tree the foliage of which let through at least a third of the sun-rays. The fiery heat of the ground so burnt and crippled the feet of the porters that we had to start each day's march very early.

At quarter of three in the morning the whistle blew; we dressed and breakfasted while the tents were taken down and the loads adjusted. Then off we strode, through the hot starlit night, our backs to the Southern Cross and our faces toward the Great Bear; for we were marching northward and homeward. The drum throbbed and muttered as we walked, on and on, along the dim trail. At last the stars began to pale, the gray east changed to opal and amber and amethyst, the red splendor of the sunrise flooded the world, and to the heat of the night succeeded the more merciless heat of the day. Higher and higher rose the sun. The sweat streamed down our faces, and the bodies of the black men glistened like oiled iron. We might halt early in the forenoon, or we might have to march until noon, according to the distance from waterhole to waterhole.

Occasionally in the afternoons, and once when we halted for a day to rest the porters, Kermit and I would kill buck for the table—hartebeest, reedbuck, and oribi. I also killed a big red ground monkey, with baboon-like habits; we had first seen the species on the Uasin Gishu, and had tried in vain to get it, for it was wary, never sought safety in trees, and showed both speed and endurance in running. Kermit killed a bull and a cow roan antelope. These so-called horse antelope are fine beasts, light roan in color, with high withers, rather short curved horns, huge ears, and bold face markings. Usually we found them shy, but occasionally very tame. They are the most truculent and dangerous of all antelope; this bull, when seemingly on the point of death, rose like a flash when Kermit approached and charged him full tilt; Kermit had to fire from the hip, luckily breaking the animal's neck.

On the same day Loring had an interesting experience with one of the small cormorants so common in this region. Previously, while visiting the rapids of the Nile below Nimule, I had been struck by the comparative unwariness of these birds, one of them repeatedly landing on a rock a few yards away from me, and thence slipping unconcernedly into the swift water—and, by the way, it was entirely at home in the boiling rapids. But the conduct of Loring's bird was wholly exceptional. He was taking a swim in a pool when the bird lit beside him. It paid no more heed to the naked white man than it would have paid to a hippo, and although it would not allow itself to be actually touched, it merely moved a few feet out of his way when he approached it. Moreover it seemed to be on the lookout for enemies in the air, not in the water. It was continually glancing upward, and when a big hawk appeared, followed its movements with close attention. It stayed in and about the pool for many minutes before flying off. I suppose that certain eagles and hawks prey on cormorants; but I should also be inclined to think that crocodiles at least occasionally prey on them.

The very most attractive birds we met in middle Africa and along the Nile were the brave, cheery little wagtails. They wear trim black-and-white suits, when on the ground they walk instead of hopping, they have a merry, pleasing song, and they are as confiding and fearless as they are pretty. The natives never molest them, for they figure to advantage in the folklore of the various tribes. They came round us at every halting place, entering the rest-houses in Uganda and sometimes even our tents, coming up within a few feet of us as we lay under trees, and boarding our boats on the Nile; and they would stroll about camp quite unconcernedly, in pairs, the male stopping every now and then to sing. Except the whiskey jacks and Hudsonian chickadees of the North Woods I never saw such tame little birds.

At Gondokoro we met the boat which the Sirdar, Major-General Sir Reginald Wingate, had sent to take us down the Nile to Khartoum; for he, and all the Soudan officials —including especially Colonel Asser, Colonel Owen, Slatin Pasha, and Butler Bey—treated us with a courtesy for

Arrival at Gondokoro
From a photograph by J. Alden Loring

which I cannot too strongly express my appreciation. In the boat we were to have met an old friend and fellow-countryman, Leigh Hunt; to our great regret he could not meet us, but he insisted on treating us as his guests, and on our way down the Nile we felt as if we were on the most comfortable kind of yachting trip; and everything was done for us by Captain Middleton, the Scotch engineer in charge.

Nor was our debt only to British officials and to American friends. At Gondokoro I was met by M. Ranquet, the Belgian Commandant of the Lado district, and both he and M. Massart, the Chef de Poste at Redjaf, were kindness itself, and aided us in every way.

From Gondokoro Kermit and I crossed to Redjaf, for an eight days' trip after the largest and handsomest, and one of the least known, of African antelopes, the giant eland. We went alone, because all the other white men of the party were down with dysentery or fever. We had with us sixty Uganda porters and a dozen mules sent us by the Sirdar, together with a couple of our little riding mules, which we used now and then for a couple of hours on safari, or in getting to the actual hunting ground. As always when only one or two of us went, or when the safari was short, we travelled light, with no dining-tent and nothing unnecessary in the way of baggage; the only impedimenta which we could not minimize were those connected with the preservation of the skins of the big animals, which, of course, were throughout our whole trip what necessitated the use of the bulk of the porters and other means of transportation employed.

From the neat little station of Redjaf, lying at the foot of the bold pyramidal hill of the same name, we marched two days west, stopping short of the river Koda, where we knew the game drank. Now and then we came on flower-bearing bushes, of marvellously sweet scent, like gardenias. It was the height of the dry season; the country was covered with coarse grass and a scrub growth of nearly leafless thorn-trees, usually growing rather wide apart, occasionally close enough together to look almost like a forest. There were a few palms, euphorbias, and very rarely scattered clumps of withered bamboo, and also bright green trees with rather thick leaves and bean pods, on which we afterward found that the eland fed.

The streams we crossed were dry torrent beds, sandy or rocky; in two or three of them were pools of stagnant water, while better water could be obtained by digging in the sand alongside. A couple of hours after reaching each camp everything was in order, and Ali had made a fire of some slivers of wood and boiled our tea; and our two meals, breakfast and dinner, were taken at a table in the open, under a tree.

We had with us seven black soldiers of the Belgian native troops, under a corporal; they came from every quarter of the Congo, but several of them could speak Swahili, the lingua franca of middle Africa, and so Kermit could talk freely with them. These black soldiers be-

The return to Redjaf, Belgian askari in the rear
From a photograph by Kermit Roosevelt

haved excellently, and the attitude, both toward them and toward us, of the natives in the various villages we came across was totally incompatible with any theory that these natives had suffered from any maltreatment; they behaved just like the natives in British territory. There had to be the usual parleys with the chiefs of the villages to obtain food for the soldiers (we carried the posho for our own men), and ample payment was given for what was brought in; and in the only two cases where the natives thought themselves aggrieved by the soldiers, they at once brought the matter before us. One soldier had taken a big gourd of water when very thirsty; another, a knife from a man who was misbehaving himself. On careful inquiry, and delivering judgment in the spirit of Solomon, we decided that both soldiers had been justified by the provocation received; but as we were dealing with the misdeeds of mere big children, we gave the gourd back to its owner with a reprimand for having refused the water, and permitted the owner of the knife, whose offence had been more serious, to ransom his property by bringing in a chicken to the soldier who had it.

The natives lived in the usual pointed beehive huts in unfenced villages, with shambas lying about them; and they kept goats, chickens, and a few cattle. Our permanent camp was near such a village. It was interesting to pass through it at sunrise or sunset, when starting on or returning from a hunt. The hard, bare earth was swept clean. The doors in the low mud walls of the huts were but a couple of feet high and had to be entered on all-fours; black pickaninnies scuttled into them in wild alarm as we passed. Skinny, haggard old men and women, almost naked, sat by the fires smoking long pipes; the younger men and women laughed and jested as they moved among the houses. One day, in the course of a long and fruitless hunt, we stopped to rest near such a village, at about two in the afternoon, having been walking hard since dawn. We—I and my gun-bearer, a black askari, a couple of porters, and a native guide—sat down under a big tree a hundred yards from the village. Soon the chief and several of his people came out to see us. The chief proudly wore a dirty jersey and pair of drawers; a follower carried his spear and the little wooden stool of dignity on which he sat. There were a couple of warriors with him, one a man in a bark apron with an old breech-loading rifle, the other a stark-naked savage—not a rag on him—with a bow and arrows; a very powerfully built man with a ferocious and sinister face. Two women bore on their heads, as gifts for us, one a large earthenware jar of water, the other a basket of ground-nuts. They were tall and well-shaped. One as her sole clothing wore a beaded cord around her waist, and a breechclout consisting of half a dozen long, thickly leaved, fresh sprays of a kind of vine; the other, instead of this vine breechclout, had hanging from her girdle in front a cluster of long-stemmed green leaves, and behind a bundle of long strings, carried like a horse's tail.

The weather was very hot, and the country, far and wide, was a waste of barren desolation. The flats of endless thorn scrub were broken by occasional low and rugged hills, and in the empty watercourses the pools were many miles apart. Yet there was a good deal of game. We saw buffalo, giraffe, and elephant; and on our way back to camp in the evenings we now and then killed a roan, hartebeest, or oribi. But the game we sought was the giant eland, and we never fired when there was the slightest chance of disturbing our quarry. They usually went in herds, but there were solitary bulls. We found that they drank at some pool in the Koda before dawn and then travelled many miles back into the parched interior, feeding as they went; and, after lying up for some hours about mid-day, again moved slowly off, feeding. They did not graze, but fed on the green leaves, and the bean pods of the tree of which I have already spoken and of another tree. One of their marked habits—shared in some degree by their forest cousin, the bongo—was breaking the higher branches with their horns, to get at the leaves; they thus broke branches two or three inches in diameter and seven or eight feet from the ground, the crash of the branches being a sound for which we continually listened as we followed the tracks of a herd. They were far more wary than roan, or hartebeest, or any of the other buck, and the country was such that it was difficult to see more than a couple of hundred yards ahead.

It took me three hard days' work before I got my eland. Each day I left camp before sunrise and on the first two I

33

came back after dark, while it always happened that at noon we were on a trail and could not stop. We would walk until we found tracks made that morning, and then the gun-bearers and the native guide would slowly follow them, hour after hour, under the burning sun. On the first day we saw nothing; on the next we got a moment's glimpse of an eland, trotting at the usual slashing gait; I had no chance to fire. By mid-afternoon on each day it was evident that further following of the trail we were on was useless, and we plodded campward, tired and thirsty. Gradually the merciless glare softened; then the sun sank crimson behind a chain of fantastically carved mountains in the distance; and the hues of the afterglow were drowned in the silver light of the moon, which was nearing the full.

On the third day we found the spoor of a single bull by eight o'clock. Hour after hour went by while the gun-bearers, even more eager than weary, puzzled out the trail. At half-past twelve we knew we were close on the beast, and immediately afterward caught a glimpse of it. Taking advantage of every patch of cover I crawled toward it on all-fours, my rifle too hot for me to touch the barrel, while the blistering heat of the baked ground hurt my hands. At a little over a hundred yards I knelt and aimed at the noble beast; I could now plainly see his huge bulk and great, massive horns, as he stood under a tree. The pointed bullet from the little Springfield hit a trifle too far back and up, but made such a rip that he never got ten yards from where he was standing; and great was my pride as I stood over him, and examined his horns, twisted almost like a koodoo's, and admired his size, his finely modelled head and legs, and the beauty of his coat.

Meanwhile, Kermit had killed two eland, a cow on the first day, and on the second a bull even better than, although not quite so old as, mine. Kermit could see game, and follow tracks, almost as well as his gun-bearers, and in a long chase could outrun them. On each day he struck the track of a herd of eland, and after a while left his gun-bearers and porters, and ran along the trail accompanied only by a native guide. The cow was killed at two hundred yards with a shot from his Winchester. The bull yielded more excitement. He was in a herd of about forty which Kermit had followed for over five hours, toward the last accompanied only by the wild native; at one point the eland had come upon a small party of elephant, and trotted off at right angles to their former course—Kermit following them after he had satisfied himself that the elephants were cows and half-grown animals. When he finally overtook the eland, during the torrid heat of the early afternoon, they were all lying down, in a place where the trees grew rather more thickly than usual.

Stalking as close as he dared he selected a big animal which he hoped was a bull, and fired three shots into it; however, it ran, and he then saw that it was a cow. As the rest of the herd jumped up he saw the form of the master bull looming above the others. They crossed his front at a slashing trot, the cows clustered round the great bull; but just as they came to a little opening, they opened somewhat, giving him a clear shot. Down went the bull on his head, rose, received another bullet, and came to a stand-still. This was the last bullet from the magazine; and now the mechanism of the rifle refused to work or to throw the empty shell out of the chamber. The faithful Winchester, which Kermit had used steadily for ten months, on foot and on horseback, which had suffered every kind of hard treatment and had killed every kind of game, without once failing, had at last given way under the strain. While Kermit was working desperately at the mechanism, the bull, which was standing looking at him within fifty yards, gradually recovered, moved off step by step, and broke into a slow trot. After it went Kermit as hard as he could go, still fussing with the rifle, which he finally opened, and refilled with five cartridges. Kermit could just about keep the eland in sight, running as hard as he was able; after a mile or two it lay down, but rose as he came near, and went off again, while he was so blown that though, with four shots, he hit it twice he failed to kill it. He now had but one bullet left, after which he knew that the rifle would jam again; and it was accordingly necessary to kill outright with the next shot. He was just able to keep close to the bull for a half-mile, then it

Giant bull eland
From a photograph by Kermit Roosevelt

halted; and he killed it. Leaving the shenzi by the carcass, he went off to see about the wounded cow, but after an hour was forced to give up the chase and return, so as to be sure to save the bull's skin. The gun-bearers and another shenzi had by this time reached the dead eland; they had only Kermit's canteen of water among them. One of the shenzis was at once sent to camp to bring back twenty porters, with rope, and plenty of water; and, with parched mouths, Kermit and the gun-bearers began to take off the thick hide of the dead bull. Four hours later the porters appeared with the ropes and the water; the thirsty men drank gallons; the porters were loaded with the hide, head, and meat; and they marched back to camp by moonlight.

It was no easy job, in that climate, to care for and save the three big skins; but we did it. On the trip we had taken, besides our gun-bearers and tent boys, Magi, the sais, and two of our East African skinners, Kiboko and Merefu; they formed in the safari a kind of chief-petty-officer's mess, so to speak. They were all devoted to their duties, and they worked equally hard whether hunting or caring for the skins; the day Kermit killed his bull he and the gun-bearers and skinners, with Magi as a volunteer, worked until midnight at the hide. But they had any amount of meat, and we shared our sugar and tea with them. On the last evening there was nothing to do, and they sat in the brilliant moonlight in front of their tents, while Kassitura played his odd little harp. Kermit and I strolled over to listen; and at once Kassitura began to improvise a chant in my honor, reciting how the Bwana Makuba had come, how he was far from his own country, how he had just killed a giant eland, and so on and so on. Meanwhile, over many little fires strips of meat were drying on scaffolds of bent branches, and askaris and porters were gathered in groups, chatting and singing; while the mighty tree near which our tents were pitched cast a black shadow on the silver plain. Then the shenzis who had helped us came to receive their reward, and their hearts were gladdened with red cloth and salt, and for those whose services had been greatest there were special treasures in the shape of three green and white umbrellas. It was a pleasant ending to a successful hunt.

On our return to Gondokoro we found Cuninghame all right, although he had been obliged single-handed to do the work of getting our porters safely started on their return march to Kampalla, as well as getting all the skins and skeletons properly packed for shipment. Heller had also recovered, and had gone on a short trip during which he trapped a leopard and a serval at the same carcass, the leopard killing the serval. Dr. Mearns and Loring were both seriously sick; so was the district commissioner, kind Mr. Haddon. One day a German missionary dined with us; the next he was dead, of black water fever. An English sportsman whom we had met at Nimule had been brought in so sick that he was at death's door; Dr. Mearns took care of him, badly off though he himself was.

Bari at Mongalla
From a photograph by Edmund Heller

We had brought with us a case of champagne for just such emergencies; this was the first time that we made use of it.

On the last day of February we started down the Nile, slipping easily along on the rapid current, which wound and twisted through stretches of reeds and marsh grass and papyrus. We halted at the attractive station of Lado for a good-by breakfast with our kind Belgian friends, and that evening we dined at Mongalla with Colonel Owen, the chief of the southernmost section of the Soudan. I was greatly interested in the Egyptian and Soudanese soldiers and their service medals. Many of these medals

showed that their owners had been in a dozen campaigns;
some of the native officers and men (and also the Reis
or native captain of our boat, by the way) had served
in the battles which broke forever the Mahdi's cruel power;
two or three had been with Gordon. They were a fine-
looking set; and their obvious self-respect was a good thing
to see. That same afternoon I witnessed a native dance,
and was struck by the lack of men of middle-age; in all

Troops at Mongalla

From a photograph by Edmund Heller

the tribes who were touched by the blight of the Mahdist
tyranny, with its accompaniments of unspeakable horror,
suffered such slaughter of the then young men that the loss
has left its mark to this day. The English when they
destroyed Mahdism rendered a great service to humanity;
and their rule in the Soudan has been astoundingly successful and beneficial from every stand-point.*

We steamed onward down the Nile; sometimes tying

* The despotism of Mahdist rule was so revolting, so vilely cruel and hideous, that
the worst despotism by men of European blood in recent times seems a model of
humanity by comparison; and yet there were nominal "anti-militarists" and self-
styled "apostles of peace" who did their feeble best to prevent the destruction of
this infamy.

520 AFRICAN GAME TRAILS

up to the bank at nightfall, sometimes steaming steadily through the night. We reached the Sud, the vast papyrus marsh once so formidable a barrier to all who would journey along the river; and sunrise and sunset were beautiful over the endless, melancholy stretches of water reeds. In the Sud the only tree seen was the water-loving ambatch, light as cork. Occasionally we saw hippos and crocodiles and a few water birds; and now and then passed native villages, the tall, lean men and women stark naked, and their bodies daubed with mud, grease, and ashes to keep off the mosquitoes.

On March 4th we were steaming slowly along the reedy, water-soaked shores of Lake No, keeping a sharp lookout for the white-eared kob and especially for the handsome saddle-marked lechwe kob—which has been cursed with the foolishly inappropriate name of "Mrs. Gray's waterbuck."

Early in the morning we saw a herd of these saddle-marked lechwe in the long marsh grass and pushed the steamer's nose as near to the shore as possible. Then Cuninghame, keen-eyed Kongoni, and I started for what proved to be a five hours' tramp. The walking was hard; sometimes we were on dry land, but more often in water up to our ankles or knees, and occasionally floundering and wallowing up to our hips through stretches of reeds, water-lilies, green water, and foul black slime. Yet there were ant-hills in the marsh. Once or twice we caught a glimpse of the game in small patches of open ground covered with short grass; but almost always they kept to the high grass and reeds. There were with the herd two very old bucks, with a white saddle-shaped patch on the withers, the white extending up the back of the neck to the head; a mark of their being in full maturity, or past it, for on some of the males, at least, this coloration only begins to appear when they seem already to have attained their growth of horn and body, their teeth showing them to be five or six years old, while they are obviously in the prime of vigor and breeding capacity. Unfortunately, in the long grass it was impossible to single out these old bucks. Marking as well as we could the general direction of the herd we would steal toward it until we thought we were in the neighborhood, and then cautiously climb an ant-hill to look about. Nothing would be in sight. We would scan the ground in every direction; still nothing. Suddenly a dozen heads would pop up, just above the grass, two or three hundred yards off, and after a steady gaze would disappear; and some minutes later would again appear a quarter of a mile farther on. Usually they skulked off at a trot or canter, necks stretched level with the back; for they were great skulkers, and trusted chiefly to escaping observation and stealing away from danger unperceived. But occasionally they would break into a gallop, making lofty bounds, clear above the tops of the grass; and then they might go a long way before stopping. I never saw them leap on the ant-hills to look about, as is the custom of the common or Uganda kob. They were rather noisy; we heard them grunting continually, both when they were grazing and when they saw us.

At last, from an ant-hill, I saw dim outlines of two or three animals moving past a little over a hundred yards ahead. There was nothing to shoot at; but a moment afterward I saw a pair of horns through the grass tops, in such a position that it was evident the owner was looking at me. I guessed that he had been moving in the direction in which the others had gone, and I guessed at the position of the shoulder, and fired. The horns disappeared. Then I caught a glimpse, first of a doe, next of a buck, in full flight, each occasionally appearing for an instant in a great bound over the grass tops. I had no idea whether or not I had hit my buck; so Cuninghame stayed on the ant-heap to guide us, while Kongoni and I plunged into the long grass, as high as our heads. Sure enough, there was the buck, a youngish one, about four years old; my bullet had gone true. While we were looking at him we sud-

denly caught a momentary glimpse of two more of the
herd rushing off to our right, and we heard another grunting and sneaking away, invisible, thirty yards or so to our
left.

Half an hour afterward I shot another buck, at over
a hundred and fifty yards, after much the same kind of
experience. At this one I fired four times, hitting him with
three bullets; three of the shots were taken when I could
only see his horns and had to guess at the position of the
body. This was a very big buck, with horns over twenty-
nine inches long, but the saddle mark was yellow, with
many whitish hairs, showing that he was about to assume
the white saddle of advanced maturity. His stomach was
full of the fine swamp grass.

These handsome antelopes come next to the situtunga
as lovers of water and dwellers in the marshes. They
are far more properly to be called "waterbuck" than are
the present proprietors of that name, which, like the ordinary kob, though liking to be near streams, spend most of
their time on dry plains and hill-sides. This saddle-marked
antelope of the swamps has the hoofs very long and the
whole foot flexible and spreading, so as to help it in passing
over wet ground and soft mud; the pasterns behind are
largely bare of hair. It seems to be much like the lechwe, a
less handsome, but equally water-loving, antelope of southern Africa, which is put in the same genus with the waterbuck and kob.

That afternoon Dr. Mearns killed with his Winchester
30–40, on the wing, one of the most interesting birds we
obtained on our whole trip, the whale-billed stork. It
was an old male and its gizzard was full of the remains of
small fish. The whalebill is a large wader, blackish-gray
in color, slightly crested, with big feet and a huge, swollen
bill; a queer-looking bird, with no near kinsfolk, and so
interesting that nothing would have persuaded me to try to
kill more than the four actually needed for the *public*
(not private) museum to which our collections were going.

It is of solitary habits and is found only in certain vast, lonely marshes of tropical Africa, where it is conspicuous by its extraordinary bill, dark coloration, and sluggishness of conduct, hunting sedately in the muddy shallows, or standing motionless for hours, surrounded by reedbeds or by long reaches of quaking and treacherous ooze.

Next morning while at breakfast on the breezy deck we spied another herd of the saddle-marked lechwe, in the marsh alongside; and Kermit landed and killed one, after deep wading, up to his chin in some places, and much hard work in the rank grass. This buck was interesting when compared with the two I had shot. He was apparently a little older than either, but not aged; on the contrary, in his prime, and fat. He had the white saddle-like mark on the withers, and the white back of the neck, well developed. Yet he was smaller than either of mine, and the horns much smaller; indeed they were seven inches shorter than my longest ones. It looks as if, in some animals at least, the full size of body and horns were reached before the white saddle markings are acquired. The horns of these saddle-marked lechwes are, relatively to the body, far longer and finer than in other species of the genus; just as is the case with the big East African gazelle when compared with other gazelles.

That afternoon, near the mouth of the Rohr, which runs into the Bahr el Ghazal, I landed and shot a good buck, of the Vaughn's kob; which is perhaps merely a subspecies of the white-eared kob. It is a handsome animal, handsomer than its close kinsman, the common or Uganda kob; although much less so than its associate, the saddle-marked lechwe. Its hooves are like those of the ordinary kobs and waterbucks, not in the least like those of the saddleback; so that, although the does are colored alike, there is no chance of mistaking any lechwe doe for any true kob doe. We found these kobs in much drier ground than the saddlebacks, and therefore they were easier to get at. The one I shot was an old ram, accom-

panied by several ewes. We saw them from the boat, but
they ran. Cuninghame and I, with Kongoni and Gouvimali, hunted for them in vain for a couple of hours. Then
we met a savage, a very tall, lean Nuer. He was clad in
a fawn skin, and carried two spears, one with a bright,
sharp, broad-bladed head, the other narrow-headed with
villainous barbs. His hair, much longer than that of a
west coast negro, was tied back. As we came toward him
he stood on one leg, with the other foot resting against it,
and, raising his hand, with fingers extended, he motioned
to us with what in civilized regions would be regarded as a
gesture bidding us halt. But he meant it as a friendly
greeting, and solemnly shook hands with all four of us,
including the gun-bearers. By signs we made him understand that we were after game; so was he; and he led
us to the little herd of kob. Kongoni, as usual, saw them
before any one else. From an ant-hill I could make out
the buck's horns and his white ears, which he was continually flapping at the biting flies that worried him; when
he lowered his head I could see nothing. Finally, he looked
fixedly at us; he was a hundred and fifty yards off and I
had to shoot standing on the peak of the ant-heap, and
aim through the grass, guessing where his hidden body
might be; and I missed him. At the shot the does went off
to the left, but he ran to the right, once or twice leaping
high; and when he halted, at less than two hundred yards,
although I could still only see his horns, I knew where his
body was; and this time I killed him. We gave most of
the meat to the Nuer. He was an utterly wild savage,
and when Cuninghame suddenly lit a match he was so
frightened that it was all we could do to keep him from
bolting.

Kermit went on to try for a doe, but had bad luck,
twice killing a spike buck by mistake, and did not get
back to the boat until long after dark.

The following day we were in the mouth of the Bahr
el Ghazal. It ran sluggishly through immense marshes,

which stretched back from the river for miles on either hand, broken here and there by flats of slightly higher land with thorn-trees. The whale-billed storks were fairly common, and were very conspicuous as they stood on the quaking surface of the marsh, supported by their long-toed feet. After several fruitless stalks and much following through the thick marsh grass, sometimes up to our necks in water, I killed one with the Springfield at a distance of one hundred and thirty yards, and Kermit, after missing one standing, cut it down as it rose with his Winchester 30-40. These whalebills had in their gizzards not only small fish but quite a number of the green blades of the marsh grass. The Arabs call them the "Father of the Shoe," and Europeans call them shoebills as well as whalebills. The Bahr el Ghazal was alive with water-fowl, saddle-bill storks, sacred and purple ibis, many kinds of herons, cormorants, plover, and pretty tree ducks which twittered instead of quacking. There were sweet-scented lotus water-lilies in the ponds. A party of waterbuck cows and calves let the steamer pass within fifty yards without running.

We went back to Lake No, where we met another steamer, with aboard it M. Solvé, a Belgian sportsman, a very successful hunter, whom we had already met at Lado; with him were his wife, his sister, and his brother-in-law, both of the last being as ardent in the chase, especially of dangerous game, as he was. His party had killed two whalebills, one for the British Museum and one for the Congo Museum. They were a male and female who were near their nest, which contained two downy young; these were on M. Solvé's boat, where we saw them. The nest was right on the marsh water; the birds had bent the long blades of marsh grass into an interlacing foundation, and on this had piled grass which they had cut with their beaks. These beaks can give a formidable bite, by the way, as one of our sailors found to his cost when he rashly tried to pick up a wounded bird.

I was anxious to get a ewe of the saddle-back lechwe for the museum, and landed in the late afternoon, on seeing a herd. The swamp was so deep that it took an hour's very hard and fatiguing wading, forcing ourselves through the rank grass up to our shoulders in water before we got near them. The herd numbered about forty individuals;

Mr. Roosevelt with the Belæniceps rex, or whale-billed stork, at Lake No

From a photograph by Kermit Roosevelt

their broad trail showed where they had come through the swamp, and even through a papyrus bed; but we found them grazing on merely moist ground, where there were ant-hills in the long grass. As I crept up they saw me and greeted me with a chorus of croaking grunts; they are a very noisy buck. I shot a ewe, and away rushed the herd through the long grass, making a noise which could have been heard nearly a mile off, and splashing and bounding through the shallow lagoons; they halted, and again began grunting; and then off they rushed once more. The doe's stomach was filled with tender marsh grass. Meanwhile, Kermit killed, on drier ground, a youngish male of the white-eared kob.

Next morning we were up at the Bahr el Zeraf. At ten we sighted from the boat several herds of white-eared kob, and Kermit and I went in different directions after them, getting four. The old rams were very handsome animals with coats of a deep rich brown that was almost black, and sharply contrasted black and white markings on their faces; but it was interesting to see that many of the younger rams, not yet in the fully adult pelage, had horns as long as those of their elders. The young rams and ewes were a light reddish-yellow, being in color much like the ewes of the saddle-back lechwe; and there was the usual disproportion in size between the sexes. With each flock of ewes and young rams there was ordinarily one old black ram; and some of the old rams went by themselves. The ground was so open that all my shots had to be taken at long range. In habits they differed from the saddle-back lechwes, for they were found on dry land, often where the grass was quite short, and went freely among the thorn-trees; they cared for the neighborhood of water merely as ordinary waterbuck or kob care for it.

Here we met another boat, with aboard it Sir William Garstin, one of the men who have made Egypt and the Soudan what they are to-day, and who have thereby rendered an incalculable service, not only to England, but to civilization.

We had now finished our hunting, save that once or twice we landed to shoot a buck or some birds for the table. It was amusing to see how sharply the birds discriminated between the birds of prey which they feared and those which they regarded as harmless. We saw a flock of guinea-fowl strolling unconcernedly about at the foot of a tree in which a fish eagle was perched; and one evening Dr. Mearns saw some guinea-fowl go to roost in a bush in which two kites had already settled themselves for the night, the kites and the guineas perching amiably side by side.

We stopped at the mouth of the Sobat to visit the American Mission, and were most warmly and hospitably received by the missionaries, and were genuinely impressed by the faithful work they are doing, under such great

difficulties and with such cheerfulness and courage. The
Medical Mission was especially interesting. It formed an
important part of the mission work; and not only were
the natives round about treated, but those from far away
also came in numbers. At the time of our visit there were

American Mission, Sobat River
From a photograph by Edmund Heller

about thirty patients, taking courses of treatment, who
had come from distances varying from twenty-five miles
to a hundred and fifty.

We steamed steadily down the Nile. Where the great
river bent to the east we would sit in the shade on the forward deck during the late afternoon and look down the
long glistening water-street in front of us, with its fringe
of reedbed and marshy grassland and papyrus swamp, and
the slightly higher dry land on which grew acacias and
scattered palms. Along the river banks and inland were

villages of Shilluks and other tribes, mostly cattle-owners; some showing slight traces of improvement, others utter savages, tall, naked men, bearing bows and arrows.

Our Egyptian and Nubian crew recalled to my mind the crew of the daha-biah on which as a boy I had gone up the Egyptian Nile thirty-seven years before; especially when some piece of work was being done by the crew as they chant-ed in grunting chorus "Ya allah, ul allah." As we went down the Nile we kept see-ing more and more of the birds which I remembered, one species after an-other appearing; familiar cow-her-ons, crocodile plo-ver, noisy spur-wing plover, black-and-white king-fishers, hoopoos,

Slatin Pasha, from the roof of the Khalifa's palace, shows how he made his escape from Omdurman

From a photograph by Kermit Roosevelt

green bee-eaters, black-and-white chats, desert larks, and trumpeter bullfinches.

At night we sat on deck and watched the stars and the dark, lonely river. The swimming crocodiles and plung-ing hippos made whirls and wakes of feeble light that glimmered for a moment against the black water. The unseen birds of the marsh and the night called to one another in strange voices. Often there were grass fires, burning, leaping lines of red, the lurid glare in the sky above them making even more sombre the surrounding gloom.

As we steamed northward down the long stretch of the Nile which ends at Khartoum, the wind blew in our faces, day after day, hard and steadily. Narrow reedbeds bordered the shore; there were grass flats and groves of acacias and palms, and farther down reaches of sandy desert. The health of our companions who had been suffering from fever and dysentery gradually improved; but the case of champagne, which we had first opened at Gondokoro, was of real service, for two members of the party were at times so sick that their situation was critical.

We reached Khartoum on the afternoon of March 14th, 1910, and Kermit and I parted from our comrades of the trip with real regret; during the year we spent together there had not been a jar, and my respect and liking for them had grown steadily. Moreover, it was a sad parting from our faithful black followers, whom we knew we should never see again. It had been an interesting and a happy year; though I was very glad to be once more with those who were dear to me, and to turn my face toward my own home and my own people.

Kermit's and my health throughout the trip had been excellent. He had been laid up for three days all told, and I for five. Kermit's three days were due, two to tick fever on the Kapiti Plains, one probably to the sun. Mine were all due to fever; but I think my fever had nothing to do with Africa at all, and was simply a recurrence of the fever I caught in the Santiago campaign, and which ever since has come on at long and irregular intervals for a day or two at a time. The couple of attacks I had in Africa were very slight; by no means as severe as one I had while bear hunting early one spring in the Rocky Mountains. One of these attacks came on under rather funny circumstances. It was at Lake Naivasha on the day I killed the hippo which charged the boat. We were in the steam launch and I began to feel badly, and knew I was in for a bout of fever. Just then we spied the hippo and went after it in the row-boat. I was anxious to hold back the attack until I got the hippo, as when shaking with a chill it is of course very difficult to take aim. I just succeeded, the

Mr. Roosevelt on his camel
From a photograph by Kermit Roosevelt

excitement keeping me steady; and as soon as the hippo was dead I curled up in the boat and had my chill in peace and comfort.

There are differences of opinion as to whether any spirituous liquors should be drunk in the tropics. Personally I think that the less one has to do with them the better. Not liking whiskey I took a bottle of brandy for emergencies. Very early in the trip I decided that even when feverish or exhausted by a hard day's tramp, hot tea did me more good than brandy, and I handed the bottle over to Cuninghame. At Khartoum he produced it and asked what he should do with it, and I told him to put it in the steamer's stores; he did so, after finding out the amount that had been drunk, and informed me that I had taken just six ounces in eleven months.

LIST OF GAME SHOT WITH THE RIFLE DURING THE TRIP

	BY T. R.	BY K. R.
Lion	9	8
Leopard	—	3
Cheetah	—	7
Hyena	5	4
Elephant	8	3
Square-mouthed rhinoceros	5	4
Hook-lipped rhinoceros	8	3
Hippopotamus	7	1
Wart-hog	8	4
Common zebra	15	4
Big or Grévy's zebra	5	5
Giraffe	7	2
Buffalo	6	4
Giant eland	1	2
Common eland	5	2
Bongo	—	2
Kudu	—	2
Situtunga	—	1
Bushbuck		
East African	2	4
Uganda harnessed	1	2
Nile harnessed	3	3
Sable	—	3
Roan	4	5
Oryx	10	3
Wildebeest	5	2
Neuman's hartebeest	—	3
Coke's hartebeest	10	3
Big hartebeest		
Jackson's	14	7
Uganda	1	3
Nilotic	8	4
Topi	12	4
Common waterbuck	5	3
Singsing waterbuck	6	6
Common kob	10	6
Vaughn's kob	1	2
White-eared kob	3	2
Saddle-backed lechwe (Mrs. Gray's)	3	1
Bohor reedbuck	10	4
Chanler's buck	3	4
Impalla	7	5

	BY T. R.	BY K. R.
Big gazelle		
Granti	5	3
Robertsi	4	6
Notata	8	1
Thomson's gazelle	11	9
Gerenuk	3	2
Klipspringer	1	3
Oribi	18	?
Duiker	3	2
Steinbuck	4	2
Dikdik	1	1
Baboon	—	3
Red ground monkey	1	—
Green monkey	—	1
Black and white monkey	5	4
Serval	—	1
Jackal	—	1
Aardwolf	—	1
Rattel	—	1
Porcupine	—	2
Ostrich	2	—
Great bustard	4 (1 on wing)	3 } (1 on wing)
Lesser bustard	1	1
Kavirondo crane	2 (on wing)	—
Flamingo	—	4
Whale-headed stork	1	1 (on wing)
Marabou	1	1
Saddle-billed stork	1 (on wing)	—
Ibis stork	2 (1 on wing)	—
Pelican	1	—
Guinea-fowl	5	5
Francolin	1	2
Fish eagle	—	1
Vulture	—	2
Crocodile	1	3
Monitor	—	1
Python	3	1
	296	216

Grand total 512

In addition we killed, with the Fox shot-gun, Egyptian geese, yellow-billed mallards, francolins, spurfowl and sand grouse for the pot, and certain other birds for specimens.

Kermit and I kept about a dozen trophies for ourselves; otherwise we shot nothing that was not used either as a museum specimen or for meat—usually for both purposes. We were in hunting grounds practically as good as any that have ever existed; but we did not kill a tenth, nor a hundredth part of what we might have killed had we been willing. The mere size of the bag indicates little as to a man's prowess as a hunter, and almost nothing as to the interest or value of his achievement.

APPENDICES

APPENDIX A

I wish to thank Sir Edward Grey and Lord Crewe for the numerous courtesies extended to me by the British officials throughout the British possessions in Africa ; and M. Renkin for the equal courtesy shown me by the Belgian officials in the Lado.

The scientific part of the expedition could not have been undertaken save for the generous assistance of Mr. Andrew Carnegie, Mr. Oscar Straus, Mr. Leigh Hunt, and certain others, to all of whom lovers of natural history are therefore deeply indebted.

I owe more than I can express to the thoughtful and unwearied consideration of Mr. F. C. Selous and Mr. E. N. Buxton, through whom my excellent outfit was obtained.

Mr. R. J. Cuninghame, assisted in East Africa by Mr. Leslie J. Tarlton, managed the expedition in the field; and no two better men for our purposes could have been found anywhere. I doubt if Mr. Cuninghame's equal in handling such an expedition as ours exists; I know no one else who combines as he does the qualities which make a first-class explorer, guide, hunter, field-naturalist, and safari manager. Messrs. Newland and Tarlton, of Nairobi, did the actual work of providing and arranging for our whole journey in the most satisfactory manner.

APPENDIX B

The following is a partial list of the small mammals obtained on the trip, except certain bats, shrews, and rodents which it is not possible to identify in the field; even some of these identifications are not final.

LIST OF SMALL MAMMALS

UNGULATA—HOOFED MAMMALS

Procavia mackinderi	Alpine Hyrax
Procavia brucei maculata	Athi Rock Hyrax
Procavia (Dendrohyrax) bettoni. . . .	Kikuyu Tree Hyrax
Procavia (Dendrohyrax) crawshayi . .	Alpine Tree Hyrax

GLIRES—RODENTS

Heliosciurus keniæ	Kenia Forest Squirrel
Paraxerus bœhmi emini	Uganda Striped Squirrel
Paraxerus jacksoni	Jackson Forest Squirrel
Paraxerus jacksoni capitis	Nairobi Forest Squirrel
Euxerus microdon julvior	Kenia Ground Squirrel
Graphiurus raptor	Kenia Dormouse
Graphiurus parvus	Pygmy Dormouse
Lophiomys testudo	Nandi Maned Rat
Tatera mombasæ	Mombasa Gerbille
Tatera pothæ	Highland Gerbille
Tatera jallax	Uganda Gerbille
Tatera varia	Sotik Gerbille
Tatera emini	Nile Gerbille
Tatera nigrita	Dusky Gerbille
Dipodillus harwoodi	Pygmy Gerbille
Otomys irroratus orestes	Alpine Veldt Rat
Otomys irroratus tropicalis	Masai Veldt Rat
Dendromus nigrijrons	Black-fronted Tree Mouse
Dendromus insignis	Greater Tree Mouse
Dendromus whytei pallescens	Athi Tree Mouse
Steatomys athi	East African Fat Mouse
Lophuromys ansorgei	Uganda Harsh-furred Mouse
Lophuromys aquilus	Masai Harsh-furred Mouse
Mus (Leggada) bellus	East African Pygmy Mouse
Mus (Leggada) gratus	Uganda Pygmy Mouse
Mus (Leggada) sorellus	Elgon Pygmy Mouse
Mus (Leggada) triton murillus	Sooty Pygmy Mouse
Mus (Leggada) triton naivashæ . . .	Naivasha Pygmy Mouse
Epimys hindei	Masai Bush Rat
Epimys endorobæ	Small-footed Forest Mouse
Epimys jacksoni	Uganda Forest Mouse
Epimys peromyscus	Large-footed Forest Mouse
Epimys hildebranti	Taita Multimammate Mouse
Epimys ugandæ	Uganda Multimammate Mouse
Epimys panya	Masai Multimammate Mouse

Epimys nieventris ulæ	Athi Rock Mouse
Zelotomys hildegardæ	Broad-headed Bush Mouse
Thamnomys surdaster polionops . . .	Athi Tree Rat
Thamnomys loringi	Masked Tree Rat
Œnomys hypoxanthus bacchante . . .	Rusty-nosed Rat
Dasymus helukus	East African Swamp Rat
Acomys wilsoni	East African Spiny Mouse
Arvicanthis abyssinicus nairobæ . . .	Athi Grass Rat
Arvicanthis abyssinicus rubescens . .	Uganda Grass Rat
Arvicanthis pulchellus massaicus . .	Spotted Grass Rat
Arvicanthis barbarus albolineatus . . .	Striped Grass Rat
Arvicanthis pumilio diminutus	Pygmy Grass Rat
Arvicanthis dorsalis maculosus	Single Striped Grass Rat
Pelomys roosevelti	Iridescent Creek Rat
Saccostomus umbriventer	Sotik Pouched Rat
Saccostomus mearnsi	Swahili Pouched Rat
Tachyoryctes annectens	Rift Valley Mole Rat
Tachyoryctes splendens ibeanus . . .	Nairobi Mole Rat
Tachyoryctes rex	Alpine Mole Rat
Myoscalops kapiti	Masai Blesmol
Pedetes surdaster	East African Springhaas
Hystrix galeata	East African Porcupine
Lepus victoriæ	East African Hare

FERÆ—CARNIVORES

Hyæna striata schillingsi	Masai Striped Hyena
Hyæna crocuta germinans	East African Spotted Hyena
Proteles cristatus septentrionalis . . .	Somali Aardwolf
Genetta bettoni	East African Genet
Crossarchus fasciatus macrurus . . .	Uganda Banded Mongoose
Mungos sanguienus ibeæ	Kikuyu Lesser Mongoose
Mungos albicaudus ibeanus	Masai White-tailed Mongoose
Canis mesomelas	Black-backed Jackal
Canis variegatus	Silver-backed Jackal
Lycaon pictus lupinus	East African Hunting Dog
Otocyon virgatus	Masai Great-eared Fox
Mellivora ratel	Cape Honey Badger

INSECTIVORA—INSECTIVORES

Nasilio brachyrhynchus delamerei . . .	Athi Lesser Elephant Shrew
Elephantulus pulcher	East African Elephant Shrew
Erinaceus albiventris	White-bellied Hedgehog
Crocidura flavescens myansæ	Giant Shrew
Crocidura alchemillæ	Alpine Shrew
Crocidura fumosa	Dusky Shrew
Crocidura argentata fisheri	Veldt Shrew
Crocidura bicolor elgonius	Elgon Pygmy Shrew
Crocidura allex	Rift Valley Pygmy Shrew
Surdisorex noræ	Short-tailed Shrew

CHIROPTERA—BATS

Scotophilus nigrita colias	Kikuyu Green Bat
Pipistrellus kuhlii fuscatus	Naivasha Pygmy Bat

Nyctinomus hindei . . . . Free-tailed Bat
Lavia frons . . . . East African Great-eared Bat
Lavia frons affinis . . . . Nile Great-eared Bat
Petalia thebaica . . . . Nile Wrinkle-nosed Bat
Rhinolophus hildebrandti eloqueus . . . Elgon Horseshoe Bat
Hipposiderus caffer centralis . . . . Uganda Leaf-nosed Bat

PRIMATES—MONKEYS

Galago (Otolemur) lasiotis . . . . . Mombasa Lemur
Papio ibeanus . . . . East African Baboon
Cercocebus albigena johnstoni . . . . Uganda Mangabey
Erythrocebus formosus . . . . . . Uganda Patas Monkey
Cercopithecus ascanius schmidti . . . Uganda White-nosed Monkey
Cercopithecus pygerythrus johnstoni . . Masai Green Monkey
Cercopithecus kolbi . . . . Kikuyu Forest Green Monkey
Cercopithecus kolbi hindei . . . . . Kenia Forest Green Monkey
Colobus abyssinicus caudatus . . . . White-tailed Colobus Monkey
Colobus abyssinicus matschiei . . . . Uganda Colobus Monkey
Colobus palliatus cottoni . . . . . Nile Colobus Monkey

LIST OF LARGE MAMMALS

UNGULATA—HOOFED MAMMALS

Diceros simus cottoni . . . . Nile Square-nosed Rhinoceros
Diceros bicornis . . . . Black Rhinoceros
Equus burchelli granti . . . . . . Northern Burchell Zebra
Equus grevyi . . . . Grévy Zebra
Hippopotamus amphibius . . . . . Nile Hippopotamus
Potamochœrus chœropotamus dœmonis . . East African Bush Pig
Hylochœrus meinertzhageni . . . . . East African Forest Hog
Phacochœrus œthiopicus massaicus . . . East African Wart Hog
Bos caffer radcliffei . . . . East African Buffalo
Bos œquinoctialis . . . . Abyssinian Buffalo
Taurotragus oryx livingstonii . . . . East African Eland
Taurotragus gigas . . . . Giant Eland
Boocercus isaaci . . . . East African Bongo
Strepsiceros strepsiceros . . . . . . Greater Koodoo
Tragelaphus scriptus heywoodi . . . . Aberdare Bushbuck
Tragelaphus scriptus dama . . . . . Kavirondo Bushbuck
Tragelaphus scriptus bor . . . . . . Nile Bushbuck
Limnotragus spekii . . . . Uganda Situtunga
Ozanna roosevelti . . . . Roosevelt Sable Antelope
Ozanna equinus langheldi . . . . . East African Roan Antelope
Ozanna equinus bakeri . . . . . . Nile Roan Antelope
Oryx beisa annectens . . . . East African Beisa
Gazella granti . . . . Grant Gazelle
Gazella granti robertsi . . . . . . Nyanza Grant Gazelle
Gazella granti notata . . . . Boran Grant Gazelle
Gazella thomsoni . . . . Thomson Gazelle
Lithocranius walleri . . . . Gerenuk Gazelle
Æpyceros melampus suara . . . . . Impalla
Redunca fulvorufula chanleri . . . . East African Rock Reedbuck

Redunca redunca wardi	Hig'.land Bohor Reedbuck
Redunca redunca donaldsoni	Uga..da Bohor Reedbuck
Kobus kob thomasi	Kavirondo Kob
Kobus vaughani	Rufous White-eared Kob
Kobus leucotis	White-eared Kob
Kobus dejassa ugandæ	Uganda Defassa Waterbuck
Kobus dejassa harnieri	White Nile Defassa Waterbuck
Kobus ellipsiprymnus	East African Waterbuck
Kobus maria	White-withered Waterbuck
Cephalophus abyssinicus hindci	Masailand Duikerbok
Cephalophus abyssinicus nyansæ . . .	Kavirondo Duikerbok
Cephalophus ignijer	Rufous Forest Duikerbok
Nototragus neumanni	East African Steinbok
Ourebia montana	Abyssinian Oribi
Ourebia cottoni	Guas Ngishu Oribi
Rhynchotragus kirki hindei	Masai Dikdik
Oreotragus schillingsi	East African Klipspringer
Connochætes albojubatus	White-bearded Wildebeest
Damaliscus corrigum jimela	East African Topi
Bubalis jacksoni	Jackson Hartebeest
Bubalis jacksoni insignis	Uganda Hartebeest
Bubalis cokei	Kongoni Hartebeest
Bubalis neumanni	Neumann Hartebeest
Bubalis lelwel niediecki	White Nile Hartebeest
Girajja reticulata	Somali Giraffe
Girajja camelopardalis tippelskirchi . . .	Masailand Giraffe
Girajja camelopardalis rothschildi . . .	Five-horned Giraffe
Elephas ajricanus peeli	British East African Elephant

FERÆ—CARNIVORES

Felis leo massaica	East African Lion
Felis pardus suahelica	East African Leopard
Felis capensis hindei	East African Serval Cat
Cynælurus jubatus guttatus	African Cheetah

The following is a partial list of those species obtained by Heller concerning which he (and occasionally I) could make observations as to their life histories. In the comparisons with or allusions to our American species there is, I need hardly say, no implication of kinship; the differences are generally fundamental, and I speak of the American animals only for the purpose of securing a familiar standard of comparison. The central African fauna is of course much more nearly allied to that of Europe than to that of North America, and were I familiar with small European mammals, I should use them, rather than the American, for purposes of illustration.

Heliosciurus keniæ (Kenia Forest Squirrel). Mount Kenia, B. E. A. Heller shot one in a tree in the heavy forest by our first elephant camp. In size and actions like our gray squirrel. Shy.

Paraxerus jacksoni. Shot at same camp; common at Nairobi and Kijabe, B. E. A. A little smaller than our red squirrel; much less noisy and less vivacious in action. Tamer than the larger squirrel, but much shyer than our red squirrel or chickaree. Kept among the bushes and lower limbs of the trees. Local in distribution; found in pairs or small families.

Graphiurus parvus (Pygmy Dormouse). Everywhere in B. E. A. in the forest; arboreal, often descending to the ground at night, for they are strictly nocturnal. Found in the woods fringing the rivers in the Sotik and on the Athi Plains, but most common in the juniper forests of the higher levels. Spend the daytime in crevices and hollows in the big trees. Build round, ball-like nests of bark fibre and woolly or cottony vegetable fibre. One of them placed in a hollow, four inches across, in a stump, the entrance being five feet above the ground. Caught in traps baited with walnuts or peanuts.

Tatera pothæ Heller (n. s.) (Athi Gerbille). Common on the Athi Plains, in open ground at the foot of the hills. Live in short grass, not bush. Nocturnal. Live in burrows, each burrow often possessing several entrances, and sometimes several burrows, all inhabited by same animal, not communicating.

Tatera varia Heller (n. s.) (Sotik Gerbille). A large form, seemingly new. Lives in the open plains, among the grass; not among bushes, nor at foot of hills. Lives in burrows, one animal apparently having several, each burrow with a little mound at the entrance. Nocturnal. In aspect and habits bears much resemblance to our totally different kangaroo rats.

Dipodillus harwoodi (Naivasha Pygmy Gerbille). Common around Naivasha, also in Sotik. A small form, quarter the size of the above; about as big as a house mouse. Same habits as above, but apparently only one burrow to each animal; much more plentiful. The burrows in the Sotik were in hard ground and went straight down. Round Naivasha the ground was soft and dry, and most of the burrows entered it diagonally.

Otomys irroratus tropicalis (Veldt Rat). Generally throughout B. E. A. but always in moist places, never on dry plains. Abundant on top of Aberdares, and ten thousand feet up on slopes of Kenia. Always in open grass. Make very definite trails which they cut with their teeth through the grass. Feed on the grass which they cut into lengths just as our meadow mice—mirotus—do. Largely diurnal, but also run about at night. The gravid females examined had in each of them two embryos only. Live in burrows, in which they place nests of fine grass six inches in diameter.

Dendromys nigrofrons (Black-fronted Tree Mouse). On Athi Plains and on the Sotik. Size of our harvest mouse. Do not go into forest, but dwell in bush country and thin timber along streams. Nocturnal; not abundant. Live in covered nests in bushes; nests made of long wiry grass, not lined, and very small, less than three inches in diameter. They are globular, and entered by a hole in one side, as with our marsh wrens. Only one mouse to a nest, as far as we saw; Heller caught two in their nests. The nests were in thorn-bushes only about a foot and a half from the ground; once or twice these mice were found in what were apparently abandoned weaver-birds' nests. If frightened, one would drop out of its nest to the ground and run off; but if Heller waited quietly for ten minutes the mouse would come back, climb up the twigs of the bush, and re-enter the nest. It never stayed away long, seeming to need the nest for protection.

Dendromys insignis. Although belonging to the genus of tree mice this large dendromys lives on the ground, seemingly builds no nest, and is most often found in the runways of the *Otomys.*

Lophuromys aquilus (Harsh-furred Mouse). Common in Rift Valley, on the top of the Aberdares, and in the Kenia forest. Go up to timber line, but are not found in the deep forest, save above the edges of the stream. Very fond of brush. Do not go out on the grassy plains. Usually, but not strictly, nocturnal; and in the cold, foggy uplands, as on the Aberdares, become diurnal.

(Leggada) Mus gratus (Pygmy Harvest Mouse). As small as our smallest harvest mouse. A grass mouse, usually entirely away from bushes and trees. Usually taken in the runways of the larger species. Occasionally come into tents. Nocturnal. Found generally throughout East Africa, but nowhere as abundant as many other species.

Epimys hindei (Masai Bush Rat). Trapped on the Kapiti and Athi Plains. About the size of the Southern wood rat of California; almost the size of the wood rat of the Eastern States. Is a ground-loving species, fond of bushes; in habits like the Mus panya; but less widely distributed, and entering houses less freely.

Epimys peromyscus Heller (n. s.) African White-footed Mouse. Externally strikingly like our white-footed mouse. Found in thick forest, along the edges of the Rift Valley and on Mount Kenia. Near our elephant camp Heller failed to trap any white-footed mice in the open glades, even when the glades were of small size, but caught them easily if the traps were set only a few yards within the dense forest. Evidently very abundant in the forest, but not venturing at all into the open. Strictly nocturnal. Dwell under logs and in decayed places around stumps, and the trunks of big trees.

Epimys panya (East African House Mouse). Common in B. E. A., coming into the houses, and acting like a house mouse, but twice the size. Frequently came into our camps, entering the tents. Very common on the edges of the forest and in brush country and long grass, and among the shambas; not in the deep forests, except along streams, and not in the bare open plains. Nocturnal. Found in the runways of *Otomys* and *Arvicanthis*. Does not seem to be a grass-feeding species, like *Otomys;* eats grain, beans, etc.

Epimys nieventris ulæ (Athi Rock Mouse). On the Athi Plains, in the Sotik, around Naivasha, and in the Rift Valley. Body only slightly larger than that of a house mouse, but tail at least a third longer than the head and body together. Yellowish-brown above and whitish beneath. Never found except among rocks; we always found it where there were cliffs or on stony koppies. Lives in crevices in the rocks and along the ledges of the cliffs. Nocturnal. Caught in traps with nuts.

Zelotomys hildegardæ (Broad-headed Bush Mouse). Looks like a small-eared, broad-headed house mouse. Rather common on Athi Plains, in same localities with Uganda mouse, but rarer, and seldom enters houses.

Thamnomys surdaster polionops (Long-tailed Tree Mouse). Arboreal; more like a mouse than a rat. On the Athi Plains, in the Sotik and Rift Valley. Not found in heavy forest, but in the open acacia woods and in bushy country. Apparently lives much of the time on the ground, and builds no nests in the trees, but runs up and down them and among their branches freely. Nocturnal.

Thamnomys Loringi Heller (n. s.) (Masked Tree Rat). In the Rift Valley; common around Naivasha. Has a black ring around each eye, the color spreading over the nose like a mask. Arboreal and nocturnal. Much the habits of our neotoma, but do not build large nests. Build nests about six inches in diameter, made of sticks, placed in the branches of the thorn-trees; also in burrows near the bottom of the trunks; runways lead from the trees containing the nests to the burrows. Trapped on the ground and in traps set in notches of the trees.

Œnomys hypoxanthus bacchante (Rusty-nosed Rat). Found in same country as above, and with similar habits, but somewhat less arboreal. A handsome species.

Dasymus helukus Heller (n. s.) (Swamp Rat). In appearance much like the Alexandrian or roof rat, but with longer hair and shorter, much less conspicuous ears. Found all over the Athi Plains where there was brush, especially along stream beds. Nocturnal.

Arvicanthis abyssinicus nairobœ (Athi Grass Rat). The commonest mouse in B. E. A. on the plains. Outnumbers any other species. Found everywhere in grass and brush, but not in deep forest. Often lives in shallow burrows round the bases of thorn-trees, from which its well-marked runways radiate into the grass. Strictly diurnal. Often seen running about in bright sunlight. Never found in traps at night. A striped mouse that has lost its stripes, vestiges of which are occasionally found in the young.

Arvicanthis pulchellus masaicus (Nairobi Striped Mouse). Diurnal. Common on the Athi Plains and on the Sotik and in Rift Valley. Around Neri we often saw them running about through the shambas. Live in brush and cultivated fields. In pattern of coloration much like our thirteen-striped gopher.

Arvicanthis pumilio diminutus (Naivasha Striped Rat). Common in Rift Valley, and on the Aberdares and around Kenia. Sometimes occurs in company with Nairobi mouse, but less widely distributed; much more abundant where found, and ascends to much higher altitudes.

Pelomys roosevelti Heller (n. s.) About the size of our cotton rat, and with much the same build. Coarse, bristly hair; the dorsal coloration is golden yellow overlaid by long hairs with an olive iridescence; the under parts are silky white. It is a meadow mouse found at high altitudes, seven to nine thousand feet high; usually lives close to streams in heavy grass, through which it makes runways. Not common.

Saccostomus umbriventer (Sotik Pouched Rat). Heller trapped several on the Sotik at the base of the southernmost range of mountains we reached. Found in the longish grass along a dry creek bed. Trapped in their rather indistinct runways. The pockets or pouches are internal; not external as in our pocket mice.

Tachyroyctes splendens ibeanus (Nairobi Mole Rat). A mole rat of B. E. A. with general habits of above, but avoiding rocky places, and not generally found many miles out on the plains away from the forest. Rarely found in the bamboos—in spite of its name.

Myoscalops kapiti Heller (n. s.) (Kapiti Blesmole). On the Kapiti and Athi Plains and in the Sotik. Smaller than German East African form and no white occipital spot. A cinnamon wash on its silvery fur. Burrows like our pocket gophers, and has same squat look and general habits. Lives in rocky ground, where bamboo rat does not penetrate. It does not run just below the surface of the soil, as the pocket gopher does in winter. The blesmole's burrows are about a foot below the surface. Eats roots.

Pedetes surdaster (Springhaas). (See body of book.) One young at birth. A colony of four to eight open burrows, all inhabited by a single animal.

Hystrix galeata. (See body of book.) Heller found in stomach the remains of a root or tuber and seeds like those of the nightshade.

Lepus victoriæ. Generally distributed on plains; much the habits and look of a small jack-rabbit. Does not burrow.

Elephantulus pulcher (Elephant Shrew). Fairly common throughout B. E. A. in bush and on hills, not in deep forests or on bare plains. Often out at dusk, but generally nocturnal. A gravid female contained a single embryo. One in a trap had its mouth full of partly masticated brown ants. A gentle thing, without the fierceness of the true shrews. Trapped in the runways of arvicanthis.

Erinaceus albiventris (Hedgehog). Fairly common in the Sotik. In certain places under trees Heller found accumulations of their spiny skins, as if some bird of prey had been feeding on them.

Crocidura fisheri. The common shrew of the Athi Plains and the Sotik in the Rift Valley. Largely diurnal. Males quite yellowish, females smoky brown. Generally trapped in runways of arvicanthis. Pregnant females contained three to five embryos, usually four. Not found in heavy forest or swamp.

Crocidura fumosa (Dusky Shrew). A darker form found in the rush swamps and sedgy places of the same region. Number of young usually three. Diurnal. Occasional in forests.

Crocidura alchemillæ Heller (n. s.). Aberdare shrew; a diurnal form, occurring above timber line on the Aberdare; perhaps identical with the foregoing.*

Crocidura allex. A pygmy shrew, taken at Naivasha.

Crocidura nyansæ. Very big for a shrew. Chiefly in the high country, near watercourses; found round the edge of the forest, at Kenia and Kijabe. A fierce, carnivorous creature, preying on small rodents as well as insects; habitually ate mice, rats, or shrews which it found in the traps, and would then come back and itself be readily trapped.

Surdisorex noræ. A shrew in shape not unlike our mole shrew. On the high, cold, wet Aberdare plateau. Diurnal.

Scotophilus migrita colias. Common at Nairobi; flying among the tree tops in the evenings. Greenish back, with metallic glint; belly sulphur. Has the same flight as our big brown bat—vespertilio fuscus.

Pipistrellus kuhlii fuscatus. Common at Naivasha and Nairobi. Very closely kin to our Myotis, or little brown bat, with same habits. Fly high in the air after dusk, and are easily shot. We never found its day roosts.

Nyctinomus hindei (Free-tailed Bat). At Naivasha. Very swift flight, almost like a swallow's, fairly high in the air. Live in colonies; one such in a house at Naivasha. On the Athi Plains they were found in daytime hanging up behind the loose bark of the big yellow-trunked acacias.

Lavia frons (Great-eared Bat). Bluish body and yellowish wings; very long ears. Almost diurnal, flies well by day; hangs from the thorn-tree branches, in the sunlight, and flies as soon as it sees a man approaching. One young, which remains attached to the mother until it is more than half her size.

Petalia thebaica (Large-eared Nycterine Bat). Caves in the Rift Valley; also in the Sotik, spending the day in the tops of the limestone wells or caverns which contained water. Both sexes occurred together in company with a bat of another genus—Rhinolophus. Fly very close to the ground, only two or three feet above it, and usually among trees and brush and not in the open, so that it is almost impossible to shoot them.

Rhinolophus. Found at the Limestone Springs in the Sotik, and in great numbers in a cave at Naivasha, no other bat being found in the cave. Same general habits as the nycteris. Specimens flew among our tents in the evening.

* *Crocidura alchemillæ,* new species (Heller). Type from the summit of the Aberdare Range; altitude, 10,500 feet; British East Africa; adult male, number 163,087, U. S. Nat. Mus.; collected by Edmund Heller, October 17, 1909; original number, 1,177.

Allied to *fumosa* of Mount Kenia, but coloration much darker, everywhere clove brown, the underparts but slightly lighter in shade; feet somewhat lighter sepia brown but much darker than in *fumosa;* hair at base slaty-black. Hair long and heavy, on back 6 to 7 mm. long; considerably longer than in *fumosa.* Musk glands on sides of body clothed with short brownish hairs, the glands producing an oily odor very similar to that of a petrel. Skull somewhat smaller than *fumosa* with relatively smaller teeth.

Measurements : Head and body, 90; tail, 55; hind foot, 15.3. Skull: Condyloincisive length, 21; mastoid breadth, 9.7; upper tooth row (alveoli), 8.3.

This species is an inhabitant of the dense beds of *Alchemilla* which clothe the alpine moorland of the Aberdare Range.

Papio ibeanus. The baboon is common all over the plains, in troops. It digs up lily bulbs, and industriously turns over stones for grubs and insects. Very curious, intelligent, and bestial.

Cercopithecus kolbi. Found in company with the Colobus in heavy forest along the Kikuyu escarpment. The subspecies *Hindei* is found on Kenia.

Cercopithecus pygerythrus johnsoni (Green Monkey). In the yellow thorns of the Sotik and Rift Valley, and along the northern Guaso Nyero. Leaves and acacia pods in their stomachs. Live in troops of from ten to twenty individually. Exceedingly active and agile. Often sit motionless on the very tops of the trees, when they cannot be seen from below. Run well on the ground.

Colobus caudatus (Black and White Monkey). Heavy mountain forests, Kijabe and Kenia, and on the Aberdares. Only foliage in the stomachs of those shot. Goes in small troops, each seemingly containing both males and females; not as agile as the other monkeys, and less wary. The natives prize their skins.

On the Guas Ngishu the small mammals were in general identical with those of the Aberdares and Mount Kenia.

In Uganda Heller shot an old male, Cercopithecus ascanius schmidti, a red-backed, red-tailed, white-nosed monkey; it was alone in a small grove of trees surrounded by elephant grass. In the same grove he shot a squirrel, Paraxerus, very different from the Kenia species. In Uganda there were fewer species of small mammals than in East Africa, in spite of the abundance of vegetation and water.

In the Lado we found rats, mice, and shrews abundant, but the number of species limited, and for the most part representing wide-spread types. Some of the bats were different from any yet obtained; the same may be true of the shrews. The small carnivores, and hyenas also, were very scarce.

North of Nimule Kermit shot another *Funisciurus*, while it was climbing a bamboo.

At Gondokoro there were many bats in the houses, chiefly Nyctinomus, the swift-flying, high-flying, free-tailed bats, with a few leaf-nosed bats, and yellow bats.

I wish field naturalists would observe the relation of zebras and wild dogs. Our observations were too limited to be decisive; but it seemed to us that zebras did not share the fear felt by the other game for the dogs. I saw a zebra, in a herd, run toward some wild dogs, with its mouth open and ears back; and they got out of the way, although seemingly not much frightened. Loring saw a solitary zebra seemingly unmoved by the close neighborhood of some wild dogs.

Once, on the Nile, while Loring and I were watching a monitor stealing crocodiles' eggs, we noticed a hippo in mid-stream. It was about ten in the morning. The hippo appeared regularly, at two or three minute intervals, always in the same place, breathed, and immediately sank. This continued for an hour. We could not make out what he was doing. It seemed unlikely that he could be feeding; and the current was too swift to allow him to rest; all other hippos at that time were for the most part lying in the shallows or were back among the papyrus beds.

APPENDIX C

The following notes were made by Loring in East Africa:

Alpine Hyrax (*Procavia mackinderi*). On Mount Kenia at altitudes between 12,000 and 15,000 feet we found these animals common wherever protective rocks occurred. Under the shelving rocks were great heaps of their droppings, and in the places where for centuries they had sunned themselves the stone was stained and worn smooth. At all times of the day, but more frequently after the sun had risen, they could be seen singly, in pairs, and in families, perched on the peaks. At our highest camp (14,700 feet), where on the 22d of September more than half an inch of ice formed in buckets of water outside the tent, they were often heard. They emit a variety of chatters, whistles, and cat-like squalls that cannot be described in print, and we found them very noisy. Whenever they saw any one approaching they always sounded some note of alarm, and frequently continued to harangue the intruder until he had approached so close that they took fright and disappeared in the rocks or until he had passed. All along the base of cliffs and leading from one mass of rocks to another they made well-worn trails through the grass. At this time of the year many young ones about one-third grown were seen and taken.

Kenia Tree Hyrax (*Procavia crawshayi*). From the time that we reached the edge of the forest belt (altitude 7,000), on Mount Kenia, we heard these tree dassies every night and at all camps to an altitude of 10,700 feet they were common. I once heard one on a bright afternoon about four o'clock, and on a second occasion another about two hours before sundown. Although I searched diligently on the ground for runways, and for suitable places to set traps, no such place was found. In a large yew-tree that had split and divided fifteen feet from the ground, I found a bed or bulky platform of dried leaves and moss of nature's manufacture. On the top of this some animal had placed a few dried green leaves. In this bed I set a steel trap and carefully covered it, and on the second night (October 14), captured a dassie containing a fœtus almost mature. We were informed by our "boys" that these animals inhabited hollow stumps and logs as well as the foliage of the live trees, but we found no signs that proved it, although, judging from the din at night, dassies were abundant everywhere in the forests.

At evening, about an hour after darkness had fully settled, a dassie would call and in a few seconds dassies were answering from all around, and the din continued for half an hour or an hour. The note began with a series of deep frog-like croaks that gradually gave way to a series of shrill tremulous screams, at times resembling the squealing of a pig and again the cries of a child. It was a far-reaching sound and always came from the large forest trees. Often the cries were directly over our heads and at a time when the porters were singing and dancing about a bright camp-fire. Although we tried many times to shine their eyes with a powerful light, we never succeeded, nor were we able to hear any rustling of the branches or scraping on the tree trunks as one might expect an animal of such size to make. The porters were offered a rupee apiece for dassies, but none was brought in.

Rock Hyrax (*Procavia brucei maculata*). These animals inhabited the rocks and cliffs on Ulukenia Hills in fair numbers. None lived in burrows of their own make, but took advantage of the natural crevices for cover. I heard their shrill calls at night, usually when the moon was out. Several were shot and two trapped in traps set in narrow passages through which the animals travelled.

Klipspringer (*Oreotragus oreotragus*). Several pairs of these little antelopes were seen on Ulukenia Hills, but never were more than two found at a time. They lived on the rocky hill-sides and were quite tame, allowing one to approach within twenty-five yards before taking fright and dashing into the rocks, invariably their shelter when alarmed. When thoroughly frightened they made a loud sneezing sound. Two were collected; one of which was a female with horns. A young Boer who had lived in that neighborhood three years told me that al' the females of proper age had horns.

Pygmy Gerbille (*Dipodillus harwoodi*). These little sand mice resemble very closely some of our American pocket mice (*Perognathus*). Heller took several on the Njoro O Solali and found them common, and I caught one specimen on the South Guaso Nyero River. On the sandy desert flats on the south-west side of Lake Naivasha they were abundant. The holes running obliquely into the ground were sometimes blocked with sand from the inside. On the opposite side of the lake there was less sand, and here the gerbilles were found only in spots. In sand alone their burrows resembled those described, but where the ground was hard they entered almost perpendicular, and were never blocked with sand. Often seed pods and tiny cockle burrs were strewn about the entrances.

Pygmy Mouse (*Mus* [*Leggada*] *gratus*). Various forms of this tiny little mouse were taken all along the route we travelled. They were caught in traps set at random in the brushy thickets in the lowland, as well as in the open grassy spots on the rocky hill-sides where they frequented the runways made by various species of *Mus*. A few were collected on Mount Kenia.

Athi Rock Mouse (*Epimys nieventris ulæ*). This mouse proved to be a new species. It was common in and about the rocks on Ulukenia Hills, which is the only place where we found them. Those taken were caught in traps baited with peanut butter, dried apple, and rolled oats and set among the rocks.

Forest Mouse (*Epimys peromyscus*). At our camp at 8,500 feet altitude we first met with this mouse, and although a good line of traps well baited and set about stumps, tree trunks, and logs for three nights, but one mouse was captured, that being taken under a large log. Several others were trapped in the thick brush bordering the bamboo. At 10,000 feet several were caught in the bamboo, and at 10,700 feet a good series was collected on a well-thicketed and timbered rocky ridge.

Masked Tree Rat (*Thamnomys loringi*). None were taken until we reached the south-west end of Lake Naivasha. Here and also at Naivasha Station a number were collected in traps baited with rolled oats and dried apple and set at the base of large trees and in brushy thickets in groves. In some of these trees and in the bushes, nests of sticks, grass and leaves were found. While setting traps one afternoon I saw what might have been one of these rats dart from a deserted bird's nest, and run down a limb to the ground. The following morning I caught a masked tree rat in a trap set beneath the nest.

Four-striped Grass Rat (*Arvicanthus pumilio minutus*). At Naivasha we first came across this species, where it was found on the east side of the lake only, although the spotted rat was common on both the east and the west side. At Naivasha these two animals inhabited slightly different regions. In the brushy and grassy thickets bordering the lake spotted rats were abundant, but a few four-striped rats were captured. As soon as the traps were transferred to thorn-tree groves where there was plenty of under-bushes, and not so much grass and weeds, the spotted rats were found in great numbers, but no four-striped rats. All the way from Fort Hall to Mount Kenia and as high as 10,700 feet, where Dr. Mearns secured one specimen, this species was common. We also caught them along the route between Kampalla and Butiaba.

Giant Rat (*Thrynomys gregorianus*). Along the skirtings of the rivers in the thick weeds, grass, and bushes at Fort Hall signs of these animals were common. There were no well-defined paths. Footprints the size and shape of those made by our muskrats (*Fiber*) were found in the mud at the water's edge, and here and there were clusters of grass and weed stems cut in lengths averaging six inches. In sections where the vegetation had been burned were innumerable holes where some animal had dug about the base of grass tufts. Their signs did not extend further than fifty feet from water. While passing through a thicket close to the water, I started a large rodent which darted through the grass and plunged into the water.

Mole Rat (*Tachyoryctes splendens ibeanus*). Mounds of earth that these rats had thrown from the mouth of their burrows at the time that the tunnels were made, were found as far west as Oljoro O'Nyon River, but none at N'garri Narok River. At our camp on the South Guaso Nyero River a pale mole-colored mole rat took this animal's place. Some fifteen miles west of Lake Naivasha mole rats became common, and on the sandy flats within five miles of the lake they were so abundant that our horses broke into their runways nearly every step. Their underground tunnels and the mounds of earth that were thrown out were similar to those made by the pocket gophers of western United States. Many were snared by the porters and brought to camp alive. They would crawl about slowly, not attempting to run away, but looking for a hole to enter. After the lapse of a few seconds they would begin to dig. In any slight depression they began work, and when small roots or a tussock of grass intervened, they used their teeth until the obstruction was removed, and then with the nails of their front feet only, continued digging. As the hole deepened they threw the dirt out between their h'.,d legs and with them still further beyond. After the earth had accumulated so that it drifted back they faced about and using their chest as a scoop, pushed it entirely out of the way. They were most active in the evening, at night, and in early morning. Several were found dead near their holes, having evidently been killed by owls or small carnivorous mammals.

Alpine Mole Rat (*Tachyoryctes rex*). Mole rat mounds were common about the West Kenia Forest Station, but none were seen between 7,500 and 8,500 feet, and from this altitude they ranged to 11,000 feet. They inhabited all of the open grassy plots in the bamboo belt and in the open timber. The "boys" snared many in nooses ingeniously placed in the runs that were opened and closed after the trap was set. While digging into the burrows, several times I found bulky nests of dried grass in side pockets just off the main runway. Most of them were empty, but one was filled with the animal's droppings.

Kapiti Blesmol (*Myoscalops kapiti*). This mole rat, which proved to be new to science, was first encountered at Potha on Kapiti Plains and it was again met with at Ulukenia Hills. I was shown several skins that were taken about fifteen miles east of Nairobi. They were the most difficult of all mole rats to catch because they lived in the very sandy soil and almost invariably covered the trap with sand without themselves getting into it. I found a number of their skulls in the pellets of barn and other species of owls.

Springhaas (*Pedetes surdaster*). Very common at Naivasha station where their burrows were numerous on a sandy flat practically in the town, and many were taken within a hundred yards of the station. They are nocturnal, although one instance came under my observation where a springhaas was seen on a dark day to run from one burrow to another. By hunting them on dark nights, with the aid of an acetylene light we were able to secure a good series of skins. When the light was flashed on them, their eyes shone like balls of fire the size of a penny, and it was not uncommon to see from two to five and six within the radius of the light at one time. They were usually flashed at a distance of about a hundred yards, and as the light drew near they would watch it, frequently bobbing up and down. Often they hopped away to right or to left, but very seldom did their fright carry them into their burrows unless a shot was fired; in fact even then we sometimes followed up one of their companions and secured it. Some allowed us to approach within ten feet before moving, and then off they would go in great bounds, but I was never able in the dim light to see whether or not their tails aided them in jumping. I once shot a fox from a cluster of eyes that I am positive were those of springhaas; this together with the fact that the stomachs of all of the foxes killed contained termites and insects, leads me to believe that these two animals are more or less congenial. Dr. Mearns saw a springhaas sitting with its tail curled around to one side of its body, similar to the position often assumed by a house cat.

Several small colonies of springhaas were discovered on sandy flats near Ulukenia Hills. Two females taken from the same burrow showed great variation in size, one having a tail several inches longer and ears larger than the other. Although I never discovered a burrow that was completely blocked with sand, in the morning one could find quantities of fresh sand that had been thrown out of the entrance during the night.

Great-eared Fox (*Otocyon virgartus*). This new species of fox we discovered at Naivasha and found it very common there. All of the seven specimens secured were taken by "jacking" at night, although while travelling over the Uganda Railroad we frequently saw them singly or in pairs in broad daylight. The white people knew nothing of a fox in this country and had always called them "jackals." They seemed to live in pairs and groups of three to six. On dark nights it was usually easy to shine their eyes and approach within shooting range. We would shine a fox, then suddenly the glare of its eyes would disappear and we would walk about casting the light in all directions until we again saw the two balls of fire glaring some fifty or a hundred yards away. Often the foxes would slink about for some time before we got within gunshot range. Frequently we saw two and sometimes three and four standing so close together that it was surprising that the spread of the shot did not kill more than one. One evening Dr. Mearns and I started out about nine o'clock and returned about midnight. Most of the hunting was done on an elevated brushy plateau within short distance of a native village where the occupants were singing, dancing, and playing their crude stringed instruments. We ran into a bunch of five of these foxes and got four of them, none of which was the young of the year. After shooting one, we would search about in the dark until the light picked up another pair of eyes, and in this way we kept circling about close to the village. One fox was killed within two hundred yards of the railroad station, and at dusk one evening I saw a fox emerge from a burrow close to a group of natives and scamper across the flat. The stomachs of several were examined and found to contain about a quart of termites and other insects.

Giant Shrew (*Crocidura nyansæ*). Giant shrews were common at Lake Naivasha, where most of them were caught in the thick reeds and rank grass bordering the lake. One was taken at Nyeri and another on Mount Kenia at an altitude of 10,700 feet. They seemed to be as much diurnal as nocturnal and were captured in traps baited with rolled oats, dried apple, and raw meat. They inhabited the dense parts of the thickets where the foliage had to be parted and a clearing made for the traps. These localities were the home of a large rat, and many of the rats captured were decapitated or partly eaten by animals that probably were giant shrews. A shrew captured alive was very ferocious and would seize upon anything that came within its reach. When fully excited and lifted into the air by its tail, it would emit a loud shrill chirping note.

Short-tailed Shrew (*Surdisorex noræ*). Collected between altitudes of 10,000 and 12,100 feet on Mount Kenia. With the exception of those collected at 10,000 feet, where they were trapped in open grassy and brushy parks in the bamboo, most of them were taken in runways of *Otomys*, and all of those taken at 12,100 were caught in such runways in tall marsh grass.

Elephant Shrew (*Elephantulus pulcher*). Both diurnal and nocturnal. While riding over the country I frequently saw them darting through the runways from one thicket to another. Nearly every clump of bushes and patch of rank vegetation in the Sotik and Naivasha districts was traversed with well-worn trails used by different species of *Mus* and shrews. The elephant shrews were most common on the dry flats where clumps of fibre plants grew, and their trails usually led into some thorny thicket and finally entered the ground.

Yellow-winged Tree Bat (*Lavia frons*). These large semi-diurnal bats lived in the thorn-tree groves and thick bush along the Athi, South Guaso Nyero, and Nile Rivers where we found them more or less common, and at the latter place abundant. At the first two named places they were almost always found in pairs hanging from the thorn-trees by their feet, their wings folded before their faces. When disturbed they fly a short distance and alight, but when we returned to the spot a few minutes later they would often be found in the same tree from which they had been started. On the Nile at Rhino Camp, and in suitable places all along the trail between Kampalla and Butiaba, it was not unusual to find three and four in a single thorn-tree. On dark days, and once in the bright sunlight, I saw these bats flying about and feeding. At evening they always appeared an hour or so before the sun went down. Their method of feeding was quite similar to that of our fly-catching birds. They would dart from the branches of a thorn-tree, catch an insect, then return and hang head downward in the tree while they ate the morsel. One was captured with a young one clinging to it head downward, its feet clasped about its mother's neck.

APPENDIX D

Dr. Mearns, accompanied by Loring, spent from the middle of September to after the middle of October, 1909, in a biological survey of Mount Kenia. I take the following account from his notes. In them he treats the mountain proper as beginning at an altitude of 7,500 feet. Mount Kenia is the only snow-capped mountain lying exactly on the equator. Its altitude is about 17,200 feet. The mountain is supposed to support 15 glaciers; those that Mearns and Loring examined resembled vast snow banks rather than clear ice-glaciers. The permanent snow line begins at the edge of the glacial lakes at 15,000 feet; on October 18th there was a heavy snow-storm as low down as 11,000 feet. For some distance below the snow line the slopes were of broken rock, bare earth, and gravel, with a scanty and insignificant vegetable growth in the crannies between the rocks. These grasses and alpine plants, including giant groundsells and lobelias, cover the soil. At 13,000 feet timber line is reached.

The Kenia forest belt, separating this treeless alpine region from the surrounding open plains, is from 6 to 9 miles wide. The forest zone is only imperfectly divided into successive belts of trees of the same species; for the species vary on different sides of the mountain. Even the bamboo zone is interrupted. On the west side the zones may be divided into:

(1) A cedar zone from 7,000 or 7,500 to 8,500 feet. The cedars are mixed with many hardwood trees.

(2) A belt composed mainly of bamboo and yellow-wood (African yew) from 8,500 to 10,700 feet. Here the true timber zone ends.

(3) A zone of giant heath, mixed with giant groundsells and shrubs, extending to 13,000 feet. The heaths may be 30 feet high and can be used as fuel. In this zone are many boggy meadows.

Loring and Mearns occupied five collecting camps in the forest zone and one above it, at 13,700 feet. One day Mearns followed the snow line for a mile without seeing any traces of large animals, although leopards and smaller cats sometimes wander to this height. The grove-toothed rat, otomys, was numerous in the grass bordering the glacial lakes at a height of 15,000 feet; so were the big mountain hyrax; and Mearns shot one of these animals at 15,500 feet, by a snow bank; it was the highest point at which any mammal was collected. Various kinds of rats and shrews were numerous about the 13,700 foot camp. Above 12,000 feet only three small birds were seen: a long-tailed sunbird, a stone chat, and a fantail warbler.

On the entire Mount Kenia trip 1,112 birds, of 210 species, were collected; 1,320 mammals and 771 reptiles and batrachians were collected, but the species represented were much fewer. Mearns also made an excellent collection of plants and a good collection of invertebrates. Freshwater crabs were numerous in the streams up to 10,000 feet, frogs went as high as 10,700, a chameleon was taken at 11,000, and a lizard at 12,100.

Loring ascended the mountain to the base of the pinnacle, at about 16,500 feet. He started from the highest camp, where the water froze each night. The ascent was easy and he carried his camera; but the glare of the snow gave him snow blindness.

APPENDIX E

PROTECTIVE COLORATION

Mr. Dugmore has made a wonderful series of photographs of African big game. Mr. Kearton has made a series of moving pictures of various big animals which were taken alive by Buffalo Jones and his two cowboys, Loveless and Meany, on his recent trip to East Africa; a trip on which they were accompanied by a former member of my regiment, Guy Scull. All three men are old-time Westerners and plainsmen, skilled in handling both horse and rope. They took their big, powerful, thoroughly trained cow horses with them, and roped and captured a lioness, a rhinoceros, a giraffe, and other animals. I regard these feats of my three fellow-countrymen as surpassing any feats which can possibly be performed by men who hunt with the rifle.

For the natural history of African big game, probably the three most valuable books—certainly the most valuable modern books—are Selous's "African Nature Notes," Schilling's "Flashlight and Rifle," and Millais's "Breath from the Veldt." The photographer plays an exceedingly valuable part in nature study, but our appreciation of the great value of this part must never lead us into forgetting that as a rule even the best photograph renders its highest service when treated as material for the best picture, instead of as a substitute for the best picture; and that the picture itself, important though it is, comes entirely secondary to the text in any book worthy of serious consideration either from the stand-point of science or the stand-point of literature. Of course this does not mean any failure to appreciate the *absolute* importance of photographs—of Mr. Dugmore's capital photographs, for instance; what I desire is merely that we keep in mind, when books are treated seriously, the *relative* values of the photograph, the picture, and the text. The text again, to be of the highest worth, must be good both in form and in substance; that is, the writer who tells us of the habits of big game must be a man of ample personal experience, of trained mind, of keen powers of observation, and, in addition, a man possessing the ability to portray vividly, clearly, and with interest what he has seen.

Experience in the field is of great value in helping to test various biological theories. One of the theories which has had a very great vogue of recent years is that of the protective coloration of animals. It has been worked out with a special elaborateness in Mr. Thayer's book on "Concealing Coloration in the Animal Kingdom." I do not question the fact that there are in all probability multitudes of cases in which the coloration of an animal is of protective value in concealing it from its prey or its foes. But the theory is certainly pushed to preposterous extremes; its ultra-adherents taking up a position like that of some of the earlier champions of the glacial theory; who, having really discovered notable proofs of glacial action in parts of Europe and North America, then went slightly crazy on their favorite subject, and proceeded to find proofs of glacial action over the entire world surface, including, for instance, the Amazon Valley. As regards many of the big game animals, at any rate, which are claimed by the ultra-exponents of the protective coloration theory as offering examples thereof, there is not the least particle of justification for the claim.

I select Mr. Thayer's book because it is a really noteworthy book, written and illustrated by men of great ability, and because it contains much that is of genuine scientific value.* I have no question whatever, for instance, that concealing coloration is of real value in the struggle for existence to certain mammals and certain birds, not to mention invertebrates. The night hawk, certain partridges and grouse, and numerous other birds which seek to escape observation by squatting motionless, do unquestionably owe an immense amount to the way in which their colors harmonize with the surrounding colors, thus enabling them to lie undetected while they keep still, and probably even protecting them somewhat if they try to skulk off. In these cases, where the theory really applies, the creature benefited by the coloration secures the benefit by acting in a way which enables the coloration to further its concealment. A night hawk, or a woodcock, or a prairie chicken, will lie until nearly trodden on, the bird showing by its action that its one thought is to escape observation, and its coloration and squatting attitude enabling it thus to escape observation; as Mr. Beddard puts it in his book on "Animal Coloration," "absence of movement is absolutely essential for protectively colored animals, whether they make use of their coloration for defensive purposes or offensive purposes." So far as Mr. Thayer's book or similar books confine themselves to pointing out cases of this kind, and to working on hypotheses where the facts are supplied by such cases, they do a real service. But it is wholly different when the theory is pushed to fantastic extremes, as by those who seek to make the coloration of big game animals such as zebras, giraffes, hartebeests, and the like, protective. I very gravely doubt whether some of the smaller mammals and birds to which Mr. Thayer refers really bear out his theory at all. He has, for instance, a picture of blue jays by snow and blue shadow, which is designed to show how closely the blue jay agrees with its surroundings (I would be uncertain from the picture whether it is really blue water or a blue shadow). Now it is a simple physical impossibility that the brilliant and striking coloration of the blue jay can be protective both in the bare woods when snow is on the ground and in the thick leafy woods of midsummer. Countless such instances could be given.

---

* In passing I wish to bear testimony to the admirable work done by various members of the Thayer family in preserving birds and wild life—work so admirable that if those concerned in it will go on with it they are entitled to believe anything in the world they wish about protective coloration!

Mr. Thayer insists, as vital to his theory, that partridges and other protectively colored animals owe their safety, not at all to being incon-
spicuously colored, that is, to being colored like their surroundings, but
to their counter-shading, to their being colored dark above and light
below. But as a matter of fact most small mammals and birds which
normally owe their safety to the fact that their coloration matches their
surroundings, crouch flat whenever they seek to escape observation;
and when thus crouched flat, the counter-shading on which Mr. Thayer
lays such stress almost, or completely, disappears. The counter-shading
ceases to be of any use in concealing or protecting the animal at the precise
moment when it trusts to its coloration for concealment. Small rodents
and small dull-colored ground birds are normally in fear of foes which
must see them from above at the critical moment if they see them at all;
and from above no such shading is visible. This is true of almost all the
small birds in question, and of the little mice and rats and shrews, and
it completely upsets Mr. Thayer's theory as regards an immense proportion of the animals to which he applies it; most species of mice, for
example, which he insists owe their safety to counter-shading, live under
conditions which make this counter-shading of practically no consequence
whatever in saving them from their foes. The nearly uniform colored
mice and shrews are exactly as difficult to see as the others.

Again, take what Mr. Thayer says of hares and prongbucks. Mr.
Thayer insists that the white tails and rumps of deer, antelope, hares,
etc., help them by "obliteration" of them as they flee. He actually
continues that "when these beasts flee at night before terrestrial enemies,
their brightly displayed sky-lit white sterns blot out their foreshortened
bodies against the sky." He illustrates what he means by pictures, and
states that "in the night the illusion must often be complete, and most
beneficent to the hunted beast," and that what he calls "these rear-end
sky-pictures are worn by most fleet ruminants of the open land, and by
many rodents with more or less corresponding habits, notably hares" and
smaller things whose enemies are beasts of low stature, like weasels, minks,
snakes, and foxes; "in short, that they are worn by animals that are
habitually or most commonly looked up at by their enemies." Mr.
Thayer gives several pictures of the prongbuck, and of the northern
rabbit, to illustrate his theory, and actually treats the extraordinarily
conspicuous white rump patch of the prongbuck as an "obliterative"
marking. In reality, so far from hiding the animal, the white rump is at
night often the only cause of the animal's being seen at all. Under
one picture of the prongbuck, Mr. Thayer says that it is commonly
seen with the white rump against the sky-line by all its terrestrial
enemies, such as wolves and cougars. Of course, as a matter of fact,
when seen against the sky-line, the rest of the prongbuck's silhouette is
so distinct that the white rump mark] as not the slightest obliterative
value of any kind. I can testify personally as to this, for I have seen
prongbuck against the sky-line hundreds of times by daylight, and at
least a score of times by night. The only occasion it could ever have

such obliterative value would be at the precise moment when it happened to be standing stern-on in such a position that the rump was above the sky-line and all the rest of the body below it. Ten steps further back, or ten steps further forward, would in each case make it visible instantly to the dullest-sighted wolf or cougar that ever killed game, so that Mr. Thayer's theory is of value only on the supposition that both the prong-buck and its enemy happen to be so placed that the enemy never glances in its direction save at just the one particular moment when, by a combi-nation of circumstances which might not occur once in a million times, the prongbuck happens to be helped by the obliterative quality of the white rump mark. Now, in the first place, the chance of the benefit happening to any individual prongbuck is so inconceivably small that it can be neglected, and, in the next place, in reality the white rump mark is exceedingly conspicuous under all ordinary circumstances, and for once that it might help the animal to elude attention, must attract at-tention to it at least a thousand times. At night, in the darkness, as any one who has ever spent much time hunting them knows, the white rump mark of the antelope is almost always the first thing about them that is seen, and is very often the only thing that is ever seen; and at night it does not fade into the sky, even if the animal is on the sky-line. So far as beasts of prey are guided by their sight at night, the white rump must always under all circumstances be a source of danger to the prong-buck, and never of any use as an obliterative pattern. In the daytime, so far from using this white rump as obliterative, the prongbuck almost invariably erects the white hairs with a kind of chrysanthemum effect when excited or surprised, and thereby doubles its conspicuousness. In the daytime, if the animals are seen against the sky-line, the white rump has hardly the slightest effect in making them less conspicuous; while if they are not seen against the sky-line (and of course in a great majority of cases they are not so seen), it is much the most conspicuous feature about them, and attracts attention from a very long distance. But this is not all. Any one acquainted with the habits of the prongbuck knows that the adult prongbuck practically never seeks to protect itself from its foes by concealment or by eluding their observation; its one desire is itself to observe its foes, and it is quite indifferent as to whether or not it is seen. It lives in open ground, where it is always very conspicuous; ex-cepting during the noonday rest, when it prefers to lie down in a hollow, almost always under conditions which render the white rump patch much less conspicuous than at any other time. In other words, during the time when it is comparatively off its guard and resting, it takes a position where it does not stand against the sky-line—as according to Mr. Thayer's ingenious theory it should; and, again contrary to this same theory, it usually lies down so that any foe would have to look down at it from above. Whenever it does lie down, the white patch becomes less conspicu-ous; it is rarely quiet for any length of time except when lying down. The kids of the prongbuck, on the other hand, do seek to escape observation, and they seek to do so by lying perfectly flat on the ground, with their heads out-stretched and the body pressed so against the ground that the effect of the white rump is minimized, as is also the effect of the "counter-shading", for the light-colored under parts are pressed against the earth, and the little kid lies motionless, trusting to escape observation owing to absence of movement, helped by the unbroken color surface which is exposed to view.   If the adult prongbucks really ever gained any bene-fit by any "protective" quality in their coloration, they would certainly act like the kids, and crouch motionless.   In reality the adult prong-buck never seeks to escape observation, never trusts in any way to the concealing or protective power of any part of its coloration, and is not bene-fited in the slightest degree by this supposed, but in reality entirely non-existent, concealing, or protective power.   The white rump practically never has any obliterative or concealing function; on the contrary, in the great majority of instances, it acts as an advertisement to all outside creatures of the prongbuck's existence.   Probably it is an example of what is known as directive coloration, of coloration used for purposes of advertisement or communication with the animal's followers.   But however this may be, it is certain that there is not the smallest justification for Mr. Thayer's theory so far as the prongbuck is concerned.

It is practically the same as regards the rabbit or the hare.   Any one who has ever been in the woods must know, or certainly ought to know, that when hares are sitting still and trying to escape observation, they crouch flat, so that the white of the tail and rump is almost concealed, as well as the white of the under parts, while the effect of the counter-shading almost or entirely vanishes.   No terrestrial foe of the hare would ever see the white rump against the sky-line unless the animal was in rapid motion (and parenthetically I may observe that even then it would only see the rump against the sky-line in an infinitesimally small number of cases). Of course as soon as the animal is in motion it is conspicuous to even the most dull-sighted beast of prey; and Mr. Thayer's idea that the white rear patch may mislead a foe as it jumps upon it is mere supposition, un-sustained by any proof, and contrary to all the facts that I have observed. Civilized man, who is much more dull-sighted than most wild things, can always see a rabbit when it runs because its white is then so very con-spicuous.   Here again I do not think there is the slightest value in Mr. Thayer's theory.   The white rump is certainly not a protective or obliterative marking; it is probably a directive or advertisement marking.

The Virginia deer, utterly unlike the prongbuck, does often seek to evade observation by lying close, or skulking.   When it lies close it lies flat on the ground like a hare, and its white tail is almost invisible, while of course even the most low-creeping foe would not under such circum-stances get it against the sky-line.   When it skulks it moves off with head and neck out-stretched and tail flattened down with the white as much obscured as possible.   The white is never shown in conspicuous fashion until the animal is frightened and no longer seeks concealment. It then bounds off openly, crashing through the brush, with its white tail flaunted, and under such circumstances the white mark is extremely conspicuous.

Indeed I feel that there is grave ground to question the general statement of Mr. Thayer that "almost all mammals are equipped with a full obliterative shading of surface colors; that is, they are darkest on the back and lightest on the belly, usually with connected intermediate shades." This is undoubtedly true as a statement of the coloration, but whether this coloration is in fact obliterative needs further investigation. Of course if it is obliterative, then its use is to conceal the mammals. Mr. Thayer's whole thesis is that such is the case. But as a matter of fact, the great majority of these mammals, when they seek to escape observation, crouch on the ground, and in that posture the light belly escapes observation, and the animal's color pattern loses very much of, and sometimes all of, the "full obliterative shading of surface colors" of which Mr. Thayer speaks. Moreover, when crouched down in seeking to escape observation, the foes of the animal are most apt to see it from above, not from below or from one side. This is also the case with carnivorous animals which seek to escape the observation of their prey. The cougar crouches when lying in wait or stalking, so that it is precisely when it is seeking to escape observation that its lighter-colored under parts are obscured, and the supposed benefit of the "obliterative shading pattern" lost. I do not intend without qualification to take ground one way or the other on this general question; but it is certainly true that any such sweeping statement as that quoted above from Mr. Thayer is as yet entirely unproved. I have no doubt that in most cases animals whose colors harmonize with their environment, and which also seek to escape observation by remaining motionless when they think there is danger, are very materially helped by their concealing coloration; but when this concealment is said to be due to the obliterative shading as described by Mr. Thayer, it is certainly worth while considering the fact that the so-called obliterative pattern is least shown, or is not shown at all, at the only time when the animal seeks to escape observation, or succeeds in escaping observation—that is, when it crouches motionless, or skulks slowly, with the conscious aim of not being seen. No color scheme whatever is of much avail to animals when they move unless the movement is very slow and cautious; rats, mice, gophers, rabbits, shrews, and the enormous majority of mammals which are colored in this fashion are not helped by their special coloration pattern at all when they are in motion. Against birds of prey they are practically never helped by the counter-shading, but merely by the general coloration and by absence of movement. Their chief destroyers among mammals— such as weasels, for instance—hunt them almost or altogether purely by scent, and though the final pounce is usually guided by sight, it is made from a distance so small that, as far as we can tell by observation, the "counter-shading" is useless as a protection. In fact, while the general shading of these small mammals' coats may very probably protect them from certain foes, it is as yet an open question as to just how far they are helped (and indeed in very many cases whether they really are helped to any appreciable extent) by what Mr. Thayer lays such especial stress upon as being "full obliterative shading (counter-shading) of surface coloring."

Certainly many of the markings of mammals, just as is the case with birds, must be wholly independent of any benefit they give to their possessors in the way of concealment. Mr. Thayer's pictures in some cases portray such entirely exceptional situations or surroundings that they are misleading—as, for instance, in his pictures of the peacock and the male wood-duck. An instant's reflection is sufficient to show that if the gaudily colored males of these two birds are really protectively colored, then the females are not, and *vice versa;* for the males and females inhabit similar places, and if the elaborate arrangement of sky or water and foliage in which Mr. Thayer has placed his peacock and wood-drake represented (which they do not) their habitual environment, a peahen and wood-duck could not be regarded as protectively colored at all; whereas of course in reality, as every one knows, they are far more difficult to see than the corresponding males. Again, he shows a chipmunk among twigs and leaves, to make it evident that the white and black markings conceal it; but a weasel which lacks these markings would be even more difficult to see. The simple truth is that in most woodland, mountain, and prairie surroundings, any small mammal that remains motionless is, unless very vividly colored, exceedingly apt to escape notice. I do not think that the stripes of the chipmunk are of any protective value; that is, I believe (and the case of the weasel seems to me to prove) that its coloration would be at least as fully "protective" without them. The striped gophers and gray gophers seem equally easy to see; they live in similar habitats and the stripes seem to have no protective effect one way or the other.

It is when Mr. Thayer and the other extreme members of the protective coloration school deal with the big game of Africa that they go most completely wide of the mark. For instance, Mr. Thayer speaks of the giraffe as a sylvan mammal with a checkered sun-fleck and leaf-colored pattern of coloration accompanied by complete obliterative shading, and the whole point of his remarks is that the giraffe's coloration "always maintains its potency for obliteration." Now of course this means nothing unless Mr. Thayer intends by it to mean that the giraffe's coloration allows it to escape the observation of its foes. I doubt whether this is ever under any circumstances the case; that is, I doubt whether the giraffe's varied coloration ever "enables" it to escape observation save as the dark monochrome of the elephant, rhinoceros, or buffalo may "enable" one of these animals to escape observation under practically identical conditions. There is of course no conceivable color or scheme of color which may not under some conceivable circumstances enable the bearer to escape observation; but if such coloring, for once that it enables the bearer to escape observation, exposes the bearer to observation a thousand times, it cannot be called protective. I do not think that the giraffe's coloration exposes it to observation on the part of its foes;

I think that it simply has no effect whatsoever. The giraffe never trusts to escaping observation; its sole thought is itself to observe any possible foe. At a distance of a few hundred yards the color pattern becomes indistinct to the eye, and the animal appears of a nearly uniform tint, so that any benefit given by the color pattern must be comparatively close at hand. On the very rare occasions when beasts of prey—that is, lions—do attack giraffes, it is usually at night, when the coloration is of no consequence; but even by daylight I should really doubt whether any giraffe has been saved from an attack by lions owing to its coloration allowing it to escape observation. It is so big, and so queerly shaped, that any trained eyes detect it at once, if within a reasonable distance; it only escapes observation when so far off that its coloration does not count one way or the other. There is no animal which will not at times seem invisible to the untrained eyes of the average white hunter, and any beast of any shape or any color standing or lying motionless, under exceptional circumstances, may now and then escape observation. The elephant is a much more truly sylvan beast than the giraffe, and it is a one-colored beast, its coloration pattern being precisely that which Mr. Thayer points out as being most visible. But I have spent over a minute in trying to see an elephant not fifty yards off, in thick forest, my black companion vainly trying to show it to me; I have had just the same experience with the similarly colored rhinoceros and buffalo when standing in the same scanty bush that is affected by giraffes, and with the rhinoceros also in open plains where there are ant-hills. It happens that I have never had such an experience with a giraffe. Doubtless such experiences do occur with giraffes, but no more frequently than with elephant, rhinoceros, and buffalo; and in my own experience I found that I usually made out giraffes at considerably larger distances than I made out rhinos. The buffalo does sometimes try to conceal itself, and, Mr. Thayer to the contrary notwithstanding, it is then much more difficult to make out than a giraffe, because it is much smaller and less oddly shaped. The buffalo, by the way, really might be benefited by protective coloration, if it possessed it, as it habitually lives in cover and is often preyed on by the lion; whereas the giraffe is not protected at all by its coloration, and is rarely attacked by lions.

Elephants and rhinoceroses occasionally stand motionless, waiting to see if they can place a foe, and at such times it is possible they are consciously seeking to evade observation. But the giraffe never under any circumstances tries to escape observation, and I doubt if, practically speaking, it ever succeeds so far as wild men or wild beasts that use their eyes at all are concerned. It stands motionless looking at the hunter, but it never tries to hide from him. It is one of the most conspicuous animals in Nature. Native hunters of the true hunting tribes pick it up invariably at an astonishing distance, and, near by, it never escapes their eyes; its coloration is of not the slightest use to it from the stand-point of concealment. Of course, white men, even though good ordinary hunters, and black men of the non-hunting tribes, often fail to see it, just as they

often fail to see a man or a horse, at a distance; but this is almost always
at such a distance that the coloration pattern cannot be made out at all, the
animal seeming neutral tinted, like the rest of the landscape, and escaping
observation because it is motionless, just as at the same distance a rhinoceros may escape observation.   A motionless man, if dressed in neutral-
tinted clothes, will in the same manner escape observation, even from
wild beasts, at distances so short that no giraffe could possibly avoid
being seen.   I have often watched game come to watering-places, or
graze toward me on a nearly bare plain; on such occasions I might
be unable to use cover, and then merely sat motionless on the grass or in
a game trail.   My neutral-tinted clothes, gray or yellow brown, were
all of one color, *without any counter-shading;* but neither the antelope
nor the zebra saw me, and they would frequently pass me, or come down
to drink, but thirty or forty yards off, without ever knowing of my presence.
My "concealment" or "protection" was due to resting motionless and
to wearing a neutral-tinted suit, although there was no counter-shading,
and although the color was uniform instead of being broken up with
a pattern of various tints.

The zebra offers another marked example of the complete break-down
of the protective coloration theory.   Mr. Thayer says: "Among all the
bolder obliterative patterns worn by mammals, that of the zebra probably
bears away the palm for potency."   The zebra's coloration has proved
especially attractive to many disciples of this school, even to some who
are usually good observers; but, as a matter of fact, the zebra's coloration
is the reverse of protective, and it is really extraordinary how any fairly
good observer of accurate mind can consider it so.   One argument used
by Mr. Thayer is really funny, when taken in connection with an argument frequently used by other disciples of the protective coloration theory
as applied to zebras.   Mr. Thayer shows by ingenious pictures that a wild
ass is much less protectively colored than a zebra; some of his fellow-
disciples triumphantly point out that at a little distance the zebra's stripes
merge into one another and that the animal then becomes protectively
colored because it looks exactly like a wild ass! Of course each author
forgets that zebras and wild asses live under substantially the same conditions, and that this mere fact totally upsets the theory that each is
beneficially affected by its protective coloration.   The two animals cannot both be protectively colored; they cannot each owe to its coloration
an advantage in escaping from its foes.   It is absolutely impossible, if one
of them is so colored as to enable it to escape the observations of its foes,
that the other can be.   As a matter of fact, neither is, and neither makes
any attempt to elude observation by its foes, but trusts entirely to vigilance
in discerning them and fleetness in escaping from them; although the
wild ass, unlike the zebra, really is so colored that because thereof it
may occasionally escape observation from dull-sighted foes.

Mr. Thayer's argument is based throughout on a complete failure
to understand the conditions of zebra life.   He makes an elaborate
statement to show that the brilliant cross bands of the zebra have great

obliterative effect, insisting that, owing to the obliterative coloration, zebras continually escape observation in the country in which they live. He continues: "Furthermore, all beasts must have water, and so the zebras of the dry plains must needs make frequent visits to the nearest living sloughs and rivers. There, by the water's edge, tall reeds and grasses almost always flourish, and there, where all beasts meet to drink, is the great place of danger for the ruminants, and all on whom the lion preys. In the open land they can often detect their enemy afar off, and depend on their fleetness for escape; but when they are down in the river-bed, among the reeds, he may approach unseen and leap among them without warning. It is probably at these drinking-places that the zebra's pattern is most beneficently potent. From far or near the watching eye of the hunter (bestial or human) is likely to see nothing, or nothing but reed-stripes, where it might otherwise detect the contour of a zebra." In a foot-note he adds that however largely lions and other rapacious mammals hunt by scent, it is only sight that serves them when they are down wind of their quarry; and that sight alone must guide their ultimate killing dash and spring.

Now this theory of Mr. Thayer's about the benefit of the zebra's coloration at drinking-places, as a shield against foes, lacks even the slightest foundation in fact; for it is self-evident that animals when they come down to drink necessarily move. The moment that any animal the size of a zebra moves, it at once becomes visible to the eye of its human or bestial foes, unless it skulks in the most cautious manner. The zebra never skulks, and, like most of the plains game, it never, at least when adult, seeks to escape observation—indeed in the case of the zebra (unlike what is true of the antelope) I am not sure that even the young seek to escape observation. I have many times watched zebras and antelopes—wildebeest, hartebeest, gazelle, waterbuck, kob—coming down to water; their conduct was substantially similar. The zebras, for instance, made no effort whatever to escape observation; they usually went to some drinking-place as clear of reeds as possible; but sometimes they were forced to come down to drink where there was rather thick cover, in which case they always seemed more nervous, more on the alert, and quicker in their movements. They came down in herds, and they would usually move forward by fits and starts; that is, travel a few hundred yards, and then stop and stand motionless for some time, looking around. They were always very conspicuous, and it was quite impossible for any watcher to fail to make them out. As they came nearer to the water, they seemed to grow more cautious. They would move forward some distance, halt, perhaps wheel and dash off for a hundred yards, and then after a little while return. As they got near the water they would again wait, and then march boldly down to drink—except in one case where, after numerous false starts, they finally seemed to suspect that there was something in the neighborhood, and went off for good without drinking. Never in any case did I see a zebra come down to drink under conditions which would have rendered it possible for the most dull-sighted beast to avoid seeing it. Of course I usually watched the pools and rivers when there was daylight; but after nightfall the zebra's stripes would be entirely invisible, so that their only effect at the drinking-place must be in the daytime; and in the daytime there was absolutely no effect, and the zebras that I saw could by no possibility have escaped observation from a lion, for they made no effort whatever thus to escape observation, but moved about continually, and, after drinking, retired to the open ground.

The zebra's coloration is certainly never of use to him in helping him escape observation at a drinking-place. But neither is it of use to him in escaping observation anywhere else. As I have said before, there are of course circumstances under which any pattern or coloration will harmonize with the environment. Once I came upon zebras standing in partially burned grass, some of the yellow stalks still erect, and here the zebras were undoubtedly less conspicuous than the red-coated hartebeests with which they were associated; but as against the one or two occasions where I have seen the zebra's coat make it less conspicuous than most other animals, there have been scores where it has been more conspicuous. I think it would be a safe estimate to say that for one occasion on which the coloration of the zebra serves it for purposes of concealment from any enemy, there are scores, or more likely hundreds, of occasions when it reveals it to an enemy; while in the great majority of instances it has no effect one way or the other. The different effects of light and shade make different patterns of coloration more or less visible on different occasions. There have been occasions when I have seen antelopes quicker than I have seen the zebra with which they happened to be associated. More often, the light has been such that I have seen the zebra first. Where I was, in Africa, the zebra herds were on the same ground, and often associated with, eland, oryx, wildebeest, topi, hartebeest, Grant's gazelle, and Thomson's gazelle. Of all these animals, the wildebeest, because of its dark coloration, was the most conspicuous and most readily seen. The topi also usually looked very dark. Both of these animals were ordinarily made out at longer distances than the others. The gazelles, partly from their small size and partly from their sandy coloration, were, I should say, usually a little harder to make out than the others. The remaining animals were conspicuous or not, largely as the light happened to strike them. Ordinarily, if zebras were mixed with elands or oryx I saw the zebras before seeing the eland and oryx, although I ought to add that my black companions on these occasions usually made out both sets of animals at the same time. But in mixed herds of hartebeests and zebras, I have sometimes seen the hartebeests first and sometimes the zebras.*

* Mr. Thayer tries to show that the cross stripes on the legs of zebras are of protective value; he has forgotten that in the typical Burchell's zebra the legs are white; whether they are striped or not is evidently of no consequence from the protective standpoint. There is even less basis for Mr. Thayer's theory that the stripings on the legs of elands and one or two other antelopes have any, even the slightest, protective value.

The truth is that this plains game never seeks to escape observation at all, and that the coloration patterns of the various animals are not concealing and are of practically no use whatever in protecting the animals from their foes. The beasts above enumerated are colored in widely different fashions. If any one of them was really obliteratively colored, it would mean that some or all of the others were not so colored. But, as a matter of fact, they are none of them instances of concealing coloration; none of the beasts seek to escape observation, or trust for safety to eluding the sight of their foes. When they lie down they almost always lie down in very open ground, where they are readily seen, and where they can hope to see their foes. When topi, roan antelope, hartebeest, and so forth, are standing head on, the under parts look darker instead of lighter than the upper parts, so that in this common position there is no "counter-shading." The roan and oryx have nearly uniform colored coats which often do harmonize with their surroundings; but their bold face markings are conspicuous.* None of these big or medium sized plains animals, while healthy and unhurt, seeks to escape observation by hiding.

This is the direct reverse of what occurs with many bush antelopes. Undoubtedly many of the latter do seek to escape observation. I have seen waterbucks stand perfectly still, and then steal cautiously off through the brush; and I have seen duiker and steinbuck lie down and stretch their heads out flat on the ground when they noticed a horseman approaching from some distance. Yet even in these cases it is very hard to say whether their coloration is really protective. The steinbuck, a very common little antelope, is of a foxy red, which is decidedly conspicuous. The duiker lives in the same localities, and seems to me to be more protectively colored—at any rate, if the coloration is protective for one it certainly is not for the other. The bushbuck is a boldly colored beast, and I do not believe for a moment that it ever owes its safety to protective coloration. The reedbuck, which in manners corresponds to our white-tailed deer, may very possibly at times be helped by its coloration, although my own belief is that all these bush creatures owe their power of concealment primarily to their caution, noiselessness, and power to remain motionless, rather than to any pattern of coloration. But all of these animals undoubtedly spend much of their time in trying to elude observation.

On the open plains, however, nothing of the kind happens. The little tommy gazelle, for instance, never strives to escape observation. It has a habit of constantly jerking its tail in a way which immediately attracts notice, even if it is not moving otherwise. When it lies down, its obliterative shading entirely disappears, because it has a very vivid black line along its side, and when recumbent—or indeed for the matter of that when standing up—this black line at once catches the eye. However, when standing, it can be seen at once anyhow. The bigger Grant's

* A curious instance of the lengths to which some protective-coloration theorists go is afforded by the fact that they actually treat these bold markings as obliterative or concealing. In actual fact the reverse is true; these face markings are much more apt to advertise the animal's presence.

gazelle is, as far as the adult male is concerned, a little better off than the tommy, because the bucks have not got the conspicuous black lateral stripe; but this is possessed by both the young and the does—who stand in much more need of concealing coloration. But as I have already so often said, neither concealment nor concealing coloration plays any part whatever in protecting these animals from their foes. There is never any difficulty in seeing them; the difficulty is to prevent their seeing the hunter.

Mr. Thayer's thesis is "that all patterns and colors whatsoever of all animals that ever prey or are preyed on are under certain normal circumstances obliterative." Either this sentence is entirely incorrect or else it means nothing; either no possible scheme of coloration can be imagined which is not protective (in which case of course the whole theory becomes meaningless) or else the statement so sweepingly made is entirely incorrect. As I have already shown, there are great numbers of animals to which it cannot apply; and some of the very animals which do escape observation in complete fashion are colored utterly differently when compared one with the other, although their habitats are the same. The intricate pattern of the leopard and the uniform, simple pattern of the cougar seem equally efficient under precisely similar conditions; and so do all the intermediate patterns when the general tint is neutral; and even the strikingly colored melanistic forms of these creatures seem as well fed and successful as the others. Mono-colored cougars and spotted jaguars, black leopards and spotted leopards, and other cats of all tints and shades, broken or unbroken, are frequently found in the same forests, dwelling under precisely similar conditions, and all equally successful in eluding observation and in catching their prey.

One of the most extreme, and most unwarrantable, of the positions taken by the ultra-advocates of the protective coloration theory is that in reference to certain boldly marked black and white animals, like skunks and Colobus monkeys, whose coloration patterns they assert to be obliterative. In skunks, the coloration is certainly not protective in any way against foes, as every human being must know if he has ever come across skunks by night or by day in the wilderness; their coloration advertises their presence to all other creatures which might prey on them. In all probability, moreover, it is not of the slightest use in helping them obtain the little beasts on which they themselves prey. Mr. Thayer's "sky-pattern" theory about skunks cannot apply, for bears, which are equally good mousers and insect grubbers, have no white on them, nor have fishers, weasels, raccoons, or foxes; and in any event the "sky-pattern" would not as often obliterate the skunk from the view of its prey as it would advertise it to its prey. It is to the last degree unlikely that any mouse or insect is ever more easily caught because of the white "sky-pattern" on the skunk; and it is absolutely certain that any of these little creatures that trust to their eyes at all must have their vision readily attracted by the skunk's bold coloration; and the skunk's method of hunting is incompatible with deriving benefit from its coloration. Besides, it usually hunts at night, and at night the white "sky-pattern" is *not* a sky-pattern at all, but is exceedingly conspicuous, serving as an advertisement.

The big black-and-white Colobus monkey has been adduced as an instance of the "concealing" quality of bold and conspicuous coloration patterns. Of course, as I have said before, there is no conceivable pattern which may not, under some wholly exceptional circumstances, be of use from the protective stand-point; a soldier in a black frock-coat and top hat, with white duck trousers, might conceivably in the course of some city fight get into a coal cellar with a white-washed floor, and find that the "coloration pattern" of his preposterous uniform was protective; and really it would be no more misleading to speak of such a soldier's dress as protective compared to khaki, than it is to speak of the Colobus monkey's coloration as protective when compared with the colorations of the duller-colored monkeys of other species that are found in the same forests. When hunting with the wild 'Ndorobo I often found it impossible to see the ordinary monkeys, which they tried to point out to me, before the latter fled; but I rarely failed to see the Colobus monkey when it was pointed out. In the tops of the giant trees, any monkey that stood motionless was to my eyes difficult to observe, but nine times out of ten it was the dull-colored monkey, and not the black-and-white Colobus, which was most difficult to observe. I questioned the 'Ndorobos as to which they found hardest to see and, rather to my amusement, at first they could not understand my question, simply because they could not understand failing to make out either; but when they did understand, they always responded that the black-and-white Colobus was the monkey easiest to see and easiest to kill. These monkeys stretch nearly across Africa, from a form at one extremity of the range which is almost entirely black, to a form at the other extremity of the range which is mainly or most conspicuously white. Of course it is quite impossible that both forms can be protectively colored; and as a matter of fact neither is.

I am not speaking of the general theory of protective coloration. I am speaking of certain phases thereof as to which I have made observations at first-hand. I have studied the facts as regards big game and certain other animals, and I am convinced that as regards these animals the protective-coloration theory either does not apply at all or applies so little as to render it necessary to accept with the utmost reserve the sweeping generalizations of Mr. Thayer and the protective coloration extremists. It is an exceedingly interesting subject. It certainly seems that the theory must apply as regards many animals; but it is even more certain that it does not, as its advocates claim, apply universally; and careful study and cautious generalizations are imperatively necessary in striving to apply it extensively, while fanciful and impossible efforts to apply it where it certainly does not apply can do no real good. It is necessary to remember that some totally different principle, in addition to or in substitution for protective coloration, must have been at work where totally different colorations and color patterns seem to bring the same results to the wearers. The bear and the skunk are both catch-ers of small rodents, and when the color patterns of the back, nose, and breast, for instance, are directly opposite in the two animals, there is at least need of very great caution in deciding that either represents obliterative coloration of a sort that benefits the creature in catching its prey. Similarly, to say that white herons and pelicans and roseate-colored flamingoes and spoon-bills are helped by their coloration, when other birds that live exactly in the same fashion and just as successfully, are black, or brown, or black and white, or gray, or green, or blue, certainly represents mere presumption, as yet unaccompanied by a vestige of proof, and probably represents error. There is probably much in the general theory of concealment coloration, but it is not possible to say how much until it is thoroughly tested by men who do not violate the advice of the French scientific professor to his pupils: "Above all things remember in the course of your investigations that if you determine to find out something you will probably do so."

I have dealt chiefly with big game. But I think it high time that sober scientific men desirous to find out facts should not leave this question of concealing coloration or protective coloration to theorists who, however able, become so interested in their theory that they lose the capacity to state facts exactly. Mr. Thayer and the various gentlemen who share his views have undoubtedly made some very interesting discoveries, and it may well be that these discoveries are of wide-spread importance. But they must be most carefully weighed, considered, and corrected by capable scientific men before it is possible to say how far the theory applies and what limitations there are to it. At present all that is absolutely certain is that it does not apply anywhere near as extensively as Mr. Thayer alleges, and that he is so completely mistaken as to some of his facts as to make it necessary carefully to reconsider most of the others. I have shown that as regards most kinds of big game which inhabit open places and do not seek to escape observation but trust to their own wariness for protection, his theories do not apply at all. They certainly do not apply at all to various other mammals. Many of his sweeping assertions are certainly not always true, and may not be true in even a very small number of cases. Thus, in his introductory, Mr. Thayer says of birds that the so-called "nuptial colors, etc., are confined to situations where the same colors are to be found in the wearer's background, either at certain periods of his life or all the time," and that apparently not one of these colors "exists anywhere in the world where there is not every reason to believe it the very best conceivable device for the concealment of its wearer, either throughout the main part of this wearer's life or under certain peculiarly important circumstances." It is really difficult to argue about a statement so flatly contradicted by ordinary experience. Taking at random two of the common birds around our own homes, it is only necessary to consider the bobolink and the scarlet tanager. The males of these two birds in the breeding season put on liveries which are not only not the "very best conceivable" but, on the contrary, are the very worst conceivable devices for the concealment of the wearers. If the breeding cock bobolink and breeding cock tanager are not colored in the most conspicuous manner to attract attention, if they are not so colored as to make it impossible for them to be more conspicuous, then it is absolutely hopeless for man or Nature or any power above or under the earth to devise any scheme of coloration whatsoever which shall not be concealing or protective; and in such case Mr. Thayer's whole argument is a mere play upon words. In sufficiently thick cover, whether of trees or grass, any small animal of any color or shape may, if motionless, escape observation; but the coloration patterns of the breeding bobolink and breeding tanager males, so far from being concealing or protective, are in the highest degree advertising; and the same is true of multitudes of birds, of the red-winged blackbird, of the yellow-headed grackle, of the wood-duck, of the spruce grouse, of birds which could be mentioned off-hand by the hundred, and probably, after a little study, by the thousand. As regards many of these birds, the coloration can never be protective or concealing; as regards others, it may under certain rare combinations of conditions, like those set forth in some of Mr. Thayer's ingenious but misleading colored pictures* serve, for concealment or protection, but in an infinitely larger number of cases it serves simply to advertise and attract attention to the wearers. As regards these cases, and countless others, Mr. Thayer's theories seem to me without substantial foundation in fact, and other influences than those he mentions must be responsible for the coloration. It may be that his theories really do not apply to a very large number of animals which are colored white, or are pale in tint, beneath. For instance, in the cases of creatures like those snakes and mice—where the white or pale tint beneath can never be seen by either their foes or their prey—this "counter-shading" may be due to some cause wholly different from anything concerned with protection or concealment.

There are other problems of coloration for which Mr. Thayer professes to give an explanation where this explanation breaks down for a different reason. The cougar's coloration, for instance, is certainly in a high degree concealing and protective, or at any rate it is such that it does not interfere with the animal's protecting itself by concealment, for the cougar is one of the most elusive of creatures, one of the most difficult to see, either by the hunter who follows it or by the animal on which it preys. But the cougar is found in every kind of country—in northern pine woods, in thick tropical forests, on barren plains, and among rocky mountains. Mr. Thayer in his introduction states that "one may read on an animal's coat the main facts of his habits and habitat, without ever seeing him in his home." It would be interesting to know how he would apply this statement to the cougar, and, if he knew nothing about the animal, tell from its coat which specimen lived in a Wisconsin pine forest, which among stunted cedars in the Rocky Mountains, which on the snow-line of the Andes, which in the forest of the Amazon, and which on the plains of Patagonia. With which habitat is the cougar's coat

* Some of the pictures are excellent, and undoubtedly put the facts truthfully and clearly; others portray as normal conditions which are wholly abnormal and exceptional, and are therefore completely misleading.

supposed especially to harmonize? A lioness is colored like a cougar, and in Africa we found by actual experience that the very differently colored leopard and lioness and cheetah and serval were, when in precisely similar localities, equally difficult to observe. It almost seems as if with many animals the matter of coloration is immaterial, so far as concealment is concerned, compared with the ability of the animal to profit by cover and to crouch motionless or slink stealthily along.

Again, there seems to be much truth in Mr. Thayer's statement of the concealing quality of most mottled snake skins. But Mr. Thayer does not touch on the fact that in exactly the same localities as those where these mottled snakes dwell, there are often snakes entirely black or brown or green, and yet all seem to get along equally well, to escape equally well from their foes, and prey with equal ease on smaller animals. In Africa, the two most common poisonous snakes we found were the black cobra and the mottled puff adder. If the coloration of one was that best suited for concealment, then the reverse was certainly true of the coloration of the other.

But perhaps the climax of Mr. Thayer's theory is reached when he suddenly applies it to human beings, saying: "Among the aboriginal human races, the various war-paints, tattooings, head decorations, and appendages, such as the long, erect mane of eagle feathers worn by North American Indians—all these, whatever purposes their wearers believe they serve, do tend to obliterate them, precisely as similar devices obliterate animals." Now this simply is not so, and it is exceedingly difficult to understand how any man trained to proper scientific observation can believe it to be so. The Indian, and the savage generally, have a marvellous and wild-beast-like knack of concealing themselves. I have seen in Africa 'Ndorobo hunters, one clad in a white blanket and one in a red one, coming close toward elephants, and yet, thanks to their skill, less apt to be observed than I was in dull-colored garments. So I have seen an Indian in a rusty frock-coat and a battered derby hat make a successful stalk on a deer which a white hunter would have had some difficulty in approaching. But when the 'Ndorobos got to what they—not I—considered close quarters, they quietly dropped the red or white blankets; and an Indian would take similar pains when it came to making what he regarded as a difficult stalk. The feathered head-dress to which Mr. Thayer alludes would be almost as conspicuous as a sun umbrella, and an Indian would no more take it out on purpose to go stalking in than a white hunter would attempt the same feat with an open umbrella. The same is true of the paint and tattooing of which Mr. Thayer speaks, where they are sufficiently conspicuous to be visible from any distance. Not only do the war-bonnets and war-paint of the American Indians and other savages have no concealing or protective quality, as Mr. Thayer supposes, but, as a matter of fact, they are highly conspicuous; and this I know by actual experience, by having seen in the open, savages thus arrayed, and compared them with the aspect of the same savages when hunting.

APPENDIX F

THE original list of the "Pigskin Library" was as follows:

Bible.
Apocrypha.
Borrow . . . . Bible in Spain.
                                 Zingali.
                                 Lavengro.
                                 Wild Wales.
                                 The Romany Rye.
Shakespeare.
Spenser . . . . Faerie Queene.
Marlowe.
Mahan . . . . Sea Power.
Macaulay . . . . History.
                                 Essays.
                                 Poems.
Homer . . . . Iliad.
                                 Odyssey.
Chanson de Roland.
Nibelungenlied.
Carlyle . . . . Frederick the Great.
Shelley . . . . Poems.
Bacon . . . . Essays.
Lowell . . . . Literary Essays.
                                 Biglow Papers.
Emerson . . . . Poems.
Longfellow.
Tennyson.
Poe . . . . Tales.
                                 Poems.
Keats.
Milton . . . . Paradise Lost (Books I and II).
Dante . . . . Inferno (Carlyle's translation).
Holmes . . . . Autocrat.
                                 Over the Teacups.
Bret Harte . . . . Poems.
                                 Tales of the Argonauts.
                                 Luck of Roaring Camp.
Browning . . . . Selections.
Crothers . . . . Gentle Reader.
                                 Pardoner's Wallet.
Mark Twain . . . . Huckleberry Finn.
                                 Tom Sawyer.
Bunyan's "Pilgrim's Progress."
Euripides (Murray's translation) . . . Hippolytus.
                                 Bacchæ.

The Federalist.
Gregorovius . . . . Rome.
Scott . . . . Legend of Montrose.
Guy Mannering.
Waverley.
Rob Roy.
Antiquary.
Cooper . . . . Pilot.
Two Admirals.
Froissart.
Percy's Reliques.
Thackeray . . . . Vanity Fair
Pendennis.
Dickens . . . . Mutual Friend.
Pickwick.

I received so many inquiries about the Pigskin Library (as the list appeared in the first chapter of my African articles in *Scribner's Magazine* [see page 29]), and so many comments were made upon it, often in connection with the list of books recently made public by ex-President Eliot, of Harvard, that I may as well myself add a word on the subject.

In addition to the books originally belonging to the "library," various others were from time to time added; among them, "Alice in Wonderland" and "Through the Looking-Glass," Dumas's "Louves de Machekoule," "Tartarin de Tarascon" (not until after I had shot my lions!), Maurice Egan's "Wiles of Sexton Maginnis," James Lane Allen's "Summer in Arcady," William Allen White's "A Certain Rich Man," George Meredith's "Farina," and d'Aurevilly's "Chevalier des Touches." I also had sent out to me Darwin's "Origin of Species" and "Voyage of the Beagle," Huxley's Essays, Frazer's "Passages from the Bible," Braithwaite's "Book of Elizabethan Verse," FitzGerald's "Omar Khayyám," Gobineau's "Inégalité des Races Humaines" (a well-written book, containing some good guesses; but for a student to approach it for serious information would be much as if an albatross should apply to a dodo for an essay on flight), "Don Quixote," Montaigne, Molière, Goethe's "Faust," Green's "Short History of the English People," Pascal, Voltaire's "Siècle de Louis XIV," the "Mémoires de M. Simon" (to read on the way home), and "The Soul's Inheritance," by George Cabot Lodge. Where possible I had them bound in pigskin. They were for use, not ornament. I almost always had some volume with me, either in my saddle pocket or in the cartridge-bag which one of my gun-bearers carried to hold odds and ends. Often my reading would be done while resting under a tree at noon, perhaps beside the carcass of a beast I had killed, or else while waiting for camp to be pitched; and in either case it might be impossible to get water for washing. In consequence the books were stained with blood, sweat, gun oil, dust, and ashes; ordinary bindings either vanished or became loathsome, whereas pigskin merely grew to look as a well-used saddle looks.

Now, it ought to be evident, on a mere glance at the complete list, both that the books themselves are of unequal value and also that they were chosen for various reasons, and for this particular trip. Some few of them I would take with me on any trip of like length; but the majority I should of course change for others—as good and no better—were I to start on another such trip. On trips of various length in recent years I have taken, among many other books, the "Memoirs of Marbot," Æschylus, Sophocles, Aristotle, Joinville's "History of St. Louis," the Odyssey (Palmer's translation), volumes of Gibbon and Parkman, Lounsbury's Chaucer, Theocritus, Lea's "History of the Inquisition," Lord Acton's Essays, and Ridgeway's "Prehistoric Greece." Once I took Ferrero's "History of Rome," and liked it so much that I got the author to come to America and stay at the White House; once De La Gorce's "History of the Second Republic and Second Empire"—an invaluable book. I did not regard these books as better or worse than those I left behind; I took them because at the moment I wished to read them. The choice would largely depend upon what I had just been reading. This time I took Euripides, because I had just been reading Murray's "History of the Greek Epic." * Having become interested in Mahaffy's essays on Hellenistic Greece, I took Polybius on my next trip; having just read Benjamin Ide Wheeler's "History of Alexander," I took Arrian on my next hunt; something having started me reading German poetry, I once took Schiller, Koerner, and Heine to my ranch; another time I started with a collection of essays on and translations from early Irish poetry; yet another time I took Morris's translations of various Norse Sagas, including the Heimskringla, and liked them so much that I then incautiously took his translation of Beowulf, only to find that while it had undoubtedly been translated out of Anglo-Saxon, it had not been translated into English, but merely into a language bearing a specious resemblance thereto. Once I took Sutherland's "History of the Growth of the Moral Instinct"; but I did not often take scientific books, simply because as yet scientific books rarely have literary value. Of course a really good scientific book should be as interesting to read as any other good book; and the volume in question was taken because it fulfilled this requirement, its eminent Australian author being not only a learned but a brilliant man.

I as emphatically object to nothing but heavy reading as I do to nothing but light reading—all that is indispensable being that the heavy and the light reading alike shall be both interesting and wholesome. So I have always carried novels with me, including, as a rule, some by living authors, but (unless I had every confidence in the author) only if I had already read the book. Among many, I remember off-hand a few such as "The Virginian," "Lin McLean," "Puck of Pook's Hill," "Uncle Remus," "Aaron of the Wild Woods," "Letters of a Self-made Merchant to His Son," "Many Cargoes," "The Gentleman from Indiana,"

* I am writing on the White Nile from memory; the titles I give may sometimes be inaccurate, and I cannot, of course, begin to remember all the books I have at different times taken out with me.

"David Harum," "The Crisis," "The Silent Places," "Marse Chan," "Soapy Sponge's Sporting Tour," "All on the Irish Shore," "The Blazed Trail," "Stratagems and Spoils," "Knights in Fustian," "Selma," "The Taskmasters," Edith Wyatt's "Every Man to His Humor," the novels and stories of Octave Thanet—I wish I could remember more of them, for personally I have certainly profited as much by reading really good and interesting novels and stories as by reading anything else, and from the contemporary ones I have often reached, as in no other way I could have reached, an understanding of how real people feel in certain country districts, and in certain regions of great cities like Chicago and New York.

Of course I also generally take out some of the novels of those great writers of the past whom one can read over and over again; and occasionally one by some writer who was not great—like "The Semi-attached Couple," a charming little early-Victorian or pre-Victorian tale which I suppose other people cannot like as I do, or else it would be reprinted.

Above all, let me insist that the books which I have taken were and could only be a tiny fraction of those for which I cared and which I continually read, and that I care for them neither more nor less than for those I left at home. I took "The Deluge" and "Pan Michael" and "Flight of a Tartar Tribe," because I had just finished "Fire and Sword"; "Moby Dick," because I had been rereading "Omoo" and "Typee"; Gogol's "Taras Bulba," because I wished to get the Cossack view of what was described by Sienkiewicz from the Polish side; some of Maurice Jokai, and "St. Peter's Umbrella" (I am not at all sure about the titles), because my attention at the moment was on Hungary; and the novels of Topelius when I happened to be thinking of Finland. I took Dumas's cycle of romances dealing with the French Revolution, because I had just finished Carlyle's work thereon—and I felt that of the two the novelist was decidedly the better historian. I took "Salammbo" and "The Nabob" rather than scores of other French novels simply because at the moment I happened to see them and think that I would like to read them. I doubt if I ever took anything of Hawthorne's, but this was certainly not because I failed to recognize his genius.

Now, all this means that I take with me on any trip, or on all trips put together, but a very small proportion of the books that I like; and that I like very many and very different kinds of books, and do not for a moment attempt anything so preposterous as a continual comparison between books which may appeal to totally different sets of emotions. For instance, one correspondent pointed out to me that Tennyson was "trivial" compared to Browning, and another complained that I had omitted Walt Whitman; another asked why I put Longfellow "on a level" with Tennyson. I believe I did take Walt Whitman on one hunt, and I like Browning, Tennyson, and Longfellow, all of them, without thinking it necessary to compare them. It is largely a matter of personal taste. In a recent English review I glanced at an article on English verse of to-day in which, after enumerating various writers of the first and second classes, the writer stated that Kipling was at the head of the third class of "ballad-mongers"; it happened that I had never even heard of most of the men he mentioned in the first two classes, whereas I should be surprised to find that there was any one of Kipling's poems which I did not already know. I do not quarrel with the taste of the critic in question, but I see no reason why any one should be guided by it. So with Longfellow. A man who dislikes or looks down upon simple poetry, ballad poetry, will not care for Longfellow; but if he really cares for "Chevy Chase," "Sir Patrick Spens," "Twa Corbies," Michael Drayton's "Agincourt," Scott's "Harlaw," "Eve of St. John," and the Flodden fight in "Marmion," he will be apt to like such poems as the "Saga of King Olaf," "Othere," "The Driving Cloud," "Belisarius," "Helen of Tyre," "Enceladus," "The Warden of the Cinque Ports," "Paul Revere," and "Simon Danz." I am exceedingly fond of these, and of many, many other poems of Longfellow. This does not interfere in the least with my admiration for "Ulysses," "The Revenge," "The Palace of Art," the little poems in "The Princess," and in fact most of Tennyson. Nor does my liking for Tennyson prevent my caring greatly for "Childe Roland," "Love Among the Ruins," "Proteus," and nearly all the poems that I can understand, and some that I can merely guess at, in Browning. I do not feel the slightest need of trying to apply a common measuring-rule to these three poets, any more than I find it necessary to compare Keats with Shelley, or Shelley with Poe. I enjoy them all.

As regards Mr. Eliot's list, I think it slightly absurd to compare any list of good books with any other list of good books in the sense of saying that one list is "better" or "worse" than another. Of course a list may be made up of worthless or noxious books; but there are so many thousands of good books that no list of small size is worth considering if it purports to give the "best" books. There is no such thing as *the* hundred best books, or *the* best five-foot library; but there can be drawn up a very large number of lists, each of which shall contain *a* hundred good books or fill *a* good five-foot library. This is, I am sure, all that Mr. Eliot has tried to do. His is in most respects an excellent list, but it is of course in no sense a list of the best books for all people, or for all places and times. The question is largely one of the personal equation. Some of the books which Mr. Eliot includes I would not put in a five-foot library, nor yet in a fifty-foot library; and he includes various good books which are at least no better than many thousands (I speak literally) which he leaves out. This is of no consequence so long as it is frankly conceded that any such list must represent only the individual's personal preferences, that it is merely a list of *good* books, and that there can be no such thing as a list of the *best* books. It would be useless even to attempt to make a list with such pretensions unless the library were to extend to many thousand volumes, for there are many voluminous writers, most of whose writings no educated man ought to be willing to spare. For instance, Mr. Eliot evidently does not care for history; at least he includes no historians as such. Now, personally, I would not include, as Mr. Eliot does, third or fourth rate plays, such as those of Dryden, Shelley, Browning, and Byron (whose greatness as poets does not rest on such an exceedingly slender foundation as these dramas supply), and at the same time completely omit Gibbon and Thucydides, or even Xenophon and Napier. Macaulay and Scott are practically omitted from Mr. Eliot's list; they are the two nineteenth-century authors that I should most regret to lose. Mr. Eliot includes the Æneid and leaves out the Iliad; to my mind this is like including Pope and leaving out Shakespeare. In the same way, Emerson's "English Traits" is included and Holmes's "Autocrat" excluded—an incomprehensible choice from my stand-point. So with the poets and novelists. It is a mere matter of personal taste whether one prefers giving a separate volume to Burns or to Wordsworth or to Browning; it certainly represents no principle of selection. "I Promessi Sposi" is a good novel; to exclude in its favor "Vanity Fair," "Anna Karénina," "Les Misérables," "The Scarlet Letter," or hundreds of other novels, is entirely excusable as a mere matter of personal taste, but not otherwise. Mr. Eliot's volumes of miscellaneous essays, "Famous Prefaces" and the like, are undoubtedly just what certain people care for, and therefore what they ought to have, as there is no harm in such collections; though personally I doubt whether there is much good, either, in this "tidbit" style of literature.

Let me repeat that Mr. Eliot's list is a good list, and that my protest is merely against the belief that it is possible to make any list of the kind which shall be more than a list as good as many scores or many hundreds of others. Aside from personal taste, we must take into account national tastes and the general change in taste from century to century. There are four books so pre-eminent—the Bible, Shakespeare, Homer, and Dante—that I suppose there would be a general consensus of opinion among the cultivated men of all nationalities in putting them foremost;* but as soon as this narrow limit was passed there would be the widest divergence of choice, according to the individuality of the man making the choice, to the country in which he dwelt, and the century in which he lived. An Englishman, a Frenchman, a German, an Italian, would draw up totally different lists, simply because each must necessarily be the child of his own nation.†

* Even this may represent too much optimism on my part. In Ingres's picture on the crowning of Homer, the foreground is occupied by the figures of those whom the French artist conscientiously believed to be the greatest modern men of letters. They include half a dozen Frenchmen—only one of whom would probably have been included by a painter of some other nation—and Shakespeare, although reluctantly admitted, is put modestly behind another figure, and only a part of his face is permitted to peek through.

† The same would be true, although of course to a less extent, of an American, an Englishman, a Scotchman, and an Irishman, in spite of the fact that all speak substantially the same language. I am entirely aware that if I made an anthology of poems, I should include a great many American poems—like Whittier's "Snow-Bound," "Ichabod," and "Laus Deo"; like Lowell's "Commemoration Ode" and "Biglow Papers"

We are apt to speak of the judgment of "posterity" as final; but "posterity" is no single entity, and the "posterity" of one age has no necessary sympathy with the judgments of the "posterity" that preceded it by a few centuries. Montaigne, in a very amusing and, on the whole, sound essay on training children, mentions with pride that when young he read Ovid instead of wasting his time on " 'King Arthur,' 'Lancelot du Lake,' . . . and such idle time-consuming and wit-besotting trash of books, wherein youth doth commonly amuse itself." Of course the trashy books which he had specially in mind were the romances which Cervantes not long afterward destroyed at a stroke. But Malory's book and others were then extant; and yet Montaigne, in full accord with the educated taste of his day, saw in them nothing that was not ridiculous. His choice of Ovid as representing a culture and wisdom immeasurably greater and more serious shows how much the judgment of the "posterity" of the sixteenth century differed from that of the nineteenth, in which the highest literary thought was deeply influenced by the legends of Arthur's knights and hardly at all by anything Ovid wrote. Dante offers an even more striking instance. If "posterity's" judgment could ever be accepted as final, it would seem to be when delivered by a man like Dante in speaking of the men of his own calling who had been dead from one to two thousand years. Well, Dante gives a list of the six greatest poets. One of them, he modestly mentions, is himself, and he was quite right. Then come Virgil and Homer, and then Horace, Ovid, and *Lucan!* Nowadays we simply could not understand such a choice, which omits the mighty Greek dramatists (with whom in the same canto Dante shows his acquaintance), and includes one poet whose works come about in the class of the "Columbiad."

With such an example before us, let us be modest about dogmatizing overmuch. The ingenuity exercised in choosing the "Hundred Best Books" is all right if accepted as a mere amusement, giving something of the pleasure derived from a missing-word puzzle. But it does not mean much more. There are very many thousands of good books; some of them meet one man's needs, some another's; and any list of such books should simply be accepted as meeting a given individual's needs under given conditions of time and surroundings.

KHARTOUM, *March* 15, 1910.

—which could not mean to an Englishman what they mean to me. In the same way, such an English anthology as the "Oxford Book of English Verse" is a good anthology —as good as many other anthologies—as long as it confines itself to the verse of British authors. But it would have been far better to exclude American authors entirely; for the choice of the American verse included in the volume, compared in quantity and quality with the corresponding British verse of the same period which is selected, makes it impossible to treat the book seriously, if it is regarded as a compendium of the authors of both countries.

INDEX

Aberdare ranges, 277, 373.

Abutilon, a flowering shrub on which elephant feed, 312.

Africa, British East, 1; English rule in, 120, 121; healthy climate of, 148; future of, 173; spring in, 278; preservation of elephant in, 288; missionary work in, 432, 433.

Africa, East, growth and development of, 42; natives of, 44.

Africa, German East, 48.

Akeley, Carl, 67, 399, 400, 401, 403, 404.

Akeley, Mrs., 399, 404.

Ali, the tent boy, 332, 390.

Allen, Mr., 404.

American flag, 22, 95, 433.

American Mission Stations, 119, 121; Industrial, 174, 426; Mission at Sobat, visit to, 527.

Antelope, 57, 148, 330; roan antelope, 383, 385, 507.

Ants, 423, 448; damage done by, 501; driver ants, 501.

Arabs, 332.

Ardwolf (a miniature hyena), 341.

Askaris, or native soldiers, 22, 98.

Asser, Colonel, 509.

Athi Plains, 52.

Attenborough, Messrs., 248.

Baboons, 261.

Bahima herdsmen, 439.

Bahr el Ghazal, 525.

Bahr el Zeraf, 526.

Baker, Sir Samuel, 72.

Bakhari, a gun-bearer, 330; ostriches described by, 332, 390.

Banana plantation, 311.

Bateleur eagle, the, 441.

Bats, 360, 462.

Beetles, Goliath, 449.

Belgian Government, courtesy of, 458.

Belgian troops, soldiers of, 511.

Birds, 41; honey bird, 125, 236; extraordinary habit of, 393, 397; whydah finches, 155, 170, 189; "lily trotters,"

251; wealth of bird life, 251, 260, 264; water birds, 269, 273, 344, 394, 441, 448, 449, 460, 470; wagtails, 508, 529, 533.

Bishops in Africa. See Hanlon, Streicher, Tucker.

Black water fever, 518.

Boar, 244.

Boers, the, 47, 48, 50; identity of interest between Britons and, 51, 131, 405, 406.

Bondoni, 46, 94.

Bongo, 420, 422, 423.

Borani caravan, a, 338.

Botha, Mr., 405.

Boyle, Mr., 429.

Brandy, moderate use of, 531.

Brooks, Mr., 404.

Browne, Mr., district commissioner, 280.

Buffalo, 67, 150, 157, *et seq.*, 290; bulls, 341; disease wiped out herds of, 342; 361; 496; great muscular power of, 497.

Bulpett, Mr., 124.

Burroughs, John, 393.

Bushbuck, 275, 330, 393, 396, 443, 483.

Bustard, 228; 340; 483; great bustard, 164; 234.

Butiaba, 451.

Butler Bey, 509.

Buxton, Edward North, 3; books on sport of, 380.

"Bwana," Swahili title of, 119, 504.

Cambridge Museum, 404.

Camp, pitching, 98; at Kilimakiu, 102; fires in, 467.

Caravan, a, 338.

Carnegie, Andrew. Appendix A.

Champagne, case of, 518, 530.

Chapman, Abel, 73.

Chapman, Captain, 406.

Cheetah, 90, 146, 340.

Christians, 333.

Christmas Day, march on, 442.

577